UFO RELIGIONS

'A truly welcome addition to work on UFO spiritualities. From introductory articles to nuanced analyses, the book presents new insights into the religious dimensions of both UFO phenomena and UFO groups'.

Jennifer E. Porter, Memorial University

March 1997, the bodies of 39 members of Heaven's Gate were discovered in a mansion outside San Diego. All had committed suicide, convinced that the passing of the Hale-Bopp comet signalled the arrival of aliens, who had come to transport them from their earthly bodies to the Kingdom of Heaven. In December 2002, the Raëlian Church, who want to build an Embassy for extraterrestrials in Jerusalem, annouced that they had finally realised another of its goals: 'Clonaid', a Raëlian organisation, had successfully cloned the first human baby. Between 1958 and 1961 the Aetherius Society, which has headquarters in Hollywood and London, travelled to 19 selected mountains around the world and charged them with spiritual energy. The popular fascination with UFOs, extraterrestrials, and alien abductions, enhanced by high-profile films, shows and books, such as *Independance Day*, *The X-Files*, and Erich von Däniken's *Chariots of the Gods?*, has been accompanied by an equally fascinating, sometimes apocalyptic manifestation of the modern spiritual quest.

UFO Religions analyses the religions and spiritualities which incorporate UFOs, extraterrestrial life and alien contact as core beliefs. The volume brings together an international group of scholars to consider the cultural and religious ideas within UFO religion, the incorporation of ufological elements within non-UFO religions, spiritual aspects of alien abduction narratives, and interpretations of UFO belief from the perspectives of psychology, sociology and religious studies.

Editor: Christopher Partridge is Senior Lecturer in Theology and Contemporary Religion at Chester College in the UK. His research and writing focuses on new religions and alternative spiritualities in the West and he is the editor of *Fundamentalisms* (2002), *Mysticisms East and West: Studies in Mystical Experience* (2003 with Theodore Gabriel) and *The Encyclopedia of New Religious Movements, Sects, and Alternative Spiritualities* (2004).

UFO RELIGIONS

Edited by Christopher Partridge

Routledge
Taylor & Francis Group

LONDON AND NEW YORK

First published 2003

by Routledge
11 New Fetter Lane, London EC4P 4EE

Simultaneously published in the USA and Canada
by Routledge
29 West 35th Street, New York, NY 10001

Routledge is an imprint of the Taylor & Francis Group

Typeset in Goudy by Taylor & Francis Books Ltd
Printed and bound in Great Britain by Biddles Ltd,
Guildford and King's Lynn

British Library Cataloguing in Publication Data
A catalogue record for this book is available from the British Library

Library of Congress Cataloging-in-Publication Data
UFO religions/ edited by Christopher Partridge; foreword by Paul Heelas.
p.cm
Includes bibliographical references and index.
1. Unidentified flying objects-Religious aspects. I. Partridge, Christopher H.
(Christopher Hugh), 1961 -

BL65.U54U38 2003
299- -dc21
2003041580
ISBN 0–415–26323 – 9 (hbk)
ISBN 0-41526324 – 7 (pbk)

FOR SARAH, STUART,
JAKE, JOSH, LUKE AND JOE

CONTENTS

PART II
Understanding narratives

CONTENTS

NOTES ON CONTRIBUTORS

George D. Chryssides studied philosophy and religion at the universities of Glasgow and Oxford. He has taught in several British universities, and is currently Senior Lecturer in Religious Studies at the University of Wolverhampton. His main research interest is new religious movements, and recent publications include *Exploring New Religions* (1999) and *Historical Dictionary of New Religious Movements* (2001).

Jodi Dean is an Associate Professor of Political Science at Hobart and William Smith Colleges, Geneva, New York. She is the author of *Aliens in America: Conspiracy Cultures from Outerspace to Cyberspace* (1998), chosen by the *Village Voice* as one of the best 25 books of 1998. Her most recent book is *Publicity's Secret: How Technoculture Capitalizes on Democracy* (2002).

Brenda Denzler is an independent scholar working as a writer and editor, living in North Carolina, USA. She received her doctorate from Duke University and has produced a number of studies of contemporary culture, and of the UFO community in particular. Her most recent book is *The Lure of the Edge: Scientific Passions, Religious Beliefs, and the Pursuit of UFOs* (2001).

Theodore Gabriel was born in Kerala State, India, and trained in Anthropology and Religious Studies at the University of Aberdeen. He was Senior Lecturer in Religious Studies at the University of Gloucestershire until 2000, and is currently Honorary Research Fellow at the same university. He has carried out research into Islam and Hinduism in Kerala, Lakshadweep and Malaysia, and has published articles on both Islam and Hinduism. Recent publications include: *Hindu–Muslim Relations in North Malabar* (1996); *Christian–Muslim Relations: A Case Study of Sarawak, East Malaysia* (1996); *Hindu and Muslim Inter-Religious Relations in Malaysia*

(2000); and (as editor) *Islam in the Contemporary World* (2000).

Andreas Grünschloß is Professor der Religionswissenschaft at the University of Göttingen. He has carried out research into new religious movements, Buddhism, the study of religion, and interreligious relations. His publications include *Religionswissenschaft als Welt-Theologie. Wilfred Cantwell Smith's religionstheologisches Programm* (1994); *Wenn die Götter landen... Religiöse Dimensionen des UFO-Glaubens* (2000).

Christopher Helland is a doctoral candidate in the sociology of religion at the Centre for the Study of Religion, University of Toronto. He is currently researching religious accommodation and innovation in relation to the scientific and technological developments of the late twentieth century. He is the author of 'Religion Online/Online Religion and Virtual Communitas', in *Religion on the Internet: Research Prospects and Promises* (2000). He has also contributed to J. R. Lewis (ed.), *UFOs and Popular Culture* (2000).

James R. Lewis is Professor of Religion at the University of Wisconsin, Stevens Point. He is a recognised authority on non-traditional religions and the author of numerous articles and several books, as well as the editor of many notable anthologies, including (with Gordon Melton) *Perspectives on the New Age* (1992), *Magical Religion and Modern Witchcraft*(1996), and *The Gods Have Landed: New Religions from Other Worlds* (1995). He has also edited several reference works in the field, some of which have won awards, one of the most recent being *UFOs and Popular Culture* (2001).

Sarah Lewis is Lecturer in Religious Studies in the Department of Theology and Religious Studies at the University of Wales, Lampeter, specialising in New Religious Movements and New Age. She has written several academic articles on new religions and her doctoral thesis focused on the theology of the Unification Church.

Jaakko Närvä has an M.Phil. in Comparative Religion and is currently completing doctoral research on the UFO phenomenon in the Department of Comparative Religion at the University of Helsinki. He is the author of a study of the religious features of the Finnish UFO phenomenon: 'Ufoilmiön uskonnollisia piirteitä', in Jussi Niemelä (ed.), *Vanhat jumalat – uudet tulkinnat. Näköaloja uusiin uskontoihin Suomessa* (2001).

Christopher Partridge is Senior Lecturer in Theology and Contemporary Religion at Chester College. His research and writing focuses on new religions and alternative spiritualities in the West. He is the author and editor of several books, articles and essays on new religions and contemporary spirituality in the West. He is the editor of *Fundamentalisms* (2001), *Mysticisms East and West: Studies in Mystical Experience* (2003, with Theodore Gabriel) and *Universal Salvation: the Debate* (2003, with Robin Parry), and author of *H. H. Farmer's Theological Interpretation of Religion: Towards a Personalist Theology of Religions* (1998). He also the Reviews Editor for the journal *Ecotheology*.

Mikael Rothstein is Associate Professor (*lektor*) in the Department of History of Religions, University of Copenhagen. He specialises in the study of new religions and has for some years carried out research into UFO beliefs and related subjects. He is the author and editor of a number of books in the field of history of religions, most recently the volumes *New Age Religion and Globalization* (2001) and *Gud er (stadig) blå* (2001). He is a member of the board of RENNER (The Research Network on New Religions) and co-editor of the Danish journal CHAOS.

John A. Saliba, a Jesuit, was born in Malta, studied philosophy and theology at Heythrop College, and has a diploma in anthropology from Oxford University and a doctorate in religious studies from the Catholic University of American in Washington. Since 1970 he has taught world religions, theology of religions and anthropology of religion in the Department of Religious Studies at the University of Detroit Mercy. For many years his principal area of research has been new religious movements. Among his recent publications are *Perspectives on New Religious Movements* (1995) and *Christian Responses to the New Age Movement* (1998).

Robert A. Segal is Professor of Theories of Religion, University of Lancaster. A specialist in psychological, anthropological and sociological theories of religion and of myth, he is the author of *The Poimandres as Myth* (1986), *Religion and the Social Sciences* (1989), *Explaining and Interpreting Religion* (1992), *Joseph Campbell* (1991), and *Theorizing about Myth* (1999), and is the editor of *In Quest of the Hero* (1990), *The Allure of Gnosticism* (1995), *The Gnostic Jung* (1992), *Jung on Mythology* (1998), *The Myth and Ritual Theory* (1997) and *Hero Myths* (2000).

Simon G. Smith is Manager of the Philosophical and Religious Studies Subject Centre of the Learning and Teaching Support Network (PRS-LTSN), based at the University of Leeds. He previously taught Indian Religions, New Religious Movements and Religion and Social Theory, in the Theology and Religious Studies Department, University of Leeds.

Garry W. Trompf is Professor in the History of Ideas in the Department of Studies in Religion, University of Sydney. He was formerly Professor of History at the University of Papua New Guinea. His best-known books are *The Idea of Historical Recurrence in Western Thought* and *Payback: The Logic of Retribution in Melanesian Religions*.

Diana Tumminia studied ethnography at UCLA where she received her doctorate in 1995. She now teaches social psychology, race relations and gender at Sacramento State University. Her publication topics range from advice on teaching to the social history of millenarian groups, including several studies of Unarius.

Daniel Wojcik is an Associate Professor of English and Folklore Studies at the University of Oregon. He is the author of *The End of the World As We Know It: Faith, Fatalism, and Apocalypse in America* (1997), *Punk and Neo-Tribal Body Art* (1995), and articles on millenarianism, vernacular religion and self-taught visionary artists.

FOREWORD

In northern Europe in particular, the decline of church attendance is relentless. Figures are down to a few per cent in countries like Sweden; in Britain figures are somewhat higher (around 7.5 per cent) but there are absolutely no signs of the year-in, year-out overall decline 'bottoming out'. If church attendance is anything to go by, the future of Christianity is bleak.

And so, it might be thought, is the future of the sociology of religion. Its traditional subject matter is disappearing. However, as is becoming increasingly apparent, the fact that ever-fewer people actually go to church does *not* mean – as some leading public figures have supposed – that Britain is becoming a nation of atheists. Far from it: for a very great deal is going on 'beyond' church and chapel. Whether it be yoga or astrology in popular culture, belief among the general population in a 'God within' or that 'there must be something out there', there is plenty for the sociologist of religion to study. Indeed, the 'sacred' is showing distinct signs of vibrancy, with 'spirituality', for example, making inroads with regard to well-being culture, education, business and health.

UFO religion provides another example of – relative – vibrancy. Prior to the later 1940s, very few would have answered affirmatively the question 'Do you believe in UFOs?' In a recent study, with which I have been involved, a quarter of those active with 'alternative' spiritualities answered the same question positively. Nothing surprising about this, one might think. But what is surprising – and surely shows the extent to which ufology has entered the culture – is that around 10 per cent of regular church attendees expressed belief. And, as one of the contributors to this volume notes, up to 50 per cent of the population of the USA think that intelligent life exists elsewhere.

The Space Age, NASA-wise, might not quite be what it once was. With regard to popular culture, however, 'space', the 'out there', 'the fountainhead of all life' (to cite one of the contributors to this book) is very much alive and well in the human 'imagination'. And this volume does an excellent job of exploring the ways in which 'the modern sacralisation of the extraterrestrial' (as the editor puts it) has taken place. In short, *UFO Religions* provides a substantial contribution to what really is 'beyond' in the territories that are (largely!) beyond traditional religion.

Paul Heelas
University of Lancaster

ACKNOWLEDGEMENTS

As is always the case for me, the writing and editing of books is made possible by my family and friends. To some of these wonderful people I dedicate this book.

For a sabbatical, some of which was spent editing this volume and researching the first chapter, I am enormously grateful to my colleagues in the Department of Theology and Religious Studies at Chester. I want also particularly to thank George Chryssides (University of Wolverhampton) who has been consistent in his willingness to discuss the project and whose advice has made this a better book than it otherwise would have been. Indeed, whilst my interest in the area goes back some years, the book had its genesis in a discussion with George following an excellent paper he gave on the Raëlian movement at Bath Spa University College. I am likewise indebted to James Lewis, who has been enthusiastic about the book from the outset and suggested several of the contributors.

The book would not be before you now had it not been for the excellent, endlessly patient staff at Routledge – Roger Thorpe, Julene Knox, Celia Tedd, Chantelle Johnson and Clare Johnson. Thanks are also due to Paul Heelas for so readily agreeing to write the Foreword. Finally, my work as editor was made a great deal easier than it might have been by the professionalism and scholarship of those who contributed to the volume. Thank you. It was a pleasure working with you and an education reading your excellent essays.

Part I
INTRODUCTION

1

UNDERSTANDING UFO RELIGIONS AND ABDUCTION SPIRITUALITIES

Christopher Partridge

There can be few people in the Western world who are unaware of the contemporary significance of UFOs, extraterrestrials and stories of alien abduction in popular culture. Alien faces with their large, dark, almond-shaped eyes can be seen everywhere; alien-contact films, such as *Close Encounters of the Third Kind* (1979), *ET* (1982) and, more recently, *Independence Day* (1996), *Mars Attacks!* (1996), *Contact* (1997), *Men in Black* (1997) and *Signs* (2002) are some of the most commercially successful ever produced; numerous television programmes have dealt with the subject matter, *The X-Files* being one of the most popular television series of all time;[1] in popular music, musicians such as Reg Presley of the Troggs[2] are committed believers, and bands such as Eat Static make their interest in the area explicit with albums such as *The Alien E.P.s*, *Implant*, *Abduction* and *The Science of the Gods*; books such as Erich von Däniken's *Chariots of the Gods?*[3] and Whitley Strieber's *Communion*[4] have appeared on best-seller lists, the former being described as 'the best-selling book of modern times'.[5] Further evidence of this popularity can be seen in the numerous UFO organisations and networks, some of which publish journals and host large annual gatherings. As well as significant national organisations such as BUFORA (the British UFO Research Association), there are international organisations, the most famous of these being MUFON (the Mutual UFO Network) and CUFOS (the Centre for UFO Studies), the latter of which was founded by the astronomer J. A. Hynek and publishes the *International UFO Reporter* and the more scholarly *Journal of UFO Studies*.

Whilst there are UFO reports and studies which are little more than ridiculous speculation, even fabrication, there are, as I have discovered when attending gatherings of UFO enthusiasts, 'ufologists' who go to great lengths to ensure that sightings are verified and that hoax encounters and shoddy researchers are exposed. It is my impression that many in the ufology community are hard working and intelligent people who, as far as they are able, are committed to the highest standards of research. Indeed, I have been genuinely impressed by the detailed (if a little obsessive) scrutiny of government documents, the critical discussions of recent publications on UFOs, the dogged determination to thoroughly investigate reported sightings, and the files apparently compiled over many years.

As for myself, I am, as I think many Westerners are, a little sceptical but nevertheless open-minded about such phenomena. On the one hand, it is difficult not to believe that there is, in the vastness of space and orbiting one of its innumerable suns, a planet on which there exist intelligent beings.[6] On the other hand, it is difficult to move from that statement of probability to the claim that such beings are so intelligent and technologically advanced that they are able, not only to leave the surface of their planet (as we have done), but to leave their solar system and travel to a tiny blue planet many millions of miles, if not light years, away. Moreover, not only is this difficult to believe, but I am one of the multitudes who have never seen a UFO or encountered an alien, let alone been abducted by one. (That said, for many years my friend has insisted that, in our late teens, together we witnessed a UFO hovering at some distance in front of us. However, as I point out to him, there are other reasons why a couple of hippies walking home from a party at three o'clock in the morning might have had an encounter of the third kind.) Nevertheless, I am always keen to listen to those who claim to have experienced such phenomena and, as might be expected of one who studies religion, I am particularly fascinated when, as is often the case, an encounter leads to the adoption or construction of a spiritual worldview.

This collection of studies, as the title makes plain, is not about the type of painstaking investigative ufology that analyses sightings, claimed encounters and government reports. Rather, the chapters in this volume focus on those within the UFO community whose belief in extraterrestrial contact has led to the construction of implicitly or explicitly religious worldviews, or those whose religious beliefs, whilst not being fundamentally ufological, have been informed by a belief in the existence of UFOs and the intervention of extraterrestrial life.

The emergence of contemporary ufology

When searching for the origins of the contemporary religious interest in UFOs, whilst, as we will see, many UFO theorists and religionists seek to construct what amounts to a sacred history of sightings and contacts stretching back into prehistory,[7] it is hard to avoid one date which appears more frequently than any other, namely 24 June 1947. This is the date on which Kenneth Arnold, an American businessman from Boise, Idaho, reported a sighting of ten shining discs over the Cascade Mountains while flying his private plane near Mount Rainier in western Washington. According to Arnold, 'they flew like a saucer would if you skipped it across the water.' Misquoted, the sighting was reported as Arnold's encounter with 'flying saucers'. Whilst there had been previous modern sightings of, for example, 'balls of fire' accompanying planes during the Second World War (nicknamed 'foo fighters'), or cigar- and disc-shaped objects in the sky[8] (such as the wave of Scandinavian 'ghost rocket' sightings in 1946[9]), these tended to be sporadic and vague, having no consistent pattern. Moreover, the research of Robert Bartholomew and George Howard has shown that before 1947 'there is not a single recorded episode involving mass sightings of saucer-like objects.'[10] It was Arnold's 'flying saucers' that both began the modern waves of sightings and ushered UFOs into the popular consciousness. Indeed, the interest in Arnold's story was immediate and massive. Despite frequent dismissals and explanations by scientists and military experts, such was the level of popular interest that, by the beginning of July the same year, the US Air Force felt it necessary to carry out an investigation. 'A Gallup poll taken on August 19, 1947, revealed that while one out of two Americans had heard of the Marshall Plan, nine out of ten had heard about the saucers.'[11] By the end of that year 850 UFO sightings were reported in America alone.

Within just a few weeks of the Arnold sighting, the most famous alleged UFO incident occurred at Roswell, New Mexico. More significant in terms of its cultural impact than in terms of its scientific verifiability, this event, perhaps more than any other UFO event, has spawned a whole body of literature, numerous television documentaries, various movements, a network of conspiracy theories, and many fictional works (e.g. The X-Files, Roswell High and Independence Day). During the night of 2 July (the Independence Day weekend) W W. 'Mac' Brazel, a farmer living at Foster Ranch, near Corona, New Mexico, heard an enormous explosion. On investigating, he discovered strange large, pieces of metal strewn over a radius of three-quarters of a mile. No sooner had rumours begun to circulate about the explosion and the subsequent discovery of the strange metallic fragments, than the US Air Force rapidly descended on the area, cleared everything up, and claimed that a new weather balloon had fallen to earth. Although this satisfied much of the curiosity for a short time, rumours nevertheless began to circulate. That said, whilst these events at Roswell exercised the minds of some suspicious individuals, being ideal material for conspiracy theories, it had relatively little impact on the international UFO community until 1980, when two such suspicious investigators, Charles Berlitz and William Moore, published their book, *The Roswell Incident*.[12] Following the publication of this book during the 1980s, it became the conviction of many that Roswell was perhaps the most significant UFO event of modern times. It was claimed that, not only had the Air Force recovered strange-looking debris, some of it having been inscribed with unfamiliar symbols, but also they had discovered a second, larger crash site, from which were recovered several bodies that did not appear to be human. Furthermore, it was claimed that one of these strange beings was still alive and was able to communicate telepathically with the authorities. The range of conspiracy theories, mythologies and controversies engendered by these speculations was further stimulated early in 1995 with the release of film footage showing, it was claimed, autopsies on an extraterrestrial cadaver.

Roswell is now firmly established as what might be described as a key ufological 'sacred site'. That is to say, whilst of course many ufologists would not interpret the significance of Roswell religiously, it does tend to inspire the same sort of behaviours as religion. In other words, it inspires *implicitly* religious attitudes and actions. For example, the 'pilgrims' who travelled to Roswell to mark the 50th anniversary of the crash in 1997 were greeted by what looked like an ancient religious site constructed from standing-stone-like obelisks. Jodi Dean relates that these had been erected at the entrance of the long path to the crash site and that, after a walk of several hundred yards, she came to 'two more obelisks and a commemorative stone'. From this point the visitors could 'view the rocky cleft where the saucer came to rest'. Inscribed in the stone 'in a runic font' (which is itself indicative of religious, particularly New Age–Pagan, significance) are the following revealing words: 'We don't know who they were. We don't know why they came. We only know that they changed our view of the universe. This universal sacred site is dedicated July 1997 to the beings who met their destinies near Roswell, New Mexico, July 1947.'[13] Indeed, as one would expect in a place of pilgrimage, the local community was not slow to make the most of the entrepreneurial opportunities offered by the growing torrent of pilgrims in 1997: 'Main Street decorated their windows with full-scale drawings of grays [a type of alien – usually spelled with an 'e']. Some had alien dummies and dolls. Others had balloons with large black eyes. You could buy alien piñatas, kites, shoes, aliens in jars, refrigerator aliens, alien puppets, alien Christmas tree ornaments, alien artificial insemination kits. You could buy alien *everything* ... Roswell's two UFO museums sponsored lectures and book signings by important ufologists.'[14] Even the local Church of Christ 'featured alternative speakers testifying to the Christian message of abduction'.[15] However, as we will see, the modern sacralisation of the extraterrestrial has been a central feature of UFO folklore from the outset.

Ufoism as theosophical religion

Beginning with Emmanuel Swedenborg (1688–1772),[16] one can produce a modern religious history of individuals who claim to have seen UFOs, encountered extraterrestrials and even travelled to other planets and experienced advanced alien civilisations. Certainly, even when such fantastic claims were not made, notions of beings from other planets and their advanced civilisations has entertained the minds of thinking people for centuries. For example, prior to the twentieth century: in *Micromégas*, Voltaire relates the story of a visit to Earth by inhabitants of Saturn and Sirius, the latter visitors being a mile high; Kant speculated about the possibility of life on other worlds; the philosopher Kurd Lasswitz's novel *Aus Zwei Planeten* (1897) explored the implications of Martians travelling to Earth; and of course the genre of science fiction which explores many of these issues has become increasingly popular and valued since the publication of novels, particularly by Jules Verne and H. G. Wells.[17] More recently, whilst the exegesis is unconvincing and generally dismissed by the academic community (not that it is ever seriously considered), there are numerous claims, for example, that the Hindu scriptures contain accounts of UFOs (see particularly Mikael Rothstein's discussion of Richard Thompson's/Sadapuda Dasa's thesis in Chapter 13), or, as we will see, that the Bible relates such material in passages about, for example, the mighty race of Nephilim (Genesis 6:4), the ascension of Elijah in a chariot drawn by 'horses of fire' (2 Kings 2:11), or Ezekiel's strange vision of mysterious creatures and gleaming wheels emerging from a 'great cloud, with brightness round about it, and fire flashing forth continually' (Ezekiel 1:4, 15).[18] However, from the perspectives of religious and cultural studies, the systematic religious interpretation of UFOs (i.e. flying saucers) and alien beings and the emergence of specific UFO religions has followed the general rise of interest following the Arnold sighting.

Whilst there are explicit contactee claims prior to 1947,[19] these are not central to the particular belief systems of the individuals[20] and, more particularly, do not involve UFOs. That said, it has been argued by Gordon Melton that the first UFO religion was Guy Ballard's I AM Religious Activity. Certainly it is true that, in his book *Unveiled Mysteries* (1934),[21] Ballard claimed not only to have met the enigmatic nineteenth-century alchemist (now ascended master) the Comte de Saint-Germain on Mount Shasta in California, but also to have been subsequently introduced to twelve Venusians who revealed Venus to be home to a race of technologically and spiritually advanced beings. Ballard thus develops H. P. Blavatsky's Venusian 'Lords of the Flame', which were, according to Charles Leadbeater's 1912 interpretation of the concept,[22] of the highest rank in the hierarchy of ascended masters.[23] This, according to Melton, is significant: 'Not only did Ballard become the first to actually build a religion on contact with extraterrestrials (as opposed to merely incorporating the extraterrestrial data into another already existing religion), but his emphasis was placed upon frequent contact with the masters from whom he received regular messages to the followers of the world contactee movement.'[24] But does this qualify it as a *UFO religion*? Whilst the I AM Religious Activity can be seen as the obvious theosophical forerunner to UFO religions such as the Aetherius Society, and to the thought of UFO religionists such as George Adamski, Ballard's esotericism was not, I would argue, fundamentally ufological, but rather theosophical. Although it is true that the hierarchy of masters included Venusians, the principal focus was not alien beings and certainly not UFOs (i.e. alien spacecraft), but rather masters such as Saint-Germain, the 'I AM presence'/'Christ self' within us all, karma, reincarnation and so on. As Stupple comments, 'Ballard's meeting with twelve tall Masters from Venus ... is only a minor item in his major work, *Unveiled Mysteries*.'[25] In other words, Ballard does what Melton claims he does not, namely incorporates 'the extraterrestrial data into another already existing religion'. Indeed, he simply develops ideas which already exist within the tradition to which he belongs. Hence, whilst we will see that the idea of ascended masters did undergo explicit ufological reinterpretation after the Arnold sighting, in this pre-1947 period Ballard's thought is more clearly theosophical than ufological.

The overall point is simply that, whilst there are claims to 'contact' with beings from other planets prior to the Arnold sighting, they are not the principal focus of such belief systems and UFOs *per se* are absent. The emergence of religion specifically focused on UFOs is a post-1947 phenomenon. That said, as noted above, it is important to understand that, although the 'I AM Religious Activity' was essentially a theosophical movement, and not a UFO religion as such, it is difficult to avoid the fact that much post-1947 UFO religion has been informed by many of the basic themes and ideas found within it. However, this is only to say that much UFO religion is, as the 'I AM' movement was, fundamentally theosophical, in that many of those who have developed religious interpretations of UFOs belong to a tradition that can be traced back, through particularly Alice Bailey (and, to some extent, Rudolf Steiner) to the ideas disseminated by the Theosophical Society and, in particular, to the thought of Helena Blavatsky (1831–91) who, with Henry Olcott (1832–1907), founded the organisation. Indeed, not surprisingly, the principal religious response to the wave of sightings provoked by the Arnold sighting was made by theosophical groups. For example, 'Maurice Doreal, founder of the Brotherhood of the White Temple in Sedalia, Colorado identified three types of flying saucers including one piloted by "serpent people" who once were ice-bound in Siberia, became defrosted and then overthrew and replaced the Communist regime in Russia.'[26] Again, a more typical religious response was made by former Theosophist, the Rev. Violet Gilbert, who, in 1956, claimed that she took 'a three hour excursion by mother ship to Venus'. Indeed, she also claimed that, whilst she could not talk about it publicly at that time, her initial contact with the 'space brothers' was actually back in 1939. (For some time Gilbert led 'the Cosmic Star Temple in Rosebud, Oregon'[27].)

Having introduced our examination of the theosophical influence on pre- and post-1947 religion, in order to continue we need to note some relevant doctrines of the Theosophical Society. The principal religious themes of the society are summed up in its three objectives. They are summarised by Blavatsky as follows:

> (1) To form the nucleus of a Universal Brotherhood of Humanity without distinction of race, colour, or creed. (2) To promote the study of Aryan and other Scriptures, of the World's religion and sciences, and to vindicate the importance of old Asiatic literature, namely, of the Brahmanical, Buddhist, and Zoroastrian philosophies. (3) To investigate the hidden mysteries of Nature under every aspect possible,

CHRISTOPHER PARTRIDGE

and the psychic and spiritual powers latent in man especially.[28]

In many ways, the central teachings of the Theosophical Society were not novel, and nor did Blavatsky claim that they were. As she discusses in great detail in *The Secret Doctrine*,[29] theosophical teachings are the result of her instruction in an 'ancient wisdom' which was, in turn, the source of the principal spiritual themes and ethical ideals found in the world religions. Indeed, she claims that enlightened masters throughout history, including Buddha and Jesus, taught theosophical truths and that her own instruction had been imparted by certain 'hidden adepts' (i.e. ascended masters). More particularly, and important for understanding much UFO religion, is Blavatsky's belief that certain masters dwelt on Venus. As Melton points out, 'Little recognized, and certainly not emphasized by either Blavatsky or modern theosophists, Blavatsky included among the hierarchy, masters who dwelt on Venus and with whom she was in contact. These masters she termed Lords of the Flame and the Lord of the World, the head of the hierarchy for humanity. Under these Venusian lords are the Lords of the Seven Rays (or colours) who have direct contact with human adepts such as Blavatsky.'[30] (This belief was subsequently developed by Leadbeater in 1907.) However, whatever her belief about these Venusian Masters (which is not clear), the notion of ascended masters *per se* lies at the heart of her thought and subsequent theosophical esotericism. As the influential Theosophist Annie Besant comments, 'That the Society was only worthy to live, if it were a witness to and a channel for the masters' teachings, was [Blavatsky's] constant declaration, and she only cared for it as an instrument for carrying out Their work in the world.'[31] Indeed, as far as Blavatsky was concerned, the true founders of the society were two such masters, namely Koot Hoomi (sometimes spelled Kuthumi and usually referred to as K. H.) and Morya (or simply M.). Their teachings were conveyed (i.e. channelled) through Blavatsky and other *chelas* (pupils of the masters) to two Anglo-Indian Theosophists, A. P. Sinnett and A. O. Hume, and subsequently compiled and published as *The Mahatma Letters*.[32] The mission of the Theosophical Society was to communicate these teachings to humanity and thereby contribute to the moral and spiritual evolution of the race. (It should perhaps be noted at this point that Theosophy has several prominent branches, and, strictly speaking, the branch which has been the most important influence on UFO religion is that developed by Alice Bailey.)

The ascended masters were living persons who had fully evolved through many reincarnations, had acquired and become the custodians of 'ancient wisdom', and now sought to impart that wisdom to humanity in order to lead it into a new age of peace, spirituality and global community. The masters introduce new scientific ideas into the history of human thought, they warn of potentially harmful developments and catastrophes and, 'having themselves solved and mastered the problems of human living, they make a periodical effort to bring more enlightenment to mankind'.[33] The masters have 'direct insight into the spiritual, psychic and physical workings of our solar system', and communicate these insights through specially chosen intermediaries. 'On their behalf', argues Theosophist T. H. Redfern, 'Mme Blavatsky gave out teachings giving a corrective lead in the fields of science, religion and ethical standards.'[34] For example, he quotes and comments on the following interesting passage from one of the channelled *Mahatma Letters*:

> '...every atmospheric change and disturbance [is] due to masses between which our atmosphere is compressed! I call this meteoric dust a "mass" for it really is one. High above the earth's surface the air is impregnated and space is *filled* with magnetic ... dust which does not even belong to our solar system'. The origin of cosmic rays is still debated and the Van Allen belt, which has been described as the Great Barrier Reef in space, was not discovered until 1957. The meteorology of the Mahatma Letters is still not confirmed, but if Mme Blavatsky forged these letters how did she know there was a magnetic mass above the atmosphere. Again, 'Science will *hear* sounds from certain planets before she *sees* them. This is a prophecy.' In 1882 ... Jodrell Bank wasn't even a dream, radar unthought of, radio-stars unheard of. Radio-planets are still not discovered, but who dare deny the possibility.[35]

Regardless of the scientific merits and demerits of such passages, the religious point to note is that the masters are beings (a) with a deep concern for the welfare of humanity, (b) who operate as supreme moral and spiritual guides, (c) who understand the physical nature of the cosmos, and (d) whose superior wisdom extends to the spheres of science and technology. Whilst there are some differences between the theosophical masters/mahatmas of wisdom (who were usually thought to reside in Tibet) and the early accounts of aliens, in actual fact the similarities between the two are striking and the differences fairly superficial. Both are highly spiritually evolved, morally superior, technologically advanced, benevolent beings with a deep salvific concern for a humanity bent on the destruction of the planet. (Particularly during the Cold War period, the concern of aliens, like that of many Westerners, was humankind's ability to destroy the planet with nuclear weapons – as discussed by Christopher Helland in Chapter 8 with particular reference to George Van Tassel and Ashtar.) Moreover, just as great spiritual founders and leaders of religious history are identified in Theosophy with the masters/mahatmas, so in much UFO religion these benevolent beings are similarly understood.[36] Mark-Age, for example, relates the following message from the extraterrestrial Sananda, who is identified as Jesus: 'I have come many times to the Earth planet as a leader and as a spiritual ruler responsible for that which does happen in this plane or cycle.' This is followed by an editor's note: 'Past incarnations of Sananda include: Khufu, Melchizedek, Moses, Elijah, Zarathustra, Gautama Buddha, Socrates, and Jesus of Nazareth. In addition, he was leader of the Abels [sic] and leader of the Noahs [sic].'[37] Similarly, another group relates the following fairly typical conversation between a contactee and a Venusian master aboard a UFO:

Q. Do people of other planets believe in God?
A. Of course we do, but not as an old man sitting on a throne. And by the way, the ones you call Jesus Christ, Buddha and Mohammed are all Venusians who volunteered to come to Earth to help you in a time of need.
Q. Do the people of other planets use money as we do on Earth?
A. We have no need for money. People of other worlds love to share. We take only what we need.
Q. Why are flying saucers visiting the Earth?
A. The Intergalactic Council is disturbed by Earth's experimentation with atomic weapons. The balance of the universe is in danger. Our space ships come as a warning.[38]

The point is that, in much UFO religion, fundamentally the same masters remain, but their location, dress and mode of transport has been updated. Hence, whilst we have seen that Theosophy did recognise Venusian masters, after 1947 spacecraft and other planets became the principal location of masters, rather than the mystical Asian locations favoured by Theosophists. That is to say, there is a clear shift of emphasis to flying saucers and the planets post-1947. Indeed, whilst Venus tended to retain its privileged position for some years amongst contactee and UFO groups,[39] other planets were increasingly identified as inhabited, including unknown ones (e.g. in his 1954 book *Aboard a Flying Saucer*, Truman Bethurum chronicled his encounters with aliens from the planet Clarion). Certainly, Venus's popularity as the home planet of advanced civilisations waned when it was discovered that it is shrouded by clouds of sulphuric acid, with an atmosphere constituted almost entirely of carbon dioxide and a surface temperature of 480°C – hardly ideal for a comfortable and civilised life. That said, some groups, such as the Aetherius Society, continue to insist that masters reside on Venus. Their life, however, is not lived in the rather uncomfortable physical dimension, but in another, less bracing dimension. Others, such as Benjamin Creme, even claim that 'It is an occult fact that all the planets are inhabited', whatever their observable physical conditions.[40]

However, as indicated above, perhaps the most dramatic change to occur in contact narratives after the Arnold sighting is the inclusion of 'flying saucers'. Gradually aliens cease simply to appear to contactees, as in the case of Ballard, but rather they descend in spacecraft. Similarly, the principal mode of travel for contactees visiting other planets becomes flying saucers, rather than 'astral travel' or mysterious transportation during sleep – though the latter modes of travel do not entirely disappear in contact narratives.

That this is so can be demonstrated by looking at the work of the most famous, and arguably the first, post-1947 contactee, George Adamski (1891–1965). Adamski was a Polish-born Californian occultist who, in 1936, founded the theosophically-oriented Royal Order of Tibet.[41] He had also been briefly involved with the California-based metaphysical group, the Order of Loving Service. Hence, it is unsurprising to find in his influential book, *The Flying Saucers Have Landed* (co-authored with the British occultist Desmond Leslie), not only numerous references to theosophical themes and doctrines, but also a bibliography that is little more than a shortlist of key theosophical and occult writings by authors such as Blavatsky, Besant, Leadbeater, Bailey, Dion Fortune, Rudolf Steiner and Paramhansa Yogananda. Furthermore, Adamski's 'Space Brothers' are not the almond-eyed aliens most commonly reported by contemporary contactees, but are rather 'humanoid', resembling popular theosophical descriptions of the masters, or indeed perhaps Yogananda Paramhansa (1893–1952), who had become increasingly influential in America since arriving from India in 1920.[42] (That contemporary abductees report encountering 'Nordics' or 'Beta Humanoids'[43], a type of alien which appears to be very similar to Adamski's alien, suggests the continuing and widespread appeal of the 'Space Brother' model.) The following account of Adamski's first meeting with an alien could almost be one of Blavatsky's accounts of an encounter with Koot Hoomi:[44]

> His hair was long, reaching to his shoulders, and was blowing in the wind ... He took four steps towards me, bringing us within arm's length of each other. Now, for the first time I fully realised that I was in the presence of a man from space – A HUMAN BEING FROM ANOTHER WORLD! ... The beauty of his form surpassed anything I had ever seen. And the pleasantness of his face freed me of all thoughts of my personal self. I felt like a child in the presence of one with great wisdom and much love, and I became very humble within myself ... for from him was radiating a feeling of infinite understanding and kindness, with supreme humility ... [He had] calm, grey-green eyes, slightly aslant at the corners; with slightly higher cheek bones than an Occidental, but not so high as an Indian or an Oriental; a finely chiselled nose, not conspicuously large; and an average size mouth with beautiful white teeth that shone when he smiled and spoke. As nearly as I can describe his skin, the colouring would be an even, medium-coloured suntan.[45]

Bearing in mind that the masters were often termed 'Brothers' in theosophical literature, it is perhaps significant that Adamski deliberately chooses to refer to aliens as 'Space Brothers'. Again, just as Ballard had claimed that Saint-Germain understood and lived according to 'the Great Laws of Life', so Adamski's Space Brothers 'adhere to the Laws of the Creator instead of laws of materialism as Earth men do'. He continues, 'Pointing to himself, then up into space – which I understood meant the planet on which he lived – he conveyed the thought to me that there they lived according to the Will of the Creator, not by their own personal will, as we do here on Earth.'[46] Moreover, as with the theosophical adepts who had once been Earthly mortals, but who had now ascended to higher realms, so Orthon (the name of Adamski's alien)[47] 'indicated that once he had lived on this Earth ... but now he is living out there'.[48] (It is worth noting that Adamski had already published, in 1949, a spiral-bound science fiction novel which contained many of these elements.[49])

Finally, as with the ascended masters, Adamski clearly believes Orthon to be the end result of a long process of reincarnation, for 'only one who through countless incarnations has attained great spirituality can hope to operate such a [spaceship] unaided'.[50] This is important because it highlights Adamski's close association of the spiritual and the technological. Only a superior spiritual being can operate 'a piece of cosmic machinery'. As with Theosophy, truly significant and positive advances in human evolution, technological or otherwise, are always fundamentally spiritual. For Adamski and much subsequent UFO religion, any material Utopia will be the end-product of a spiritual evolution. In the utopian future, everything from the ordering of society to the operating of machinery is spiritual work. Indeed, for contactee Brad Steiger the synthesis of the scientific and the spiritual is crucial to an accurate understanding of UFOs: 'In my opinion, the UFO phenomenon is an important factor in the total experience of a new age: the merger of "science" and "religion".'[51] Interestingly, Jennifer Porter has shown that this close correlation of the scientific and the spiritual in the understanding of extraterrestrials is also evident in contemporary North American Spiritualism, where aliens have been adopted as spirit guides.

> ... the incorporation of extraterrestrials as spiritual guides by some contemporary Spiritualists can be directly attributed to the presumed scientific and technological superiority that extraterrestrials are held to display. This scientific superiority becomes linked in Spiritualist perceptions to a 'spiritual' superiority. Extraterrestrials are seen as spiritually superior because they are scientifically more advanced than human beings. Concurrently, their superior 'science' is perceived as more advanced than ours, because, unlike contemporary earthly science, the science of extraterrestrials incorporates a recognition of spiritual 'truth'. Consequently, within the North American Spiritualist context, the adoption of extraterrestrials as spirit guides can be seen both as a reflection of the 'rationalisation' of Spiritualist belief

through the strong idealisation of 'science', and as a critique of orthodox science for ignoring the 'spiritual' realm.[52]

To return to Adamski's and Leslie's understanding of aliens, the following passages not only emphasise an identification of the spiritual and the scientific, but also closely correspond to beliefs about the masters found in theosophical literature. Also note that, whilst it is something of a 'chicken and egg' problem, in that which comes first is difficult to determine, it would seem that, whereas Porter argues that, for Spiritualists, 'extraterrestrials are seen as spiritually superior because they are scientifically more advanced than human beings', for Adamski and Leslie it is the other way around – increased spirituality leads to scientific progress.

> The Venusians have scientific knowledge, spiritually scientific, which has not yet reached Earth. When man becomes a truly spiritual being, he too will discover the secrets of spiritual science. Some day visitors will come in Venusian bodies, bringing with them a great spiritual power as before. They will bring knowledge that the more advanced on Earth will be able to hear and understand, although the masses will be unaffected and untouched.[53]

[54]The overall point to note is that Adamski's fundamental thesis is little more than a modified version of popular theosophical teaching which stresses spiritual evolution and the role of the masters/aliens in that process. Indeed, it is arguable that much of Adamski's work supports the three objectives of the Theosophical Society (quoted above on page 7-8), particularly the second and third. For example, not only is there an explicit emphasis on Indian spirituality (and a reference to 'The Lords of the Flame' – which appears in both Blavatsky's and Ballard's writings), but there is also an attempt to unite humanity and the religions of the world by identifying a common alien origin.

> About eighteen million years ago ... at a time when Mars, Venus and Earth were in close conjunction, along a magnetic path so formed came a huge, shining, radiant vessel of dazzling power and beauty, bringing to Earth 'thrice thirty-five' human beings, of perfection beyond our highest ideals; gods rather than men; divine kings of archaic memory, under whose benign world-government a sham-

bling, hermaphrodite monster was evolved into thinking, sexual man.[55]

Venus is the 'Home of the Gods'. From Venus in the year BC 18,617,841 came the first vehicle out of space to alight on our planet ... A point was reached about eighteen million years ago, say the old teachings, when something resembling man had evolved; but it was mindless, for it was born from Earth alone ... Evolution had gone so far but could go no farther until it received some tremendous stimulus outside the ordinary powers of Earth. And so from our nearest neighbour came the greatest of Venus, 'the Sanat Kumara', 'The Lord of the Flame', the Spirit of the Venusian Logos Itself, whose memory is revered and held sacred in every ancient religion. From Venus, say the old teachings, came the elder brothers, the 'Lords of the Flame', the highly perfected humans from an older branch of the planetary family. Of their free will they came; out of love and compassion for the groping, mindless things in the steaming primal jungles ... The 'Lord of the Flame' can be found under many names. He is the 'Ancient One', 'The Mighty Lord of Fire', 'The Youth of Timeless Aeons', 'The Eternal Virgin', 'The Point of Blue within the Hidden Diamond'. And in our own Bible He is 'The Ancient of Days' ... Every legend, Greek, Roman, Egyptian, South American, Indian or Persian, of the gods coming to Earth can be traced back as a race memory of this one tremendous event. But like all legends, they became distorted and overlaid, or confused ...[56]

Furthermore, as some confirmation of this, the soles of Orthon's shoes left a number of symbols impressed in the ground (helpfully illustrated by Adamski) that are similar to ancient religious symbols. Most notably, two of these are clearly intended to look like swastikas.[57] This is significant because, although culturally tainted because of its appropriation by the Nazi Party, the swastika is actually a positive symbol found in several ancient religions from Mexico to India, thereby confirming, to Adamski's satisfaction, the alien origins of the world's spiritual traditions. From our perspective, it is perhaps also significant that the swastika is the principal Hindu symbol adopted by the Theosophical Society. (Interestingly, Raël, the founder of the Raëlian Church, also claims to have seen a swastika printed both on the side of a flying saucer and also on an alien space-suit.[58])

From speculation about Atlantis to beliefs about the significance of the pyramids, from quoting the *Mahabharata* to discussions of *The Secret Doctrine*, from the practice of Yoga to the recognition of ancient adepts, from teachings about *chakras* to the claim that 'everything that exists is composed of Light',[59] the key elements of Adamski's worldview are thoroughly theosophical.

Another example of someone in this tradition with an interest in UFOs is Benjamin Creme. Creme has consistently proclaimed that the masters of wisdom, who have for millennia 'guided humanity's evolution', are re-emerging in the world. More particularly, on 19 July 1977, their leader, 'Maitreya, the Christ', 'the World Teacher', 'entered a certain country in the modern world'.[60] Whilst Creme's teaching focuses almost entirely on the advent of Maitreya, and whilst much of his thought is typically theosophical, being particularly indebted to the teaching of Alice Bailey, he not only believes that 'what we call UFOs (the vehicles of the space people from the higher planets) have a very definite part to play in the building of a spiritual platform for the World Teacher, preparing humanity for this time', but also claims that he himself is working for and with 'the Space Brothers'.[61] Indeed, the same themes of theosophical UFO religion found in Adamski's work are clearly evident in Creme's teaching. (1), It is very clear that Creme understands 'Space People' in terms of benevolent ascended masters who are concerned for the welfare of humanity and the planet. Not only have they 'placed around this planet a great ring of Light, which holds it intact and protects it from an overflow of force from the cosmic astral plane', but they 'release into our world tremendous cosmic energies which have a great effect in transforming humanity and sustaining the planet as an integral being. Their work is continuous and endless, and we all owe them a great debt.'[62]

(2), It is clear from what has already been said that, not only are spirituality and science related, but also the emphasis is firmly placed on the spiritual, in that, for example, any understanding of scientific progress is understood spiritually: 'when the time is right – when our science, under the stimulation of the masters of the Hierarchy, has reached the point where we can utilise what the Space People can show us – they will come and live and work with us for longer periods, and release their great, divine science (it is a divine science) into the world'.[63] Even life on other planets is interpreted pseudo-spiritually: 'It is an occult fact that all the planets are inhabited.

They are not necessarily inhabited by people we would recognise in a physical body; for instance, on Mars or Venus they are in etheric matter and UFOs are in fact of etheric substance.'[64]

(3), Finally, once we have evolved, 'we will recognise where we come from ... We will accept the fact that we are brothers and friends, brothers within one integrated system – the Solar System; that we are all at different stages of evolutionary development, some more advanced and some less. Gradually, we shall take our place, a place which we once held, in the cosmic brotherhood.'[65] As in Adamski's writings, the ideal of a 'Universal Brotherhood of Humanity', central to the thought of the Theosophical Society, is extended to other planets and becomes the 'interplanetary brother-hood'.[66]

Many of these theosophical themes can be found, in one form or another, in several of the prominent UFO religions discussed in this volume. For example, Norman Paulsen's thought appears to be a complex combination of von Däniken's and Blavatsky's interpreta-tions of ancient history and of mythic civilisations such as Mu and Atlantis (see Trompf's fascinating discussion in Chapter 11), and the notion of the ascended master is particularly clear in the under-standings of Ashtar[67] (see Helland's informed treatment of the development of the concept of Ashtar in Chapter 8) and Aetherius (see Simon Smith's discussion in Chapter 4). Similarly, we have seen that in such groups there is a basic understanding that the human race, in its current spiritually immature state, is the problem; we are in danger of the destroying the planet, and even upsetting a balance of cosmic universal forces. Indeed, according to Mark-Age, 'the human race is responsible for evil ... There is no such thing as Satan, except the evil that lives in men's minds, hearts, desires, ambitions and greed.'[68] We are in need of salvation from space. For example, Phyllis Schlemmer, in her 1994 book *The Only Planet of Choice*, relates channelled messages from the interstellar organisa-tion, the Council of Nine, to the effect that humanity is hindering the spiritual development of the entire universe. Consequently, such groups understand their mission in much the same way as Blavatsky understood the mission of the Theosophical Society, in that it exists to serve 'the masters' for the sake of the spiritual evolution of the human race. For example, 'the Aetherius Society', says its founder, George King (1919–97), 'is one of the metaphysical foundations which has gone out of its way ever since its inception, to educate its members so that they may not only realize their God-potential, but use it for mankind as a whole. It is now standing by, geared up, waiting to be used in any way the masters see fit. Not in any way we see fit, but we are awaiting the dictates of the great cosmic masters – not the directives of our own petty likes. Directors and members alike have dedicated themselves, have formed themselves into a body of disciples awaiting their next task.'[69] Within their literature, particularly the writings of King, there are numerous references to ascended masters, adepts, spiritual hierarchies, the Great White Brotherhood, as well as other subjects central to Theosophy, such as yoga (it is claimed that King himself was a master of yoga), kundalini, *chakras*, the New Age, Atlantis, karma, reincarnation and so on.

Finally, a religious practice common to both Theosophy and to many UFO religions is 'channelling'. Blavatsky, for example, claims that parts of *Isis Unveiled* and *The Secret Doctrine* were in fact the channelled words of Koot Hoomi. It is important to understand that, unlike traditional Spiritualism, theosophical messages were not those of departed loved ones, but teachings of highly evolved entities.[70] The complex cosmology to emerge emphasised, as we have seen, the gradual evolution of the cosmos and, consequently, a hierarchy of beings at various stages of evolution which seek to assist and educate those below them. The point is that the notion of highly evolved beings channelling advanced teachings through sensitive individuals is wholly adopted by many UFO religions. The entities reside on other planets or occupy spacecraft and, whilst the process of channelling may be interpreted in much the same way as it is in Theosophy, it is usually described using scientific (often pseudo-scientific) terminology. For example, the Aetherius Society describes the channelled messages as 'transmissions' which are 'transmitted by light beams operating upon mental frequencies capable of impressing themselves upon THE mind in such a way that translation into the English language was possible. This process of mental reception is called telepathy, which is now regarded by science as an indisputable fact.'[71] Indeed, many Aetherius Society publications claim to be transcripts of lectures by Aetherius (who is 'now alive in a physical body upon the planet Venus') channelled through King. Again, as with the channelled teachings of the Theosophical Society, entities such as Aetherius and Ashtar do not communicate the type of personal messages for individuals one would expect in a Spiritualist séance, but rather 'transmit' grand statements of universal import. For example, the following is taken from a fairly typical 'transmission' from Aetherius, through King:

The New Age will be brought in by a series of catastrophies [sic], which have to come in order to balance Karma in one way or another. *Because you have three adepts on your Earth just now, risking their very salvation for you, the blow has been softened greatly,* but nevertheless, earthquakes, tidal waves, droughts, fierce winds, hurricanes, floods, and so on have, as you know, already started. Strange weather conditions have, just as I prophesized [sic] about this time last year, already started. I also told you only a short time ago what type of conditions you could expect and you have had them exactly as I stated you would.[72]

Most channelled messages from extraterrestrials have similar universal, anthropocentric, and spiritual emphases. For the sake of the planet, the human race must progress spiritually. Everything from war to natural disasters is related to the slow progress of human spiritual evolution.

Ufoism as physicalist religion

Whilst much UFO religion contains typically religious themes, including the belief in God, salvation, reincarnation, karma and so on, we have seen that it is also 'physicalist'. That is to say, whilst the components of a religious worldview may be there, they are often reinterpreted in terms of physical phenomena. Having said that, it is important to understand that, whilst all UFO religion is physicalist to some extent, there are varying degrees ranging from a group such as the Raëlian Church which has what might be described as a *strong* physicalist belief system, to a *weak* physicalist organisation such as Mark-Age which is far more supernaturalist in the Theosophy-I AM-New Age tradition. Indeed, it is possible to construct a 'physicalist scale', at the strong end of which are those forms of religion influenced by the modern, secular, scientific worldview and at the weak end of which are those far more influenced by religious, usually theosophical, worldviews (see Figure 1.1). Groups situated at the strong end of the spectrum tend to be essentially atheist and anti-supernaturalist, whilst those situated at the weak end often claim, for example, that extraterrestrials worship God and, like the saints, understand more about God, are closer to God, and, unlike humans, live according to the cosmic laws of God.[73] On such a physicalist scale, the Raëlian Church would be situated at the former end, the Aetherius Society would

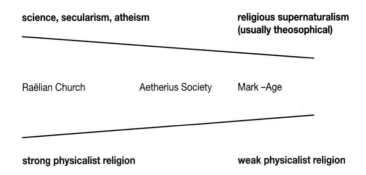

science, secularism, atheism   religious supernaturalism
(usually theosophical)

Raëlian Church   Aetherius Society   Mark –Age

strong physicalist religion   weak physicalist religion

Figure 1.1

be closer to the middle, and Mark-Age would be located towards the religious end.

I use the term 'physicalist religion', rather than 'scientific religion' (which is sometimes used), simply because I am not convinced that the beliefs of UFO religions can, strictly speaking, be described as 'science'. Whilst there is a reinterpretation of religious beliefs in *physical* terms, this is, it seems to me, rather different from producing a belief system based on *science*. Though rather negative, the term 'pseudo-scientific' would perhaps be more appropriate. Having said that, from an *emic* perspective (i.e. a believer's/insider's perspective), the description does have some merit, in that many members of UFO religions clearly do understand their beliefs to be 'scientific', even if conventional science hasn't yet caught up. Certainly, UFO religionists always seem delighted when their beliefs appear to have been formally scientifically verified. (As we have seen, it is not unusual for some to claim formal scientific verification for beliefs such as telepathy, even when such verification is lacking.) That said, we have seen that the emphasis is often on '*spiritual* science' or '*divine* science', 'spiritual' and 'divine' being the key words. Hence, the point is that, whilst many of their beliefs can be described as 'physicalist', the conventional meaning of the word 'science' is almost absent.

An example of the physicalist turn in UFO religion can be seen in the beliefs of the Aetherius Society. Whilst still a fundamentally theosophical New Age group, and whilst maintaining some religious beliefs such as karma and reincarnation, the society also provides physicalist, pseudo-technological interpretations of traditional religious beliefs – hence its position on the physicalist scale in Figure 1.1. For example, not only are channelled messages described as 'transmissions' from one physical being to another by what they claim to be the scientifically verifiable process of telepathy, but also they use special equipment designed by King to maximise the effectiveness of prayer. Hence, central to their Operation Prayer Power is a distinctive box, sometimes mounted on a tripod, which, it is claimed, is a unique 'prayer battery' that can store up to 700 hours of the psychic energy produced by praying members. This stored psychic energy can then be beamed to anywhere in the world in order to disperse violence and hatred, and to promote love, harmony and spirituality. The point is that this is a typical example of the physicalist interpretation of a spiritual practice: prayer is energy which, in much the same way as electrical energy, can be stored in batteries and used when and where required.

Very common in UFO religions, as already indicated, is the physicalist interpretation of scriptures and ancient mythologies: 'As far as contacts between terrestrial and extraterrestrial beings are concerned, mythology is a treasure trove with more than a little importance. Extraterrestrials visited this and other solar systems, and on the planets that seemed suitable, they left behind scions "in their own image"' (Erich von Däniken).[74] This physicalism is explicit in the writings of all the principle individuals and groups, from Adamski to von Däniken and from the Raëlian Church to Heaven's Gate. The following extract discussing the first chapter of Ezekiel and the Ark of the Covenant, taken from von Däniken's bestseller *Chariots of the Gods?*,[75] is a typical example of a physicalist hermeneutic.

> The Old Testament gives some impressive descriptions in which God alone or his angels fly straight down from heaven making a tremendous noise and issuing clouds of smoke. [Ezekiel] describes a craft that comes from the north, emitting rays and gleaming and raising a gigantic cloud of desert sand ... He likens the din made by the wings and wheels to a 'great rushing'. Surely this suggests that this is an eyewitness account ... In Exodus xxv, 10, Moses relates the exact instructions which 'God' gave for the building of the Ark of the Covenant. The directions are given to the very inch, how and where staves and rings are to be fitted and from what alloy metals are to be made ... No one, he told Moses, should come close to the Ark of the Covenant, and he gave precise instructions about the clothing to be worn

and the footwear appropriate when transporting it. In spite of all this care there was a slip up (2 Samuel vi, 2). David had the Ark of the Covenant moved and Uzzah helped to drive the cart it was in. When passing cattle shook and threatened to overturn the Ark, Uzzah grabbed hold of it. He fell dead on the spot, as if struck by lightening. Undoubtedly the Ark was electrically charged! If we reconstruct it today according to the instructions handed down by Moses, a voltage of several hundred volts is produced ... If, in addition, one of the two cherubim on the mercy seat acted as a magnet, the loudspeaker - perhaps a kind of set for communication between Moses and the spaceship - was perfect.[76]

For von Däniken, the beings ancient cultures referred to as gods were actually astronauts. Similarly, says von Däniken, 'if our own space travellers happen to meet primitive peoples on a planet one day, they too will presumably seem like "sons of heaven" or "gods" to them'.[77] Indeed, for von Däniken, not only can all ancient icons and texts, from cave paintings and the stone statues on Easter Island to the *Mahabharata* and the Bible, be accounted for ufologically, but so also can the world's mystical traditions, such as *Kabbalah* (which he claims – without much evidence – to have studied in detail[78]) and much contemporary paranormal phenomena.[79]

At this point, it should be noted that, unlike other individuals and groups discussed thus far, von Däniken is not a UFO religionist and does not claim any extraterrestrial guidance. He simply puts his theories down to an inquisitive mind and an unwillingness to accept conventional explanations of human origins: 'I have never had a revelation, it was a slow development.'[80] Hence, whilst coming to similar conclusions regarding the origins of humanity and the world's religions, *Chariots of the Gods?* is very different from books such as Leslie and Adamski's *Flying Saucers Have Landed*. That said, his theories provide a clear (and enormously influential) example of the physicalist interpretation of religious history.

Much discussion about religious and human origins draws on a popular thesis – of which von Däniken is the principal architect – namely, 'the ancient astronaut hypothesis'. Whilst we see embryonic versions of the idea posited by such writers as Adamski and Leslie, it only attracted widespread interest as a result of von Däniken's books. After a decline in the 1970s and early 1980s, interest in the area has soared in recent years. The rising sales of popular books such as Jack Barranger's and Paul Tice's *Mysteries Explored: the Search for Human*

Origins, UFOs and Religious Beginnings,[81] David Childress's *Extraterrestrial Archaeology*[82] and, of course, von Däniken's volumes, as well as the publication of journals such as *Legendary Times* and the founding of organisations such as AASRA (Archaeology, Astronauts and SETI Research Association), all testify to the enormous growth of contemporary interest in the ancient astronaut hypothesis. This is interesting, not least because religious texts and experiences are taken seriously as accurate records – though not of divine–human encounters but rather of alien–human encounters. In one sense, therefore, the hypothesis undermines religion, in that God, spiritual beings, providence and miracles are all explained in physical terms. In another sense, organisations such as the Rëlian Movement have founded a physicalist religious belief system on such interpretations. Indeed, once one is familiar with von Däniken's ideas, it is difficult not to see aspects of his thought sacralised and replicated in contemporary UFO religions. As Andreas Grünschloß puts it, 'UFO faith ... can be understood to oscillate between *disenchantment* and *re-enchantment*' (Chapter 9).

A specific example of the way the ancient astronaut hypothesis can be developed religiously is the belief in the alien creation of the human race. With a similar thesis to Adamski's, but going significantly beyond him, von Däniken raises the question as to whether the human race is in fact the result of 'deliberate "breeding" by unknown beings from outer space'.[83] The Genesis account not only speaks of God creating humanity in his own image (a significant text for many UFO religionists), but also of further visits of the 'sons of God' and of their sexual relations with 'the daughters of men' (Genesis 6:1–4), all of which indicates continuing fertilisation experiments. The subsequent flood narrative, he explains, is actually a record of the alien extermination of unsuccessful specimens. Our ancient ancestors, the survivors, were the specimens our alien creators were pleased with. He concludes by making the point that 'today the possibility of breeding an intelligent human race is no longer such an absurd theory'.[84] The point is that very similar theses appear in UFO religious narratives. In particular, one cannot help immediately thinking of the rationale for the enthusiastic promotion of contemporary advances in cloning technology by the largest of the UFO religions, the Raëlian Movement. (See George Chryssides' excellent treatment of this aspect of Raëlian belief in Chapter 2.) On 13 December 1973, four years after the publication of *Chariots of the Gods?*, Claude Vorilhon claims to have encountered aliens in the volcanic Clermont-Ferrand mountains in France. These extraterrestrials telepathically provided an interpretation of the Bible very similar to von Däniken's. In particular, it was explained that 'the Elohim' mentioned in Genesis were alien beings.[85] It was also explained that Elohim scientists had produced the first humans by mixing the DNA of the Elohim with that of our primate ancestors. This, argues Raël, was the beginning of a history of alien intervention that has consistently involved cloning. Jesus, for example, was a son of the Elohim who, having being murdered by an unenlightened society, was resurrected, in the sense that a cell from his dead body was cloned. The new body then underwent an 'advanced growth process' (AGP) and had the personality from the murdered body transferred to it. (Raël speaks of the personality in terms of software that can be downloaded into cloned corporeal hardware.[86]) As Susan Palmer comments, this has led the Raëlian Movement to become 'the first organization to forge a religious rationale for cloning'.[87] As one Raëlian put it, 'Now that humanity can create life from its own DNA, just like our Fathers did for us, this means the human race is undergoing elohimization [becoming equal to the Elohim]!'[88] Indeed, Palmer notes that the Raëlian Movement 'has the motivation, and perhaps the resources, to produce the first human clone'.[89] Certainly, Raël's company, Clonaid, claims to have done just that.

As noted above, whilst the Raëlian Movement presents perhaps the most systematic form of physicalist religion, aspects of it, particularly the physicalist interpretation of sacred texts, can be found in all UFO religions and abduction spiritualities.

Abduction spiritualities

It is hard to avoid the fact that the centre of gravity in popular UFO interest has shifted from alleged sightings and discussions of, for example, the possible technologies that might propel alien craft, to alien contact and particularly to alien abduction. As John Whitmore comments, 'In recent times, the subject of UFO abductions has gained immense popularity, both with the public and with a small group of scholars and writers who have turned their attention to the UFO phenomenon. The number of people who claim to have been abducted by occupants of UFOs has been rising almost exponentially since the early 1970s'.[90] The beings, not the machines, dominate UFO discourse. This, of course, has always been the case in the theosophical contactee tradition. Whilst the general interest in ufology focused on flying saucers, UFO religionists focused on those who travelled in them and, in particular, on their messages for humanity.

It is these latter emphases that have come to the fore in abduction narratives.[91]

Whilst Brenda Denzler has shown that there are those in the UFO community who consider themselves to be engaged in a purely scientific enterprise, eschewing religious interpretations, this is not the case for abductees (see Chapter 15). As she points out, 'The greatest levels of confidence in religion combined with a diminished regard for science come from a segment of the UFO community that has achieved particular notoriety only in the last fifteen years – the abductees.' More specifically, there is a conspicuous emphasis in abduction narratives on personal spiritual experience. Many abductees, notes David Jacobs, the Temple University historian and UFO researcher, 'found spiritual enlightenment and an expansion of their consciousness'.[92] Some even explicitly refer to such experiences as 'sacred encounters'.[93] Indeed, it is arguable that the majority of abduction narratives are essentially religious narratives. If the findings of John Mack, a Harvard psychiatrist and the most experienced academic psychologist working in the field, are to be trusted, this is not surprising. For example, in his principle study of abductees, *Abduction: Human Encounters with Aliens*, he makes the following point: 'Many abduction experiences are unequivocally spiritual, which usually involves some sort of powerful encounter with, or immersion in, divine light ... The alien beings, although resented for their intrusive activities, may also be seen as intermediaries, closer than we are to God or the source of being. Sometimes ... they may even be seen as angels or analogous to God. A number of abductees with whom I have worked experience at certain points an opening up to the source of being in the cosmos'.[94]

Most spiritually oriented abductees (and most abductees do seem to be spiritually oriented) are what Jacobs terms 'Positives', in that the aliens' intentions are viewed positively (i.e. extraterrestrials are benevolent beings concerned for the welfare of humanity and the Earth) and alien encounters are felt to be psychologically, spiritually and often physically positive for the individual. Interestingly, this view tends to contrast with the views of believers in UFOs who are less spiritually inclined. Jacobs himself is not a 'Positive'. He is, indeed, very critical of spiritual interpretations of aliens and, believing extraterrestrials to be a serious threat to the human race, he argues that the views of Positives such as Mack are naïve and dangerous. In his book *The Threat*, he insists that 'all the evidence seems to suggest that integration into human society is the aliens' ultimate goal. And all their efforts and activities appear to be geared toward complete control of the humans on Earth.'[95]

Having said that, abductee spiritualities which are positive about aliens often also incorporate a belief in certain species of aliens that are malevolent. For example, like many believers in the alien abduction phenomenon, Gail Seymour (a contactee, rather than an abductee) is very clear that there are several types of alien, including greys, zetas, Arcturians, reptilians, reptoids and Nordics. Referred to as 'friends' and 'family', Arcturians are clearly understood to be benevolent beings. They even help her in her work of psychic therapy and healing. At the other end of the spectrum, however, are the reptilians and reptoids that rape, torture and murder. Needless to say, they are also a threat to spiritual growth, one victim of 'possession' experiencing 'a sucking effect in her solar plexus "like a vacuum cleaner"'.[96] In short, the reptilians seem to provide abduction spiritualities with a demonology – which, interestingly, is sometimes explicitly related to Christian demonology: 'Satan was real alright. I think he was a big deal and the head of the reptilian invasion ...'[97] (A controversial British writer and speaker whose work is devoted to exposing Reptilian agendas and activities is David Icke. Icke's conspiracy theories, which Seymour told me she agreed with, include the belief that many of the world's leaders, including US Presidents and the British Royal family, are Reptilians in disguise.[98])

As with UFO religionists in the theosophical tradition, it would seem that many contemporary abductees (not all) have a spiritual worldview in place prior to their abduction experience. Interestingly, when I asked Seymour whether, in her own experience of working with abductees, she had found that individuals with an interest in spiritual matters were more likely to have abduction experiences, she quickly replied, 'Yes, absolutely. They carry more light and they stick out like a beacon in the night. Kinda like a lighthouse.' This, of course, again raises the question as to whether this is simply the repackaging of a contemporary religious worldview. Certainly, it is hard to avoid the fact that the 'enhanced spirituality' (Mack) typical of abductees is consistent with the Eastern-influenced New Age spirituality that has emerged in the West, particularly since the 1960s, much of which can be traced back to theosophical thought. That is to say, whilst strictly speaking much of it is *not* theosophical, it is part of a stream of alternative spirituality which is indebted implicitly to Theosophy and explicitly to ideas found within the Indian religious tradition. For example, in abduction spirituality, one can identify variations of the four principles identified by Andrew Rawlinson as central to contemporary Eastern-based Western spirituality:

1   Human beings are best understood in terms of *consciousness* and its modifications.
2   Consciousness can be transformed by *spiritual practice.*
3   There are *gurus/masters/teachers* who have done this.
4   They can help others to do the same by some form of *transmission* ... [which] ranges from formal initiation to a glance from the eye of the beloved.[99]

This spiritual interest in consciousness, he continues, 'affects every aspect of the human condition: what it is to be alive, to be born, to have a body, to die ... how society should be organized and according to what principles (politics, economics, ethics) ... the world and its origin (including space [and cosmology], time [and history and eternity], matter and energy; how consciousness works from the most mundane levels (drinking a glass of water) to the most rarefied (meditative states that are beyond all attributes) via the extra-ordinary (visionary encounters of every conceivable hue)'.[100] All four of the above principles and their broader implications can be found in UFO religions and abduction spiritualities, as can a host of other beliefs popular within the New Age network: e.g. reincarnation, *chakras,* past lives, future lives, psychic therapy, oneness with the Earth, channelling, astral travel and so on.

Even a cursory reading of abduction literature will reveal that aliens and alien cultures are understood to be vastly superior to our own in every respect. For example, one contactee pointed out to me that 'The Arcturians and other ET cultures have found ways in their evolutionary experience to have everything they need without striving, struggling and persevering, and competing – they are a "we" cooperative group – a collective consciousness. Lots of ET groups have evolved to a higher level where individuality and competition is not as important as the whole. We haven't gotten to that level yet.' And Porter has shown that, even in some sections of the North American Spiritualist community, alien beings are understood to be vastly spiritually superior to the usual spirit guides.[101] More specifically, aliens, when they are not believed to be malevolent beings, are very often understood to be concerned with the transformation of the human *consciousness,* both individually and collectively. Hence, aliens are understood to be *super-*gurus/-masters/-teachers who can be trusted with both the development of human consciousness and also the transmission of positive direction in all areas of human life, from personal preferences to the ordering of society. Life under the aliens cannot but be better for humans – individually and collectively – and for the planet.

This emphasis on the superiority of aliens has, quite understandably, influenced the way those who have met them and who work with them are perceived. Just as those who have faithfully sat at the feet of a guru and now relate the master's teachings are perceived to be wiser or further along the path to true knowledge, or just as channellers, like George King, are understood to be reliable sources of knowledge because of their role as conduits for advanced celestial beings, so it is often claimed that contactees and abductees have a greater awareness of 'the truth' than most of their fellow humans. They are the 'enlightened' ones and, according to Jacobs, 'they become angry when "less enlightened" abduction researchers question their interpretation'.[102] It is, he says, sometimes even suggested that, not only are abductees privy to advanced alien teaching, but they also 'possess an alien's "consciousness", which imbues their present human form'. Discussing the work of Massachusetts researcher Joseph Nyman, Jacobs makes the following observation:

> For Nyman, the evidence is 'overwhelming' that the aliens impose these dual feelings – human and alien – on the abductees. 'It implies the taking up of residence in the human form at birth (or before) of a fully developed intelligence which for a while is aware of both its human and non-human nature and of the pre-arranged monitoring to be conducted throughout life.' Abductees and aliens have 'melded' together in some way and in a sense abductees and aliens are the same. Abductees live their present lives with a 'dual reference', human and alien.[103]

For obvious reasons, this quite naturally leads to a sense of abductees being the *chosen ones*. 'An experiencer is a person specially chosen for a very important task.'[104] ('Experiencer' is increasingly the preferred term to 'abductee' in many abduction narratives. This, it would appear, is primarily because the latter has negative connotations when the overall experience should be understood positively, often in terms of privilege.) Outlining the views of many abductees, Jacobs comments that 'abductees have been chosen to undertake a mission to help humanity, Earth, the aliens and the universe. Abductees are not victims – they are important players in a majestic alien plan for the betterment of humanity. Enduring a little fear and pain is a small price to pay for taking part in such an important task.'[105] Whilst cautious about what she calls 'the chosen-one reaction' ('a common way of coping with abduction events'),[106] the idea of election is implicit in abductee Michelle LaVigne's *The Alien Abduction Survival Guide* (written specifically for abductees). For example, she writes of abductees belonging to 'the Secret Community' (of aliens, hybrids and abductees), and of being one of the 'Gemini people' – 'the main building blocks of the ET-built Community ... [who] have more control over what happens during abduction events and can have strong social bonds with ETs ... '[107] Again, this serves to elevate abductees to an enormously important and responsible position. According to LaVigne, abductees are pioneers entrusted with the preparation of the rest of humanity for the coming 'new world order'. Moreover, they will also have a special position in that new world order: 'The ETs are telling us that the world is going through some dramatic changes and will soon "end" as we know it. But it will not end completely. There will be people who survive past this "end" and make a new life on a new Earth ... The abductees will take over positions of teachers and caretakers of the populations.'[108] Hence, it is not unusual for abductees to understand themselves missiologically. 'Many if not most of the abductees with whom I have worked', claims Mack, 'intensively come to feel that their enhanced spiritual awareness must be translated into some form of teaching or higher purpose.'[109] Abductees are the new missionaries and, to slightly misquote John Wesley, 'the Earth is their parish'.

As to the gospel preached by these new missionaries, although new, it is nevertheless still one of sin and salvation. The human race has sinned, in the sense that we have, in particular, not cared for the Earth, misused the knowledge we have, and developed technologies capable of destroying ourselves and the planet. This notion of human transgression was of course very common in earlier theosophical UFO religions, many of which focused on the sin of nuclear power (see particularly Christopher Helland's discussion of George Van Tassel and Ashtar Command in Chapter 8). However, it is also one of salvation in that, as we have seen, there are beings from other worlds able to save us both spiritually and physically. These themes, which can be found in most, if not all, abduction spiritualities, are informed by a range of theologies and philosophies. For example, at one end of the spectrum there are abduction spiritualities tending towards monotheism. Psychologist Richard Boylan claims that aliens 'realize that there's a supreme being or a supreme source of everything. They are not kidded that they are at the top of the pile ... They acknowledge a supreme source out there – the fountainhead of all life.'[110] However, the dominant religious worldview within the abductee community lies at the other end of the spectrum and articulates what might be understood as a form of New Age self-spirituality.[111] Much abduction spirituality is detraditionalised, in the sense that the source of religious authority is located within, rather than being external. Whilst, as we have seen, it is true that consciousness transformation/evolution is alien-assisted – and therefore, from an *emic* perspective, there are *external* authorities – in the final analysis, the emphasis is on the self, on discovering what it is to fulfil one's destiny, on being in tune with one's innate spirituality, on experiencing one's connectedness to 'life', on the transformation of the self to a higher mode of being. For example, whilst LaVigne describes her alien guide, Hetar, as her 'mentor',[112] and whilst her own relationship seems to be one of guru and disciple (although it is clearly understood to be a friendly, even loving relationship), she provides the following advice for other abductees:

> ... follow your heart – and not your head – when making decisions about anything of a spiritual nature ... Only your heart can tell you what you really believe. If your heart tells you what the ETs are showing you is not real, then don't waste time believing it. If someday your heart's view changes, you may find yourself rethinking your position about what you have been taught ... I suggest that you spend some time meditating and thinking about it. Focus on your place in the eternal universe. Contemplate your right to exist in the vastness of time. It will reveal to you a world you know little about – the world of your heart.[113]

Similar illustrations of self-spirituality can be found Mack's work. For example:

> Abductees come to appreciate that the universe is filled with intelligences and is itself intelligent. They develop a sense of awe before a mysterious cosmos that becomes sacred and ensouled. The sense of separation from the rest of creation breaks down and the experience of oneness becomes an essential aspect of the evolution of the abductee's consciousness ... As their experiences are brought into full consciousness, abductees seem to feel increasingly a sense of

oneness with all beings and all of creation ... Each abductee experiences in some sense an expansion of his or her sense of self, of identity in the world ... The change that abductees experience is fundamentally that they may no longer feel themselves to be separate from other beings. They shed their identification with a narrow social role and gain a sense of oneness with all creation, a kind of universal connectedness ... With the opening of consciousness to new domains of being, abductees encounter patterns and a design of life that brings them a profound sense of interconnectedness in the universe.[114]

To broaden this discussion a little, it is I think significant that many therapists are themselves part of and contribute to an abduction self-spirituality culture. Hence, although Jacobs's comments have to be treated carefully because of his own anti-Positive agenda, he makes a worthwhile point when he argues that 'Many hypnotists and therapists who work with abductees adhere to New Age philosophies and actively search for confirmational material. During hypnosis, the hypnotist emphasizes material that reinforces his own worldview.'[115] This is certainly the impression one gets reading through Mack's interviews with abductees. His claim that 'Abductees become open to the presence of a divine source, which fills their being and gives them a sense of connection with a universal consciousness from which they have come and to which they will return',[116] corresponds to his often explicit sympathy with New Age spirituality and particularly Eastern perspectives, as well as his clearly positive understanding of the spiritual and psychological effects of alien contact. A notable example is the hypnosis session an abductee called Dave had with Mack and Kishwar Shirali.

Dave talked of what he was learning about Chi and its relationship to spiritual evolution, superstrings, and primal sources of energy in the universe ... He said he was learning to open his Chi and control it through his hands ... Dr Shirali spoke of similar processes with which she is familiar in yoga and Buddhist meditation. Dave said he had talked with Master Joe about the possibility that the alien beings have mastered the capacity to communicate telepathically using something like Chi ... Dave wondered ... if the aliens 'have known us before in other lifetimes' and if he had known them. Perhaps 'it's an ages-long kinship', he suggested. 'Maybe they help recycle souls or something, that they're not just concerned with our individual lifetimes but all our lifetimes as they relate to the development of the soul, the evolvement of the earth' ... As the session was ending Dr Shirali ... was struck by the way the conscious use of breath in the session had created a line or thread between my 'inner being' and Dave's ... The day before the last regression, Dave disclosed that he had once had an image several years before of having once been a cavalry spy during the Civil War ... This led to a discussion of the reality status of past life experiences. I suggested the possibility that consciousness is a 'continuous fabric' and that potentially we could be identified with any object in the cosmos, depending on the evolutionary task at hand. Dr Shirali spoke of the Hindu understanding 'of the whole divine thing that's also within you. The Brahma, the whole, the part reflects the whole, and the whole is reflected in the part ... There can't be a linear time.'[117]

It is not difficult to find abduction therapists who take similar explicitly Eastern-based self-spirituality approaches. For example, transpersonal psychotherapists Janet Colli and Thomas Beck claim that, following twelve years research, their approach 'brings together the psychology of close encounters, spiritual experience and, ultimately, enlightenment'. They go on to discuss their theories about Eastern mystics who 'have long been communicating with ... alien beings' who are, in turn, 'facilitating unity consciousness on our planet'. Furthermore, they claim that, in their forthcoming book, 'startling evidence establishing this connection will be revealed – evidence relating to the teachings of Maharishi Mahesh Yogi and Lamas of the Tibetan Buddhist tradition'. They then mention one client, Joy Gilbert, who was 'taken aboard a craft and warmly greeted by benevolent beings ... Standing before the craft's curved window, overlooking a mountainous terrain, Joy entered the state of consciousness that unites all of Creation: *Enlightenment!*' In the final analysis, for such therapists, aliens are central to the maximising of 'human potential' and play a 'pivotal role ... in the transformation of the human consciousness'.[118]

That Colli and Beck also mention 'ushering in [the] new era' is likewise fairly typical of New Age abduction spiritualities. Unlike many of the earlier 'new agers' who viewed the coming new era in strongly evolutionary terms (claiming that the Age of Aquarius, a new, better, more spiritual way of life, is dawning – its progress can be charted astrologically and its appearance is inevitable), whilst there are UFO religionists who understand it in this way, and others who, like some new agers, see the New Age in post-apocalyptic terms (see Jodi Dean's interesting study of abduction narratives in Chapter 12), generally speaking, spiritual abductees believe alien intervention and guidance to be crucial to the process. Likewise, as we have seen, most speak in utopian terms of the future of the planet under alien rule. Along with a gloomy view of the present order under human rule, there is a rosy view of the future order. LaVigne, for example, claims that the 'new world will be one of peace, art and unconditional love'.[119] Again, one of Mack's clients, Peter, 'envisages a future "Golden Age" of learning and opportunity, which he hopes to help bring about'.[120]

Finally, not unrelated to the above discussion is the ambiguous relationship with conventional science within the abductee community. Whilst, on the one hand, there is a desire to have abduction formally scientifically verified, on the other there is – as there is in much New Age thought – a strident critique of the reductionist methodology utilised by much Western science. As in UFO religion generally, anathema is the separation of the material and the spiritual, a separation often characterised by a denial of the reality of the latter. For example, Mack argued in a recent interview:

> The difficulty for our society and for our mentality is, we have a kind of either/or mentality. It's either literally physical, or it's in the spiritual other realm, the unseen realm. What we seem to have no place for – or we have lost the place for – are phenomena that can begin in the unseen realm, and cross over and manifest and show up in our literal physical world ... It's both literally, physically happening to a degree, and it's also some kind of psychological, spiritual experience occurring and originating in another dimension.[121]

Again, after commenting on obscure events such as abducted bodies passing through walls and deep wounds caused by alien surgery healing up within a very short period of time, he makes the following comment: 'we cannot begin to answer any of these questions within the framework of modern science ... multidisciplinary studies combining physics with comparative religion and spirituality are

needed to further consider how the interdimensional bridging proper-
ties of the abduction phenomenon might work'.[122]

Conclusion

Regardless of the veracity of claims of UFO sightings, extraterrestrial
contact and alien abduction, far from simply dropping out of the sky,
these religions and spiritualities are profoundly influenced by their
contexts and can be placed within certain traditions. We have seen
that, whilst the interest, religious or otherwise, in extraterrestrial life
has a long history, UFO religion *per se* emerged within the tradition
of theosophical esotericism, becoming firmly established as 'UFO
religion' during the wave of public interest following the 1947
Arnold sighting. Consequently, on the one hand, flying saucers and
alien technology are fundamentally a post-1947 phenomenon. On
the other hand, although individual groups and movements have
broken away from Theosophy to varying degrees, most retain key
theosophical themes and ideas. Although several fruitful lines of
thought could have been followed, and connections established
between, for example, idealised Venusian societies and esoteric
notions of Atlantis and other 'lost civilisations' (some believing the
mythic continents of Atlantis and Lemuria – or Mu – to have been
populated by aliens), perhaps the principal theosophical idea to
continue into ufoism is that of the ascended master. Whilst some
UFO religious belief systems continue explicitly to include *ascended*
masters, most work with what might be described as *descended*
masters. That is to say, the theosophical components are still there,
but the highly evolved entity is not now understood to have originated on Earth and *ascended*, but rather to have originated on
another planet and *descended* to Earth.

Such descended masters are clearly apparent in abduction spiritu-
alites. However, as we have seen, abduction spiritualities tend to be
more explicitly detraditionalised and New Age, the turn to the self in
abduction spiritualities mirroring the general shift towards self-spirituality that is taking place in Western cultures.[123] Moreover, bearing
in mind that much New Age thought emerges out of the theosophical tradition (particularly the branch that can be traced to Bailey
and the Arcane School), and also that aspects of it can be traced
back to post-1947 UFO religion which understood aliens to be
heralds of a new era,[124] it is not surprising that abduction spirituality
also has theosophical survivals within it.

Finally, we have also seen that, not only does much UFO religion understand itself to be a scientific pursuit, the focus of attention being advanced technologies, but this has, quite naturally, become particularly characteristic of it. Hence, whilst I have argued that UFO religions and spiritualities belong within the Theosophy–New Age tradition, they are distinctive in that, to one degree or another, they claim to offer a 'scientific' belief system. Some, such as the Raëlian Church, teach a form of ufological atheism which believes that traditional religious cosmologies and mythologies are explicable in physical terms; others, such as the Aetherius Society and Mark-Age, whilst fundamentally physicalist, expound a more traditionally theosophical worldview.

NOTES

1 For an excellent collection of essays which helpfully situates *The X-Files* in cultural, political and psychological contexts, see D. Lavery, A. Hague and M. Cartwright (eds), *Deny All Knowledge: Reading the X-Files*, London, Faber & Faber, 1996.

2 Reg Presley has invested much of the money he has made as lead singer of the Troggs into crop circle research. He believes that at least 20 per cent of the patterns that appear in fields overnight are messages created by UFOs.

3 E. von Däniken, *Chariots of the Gods? Unsolved Mysteries of the Past*, trans. M. Heron, London, Souvenir Press, 1969.

4 W. Strieber, *Communion: a True Story of Encounters with the Unknown*, London, Century, 1987.

5 B. Singer and V. A. Benassi, 'Occult Beliefs', *American Scientist*, vol. 69, 1981, p. 49.

6 See the excellent and fascinating study by Steven J. Dick, *Life on Other Worlds: the 20th-Century Extraterrestrial Life Debate*, Cambridge, Cambridge University Press, 1998.

7 See J. Clark, *The Emergence of a Phenomenon: UFOs from the Beginning Through 1959. The UFO Encyclopaedia*, vol. 2, Detroit, Omnigraphics, 1992.

8 These sightings had been reported throughout America, Europe and Scandinavia. Indeed, three days prior to Arnold's sighting, Harold Dahl reported several disc-shaped objects flying towards the Canadian border.

9 See R. E. Bartholomew and G. S. Howard, *UFOs and Alien Contact: Two Centuries of Mystery*, New York, Prometheus Books, 1998, ch. 8.

10 *Ibid.*, p. 189.

11 P. Lagrange, 'Kenneth Arnold', in J. R. Lewis (ed.), *UFOs and Popular Culture: an Encyclopaedia of Contemporary Myth*, Santa Barbara, ABC-Clio, 2000, p. 34.

12 C. Berlitz and W. L. Moore, *The Roswell Incident*, New York, Grosset & Dunlap, 1980. Charles Berlitz had already made a name for himself with his enormously popular *The Bermuda Triangle*, New York, Doubleday, 1974.

13 J. Dean, *Aliens in America: Conspiracy Cultures from Outerspace to Cyberspace*, Ithaca, Cornell University Press, 1998, p. 185.

14 *Ibid.*, pp. 182–3.
15 *Ibid.*, p. 183.
16 See J.-F. Mayer, 'Les Sauvers Venus de L'espace: Croyance aux Extraterrestres et Religions Soucoupistes', *Question de*, vol. 122, 2000, pp. 70–4.
17 See Dick, *Life on Other Worlds*, especially ch. 4.
18 See, for example, the claims made in R. L. Thompson, *Alien Identities*, Alachua, Govardhan Hill Publishing, 1995, and in B. Downing, *The Bible and Flying Saucers*, New York, Lippincott, 1968. See also Mikael Rothstein's discussion in Chapter 13 below.
19 See J. G. Melton, 'The Contactees: a Survey', in J. R. Lewis (ed.), *The Gods Have Landed: New Religions from Other Worlds*, Albany, State University of New York Press, 1995, pp. 2–8.
20 For example, whilst at the turn of the twentieth century Sara Weiss, a Spiritualist, reported contact with Martians, as Melton points out, 'Weiss's contacts with Mars were meant to validate Spiritualism while more clearly defining points upon which Spiritualists had failed to reach consensus. Immo, her Martian contact, talks through Weiss to the larger Spiritualist community ... [and verifies] a major spiritualist doctrine of belief in the necessity of mediums. Such conclusions far outweigh any information about life on Mars that were also included in the contact.' Melton, 'The Contactees: A Survey', pp. 5–6.
21 Ballard used the pseudonym Godfre Ray King: *Unveiled Mysteries*, Chicago, Saint-Germain Press, 1935.
22 C. Leadbeater, *A Textbook of Theosophy*, Adyar, Theosophical Publishing House, 1912.
23 See D. Stupple, 'Mahatmas and Space Brothers: the Ideologies of Alleged Contact with Mahatmas' and 'Space Brothers: the Ideologies of Alleged Contact with Extraterrestrials', *Journal of American Culture*, vol. 7, 1984, p. 131.
24 Melton, 'The Contactees: a Survey', p. 7.
25 Stupple, 'Mahatmas and Space Brothers', p. 133.
26 *Ibid.*, p. 134.
27 *Ibid.*134
28 H. P. Blavatsky, *The Key to Theosophy*, London, Theosophical Publishing House, 1889, p. 39.
29 H. P. Blavatsky, *The Secret Doctrine: The Synthesis of Science, Religion and Philosophy*, 2 vols, London, Theosophical Publishing House, 1888; Adyar, Theosophical Publishing House, 1978.
30 Melton, 'The Contactees: a Survey', p. 6.
31 A. Besant, *H. P. Blavatsky and the Masters of Wisdom*, London, Theosophical Publishing House, 1907, p. 60.
32 These communications can be found in T. A. Barker (ed.), *The Mahatma Letters to A. P. Sinnett*, 3rd edn, C. Humphries and E. Benjamin (eds), Adyar, Theosophical Publishing House, 1962.
33 T. H. Redfern, *The Work and Worth of Mme Blavatsky*, London, Theosophical Publishing House, n.d.
34 *Ibid.*, p. 32.
35 *Ibid.*, pp. 33–4 (emphasis in the original).
36 The Aetherius Society and Mark-Age are particularly prominent examples of theosophical religion which understands religious leaders in this

way. In the case of Mark-Age see, for example, the channelled text by Mark-Age's Nada-Yolanda, *Reappearance of Christ Consciousness on Earth*. This can be downloaded from the Mark-Age website. Available online: http://www.islandnet.com/arton/markage.html.

37 Mark-Age, *Reappearance of Christ Consciousness on Earth*.
38 Quoted in Stupple, 'Mahatmas and Space Brothers', pp. 134–5.
39 There was even a 'Venusian Church' established in Seattle in 1975 by former Seventh-Day Adventist, Ron Peterson. The church has attracted significant controversy as a result of its promotion of pornography and sexual promiscuity.
40 B. Creme, *The Reappearance of the Christ and the Masters of Wisdom*, London, Tara Press, 1980, p. 205.
41 See A. Grünschloß, *Wenn Die Götter Landed ... Religiöse Dimensionen des UFO-Glaubens*, EZW-Texte 153, Berlin, EZW, 2000, pp. 5–6.
42 Yogananda eventually established the Self-Realization Fellowship in 1935. Another example of Yogananda's influence would be the Brotherhood of the Sun, its founder Norman Paulsen being understood to be Yogananda's true successor (see Trompf's comments in Chapter 11, n. 53, below). Similarly, his influence is evident in Ruth Montgomery's writings. See, for example, R. Montgomery, *Aliens Among Us*, New York, Fawcett Crest, 1985, p. 146ff.
43 Steiger identifies various types of Beta Humanoids, all of which appear to be very good-looking humans. They are 'tall, blond, light-complexioned, idealized Nordic types'. B. Steiger, *Gods of Aquarius: UFOs and the Transformation of Man*, New York, Berkley, 1976, p. 99. See also his descriptions of the handsome Beta-2 Humanoid (p. 74), the beautiful Beta-F (i.e. female) Humanoid (p. 61) and the 'smelly, apelike monster' he identifies as 'the Gamma-Form Humanoid' (p. 141).
44 See, for example, A. Besant, *Blavatsky and the Masters of Wisdom*, p. 12.
45 D. Leslie and G. Adamski, *Flying Saucers Have Landed*, 2nd edn, London, Futura Publications, 1977, pp. 210–11.
46 *Ibid.*, pp. 216–17.
47 Desmond Leslie explains in a footnote that Orthon is 'the name Adamski's visitor allowed him to use, though he felt names quite unnecessary'. *Ibid.*, p. 269.
48 *Ibid.*, p. 220.
49 G. Adamski, *Pioneers of Space: a Trip to the Moon, Mars and Venus*, Los Angeles, Leonard-Freefield, 1949.
50 Leslie and Adamski, *Flying Saucers Have Landed*, p. 276.
51 Steiger, *Gods of Aquarius*, p. 236.
52 J. Porter, 'Spiritualists, Aliens and UFOs: Extraterrestrials as Spirit Guides', *Journal of Contemporary Religion*, vol. 11, 1996, p. 339.
53 Leslie and Adamski, *Flying Saucers Have Landed*, p. 272.
54 *Ibid.*, p. 236.
55 *Ibid.*, p. 9.
56 *Ibid.*, pp. 180–3.
57 *Ibid.*, pp. 221, 227.
58 A picture of the emblem is reproduced in G. Chryssides, 'Is God a Space Alien? The Cosmology of the Raëlian Church', *Culture and Cosmos*, vol. 4, 2000, p. 43.
59 Leslie and Adamski, *Flying Saucers Have Landed*, p. 277.

60 Creme, *Reappearance of the Christ*, p. 24.
61 *Ibid.*, p. 11.
62 *Ibid.*, p. 206.
63 *Ibid.*, p. 207
64 *Ibid.*, p. 205.
65 *Ibid.*, p. 207.
66 A similar point is made with regard to *fraternité interplanétaire* and *cosmopolitism transcendental*, by Jean-François Mayer in 'Les Sauvers Venus de L'espace', p. 77.
67 See also A. Grünschloß, *Wenn Die Götter Landed ... Religiöse Dimensionen des UFO-Glaubens*, pp. 12ff.
68 Mark-Age, *I Am Nation Newsletter*. Availableonline:http://www.island net. com/arton/markage.html (10 May 2002).
69 G. King, *Become a Builder of the New Age!*, London, Aetherius Society, 1963, p. 3.
70 Of course, as noted above, Porter has shown that some Spiritualists claim to have alien guides. See J. Porter, 'Spiritualists, Aliens and UFOs: Extraterrestrials as Spirit Guides', pp. 337–53.
71 G. King, *The Practices of Aetherius*, London, Aetherius Society, 1957, p. 5.
72 King, *Become a Builder of the New Age!*, p. 7.
73 This often seems to be understood in the following way: God is situated at the top of the celestial hierarchy, other key beings, such as the Archangel Michael, Christ, the Buddha, El Morya and other masters (often identified as extraterrestrial beings), are further down, spiritually evolved aliens may be yet further down, and the poor unenlightened human race is lower down still.
74 E. von Däniken, *Miracles of the Gods: a Hard Look at the Supernatural*, trans. M. Heron, London, Book Club Associates, 1976.
75 Because it is difficult to recall von Däniken's massive cultural impact, it is worth noting the following comment by Ronald Story, a strident critic of von Däniken, written only three years after the publication of *Gold of the Gods*:

> Few books have captured the imagination and appealed to the religious yearnings of the general public as much as *Chariots of the Gods?* (1968), *Gods from Outer Space* (1968), and *The Gold of the Gods* (1973) by Erich von Däniken. The arrival of the 'ancient astronauts' has been heralded by two major network television specials, two 'major motion pictures', and more than sixty books that refer either directly or indirectly to von Däniken's theories. The American NBC-TV special 'In Search of Ancient Astronauts' gave the Swiss amateur archaeologist the boost needed to attain super-best-sellerdom (sales of more than 12 million copies in the United states, 34 million worldwide) and spawned what the Australian press has diagnosed as 'Dänikenitis'. (R. Story, *The Space-Gods Revealed: a Close Look at the Theories of Erich von Däniken*, London, Book Club Associates, 1977, p. 1.)

76 Däniken, *Chariots of the Gods?*, pp. 58–63.
77 *Ibid.*, p. 67.

78 See Däniken, *Return to the Stars: Gods from Outer Space*, trans. M. Heron, London, Souvenir Press, 1970, pp. 146ff.
79 See Däniken, *Miracles of the Gods*.
80 From an interview: 'The Real Erich von Däniken', Channel 4 (5 February 2001).
81 J. Barranger and P. Tice, *Mysteries Explored: the Search for Human Origins, UFOs and Religious Beginnings*, London, Book Tree, 2000.
82 D. H. Childress, *Extraterrestrial Archaeology*, Illinois, Adventures Unlimited, 2000.
83 Däniken, *Chariots of the Gods?*, p. 66. Whilst there is no explicit reference to Adamski's ideas in *Chariots of the Gods?*, it seems unlikely that von Däniken was not influenced to some degree by him.
84 *Ibid.*, p. 66.
85 The leader of the Elohim, Yahweh, gave Vorilhon his new name, Raël.
86 This was explained in an interview on the Sunday programme, BBC Radio 4 (10 February 2002).
87 S. J. Palmer, 'The Raël Deal', *Religion in the News*, vol. 4:2, 2001. Available online: http://www.trincoll.edu/depts/csrpl/RIN.html.
88 *Ibid.*
89 *Ibid.*
90 J. Whitmore, 'Religious Dimensions of the UFO Abductee Experience', in Lewis (ed.), *The Gods Have Landed*, p. 65.
91 I should note at this point that I am not interested in debunking abductee experiences, since (a) as with religious experience *per se*, it is difficult to see how such accounts could convincingly be verified or falsified in the absence of aliens willing to testify to their activities, and (b) often attempts to debunk produce less convincing explanations than the accounts themselves.
92 D. Jacobs, *The Threat*, London, Pocket Books, 1999, p. 19.
93 See the website of transpersonal psychologists Janet Elizabeth Colli and Thomas Beck. Available online: http://4aliens.4anything.com/network-frame/0,1855,1361–47891,00.html (August, 2002).
94 J. E. Mack, *Abduction: Human Encounters with Aliens*, London, Simon & Schuster, 1994, p. 397.
95 Jacobs, *Threat*, p. 251.
96 Gail Seymour. Available online: http://www.abduct.com/irm.htm (July 2002).
97 *Ibid.*
98 See particularly D. Icke, *The Biggest Secret*, Ryde, Bridge of Love, 1999.
99 A. Rawlinson, *The Book of Enlightened Masters: Western Teachers in Eastern Traditions*, Chicago, Open Court, 1997, p. xvii.
100 *Ibid.*, pp. xvii–xviii.
101 Porter, 'Spiritualists, Aliens and UFOs: Extraterrestrials as Spirit Guides', pp. 343–4.
102 Jacobs, *Threat*, p. 218.
103 *Ibid.*, p. 211.
104 *Ibid.*, p. 214.
105 *Ibid.*, p. 218.
106 See M. LaVigne, *The Alien Abduction Survival Guide*, Newberg, Wild Flower Press, 1995, pp. 10, 107.

107 See *ibid.*, pp. xi, 6–7. 'The name "Gemini" was chosen by the people of the Secret Community. It was not chosen because of astrological signs, but because it is symbolic of the double life we lead' (p. 6).
108 *Ibid.*, pp. 75–6.
109 Mack, *Abduction*, p. 408.
110 Quoted in Jacobs, *Threat*, p. 211.
111 For a good recent discussion of New Age self- and life-spirituality, see P. Heelas, 'The Spiritual Revolution: from "Religion" to "Spirituality"', in L. Woodhead *et al.* (eds), *Religions in the Modern World: Traditions and Transformations*, London, Routledge, 2002, pp. 357–78.
112 LaVigne, *Survival Guide*, p. xii.
113 *Ibid.*, p. 80.
114 Mack, *Abduction*, p. 418.
115 Jacobs, *Threat*, p. 220.
116 Mack, *Abduction*, p. 409.
117 *Ibid.*, pp. 280, 283, 284, 288.
118 Colli and Beck. Available online:http://4aliens.4anything.com/network -frame/0,1855,1361–47891,00.html.
119 LaVigne, *Survival Guide*, p. 76.
120 Mack, *Abduction*, p. 408.
121 J. E. Mack, Interview with *Nova*. Available online:http://www.pbs.org/ wgbh/nova/aliens/johnmack.html (30 April 2002).
122 Mack, *Abduction*, pp. 403–4.
123 Again, see Paul Heelas's discussion of this general shift: 'Spiritual Revolution', pp. 357–77.
124 This connection with the emergence of contemporary New Age religion has been noted by Wouter Hannegraaff: 'New Age Religion', in L. Woodhead *et al.* (eds), *Religions in the Modern World*, pp. 250–1.

Part II

OBSERVING RELIGIONS

2

SCIENTIFIC CREATIONISM

A study of the Raëlian Church

George D. Chryssides

Those who are outside the UFO religions often find them difficult to take seriously. While there seems to be nothing abnormal about watching cult programmes such as *The X-Files*, or even believing that extraterrestrial life exists, making a religion out of ufology seems to be going a step too far. On explaining the Raëlians' worldview to others, even at academic conferences where colleagues are trained to display empathic understanding, the movement's ideas are met with incredulity or even mirth. Yet, in common with many new religious movements (NRMs), the Raëlians have a perfectly coherent worldview, to which its followers sincerely subscribe.

The Raëlian Church appears to offer a radical alternative to conventional religion. It purports to be scientific; it is hedonistic; and it is materialistic and atheistic, dispensing entirely with the supernatural. In our twenty-first-century religious climate, religion is beset by an array of challenges – secularisation, empiricism and verificationism – all of which have contributed towards a crisis of faith, even among religious leaders, about whether traditional belief in God is outmoded, how suffering is to be explained, whether one can really expect continued existence after death, and even whether it might be possible to have a religion without metaphysics. The Raëlian movement appears to afford a solution to these problems, not only apparently reconciling science and religion, but offering a synthesis which incorporates the paranormal, seeking to explain claims made within 'fringe science' in scientific terms. Yet the Raëlian movement remains small: about 55,000 members worldwide, with a mere 40 members and 200 'sympathisers' in Britain.

In this chapter I aim to show that, while the Raëlian Church appears effectively to address several salient issues that threaten contemporary religion, it possesses other features that distance it from the dominant intellectual climate. In particular, I shall argue that Raëlianism is characterised by being at a very early developmental stage, and by an intellectual introversion that creates an absence of dialogue with relevant interest groups in wider society. In order to do this I shall first outline the current problems, which are often judged to place religion under attack: these are principally secularisation, verificationism and the rise of science, all of which have profoundly affected the Raëlian movement. Second, I shall offer a survey of the Raëlian Church, indicating how it appears to address such issues; and finally I shall make some observations about the factors which, in my judgement, currently inhibit the organisation's further development.

Challenges to traditional religion

Secularisation

In 1979 the sociologist Roy Wallis produced his well-known typology of religions in which he distinguished between the world-affirming, the world-renouncing and the world-accommodating.[1] The world-affirming religions, he contended, portray the world as real, good (although not perfect) and worth entering into, emphasising virtues like family life and work. By contrast, the world-renouncing religions portray the world as evil, as unreal, and as something to be transcended, and frequently separate themselves off from the world by establishing monastic orders, or living in communities apart from the world. The third category – the world-accommodating – occupies a medial position between the other two, and is not particularly relevant to the ensuing discussion.

I have elsewhere argued that religions, whether old or new, do not fit neatly into any one of Wallis's three categories: most, if not all, tend to have elements of each.[2] Religions typically identify a serious condition to which humanity, or the universe more generally, is subject – *maya* (illusion, in Hinduism), *dukkha* (unsatisfactoriness, in Buddhism), or sin (in Christianity), and religions typically prescribe remedies, involving spiritual paths, the pursuit of which runs contrary to human desire. Most versions of Christianity – the religious tradition in which Claude Vorilhon, the Raëlians' founder – leader was raised – have their world-renouncing elements, ranging from celibacy and monasticism to simple acts performed by the laity such as giving up trivial pleasures for Lent. World-renunciation is particularly difficult in an age when scientific and technological advance affords so many luxuries and creature comforts, tempting believers away from world-renouncing aspirations.

As Western Christianity becomes eroded by the secularisation process, people turn to secular solutions for problems that religion traditionally addressed: non-judgemental counselling, for example, is more prevalent than a member of the clergy hearing confession or giving admonition. Christian ethics often (and intentionally) runs counter to desire, by typically insisting that sexual activities should be confined to marriage, that same-sex relationships are unacceptable, that abortion should only be permitted to save the life of the mother, or that terminally ill patients who are in great pain should not be permitted to end their misery. As the proponents of the secularisation thesis have pointed out, not only has church attendance dwindled, with less than 10 per cent of the English population attending church, but the Church has lost its hold on people's values and behaviour. As one colleague recently remarked to the present writer, although some 70 per cent still claim to believe in God, the British population is 'functionally atheist'.

It is within this content of secularisation that Raëlianism can be understood. Raëlianism claims to be an atheistic religion: as Bryan Sentes and Susan Palmer claim, it exists 'within the horizon of the death of God'.[3] Its values are worldly and hedonistic, rather than based on a deferential relationship to a supreme metaphysical deity, although it is important to note that it does not claim that 'anything goes' in morality, only that pleasurable or self-interested actions that harm no one should not be proscribed.

Science and verificationism

A further type of challenge to traditional religion has been verifiability. Christianity typically has emphasised faith, discouraged doubt and insisted that tangible signs of its veracity are not needed. 'Blessed are those who have not seen, and yet have believed', Jesus says to doubting Thomas (John 20:29) when the latter insists on empirical proof that Jesus has indeed risen from the dead in bodily form. From the standpoint of faith, this may seem acceptable enough. However, modern science rests on observation, experimentation and empirical proof – the antithesis of faith. The rise of empiricism in philosophy has cast aspersions, not merely on religions' claims to offer truth, but on their very intelligibility, creating a problem that Christian philosophers of religion are still attempting to address.

Christianity and science have had an uneasy relationship during the last 500 years, with mainstream Christianity attempting to stem the flow of scientific and technological advance. The Roman Catholic Church opposed the work of Galileo and Copernicus, preferring to rely on its own traditional authority and on scriptures that presented an 'unscientific' and outmoded worldview, with a flat Earth that was created around 4000 BCE, demons, miracle workers and so on. The nineteenth century saw the rise of historical science, which cast aspersions on the Bible's historicity and its special status as a sacred book. Darwinism is still unwelcome in many conservative Christian circles, being perceived as incompatible with the account of creation given in the book of Genesis.

In more recent times, advances in genetic engineering have proved disturbing, not only to religious believers, but to the public more widely. Although many of the expressed fears relate to alleged health risks (for example, fear of contracting new illnesses by consuming genetically modified foods) or problems of cross-pollination with conventional crops, the principal objection is a quasi-religious one, namely that the creation of life ought to be the exclusive prerogative of a divine being. With genetic engineering, it looks as if humanity is now 'playing God', by being able to create and modify life, creating 'designer babies' and eliminating genetic characteristics that potentially may lead to serious medical conditions.

All this is the background against which it is important to view Raëlianism as an attempt to devise a form of religion that does justice to science, to intellectual advance and to human well-being, which regards metaphysics as outmoded and seeks to devise a form of religion that is empirical and world-affirming. The Raëlian Church finds few problems with these attacks on traditional Christianity, and indeed endorses them. Raëlians complain that traditional religion has 'mysticised' God. For the Raëlian Church, by contrast, there is no problem: Raëlianism proposes a system of belief in which there is no truth-claim that lacks verifiability, since there is nothing that does not exist at a physical level. The Elohim are physical beings, who can be empirically observed; they are scientifically and technologically advanced, and hence their knowledge is to be appropriated and used for their creatures' well being. Human welfare is to be furthered, and human pleasure encouraged; hence the Raëlians promote the antithesis of a religion that involves self denial or austerity. Since religion is to be used for human benefit, its ethical codes of practice should benefit human beings and not exacerbate their problems: Raëlianism is unashamedly hedonistic, and, if science and technology can benefit humanity, their progress should not be halted by outmoded religious principles, but should be positively encouraged.

Also worth mentioning at this juncture is the current interest in the paranormal, in particular in UFOs and crop circles. Such phenomena have attracted widespread interest and, as yet, no convincing explanations are forthcoming. The phenomena are undoubtedly real enough: there are certainly UFOs in the sense of objects that appear to fly and defy identification, and the existence of crop circles, if not their true explanation, is well-documented. The Raëlian Church not only offers an explanation for such phenomena, but one which purports to be compatible with science: it involves no Kuhnian paradigm shift, suggesting that conventional science must be superseded, but explains the phenomena in terms that are thoroughly compatible with a present-day Western scientific worldview.

The origins of the Raëlian religion

In order to see how these ideas are worked out in Raëlian thought, we must turn to the origins of the movement. The Raëlian religion was founded by Claude Vorilhon (1946–), who was born and raised in France, and whose ambition was to become a racing car driver. Vorilhon never achieved this goal, mainly because of the expensive nature of the sport and his lack of success in gaining the necessary sponsorship. Vorilhon had to remain content with editing a small-scale motor sport journal; he also enjoyed writing songs and poems, and made some headway as a singer. On 13 December 1973, however, Vorilhon relates, he was walking in the extinct volcanic region near Clermont-Ferrand in the French Auvergne when he discovered a spacecraft. A small man emerged from the spacecraft, only 4 feet tall, with a beard and almond shaped eyes, and began to engage Vorilhon in conversation. If it seems surprising that space aliens in films always manage to speak Earth languages (usually English) fluently, this remarkable phenomenon presents no problem for the Raëlians, for the amazing knowledge the 'creators' possess, they aver, includes the ability to speak every human language.

Vorilhon was instructed to return the following day, and to bring his Bible. If it seems initially surprising that Raëlianism should be based almost as much on Judaeo – Christian scripture as on ufology, it should be remembered that the Raëlian Church does not accept the Bible literally. Much of it, the alien explained, consists of 'poetic babblings',[4] but amidst much unprofitable material, there exists a core of deeper meaning which has survived the continual process of scribal copying throughout the millennia. The alien claimed to be able to shed proper light on the meaning of scripture, and the name by which Vorilhon is better known to his followers, 'Raël', is said to mean 'the one who brings the light' or 'the light of the Elohim'. This name, apparently, was given to him on a subsequent space journey, by Yahweh, the Elohim's leader.

The next day, Raël returned with his Bible and was given an extended lesson in biblical exegesis, starting with the book of Genesis and the story of creation. The first point that was explained to him was that the word 'Elohim', generally translated as 'God', is plural rather than singular – a point that tends not to be satisfactorily explained within either Judaism or Christianity. This demonstrates that the human race has not been created by one single creator god, but by several. As the alien explained, 'Elohim' means 'those who came from the sky'. They are extra-terrestrial scientists who discovered the Earth's existence in their travels through space, and judged it to be capable of sustaining life. The alien went on to describe the various stages of the world's creation: this took an extended period of time, not six literal earth days; the six 'days' are six zodiacal periods each spanning some 2,000 years.

The human race is thus an 'artificial' life form, created by the Elohim. The Elohim too have had their own physical creators, who in turn had their creators also, and so on ad infinitum. This cosmology entails an infinite regression of creators, each one larger than their respective creations, but Raëlianism sees nothing wrong with postulating such a regression. After all, the universe is infinite, so why should it not contain an infinite number of creators and creations?

Although Raëlianism is a religion that welcomes scientific discovery and advance, the one widely held scientific theory to which it cannot subscribe is Darwin's theory of evolution. Both biblical fundamentalism and Raëlianism agree that humanity came into being as a special creation, not from some pre-human species as part of an evolutionary process. However, Raëlianism's objection to evolutionism does not derive from the fact that creationism is enshrined in holy writ, but from scientific considerations. One's genes, Raëlians argue, contain within themselves an anti-evolutionary system, being designed to avoid mutation. Irregularities in one's system are corrected rather than perpetuated. Hence there is a tendency for any species to remain as it is, and for mutations to be kept in check, rather than for mutated species to develop into separate new ones. Thus Raëlianism is creationist, but, unlike biblical fundamentalism, for purportedly scientific reasons. Raëlians thus refer to their position as 'scientific creationism'.

The Elohim, who have specially created the human race, have made contact with their creatures at various points in history, particularly through prophets such as Moses, Elijah, Ezekiel and Jesus. They have made spiritual links for humanity, by providing teachings that were geared to humanity's readiness for truth. Raëlians thus hold a theory of progressive truth, rather like Mahayana Buddhism's concept of 'provisional truth': a truth that falls short of the absolute, complete truth, but which is adapted according to humanity's readiness at any particular time and place. In the Bible, it is argued, spacecraft explicitly feature: for example, the celestial chariots of Elijah (2 Kings 2:11) and Ezekiel (Ezekiel 1) are both spaceships belonging to the Elohim. The pillar of fire that guides the Israelites through the desert (Exodus 13:21–2) is identified as a spacecraft, as is the 'star' that the Magi follow to find the infant Jesus (Matthew 2:1–9). Jesus, it is said, will return to earth on the 'clouds of heaven' (Mark 14:62): what else can this mean other than a spaceship? If the Bible's descriptions seem somewhat crude and imprecise, this is because of the difficulty that primitive people had in explaining highly technological devices: after all, as the Raëlians argue, how would a twenty-first-century individual describe a helicopter to someone living a millennium ago?[5]

In Raël's first lesson from the space alien, the teachings are confined to those of the Jewish–Christian tradition. Later Raëlian literature finds support for its ideas in the writings of other religious traditions. For example, the ancient Egyptians spoke of 'circles of fire', and the Romans of 'spheres' in the sky. Taoism tells of the 'sons of the sky' descending to earth to herald the birth of Huang Ti and Chi You, and in Islam, Muhammad on his journey travels through the sky on al-Buraq. The Buddhist scripture, the Lotus Sutra, portrays the Buddha Prabutaratna arriving in his 'treasure tower' to meet Shakyamuni, the historical Buddha. Through time, however, the teachings of all these religions became distorted, and humans came to believe that the gods (or one single god) were some kind of invisible metaphysical beings, rather than a thoroughly physical race of beings who came from another planet.

Sometimes the Elohim leave physical traces of their presence among humankind. One recent example is the proliferation of crop circles in Britain, which the Raëlians believe are marks made by alien spacecraft landing in fields. Raëlianism therefore endeavours not only to reconcile religion and science, but also to appropriate and explain the claims of 'fringe science' as well. It will be obvious that the Raëlian Church's interpretation of ancient religion is somewhat reminiscent of

Erich von Däniken's, whose *Chariots of the Gods?* was a popular piece of fringe science first published in 1969. Raëlians deny von Däniken's influence, maintaining – as one would expect – that their ideas derive from Raël's own encounters with extraterrestrials. However, one member, in personal correspondence, acknowledged that von Däniken 'wrote some great books'.

The Elohim continue to make various journeys to Earth to examine how their experiment in genetic engineering is faring, and they have made contact through the ages with those who seem sympathetic to their ideals. In their earlier years, Raëlians regarded their founder–leader as one such human contactee. However, even within its short period of existence, Raëlian teachings have developed, raising the status of Raël, who is now regarded as no ordinary human being, but as having had a miraculous birth as a result of the union between one of the Elohim and Raël's human mother. Raël is now described as the Elohim's messiah, who heralds a new zodiacal age. The age of Jesus, the messiah of the Christian era, has now ended, and the Raëlian Church is the new religion that supersedes Christianity, which it regards as a phenomenon of the past.

Politics and ideology

As the new messiah, Raël's role is to bring about the new society, heralded by the arrival of the Elohim. The time has come for the Elohim to return, since they now want to see the results of their genetic experiment. They come in peace, not to conquer the earth, but to establish a system of world government, in which the virtues of education, human merit, science and technological advance will be respected and pursued. The Elohim have no wish to impose this new political system on humankind, who must first demonstrate that they wish to accept it freely. The circumstances of their arrival and reception by humankind must be carefully planned, however. If the Elohim were simply to descend unannounced in their spacecraft, their arrival would constitute an invasion; it would be illegal, and in all probability would provoke a dangerous armed confrontation, which would thwart their purpose in coming. In order to receive an appropriate welcome on earth, the Elohim have therefore asked Raël to prepare an embassy for them, and have provided appropriate plans for its construction.

The embassy will not only receive the extraterrestrial visitors when they arrive; it will host the annual gathering of 144,000 Raëlians. Being a government building, the embassy will not be generally accessible either to the public or to its own members; however, a second, replica embassy, which will be publicly accessible, will be constructed alongside. Obviously, such a project will be expensive: the current esti-mated cost is US $20 million, of which the Raëlians claim already to have collected US $7 million.

The country that the Elohim have selected for the embassy is Israel. This is because the Jewish people play a particular significance in Raëlian thought. The Jews are believed to be descendents of the 'Nephelin' (i.e. Nephilim: Genesis 6:4), a special race of people who came into existence from sexual relationships in ancient times between some of the Elohim and humans. As we have seen, in some of the organisation's more recent writings Raël himself is believed to be a hybrid between Elohim and human, having been born as a result of a sexual relationship between Yahweh, the Elohim's leader, and Raël's human mother. Raël is, therefore, as noted above, sometimes described as the messiah; the embassy will effectively be the Third Temple, for which some Jews have been campaigning in recent years.

Time is getting short. The Elohim are expected to arrive around the year 2035, and already the Raëlians have attempted to make prepara-tions. In 1990 they took the decision to modify their symbol, which ironically was a swastika – hardly conducive to fostering good relation-ships with the Israeli government. Raël claims that he saw this symbol on an Elohim spacecraft: it connotes the ancient Aryan symbol of power, rather than Nazism, and the recent modification of its symbol rounds out the angles of the former swastika, making it look more like a swirl. Having done this, the Raëlians first made representations to the Israeli government and also to Jerusalem's Chief Rabbi. Permission to prepare for the embassy was withheld, and various subsequent over-tures have resulted in a similarly negative outcome. At the time of writing the Raëlian Church is considering alternative locations, antici-pating that the Jews may once again reject the new messiah, just as they rejected Jesus.

The Elohim's arrival will herald a new political system. They do not come to conquer, but to assist humanity in establishing a new govern-ment, based on love and respect for all human beings. The present political system, Raëlians believe, is deficient in a number of ways. It has not fully reaped the benefits that are available through advancing science and technology, and those who are now in government are not invariably those who have the intelligence to govern, or the will to bring appropriate scientific and technological progress or to ensure that sufficient education is available to facilitate such advance. When the Elohim arrive, they will help to establish a superior government on this planet. This government will create a paradise on Earth, and will solve humanity's problems by applying technological solutions to them.

The Raëlian system of government is somewhat reminiscent of Plato's *Republic*. It is important, Raël teaches, that one's rulers have appropriate personal and educational development. Democracy does not ensure that the best rulers come into office, since the electorate is often ill-educated, misguided and content with a society that falls short of a perfect utopia. When the Elohim arrive on Earth, they will assist humanity to set up a 'geniocratic world government' in which only those who are at least 50 per cent more intelligent than average will be allowed to rule. The unintelligent, the uneducated and the reactionary have no place here.

Being a world government, it will have a single currency, which will be a prelude to the abolition of the monetary system altogether, since the affluence of the future utopia will make rationing by money unnecessary. There will be a unified world calendar, which will not be based on any single religion: Raëlians deplore the fact that Christianity, which to them epitomises human repression, should define calendrical dates worldwide. (Raëlians themselves currently define their dates from the year of Raël's birth.) The Elohim will bring with them the great prophets of the past (Moses, Elijah, the Buddha, Jesus and Muhammad are explicitly named), who are not dead but have been living on their planet, and who will help to establish on Earth the Elohim's religion, with Raëlian 'guides' (those occupying the highest echelons of its hierarchy) as its priests. This religion will not be imposed, however, but the Elohim will present it to humankind for men and women to choose.

The new paradise on Earth will involve a society in which pleasure is encouraged. Christianity, Raëlians believe, has been repressive, emphasising restraint and imposing taboos, for example regarding sexuality. The Raëlian Church holds that everything should be permitted, so long as it does not harm anyone or impede scientific and technological advance. Raëlians have no problems about extramarital sex, for example, or about homosexuality, nudity, contraception and abortion. On his visit to the Elohim's planet, Raël claims to have been entertained by robotic simulated nude dancers, who were freely available for entertainment and sexual gratification. After all, as Raël has pointed out, the book of Genesis sets Adam and Eve in a primordial paradise in which they were 'naked and not ashamed' (Genesis 2:25). The human body therefore should give no cause for shame.

This government will use technology to solve the world's problems. Armed conflict will be a thing of the past: weapons and military forces will no longer be used for aggression but for the maintenance of law and order in society. Crime will be solved by medical science: if someone is socially deviant, then genetic engineering can be used to modify the offender's cells. Raëlians see no problem with this: after all, they believe that humanity's creation was itself an experiment in genetic engineering on the part of the Elohim. In contrast with the majority of the public, who are very wary of genetically modified (GM) foods, and often seek to avoid them, GM foods are positively welcomed by the Raëlians. They are the results of scientific and technological progress, and can help towards solving present-day problems of world hunger. At a more mundane level, robots will assume the menial tasks that humans now perform out of necessity. The time humans save can then be spent enjoying life – furthering one's education, reading, or playing at some sport. If one prefers simply to do nothing, then this is permissible too.

This technological utopia purportedly offers hope beyond one's present life: the Elohim have the power to clone and recreate those who have died. However, they will only use those powers on those who merit it. During one's lifetime, everyone will have their deeds monitored by computer, so that accurate evidence will be available to enable the Grand Council of the Eternals to make an appropriate decision. Some of one's cells will be deposited in a clone bank before one dies, whereupon the creators will then decide whether the deceased is worthy of a replica. Immortality will be conferred on these cloned individuals, while the others will simply enter oblivion. Thus, Raëlianism teaches a kind of 'conditional immortality' – a doctrine that posits immortality as a possible expectation after death, but not an automatic right to be bestowed on all. Immortality will, of course, be in the form of a physical body rather than any disembodied soul. The great prophets who live on the Elohim's planet – presumably with the exception of Elijah, who escaped death – have been cloned by the creators and continue to survive: Jesus' resurrection, Raël has stated, was due to the Elohim's cloning technology, rather than a supernatural miracle.

In exceptional circumstances, it might be desirable to clone the unworthy. The Elohim have it in their power to make replicas of individuals to experience eternal punishment as well as eternal pleasure. The idea of after-death punishment has not loomed large in Raëlian thought; however, following the events of 11 September 2001, when suicide hijackers crashed planes into the World Trade Center in New York and the Pentagon in Washington, the Raëlian Church commented on its website that their policies could provide due redress for victims and assassins alike. The perpetrators would be revived to stand trial, and the victims could be cloned, but with erasure of the memories of their final traumatic movements.

Raëlian projects

Already, the Raëlian movement has set up a number of projects to further their ideology, mainly in the field of genetics, under the name of Valiant Venture Ltd. Media attention has particularly focused on 'Clonaid', founded in February 1997, a venture that was assigned to Dr Brigitte Boisselier, a Raëlian bishop. The project, when in operation, will enable subscribers to secure their own cloned replica by banking a sample of their DNA while they are alive. Two conditions apply: only one cloned replica is allowed for each individual, and the clone can only be made after the subscriber's death, not before. Apparently the same rules apply on the Elohim's planet. In the year 2001 the first human cloning laboratory was established in the United States, but on account of legal issues relating to human cloning, the project had to be transferred to another (unspecified) country – possibly in the Bahamas.

Another project, 'Ovulaid', offers services to couples who are incapable of having children, either on account of sterility, or where there are same-sex partners. Ovulaid unashamedly aims to create 'designer babies', gestated to the clients' specification. 'Insuraclone' seeks to preserve a human being's cells for the purposes of future cloning or future organ replacement: this could avert or reverse bodily conditions that give rise to numerous diseases: diabetes and Alzheimer's disease are specifically mentioned. Finally, 'Clonapet', as the name suggests, would enable pet owners to deposit cells of their favourite pets, so that they can be cloned after their deaths. These projects still await fruition, but Raëlians insist that, in the light of recent scientific advance, these are live possibilities and no longer science fantasies. However, at least in their early days, they will prove costly: at the time of writing the Raëlian Church mentions US $5,000 as the cost of buying and selling a human egg, and US $200,000 as the fee for the complete Ovulaid service; the rate for Insuraclone is set at US $175 per year.

Some critical reflections on Raëlianism

Is all of the above science fantasy or future reality? Particularly in the field of genetics, much of the Raëlians' agenda could soon become genuine possibility; at present, it is questions of ethics that hold scientists back from achieving them. Given that science is creating such exciting prospects, why should there not be a religion that anticipates them, welcomes them and formulates a detailed and considered policy about how they might be used? Why is it, then, that Raëlianism tends to meet with incredulity? Inherently, the movement has a coherent worldview, and in many respects, as I have shown, offers a healthy alternative to the constraints that conventional Christianity typically imposes on its members. Its belief in ufology should not mark it out as absurd, since recent surveys have indicated that 50 per cent of the US population believe that UFOs are real and not imaginary; 46 per cent believe that extraterrestrial life forms exist, with a further 18 per cent unsure; and 14 per cent actually claim to have seen a UFO.[6]

The central problem, I believe, that prevents Raëlianism from becoming more widely accepted, is that it is based on an exclusive revelation afforded to one single individual, Raël. Apart from its 'high-tech' details, the story of Raël's initial encounter at Clermont-Ferrand has all the aspects of a typical religious foundation myth, which purportedly demonstrates Vorilhon's authority and legitimates his role as prophetic leader. It is a kind of inaugural vision, in which he effectively receives a commission to carry out an important task on behalf of the Elohim. In this regard it is similar to the stories of Isaiah's vision in the Temple (Isaiah 6), Jesus's seeing God's Spirit descend at his baptism (Mark 1:9–11), or Joseph Smith's vision in the sacred grove at Palmyra, New York. As Carl Jung argued, UFO stories are themselves present-day myths, featuring visions of spacecraft and alien abductions.

Raël's two decisive encounters, it seems, were only experienced by himself, and afforded to no-one else. In the absence of verification in the form of the Elohim's expected arrival, his encounters, instructions and messianic status can only be taken on trust. Although the existence of extraterrestrial life forms is verifiable in principle, only a very small sector of the world's population would claim to have verified it in practice. For the vast majority who have not experienced any 'close encounters', any such claims to be contactees must either be met with scepticism, or at best accepted in faith. Raëlians themselves appear to accept Raël's testimony, deriving their beliefs largely from Raël's own writings and speeches. Seeking for UFOs and directly communicating with extraterrestrials, although not prohibited, does not play a significant role in the Church's agenda. As their web site explains:

> The UFO dimension alone is totally boring. It is the philosophical, the religious dimension which interests us. What do

Extraterrestrials change in the minds of human beings is the
interesting question![7]

Any verification, therefore, comes from the effects of the Elohim's
teaching on one's lifestyle, rather than empirically verifying the religion's teachings for oneself.

Not only does the myth of Raël's inaugural vision require faith:
Raëlianism presupposes that this myth is believed as a matter of
doctrine. Western scholars have come to use the term 'myth' as
synonymous with narrative, pointing out that such narratives may or
may not be true at a literal level, but that what is important is the spiritual truth that they enshrine. It is the Christian fundamentalist, in
contrast with the Christian liberal, who regards the biblical myth as
having a literal claim to truth, thus according its historical, scientific,
ethical and doctrinal claims priority over spiritual meaning. Since
Raëlianism is a very new religion (less than 30 years old at the time of
writing), it has not yet experienced its de-mythologisers or revisionists,
who tend to come at a later stage in a religion's development. Raël's
followers are thus committed to a literal belief in Raël's encounters, to
a belief in a colony of extraterrestrials whom they have not (or not yet)
met, and to an interpretation of the Bible that is presumed to be
definitive, but which runs entirely counter to any interpretation
offered by any present-day biblical scholar.

The Raëlian movement is characterised by several factors that
perpetuate this literalism. Not only is Raëlianism a new faith that still
awaits developments and modifications. The organisation is currently
focusing on establishing its embassy, fund raising, developing its
research into genetics, and gaining converts. All these involve ambitious targets, which distract from the possibility of critical reflection on
their teachings. They are introverted activities, carried out by their
own members, and outside contacts tend to be with obstructive authorities and with journalists. Raëlianism still has to go through the stage
of becoming more outward-looking and entering into dialogue with
other religions, and with the wider academic community, as has
happened with the Unification Church, the International Society for
Krishna Consciousness (ISKCON), and the Family. If and when this
occurs, Raëlians will be made to consider some of the difficulties
inherent in their position, and to formulate responses or modifications.

Just as this intellectual introversion creates an uncritical acceptance
of its biblical exegesis, the movement displays an intellectual blindness
in other areas. There is no dialogue with those who perceive problems
about genetic engineering and human cloning. Raëlian literature

simply affirms that it is 'a good thing', with no engagement even with the concerns that are expressed at a popular level – for example, that GM foods might cause disease, that pollen from GM plants might contaminate conventional crops, or that 'designer babies' could create gender imbalances in the population or cause conventionally conceived children who have disabilities to be regarded as inferior. This conclusion seems to be reinforced by the Raëlian view of abortion, which entails that children who are unwanted for any reason can simply have their existence terminated before birth. The Raëlians' proposed geniocratic system of government also runs counter to society's more prevalent view that all humanity is of equal inherent worth and worthy of equal respect. A country's population may not invariably make the best choice of leaders, but Western democracy has championed the right of all to participate in democratic government. Universal suffrage has been viewed as an achievement, and any erosion of citizens' right to vote is inevitably viewed as a retrograde step. The Raëlian grading of human beings according to intelligence, which can be controlled by genetic engineering, seems somewhat reminiscent of the Nazi ideology that sought to ensure the supremacy of the Aryan race. Such arguments are not rebutted by the Raëlian Church, but simply ignored.

The Raëlians seem equally oblivious to the philosophical problems associated with human cloning. To say the least, it is questionable whether a new being who was cloned from my DNA bank after I had died would be the real 'me', or merely a replica. A replica is not the same as the original entity that it replicates – a point ably made by the philosopher John Hick in his discussion of personal identity and survival after death. To count as the 'real me', this new person would have to share more than an identity of physical characteristics. After all, a pair of identical twins could be alike in all physical respects, but of course they are not 'one and the same'. The Raëlian cloning programme, if it were ever successfully accomplished, could bring into existence a being who is – qualitatively – the same as me, but not a being who is, somehow, one and the same. For person X to be identical with person Y, qualitative sameness is insufficient: what is needed is 'one-and-the-same-ness'. What this 'one-and-the-sameness' consists of remains a matter of debate among philosophers, but it is generally agreed that qualitative sameness is not enough. To be told that someone will create a replica of me after I die scarcely offers me hope of survival after death: it is little better than being told that a sculptor will build my statue.

In any case, as Hick argues, it would be possible to create a replica of me before I died, or to create more than one replica of me after I had died. Thus the replica (or 'clone') cannot be the real 'me', since the before-death replica and the multiple replicas all stand in the same relation to the uncontroversially 'real me', the person who exists prior to cloning.[8] Raëlianism seems vaguely to acknowledge this problem by stipulating that clones may not be made before death or severally, but this qualification is simply made as a pragmatic matter, and does not address the philosophical problems to which Hick draws attention.

Conclusion

Raëlianism provides an interesting example of a religion that is world-affirming, inclusive, and in favour of scientific advance. However, while there is much that is progressive about Raëlianism, its present state of early development, combined with its ambitious pragmatic programme of activities, prevents it from engaging in external dialogue. As a consequence, the movement experiences an intellectual introversion which can only hamper its progress, since it fails to subject to critical discussion beliefs that the dominant culture finds problematic. Such beliefs are principally its belief that extraterrestrials are in contact with humanity, Raël's idiosyncratic biblical exegesis, its undemocratic élitism, and its failure to address ethical issues associated with politics and genetics.

The time may come when its embassy is built and complete. Assuming this goal is achieved, the approximate date of 2035 will have come much closer, thus causing the movement to become like those Christian groups with imminent eschatological expectations, the principal difference being that Raëlians await the return of the Elohim, rather than Christ's second coming. Unless the Elohim do arrive and surprise all the sceptics who remain outside the Raëlian Church, Raëlians will have to cope with an unrealised eschatology. If this happens, Raëlianism may find it even more difficult to be taken seriously by a sceptical public or by spiritual seekers. Journalists, by contrast, will no doubt continue to find them a source of good copy: as one journalist has commented, 'They worship space aliens, they're sexy, goodlooking nudists – and now they might even clone a human!'[9]

One final word on the subject of cloning, by way of a postscript. This chapter was substantially written before the end of 2002, when Dr Brigitte Boisellier claimed to have successfully cloned a number of human babies. The Raëlian Church never substantiated these claims to the wider scientific community, although the stories were reported widely in the press and aroused considerabled public interest. The

Raëlians claim to have gained an extra 5,000 members as a result, bringing current world membership to around 60,000.

NOTES

1   See particularly R. Wallis, 'The Sociology of the New Religions', *Social Studies Review*, 1985, vol. 1, pp. 3–7.
2   G. D. Chryssides, *Exploring New Religions*, London, Cassell, 1999.
3   B. Sentes and S. J. Palmer, 'Presumed Immanent: The Raëlians, UFO Religions, and the Postmodern Condition', *Nova Religio*, 2000, vol. 4:1, p. 87.
4   Raël (Claude Vorilhon), *The Message Given to Me by Extra-Terrestrials: They Took Me to Their Planet*, Tokyo, AOM Corporation, 1992, p. 15.
5   Raëlian Church, 'Summary of the Messages: Scientists from Another Planet Created All Life on Earth Using D.N.A.' Available online: http://www.rael.org (31 December 2001).
6   P. Cousineau, *UFOs: A Manual for the Millennium*, New York, HarperCollins, 1995.
7   Raëlian Church. Available online: http://www.rael.org (10 May 1999).
8   J. Hick, *Death and Eternal Life*, Glasgow, Collins, 1979, pp. 279–85.
9   S. J. Palmer, 'The Raël Deal', *Religion in the News*, 2001, vol. 4:2, p. 19.

3

WHEN THE ARCHANGEL DIED

From revelation to routinisation of charisma in Unarius

Diana Tumminia

The history of Unarius, an American millenarian group, speaks of movement from an earlier period of charismatic authority to an eventual routinisation of charisma. Unarius purports the advent of one flying saucer from the planet Myton, followed by the arrival of thirty-three spaceships 'when Earth understands their peace mission'. Adherents define their practice as a science that teaches the spiritual understanding of high-energy physics and reincarnation. Since 1986, I have been involved in an in-depth case study of the group.[1] The core group of dedicated members has always remained small (around sixty people). However, Unarius still maintains a broader home-study program bolstered by an active business in mail-order books and videos. In 1989 I began participant observation, periodically staying at the apartment of a member. During the following years of research,[2] I observed and recorded the various transitions of power that are detailed in this chapter.

Unarian leadership typifies Max Weber's theories about the unstable nature of charisma and the eventual transition of power into routinisation. From its inception, Unarian leaders explained their charismatic powers with 'channelled' messages from the great beyond and by identifying their past lives through psychic visions. As time passed, the most accomplished student devotees entered into reciprocal relationships of charismatic validation with their teachers. These 'students' did the interpretive work needed to verify the extraordinary natures of their leaders by producing 'inspired' information about them. By producing and accepting divine revelations, Unarians historically negotiated their path of authority and succession for their principal leaders. Adept students relayed messages from the 'Space Brothers', whose millenarian prophecies added to the glorification of the leaders. Such messages, or transmissions as they are called, are believed to emanate from Infinite Intelligence. After the sudden death of the last of their charismatic lineage, Unarian students moved towards the establishment of a board of directors. Unarians again used revelation and channelling to fashion the legitimacy of this shared authority as they progressed toward a routinisation of charisma.

Max Weber on charisma

German sociologist Max Weber wrote on the ascendance of charisma, as well as on its eventual routinisation. Entwined within the dynamics of charisma are the duties of followers to *recognise* and *promote* the specialness or extraordinary nature of their leaders. Weber states:

> The holder of charisma seizes the task that is adequate for him and demands obedience and a following by virtue of his mission. His success determines whether he finds them. His charismatic claim breaks down if his mission is not recognized by those to whom he feels he has been sent.[3]

Charismatic leadership can be volatile and unstable[4] because the decisions of charismatic leaders can be arbitrary and disruptive, having no validity in legal-rational terms.[5] While some charismatic leaders pilot organisations benignly, others clearly do not, for their very appeal derives from the excitement and adventure their impulses produce. Lucy DuPertuis cites the Weberian notion that attributes charisma to the 'eye of the beholders'.[6] Weber states that a charismatic individual is 'treated as endowed with supernatural, superhuman, or at least specifically exceptional powers or qualities'.[7] Drawing on the writings of Weber and Shils, DuPertuis stresses the importance of the recognition of charisma by followers.[8] Strong displays of devotion towards a charismatic leader validate the power of his or her message, while also providing emotional gratification for devotees.

From Weber's writings and subsequent empirical study,[9] we can infer that leaders and followers share the work involved in the presentation and recognition of charisma. While charismatic leaders are expected to display their extraordinary abilities, close followers are reciprocally expected to facilitate these displays, sometimes playing assistant or even managerial roles. Close followers bear the burden of managing the contexts that support the social production of charisma. The staging and the maintenance of charisma involve any number of tasks, like the organisation of appropriate events, costuming, emotional displays of devotion and deference, and protection of the leader from outsiders. The emotional and interpretive work of followers renders charisma intelligible to others as well as to themselves. The resulting division of labour can be summed up under the following aphorism: behind every successful charismatic leader there are close followers who work at the recognition and promotion of charisma.

Because charismatic authority is 'precarious' by its very nature and has features foreign to the stability of everyday life, it must eventually alter itself to become part of a stable community of followers.[10] Weber delineates six methods for the routinisation of charisma to occur:

1   the search for a new leader (e.g. the Dalai Lama);
2   the divine 'revelation' of a new leader;
3   the designation of a successor by the original leader;
4   the designation of a successor by administrative staff;
5   charisma through heredity;
6   the charisma acquired through holding office and performing rituals.[11]

In Unarius, the interpretive path of authority and succession has always been legitimated by revelation, or so-called inspired messages.[12]

The notion of a charismatic division of labour is particularly helpful in understanding Unarius. It accounts both for charismatic legitimisation and for the successor's recognition. The devoted students themselves testified to the 'truth' of the legitimacy of Unarian leadership by means of channelled messages and testimonials. Loyal members also wrote books and made films celebrating the specialness of their leaders. Several students played important roles in producing these stories of legitimacy, and at one time or another they became contenders for the mantle of authority. In the Weberian sense, Unarian students originally created the charisma of Uriel the Archangel (Ruth Norman – who, with her husband, founded and led the group). The spiritual careers of students (Cosmon, Antares, Arieson, Lianne and the Polarity of Four) illustrate the shared burden and the protean nature of her charisma before and after Uriel's death. Legitimating the transfer of power through divine revelation, members eventually made sense of every change. In their last development, they routinised charisma by forming a bureaucratic body in order to share the responsibility among equals.

Unarian history and social structure

Throughout its history Unarius has functioned with a somewhat benign authoritarian structure based on the charismatic authority of its leaders Ernest and Ruth Norman, who are called 'the Moderator' and 'Uriel the Archangel' respectively. From a sociological standpoint, the Normans created an incipient mythology about their divinity that would emerge as a foundation for the standard interpretive practices of the ensuing group. Followers treated their leaders with friendly but absolute deference, producing in exchange for their attention narratives about past lives together. Over the many years, many published stories emerged into a full-blown mythology that the group would refer to as 'true stories of the science of past life therapy'. These multitudes of stories endorsed the perceived charisma of Ruth Norman, and her legitimacy endured many crises, and even failed prophecies.[13]

The Archangel

(1970).[15] The Unarius Science of Life (as it was then called) Unarius began in 1954 when Ernest Norman, a psychic who gave past-life readings, met Ruth Marian at a psychic fair. Unarians idealise this time as the meeting of two cosmic visionaries destined to carry out their mission to enlighten souls by giving them the logic and reason of 'the fourth-dimensional science', sometimes referred to simply as 'the Science'. Mrs Ruth E. Norman was very much a helpmate, typing out the messages Ernest Norman channelled from beyond. His first book, *Voice of Venus* (1956),[14] detailed his psychic trip to Venus where he encountered the advanced wonders of that civilisation. Now known as 'the Moderator', he explained the existence of 'healing wards' on that planet where troubled souls go to rest and recuperate from their traumatic experiences. He also gave psychic readings through the mail, in addition to channelling his magnum opus, *The Infinite Concept of Cosmic Creation* published books as the Normans moved to different cities in California, eventually settling near San Diego.

Coupling their channelling with past-life readings, they developed a devoted following. Of particular note in this respect is Charles Spaegel (also known as Vaughn Spaegel and Louis Spiegel, and later named Antares). Ernest Norman had over the years remembered his life as Jesus of Nazareth, a 'true fact' that his followers accepted and embellished with written testimonials.[16] Like other long-distance students, Charles Spaegel, who had corresponded with the Moderator, came to the realisation that he had played a role in the death of Jesus (Ernest

Norman). Unarian myth began to take shape with the earliest revelations of the past lives of Ernest and Ruth Norman. But over the many years, the themes evolved into collective biographies of members, who are believed to have lived together in past lives. Inclusion in the myth reflects the status of a member. Members with favoured status received important roles because they were so instrumental in producing the elaborate stories.

When Ernest Norman died in 1972, Spaegel came to California to serve the Moderator's widow. Like all good students of Unarius, he reproduced for his spiritual teachers several kinds of intelligible evidence that supported their claims about themselves. He was expected to legitimate their charismatic authority by expressing deference in the form of gratitude and awe, and by attesting that he had perceived their higher transcendental forms. The death of the Moderator meant the birth of the Archangel. When Ernest Norman died, Spaegel played a pivotal role in legitimising Ruth Norman as the new head of Unarius. Unless it is perceived by others, charisma amounts to nothing. Spaegel wrote volumes celebrating his visions of Ruth's spiritual identity. In the following passage, he tells us how he recognised Ruth's true authority:

> Then it was, in February 1972, when I came from Massachusetts to California and as I stepped from the car and walked toward the house of Ruth Norman that here I again saw this vision! I then knew it to be the higher self of this person, Ruth, the teacher of Truth, or as she is called Ioshanna. Her husband, Ernest, who has authored the twenty books – which is the Unarius Library – had just within these last few weeks, passed on to higher dimensions, and I came from my home state to help in the dispensing of the great work of Truth they had brought to planet Earth. Then as I again viewed this lovely (as I call her) Madonna, I knew it to be the higher or spiritual Self of Ioshanna.
>
> At this point, I sensed no connection or thought regarding the Mona Lisa. It was not until about eighteen months later, at the time she and I were experiencing a period of twenty days, to be exact, of inner visitation and vision upon one of the most high Spiritual Worlds that it happened. It was during this time we both viewed and 'saw' psychically the great Spiritual conclave that was taking place on this great Spiritual World. This was a truly vast gathering of Higher Beings. There were many thousands of Advanced Souls in a great

celebration in honor of the new Golden Age and their new Queen of Archangels.[17]

This passage explains how Ruth Norman garnered the honour of being crowned 'Queen of the Archangels'. Within a few years, she came to use more exclusively her new title and name, and became the public persona known as Uriel the Archangel. As Uriel, Ruth Norman dressed in regal costume to have her picture taken by scores of photographers. She made predictions about the landing of flying saucers, much to the delight of the news-hungry media,[18] and she also starred in her own films about her divinity. Initially, she succeeded as leader of Unarius, largely as a result of Spaegel's interpretive work that sought to verify her special qualities as a 'fourth-dimensional being' dispensing grace to her followers. Besides Spaegel, another student, Cosmon, assisted Ruth in channelling the messages of thirty-three new Space Brothers who promised to land in giant spaceships in order to bring about a 'new age'. Other students won her favour and helped in the myth making, but they did not endure like Spaegel.

Antares as humble assistant

Ruth's narrative of herself as Uriel, the Cosmic Bride, increased her authority with the group. The story seemed to imply that she was now making new powerful spiritual alliances. Her students immortalised her story in their paintings as an ageless heavenly queen radiating waves of light and energy. In subsequent years, Unarians celebrated the divine coupling and coronation in annual observances where Uriel, dressed in a wedding gown, received guests at a re-enacted reception. Some Unarian women dressed as bridesmaids, while certain men donned tuxedos. On one occasion Antares escorted her, although she was more likely to choose Cosmon, a younger student.

In her persona as Uriel, Ruth Norman dressed in floor-length gowns, capes, elaborate wigs and tiaras. She posed for endless photos with her royal sceptre or a bouquet of roses. Her students referred to her as the 'Light', as her name was said to stand for 'Universal Radiant Infinite Eternal Light'. Eventually she claimed over two hundred previous incarnations, including Isis, Queen Elizabeth I, Bathsheba, Queen Maria Theresa, Socrates and Peter the Great.[19] Students endlessly commemorated her past lives. Antares consistently found 'proof' for all her incarnations, including the 'fact' that Uriel looked just like the Mona Lisa.[20] The students at the Academy painted hundreds of paintings of her many manifestations, and filmed her as a magical 'goddess' calling to the people of Earth from a vortex of stars.

It is doubtful that Uriel would have convinced many others that she was an archangel without this interpretive help from her close students. They produced the public image of Uriel. Besides their devotion and adoration, students contributed volumes of channelled books that were attributed to her authorship. These students, as well as others, helped her buy property for a landing site, and they would drive out to the site dozens of times in vain attempts to witness spaceships landing. Antares' devotion remained constant, unquestioning and unwavering, unlike that of others who only temporarily served Uriel. In return for this devotion, Antares received a special role in Unarius. When Uriel awoke from a nap one day, she related her dream to him. She told Antares that he was the Fallen Angel, Satan, who had come to her to redeem himself. Whether as Satan or Tyrantus ('the Terror of the Orion constellation'), in all the subsequent past life stories that emerged, Antares was cast as Uriel's evil foil. He relished this role, because he could humbly 'work out his *karma*'. When Uriel's other favourites left, Antares stood alone having proved his devotion. By 1984, Uriel declared that, because he had now overcome all his negativity through the study of 'the Science', she would change his name to Antares. Subsequently, he channelled new elements of the millenarian prophecy, introducing a new planet, Myton, which would send a spaceship in the year 2001.

Nevertheless, while Antares was clearly very important to Uriel and Unarian mythology, for a time she pushed him into the background, choosing instead to privilege other students as her most pampered companions. Cosmon and then Arieson were declared to be the heirs to the Unarian leadership, for they once served as Uriel's 'polarities'.[21] Being designated as Uriel's polarity meant having an honoured status in the group. It also meant that 'waveforms of oscillating loving energies' flowed between Uriel and her polarity. Cosmon and Arieson assisted Uriel with enthusiasm and style, indulging her whimsy and theatricality as Unarius turned into a psychotherapeutic playhouse. However, today Unarius considers Cosmon and Arieson renegade heretics with misguided souls, evidenced by the fact they defied Uriel's authority. Just as their status as 'polarities' was legitimated by revelations from Uriel, so were their ex-communications!

The death of the Archangel

The sudden death of a charismatic leader can throw a group into chaos. Fortunately, Unarian students had time to prepare for the inevitable transition. Ruth Norman's death was not unanticipated, but to a large extent students entertained a certain amount of denial about its eventuality. Unarian prophecy had long stated that the Space Brothers would arrive during Uriel's lifetime. With the prophesied year of landing being 2001, it meant she had to live to be 101 years old. Ruth Norman was, however, a mortal. In 1988, as a result of osteoporosis and her advanced age (eighty-seven years old), she broke her hip. Needless to say, members were greatly distressed to witness their once robust leader now enduring agonising treatments and gradually becoming disabled.

As to how this deterioration of the archangel's health was dealt with by Unarians, essentially there was a combination of denial, acceptance and the use of past-life therapy. Concerning the significance of past lives, students were understood to have injured Uriel in some past existence when she had graciously come to save their souls, but now their evil actions had caught up with them. They had to atone by acknowledging these actions and recovering the memories from that dark time when they had tortured their beloved leader. Several things were done to facilitate this. For example, students attended classes and confessed to the torture of Uriel in a past life. In early December 1989, Uriel fell gravely ill and the mood at the Center became hushed and sombre. Antares reported to the class that he had taken Uriel to the emergency room, because she had vomited 'buckets of blood'. He cautioned the students to avoid the mistakes he had made. According to Antares, when he first met Uriel he would 'get upset' if she had physical problems, but, he claimed, those emotions only covered up the truth of the matter, namely that he was 'reliving' his past life on the planet Orion. Millions of years ago when we had all served Antares (at that time Tyrantus), the students had tortured Uriel at his bidding. The picture presented was one of torment in which Uriel was strapped to a chair with thousands of electric wires dangling from her head. The computers of the Orion Empire used the energy from her brain to run all its facilities. The students, her parasitic torturers, were now 'reliving' that time, and Uriel was again suffering the pain of their torture. As 'good' students, they were each expected to confess this during the testimonial portion of the class. The underlying rationale was that not only would they progress spiritually by remembering, but, as a consequence, Uriel would also recover. Antares exhorted them, for their own sakes and for Uriel's, to look deeply into their pasts.

At one meeting I attended, Antares began with his own confession. His realisation came to him while attending to Uriel in hospital. Antares said, 'I was holding a plastic bag. Uriel was vomiting blood. I realised this was the poison I had given to Dalos [Uriel in a past life]. Here was the victim in front of the aggressor. Only because of the Science could I stand up to this time.' Uriel complained heavily that there was 'no feeling of spirit' in the sterile, cold hospital. According to Antares, Uriel's doctor did not know her 'true identity' as he subjected her to numerous medical tests. Antares argued for more humane treatment and less invasive procedures, but her doctor insisted he would proceed with the prescribed course of treatment and testing, unless Antares produced the legal papers to stop it. Antares explained he was powerless, as 'the energy from the past spilled over into the twentieth century'. Heavy and morose, the meeting continued as Antares disclosed more and more. Following this, we proceeded by reading a chapter from a forthcoming book, channelled by the student Lianne. This chapter explained in detail how Uriel was tortured. Each of us in turn stood to read a paragraph. Eventually the time for testimonials arrived. Pale and shaken, a student, Nannette, went up to the front of the class to speak into the microphone. She took a deep breath, paused and then, clearly struggling, spoke: 'Unfortunately, I was there when Uriel came to the hospital. I realised I was part of the torture of Dalos [Uriel]. I was working as an experimentation attendant.' At this point, tears welled up in her eyes, then rolled down her face. The students supportively waited for her next words. She continued to weep as she spoke: 'I was involved in the poisoning. She asked for water, but I refused Dalos [Uriel] drink. I relived all of this whilst lifting Uriel into her bed. I wanted to stay by Uriel's side, but I was afraid my supervisor would say something, so I left.' At this point, Nannette began to break down again. When she regained control of herself, she continued. Silently, the night class weighed the impact of Nannette's testimonial along with the testimonials of the others who spoke.

Antares closed the meeting by reiterating that everything that had been related was historical fact and that it had happened millions of years ago on another planet. 'I, Tyrantus, was keeping Uriel a prisoner.' He then spoke about reconvening the class 'to do a reliving'. Finally he added, 'You are spirit beings in the making. We're not here to kick anyone's butt. It is not my intention to interfere in the private life of any student, but we all here must face the fact of this torture.' I left the class stunned by its emotional impact.

About a week later I was informed that Uriel had miraculously recovered. Unarians attributed her recovery to the 'fact' that students got in touch with the 'guilt' from the past. Indeed, for a while it seemed that Uriel would fulfil her prophecy to live to the year 2001. However, the next couple of years were difficult for the students. Every time Uriel had a health crisis, which was often, the students were again called upon to confess their guilt. Moreover, members were also instructed to clear up their *karma* with Antares, who would eventually succeed Uriel. She announced that anyone who had 'trouble dealing with Antares' should have a psychic reading from him. When students in the nucleus avoided making appointments, the appointments were made for them. Following this, students were expected to write testimonials about the information they derived from the reading. Most testimonials were given back to the students, who rewrote them several times until they were approved. Unsurprisingly, this cycle of psychic readings led to an unprecedented number of attritions. The stress of producing more confessional stories proved too onerous for some. Several 'good' students left the group. Departure was explained as the student's unwillingness to face the information presented in his or her psychic reading.

As time passed, Uriel's health significantly deteriorated. Notwithstanding the endless therapeutic confessions, Uriel suffered increasing pain, finding herself, in her own words, 'in a pickle'. Three Unarians with nursing backgrounds tended to her needs at home and she only came to the Center a couple times a year for special occasions. Eventually these appearances also ceased, and the students started to visit her in her home.

In a letter dated 8 December 1991, Uriel wrote to her students to tell them that she might die before the landing. She had contacted the Space Brothers through Antares, who had channelled the message. The Space Brothers affirmed that her mission had been completed. She could leave at any time. Unarians prepared for the inevitable, except for two students who had been with the group since the early seventies. They disputed the message, because they believed Antares was trying to take over the organisation. Uriel responded by asking those students not to return to the group.

On 14 February 1991, Uriel invited students to her home, where she gave each one a personal audience. Each student was photographed with Uriel as she blessed him or her, and she told each to study the Science. As the months passed, students sensed that this might have been the last opportunity to see her. The students swung between hope and resignation until finally Ruth Norman died on 12 July 1993.

Antares cremated her body according to her wishes, but no cere-mony and public funeral emerged. Unarians wept quietly and privately, for Uriel did not want them to grieve. Rather she had wanted them to be happy because she had finally returned to her celestial home. Following the funeral, students gathered at an evening class to hear the reading of her will. Her last will and testament stated that she would return with the Space Brothers in 2001, and requested that Antares look after her 'Space Cadillac' (with the flying saucer on the roof) for she would pick it up when she returned.[22] During the weeks that followed, Antares invited numerous students up to the 'Light House' where he gave them pieces of her costume jewellery as mementos of their 'Goddess of Love'. The students accepted the task of carrying on the Archangel's mission and telling the world about her extraordinary power as a redeemer.

Apart from the belief that Uriel had returned to her celestial home, it is important to understand that Unarian belief states that there is no death and that life simply passes to 'another form' – i.e. to 'a higher statement on a higher dimension' (that is, if one's *karma* does not take one's spirit elsewhere). As 'a part of fourth-dimensional energy', Uriel could never die. According to Unarius, Uriel lives as 'the higher self' of Ruth Norman, indestructible and immortal on a super-celestial planet.

The Polarity of Four and the problem of succession

Over the period of the gradual demise of Uriel it was apparent that students at the Center had been mentally and emotionally preparing themselves for a transition of leadership. When I began the study, outsiders continually posed questions of succession to me. Who would take over after Uriel died? Would there be a new Uriel? Would they channel her voice from beyond the grave? While it seemed clear that Antares would succeed Uriel – if he outlived her (he was in his seven-ties) – the next successor was not so obviously identifiable. That said, while Antares had been central to the construction of Uriel's charisma, he possessed none of his own. This was clearly a problem for a future leader. Moreover, Uriel was an autocrat who could change her mind at any time and name someone else as her successor. Hence, in the period immediately before and after her death, several other pretenders started to take on prominent roles.

Some of these students had risen from the ranks in mid-1989, prior to Uriel's passing. Of particular note are Lianne, Rafael, Joseph and

Michael, who decided to form a polarity (a unit of oscillating energy) by living together. They united to develop their channelling abilities, calling themselves 'The Polarity of Four'. On 28 August 1989, they collectively 'transmitted' a long message from the Space Brothers, 'The Fountainhead of Cosmic Love'. They channelled the Space Brothers' message on 'Interplanetary Confederation Day'. This won them much praise from Uriel and Antares, as well as from the other students. Although other students had been given approval to begin channelling, none had actually accomplished the task. Consequently the Polarity of Four appeared especially gifted with 'grace', the inspired energy of the Space Brothers. Although the foursome broke up after a year, they continued to serve Unarius individually as they struggled to balance their personal lives with the demands of the organisation. For a time they appeared to be likely candidates in the line of succession. Their spiritual careers speak of the supportive role that members play in the social construction of charisma.

Rafael

In his late thirties, Rafael (Doug) of the Polarity of Four certainly emerged as a contender. Rafael worked as an accomplished airbrush artist and carpenter – he made a colourful surfboard depicting a flying saucer that hung in the Academy. He had formerly abused drugs and alcohol, as a result of which he spent some time in prison.[23] He became interested in Unarius after reading *The Voice of Venus* in a public library. Although in 1991 he was asked by Uriel to repaint a mural he had done for the outside of the building because 'it was the wrong frequency', Rafael was considered 'a good student' and the community valued his artistic talents. Indeed, his stories of himself as the space captain Steelon initiated what came to be known as 'the Steelon Cycle' in 1992, a productive period for past life 'memories' and testimonials. Rafael paid much homage to his teacher. Of Uriel, Rafael wrote the following:

> Uriel is a Universal Radiant Infinite Eternal Light. To put it simply, She is the Master Teacher who has overcome all opposition by always expressing Love to her fellowman. She is the example and continuity of all great Illumined Souls who have put on the cloak of an earth body in order to help those who

were too lost and crippled to help themselves and who knew not of their terrible plight.[24]

When Antares left his post at the beginning of 1992 to take care of Uriel at home, he gave the positions of co-directors to Rafael and Lianne. However, Rafael resigned his position, saying that the demands were too great. He took some time off, moved, and got a new job. When he sold his paintings to a greetings card company to make some cash, Uriel disapproved because the paintings were considered Unarian property. While this disapproval did not seem to warrant it, Rafael's next move was the formation of a splinter group with other ex-students, and the teaching his own derivative brand of UFO religion. Unarians say he left because 'he was afraid to confront his guilt for the past'. When I asked him why he left, Rafael replied that it was time for him to leave the nest, even though he appreciated what Unarius taught him.

Michael

Michael, another member of the Polarity of Four, grew up in a strongly religious Roman Catholic family in Nebraska. He also spent five years in and out of mental hospitals before his involvement with Unarius, to which he was introduced by a neighbour who had given him a Unarian book to read. He has subsequently claimed to have been '100% cured' as a direct result of his involvement in Unarius. Perhaps not surprisingly, given his previous history, past-life therapy sessions revealed that he was tortured and killed as a heretic by the Roman Catholic Church. Learning the skill in Unarius, Michael worked as a printer for the Academy, receiving a small salary of $500 a month. When I asked why the Polarity of Four was formed, Michael told me they 'wanted to work as a team to help in the Mission'.

As to his understanding of Uriel, Michael, doing his interpretive duty, wrote about his experience of her charisma:

> I have never been as close to Uriel as I was yesterday. This was the first for me when she actually asked me to come and be with her, and it lifts one out of his body! [sic] How else can you explain being with an Archangel? It changes every person's life! Now anybody I touch will change also because it is there whether I can do it or not! The Power that she has

touched me with, will flow to any person, whether I know it or not![25]

In the Unarian art-therapy class, Michael produced numerous praiseworthy paintings and sculptures. Like Rafael, Michael was considered a 'good student', and clearly had every intention of staying with the group for the rest of his life. But, again like Rafael, he eventually left after the 1992 psychic readings, when he refused to write a testimonial. Interestingly, this was curiously out of character for Michael. No one had more hopes for him than Antares, who believed that Michael had once been his illegitimate son when he, Antares, had lived as Napoleon.[26] No one could explain Michael's behaviour, except in terms of *karma*. After his departure from Unarius, Michael worked as a print shop manager, and reportedly joined Rafael's splinter group. That said, at the turn of the millennium, Michael had again chosen to become a 'home-study student' with Unarius. He currently remains connected, though at a distance. He now sells his paintings of flying saucers over the Internet.

Joseph and Lianne

After the departure of Rafael and Michael, it appeared that the Space Brothers had chosen the two remaining members of the Polarity of Four. Joseph and Lianne emerged as leaders.

Joseph joined Unarius when he was in his teens, having discovered the group by chance when he was walking by the Center in 1988. Heavily addicted to drugs and in trouble with the juvenile justice system, he wore the standard accoutrements of 'heavy metal' when he received his first reading. In one lifetime, it was claimed, Joseph had lived as a Mongol warrior who had had his head shorn to disgrace him. In another lifetime, as a punishment for witchcraft, Joseph was drowned, choking on his long hair. Unarians befriended Joseph, although most were worried about his 'drug obsession'. When he became a serious student he cut his hair, and wore a shirt and tie for the public meetings of Unarius. He found employment as a salesman for another Unarian. By the time Joseph joined the Polarity of Four, he was the epitome of the 'clean-cut kid'. After Rafael abandoned the post, Joseph was made co-director with Lianne. Antares said that Joseph was a 'Brother'. The students generally admired Joseph for his peaceful disposition. Joseph was in a position to grow into leadership, although his abilities were for the moment eclipsed by those of Lianne, whom he married in 1994.

Achieving the role of subchannel and Center co-coordinator, Lianne rose in status due to her ability to contribute to the ongoing narrative. In the early 1990s, I noted that Lianne was the likely candidate to succeed Uriel as the next leader of Unarius. I based my prediction on her prodigious channelling abilities, accompanied by a change in dress and demeanour that accorded with Uriel's style. Lianne was also articulate, a bold apologist for the group, and indeed took risks with outsiders to defend Unarius.

As to how Lianne came to be involved with the group, as a college student she had seen a poster on Unarian classes. She said, 'I was one miserable, confused, mean-tempered, overweight and depressed 19-year-old!'[27] Sixteen years later, Lianne worked as a freelance writer, devoting all her spare time to Unarius. (As an indication of her evangelistic boldness, it is worth noting that her employer once suspended her when she protested at her newspaper's report of Uriel.) In 1989, Lianne wrote her *Biography of an Archangel*,[28] a beautifully illustrated book about her teacher. In 1990, she channelled the unpublished book *The Liberator* (about Dalos and Tyrantus – i.e. Uriel and Antares in their previous incarnations), the text of which was read in classes chapter by chapter as they were completed. I once spoke with her about the problems of writing about Unarius, bearing in mind that many people would find it difficult not to laugh at their beliefs, and that many would simply understand them in terms of popular cultic stereotypes. She responded that, at a certain point in time, she completely stopped bothering about such opinions and compromising with outsiders. Once she found that courage, she never apologised for Unarius again.

Lianne received awards for her books from Uriel. The Archangel gently encouraged Lianne with gifts of costume jewellery. She was told to wear her hair up, accented with rhinestone accessories, because, Uriel claimed, the reflected light of the rhinestones 'tuned people into the higher frequencies'. She also advised Lianne to look out for some special dresses at the Salvation Army store. Uriel predicted that a rich woman, Lianne's size, would donate them. When Lianne found several silk dresses in her size, she thanked her teacher, for surely this was a sign that the Space Brothers were watching over her. Gradually Lianne started to sparkle in her clothing and attitude, her sequined hair ornaments reminiscent of Uriel's glittering tiaras. Again, this seemed like the grooming of Uriel's successor. As she emerged, Lianne began to exhibit the necessary qualities of a Unarian leader: beauty, charm and a talent for storytelling.

After Uriel's death, however, while she played a prominent role, she did not become the next leader. Concerned with their finances, and tired of the constant pressure to serve Unarius, after a couple of years Lianne and Joseph surrendered their posts and moved away from the influence of the group.

After Uriel's death, and following Lianne's and Joseph's exit, Unarius continued to lose long-term students. Although a few students found the ability to channel messages, the task of waiting for the Space Brothers proved difficult in the absence of the excitement that Uriel had produced. Antares held the mantle of Uriel's authority until his unexpected death on 22 December 1999. Although he was seventy-eight at the time, no one expected him to 'pass on' so suddenly. The students were clearly shocked, but they have managed to carry on regardless. After all, they had to prepare for the landing of the Space Brothers under a new phase of leadership. It is this new phase of leadership that demonstrates the routinisation of charisma, the passage from the volatile charismatic stage into a more stable bureaucratic administration.

Routinisation through revelation

Antares died suddenly, leaving Unarius with a $40,000 debt and without a clear-cut plan for succession. Although the group had a Board of Directors in name only, it swung into action in response to Antares' death. In the void, sixteen extremely dedicated students emerged as the newly formed board. Although it appeared bureaucratic and stable, the board did not seek advice from the established world of business management. Rather, it sought advice from the Space Brothers, so that its course of action would be founded on higher authority. They legitimated their new social structure through the improvised wisdom of channelling. They believed that Antares was not dead, but was rather still spiritually available to give advice. Thus, Unarius gained a 'new Space Brother' in the form of 'fourth-dimensional Antares', who they turned to for guidance and comfort.

Jack Appel of the new Unarius Board of Directors channelled a message entitled *The Homecoming (A Message from Antares)* on New Year's Day, 2000. This communication from Antares began as follows: 'I am currently addressing you from the city of Parhelion located on planet Eros.'[29] With Uriel at his side, the spirit of Antares addressed the problem of succession by saying that everyone should cooperate with one another. Another channelled communication dated 4 January 2000 revealed a previously hidden history of the Orion Empire. It stated that, after Tyrantus (Antares in a past life) died, his followers

77

fought amongst themselves, splitting into various factions. The following warning was related: 'In essence the student body, not recognizing this particular past, has provided an inroad for the negative forces to de-tune them from their positive consciousness.'[30] Again the message stressed cooperation among the Unarian students to bring about their spiritual mission.

When I interviewed members of the newly-formed Board of Directors, they discussed what had happened to foster a new egalitarianism. In addition to the channelled messages from beyond, past-life memories had been awakened in the group, spurring higher levels of resolve. A student, Thelma, told me how the students discussed Antares' death as an experience of reliving a past life. Thelma explained to me that, when Antares had been Tyrantus long ago in the Orion Empire, the students had fatally poisoned him. In those past lives, the students fought each other to take control of his evil empire. Once they started to realise collectively what had happened in past lives, they prepared themselves to deal with the 'ego' problems of succession. Not one student, but a group of students stressed that cooperation and selflessness should guide the future of Unarius. In the year 2001, Unarians hoped to witness the fulfillment of the prophecy uttered by the great Archangel Uriel, which promised a spaceship landing. Although the anticipated Space Brothers did not become visible, members of the Board of Directors experienced little disappointment as they continued to volunteer their time to running the organisation. Two members, Jack and David, had become regular channellers who brought the voice and wisdom of Uriel back to planet Earth. Death has not silenced her ability to guide the organisation, because channellers voiced her supposed words in their trance state. Channelled messages from Uriel have explained that the Space Brothers cannot become visible until people stop their warlike attitudes and practices. The prophecy has not failed, because the Space Brothers have arrived to guide world affairs with invisible hands. For the time being, routinisation has gone smoothly, principally as a result of channelled advice and the further production of past-life memories that attest to the present need for cooperation.

Conclusion

Many define charisma as the gift of grace or the possession of extraordinary ability and attractiveness. Max Weber reminds us that charisma is often as much created by the actions of followers as it is derived from the qualities of leaders. Dutiful followers, who recognise and promote charismatic leadership, can in some cases stage the kind of events that make their loyalty seem wholly justified. These followers can sustain leaders that they find captivating. Yet Weber argues that charisma rules in a volatile and capricious manner, such that it cannot be maintained indefinitely. Eventually, this unstable process will lead to a contrasting form of leadership in the form of rountinisation of charisma, which is often legitimised by divine revelation.

Unarius serves as an example of this Weberian model of charisma, because its history reveals a clear picture of the reciprocal roles of leader and followers. The group was transformed from its initial psychic orientation into a millenarian flying-saucer cult by means of a charismatic division of labour. Followers shared the burden of supporting charisma by constructing a mythology of the divinity of the leaders through channelled messages, visions and devotional behaviour. Initially all charismatic authority in Unarius stemmed from Ernest Norman, who saw himself as the reincarnated Jesus. Following his death, power transferred to his wife, Ruth Norman, otherwise known as Uriel the Archangel. Charles Spaegel (Antares) validated her charismatic authority with his visions, helping her to build her other-worldly persona while communicating her millenarian prophecies to others. As devoted as he was, Antares still endured displacement by others as a result of her capriciousness. At the top of the organisation, several males contested for Uriel's favour, while ordinary students supported her reign by producing stories about her in past-life therapy classes. In their confessional testimonials, students bound themselves to Uriel's power, asking for release from their past transgressions. Students sang songs about her cosmic connections to the Space Brothers, and they made films about her redemptive power. Students on every level assumed tasks and they constructed narratives that validated Mrs Norman as a cosmic scientist, healer and leader of an invisible space fleet.

From the Unarian point of view, the group survived because of the enduring truth of 'the Science'. From a sociological standpoint, Unarius somehow perpetuated its longevity by attracting the type of student who would take on the tasks needed to sustain its charismatic authority. In itself, everyday life under the rule of a charismatic leader can prove enjoyable and meaningful. However, when the leader dies, organisations may face collapse or wars of succession. Because other contenders, most notably Cosmon, Arieson and the Polarity of Four, for various reasons proved unworthy, Antares eventually assumed leadership after Ruth Norman's death. However, Antares' authority rested, not upon his own charismatic authority, but rather upon Uriel's. Uriel had declared that, although he had been Satan, through repentance and service to Uriel Antares had been healed, earning his spiritual leadership ability. Finally, with Antares' unexpected death in 1999, a collective egalitarian leadership emerged with a student Board of Directors legitimated by channelled messages from outer space, Antares, and Uriel herself. Weber writes that groups may choose several solutions to the problem of succession, including legitimising new leaders through divine revelations.[31] Following long-standing practices, a core group of students produced channelled messages that guided the norms of succession as egalitarian and cooperative. This nucleus of students stepped into the power vacuum in order to maintain the group's viability and to keep the millenarian prophecy alive. So far it has succeeded in stabilising the Unarian Mission. The process of routinisation has run its course in the Unarius Academy of Science – though, of course, not without the help of the elusive Space Brothers.

NOTES

This essay began life as a paper presented at the meeting of the American Sociological Association, Anaheim, California, 18–21 August 2001. Portions of this chapter are also taken from D. Tumminia, 'Brothers from the Sky: Myth and Reality in a Flying Saucer Group', UCLA, unpublished doctoral thesis, 1995 – completed under the supervision of Ralph H. Turner.

1 R. G. Kirkpatrick and D. Tumminia, 'A Case Study of a Southern Flying Saucer Cult', unpublished paper presented to the annual meeting of the American Sociological Association, San Francisco, August 1989.
2 See D. Tumminia, 'How Prophecy Never Fails: Interpretive Reason in a Flying Saucer Group', *Sociology of Religion*, vol. 59, 1998, pp. 157–70; D. Tumminia and R. G. Kirkpatrick, 'Unarius: Emergent Aspects of a Flying Saucer Group', in J. R. Lewis (ed), *The Gods Have Landed: New Religions From Other Worlds*, Albany, State University of New York Press, 1995, pp. 85–100; R. G. Kirkpatrick and D. Tumminia, 'California Space Goddess: the Mystagogue in a Flying Saucer Group', in W. H. Swatos (ed), *Twentieth-Century World Religious Movements in Neo-Weberian Perspective*, Lewiston, Edwin Mellen Press, 1992, pp. 299–311.
3 S. N. Eisenstadt, *Max Weber: On Charisma and Institution Building*, Chicago, University of Chicago Press, 1968, p. 20.
4 See H. H. Gerth and C. Wright Mills (eds), *From Max Weber: Essays on Sociology*, trans H. H. Gerth and C. Wright Mills, New York, Oxford University Press, 1946; R. Wallis, 'The Social Construction of Charisma', *Social Compass*, vol. 29, 1982, pp. 25–39.
5 T. Robbins, *Cults, Converts and Charisma: the Sociology of New Religious Movements*, Beverly Hills, Sage, 1988.

6 L. Du Pertuis, 'How People Recognize Charisma: the Case of Darshan in Radhasoami and the Divine Light Mission', *Sociological Analysis*, vol. 47, 1986, p. 111.

7 See *ibid*.

8 *Ibid*., pp. 111–24.

9 See *ibid*.; Gerth and Mills, *From Max Weber*; Eisenstadt, *Max Weber*; Wallis, 'The Social Construction of Charisma'; Robbins, *Cults, Converts and Charisma*.

10 Gerth and Mills, *From Max Weber*; Eisenstadt, *Max Weber*.

11 Eisenstadt, *Max Weber*, p. 55.

12 Unarians themselves, however, would object to this assertion. Unarius' self-definition as a science rejects the idea of divine revelation in the more conventional sense of the term. The group talks about God, a Spiritual Hierarchy and the super-celestial realms where beings of Higher Intelligence reside, yet it insists that knowledge from those sources is transmitted through a scientific means of energy frequency attunement. Thus, from their point of view, ascended masters or Brothers believed to exist on higher planes of spiritualised energy transmit inspired messages, a phenomenon not to be confused with outmoded non-scientific concepts like divine revelation.

13 Tumminia, 'How Prophecy Never Fails'.

14 E. Norman, *Voice of Venus*, 6th edn, El Cajon, Unarius Educational Foundation, 1956.

15 E. Norman, *The Infinite Concept of Cosmic Creation*, Glendale, Unarius Science of Life, 1970.

16 R. Norman and Unarius Students, *Return to Jerusalem*, El Cajon, Unarius Educational Foundation, 1983; A. Smyth, *The Occult Life of Jesus of Nazareth*, Chicago, The Progressive Thinker Publishing House, 1899 – reprinted in the Unarius publication *The True Life of Jesus of Nazareth: the Confessions of St. Paul*.

17 R. Norman and V. Spaegel, *Who is the Mona Lisa?*, El Cajon, Unarius Science of Life, 1973, pp. 2–3

18 Tumminia, 'How Prophecy Never Fails'.

19 Kirkpatrick and Tumminia, 'California Space Goddess'.

20 Norman and Spaegel, *Who is the Mona Lisa?*

21 R. Norman, *Thwarted: Effort to Destroy the Unarius Mission Thwarted*, El Cajon, Unarius Educational Foundation, 1984; Arieson, *The Visitations: a Saga of Gods and Men*, El Cajon, Unarius Educational Foundation, 1987; A. Parfrey, *Cult Rapture*, Portland, Feral House, 1995.

22 I noted this statement from Uriel's will in my fieldnotes at the time of the reading. Unarians now dispute that she will return, and they claim that her mission was completed.

23 R. Norman, *Testimonials by Unarius Students: to Help the New Seeker Conceive of the Various Benefits of Unarius*, El Cajon, Unarius Educational Foundation, 1985.

24 Uriel and Her Students, *The Proof of the Truth of Past Life Therapy*, El Cajon, Unarius Publishers, 1988, p. 49

25 *Ibid*., p. 107.

26 L. Spiegel (Antares), *I, Bonaparte: an Autobiography*, El Cajon, Unarius Publishers, 1985.

27 R. Norman, *Testimonials by Unarius Students*, p. 38.
28 R. Norman, *Biography of an Archangel*, El Cajon, Unarius Educational Foundation, 1989.
29 J. Appel, *The Homecoming (A Message from Antares)*, El Cajon, Unarius, 2000, p. 1. This publication is a pamphlet.
30 *Ibid.*
31 See Eisenstadt, *Max Weber*.

4

OPENING A CHANNEL TO THE STARS

The origins and development of the Aetherius Society

Simon G. Smith

This is not a new religion ... it's a spiritual path to enlightenment and the cosmic evolution of mankind

Read and evolve

For the first time the connection between the science of Yoga,
the theology of all major religions and the mystery of UFOs is
explained.[1]

The Aetherius Society is one of the oldest and best-known UFO-
related religious organisations.[2] Founded in 1956 by George King
(1919–97), a Briton who had been a member of a number of theosophical and occult groups in London since the 1930s, it has developed into
a worldwide movement with a small but stable membership. As we can
see from the above quotation from the website, the Aetherius Society
does not regard itself as a religious movement *per se*, but rather as the
provider of a 'spiritual path' which enables human beings to evolve to
a higher spiritual level. This has been made possible through med
iumistic contact with beings from other planets, usually within our
solar system, who not only act as spiritual guides and facilitators of spiritual evolution, but also help to protect the Earth from evil and natural
disasters through the regular delivery of spiritual energy by spacecraft
that frequently orbit Earth. Contact with these beings, who include
religious figures such as Buddha, Jesus and Krishna, can only be made if
the individual is able to attain, as King did, certain levels of consciousness through yogic practice. King referred to these extraterrestrial
contacts as 'Cosmic Masters', and he gradually built up his own powers
to the extent that he came to be regarded as one of them. With this
'privileged' knowledge he developed a coherent set of beliefs that have

proved attractive enough for the movement to persist for nearly half a century.

In this chapter I shall map out the history and development of the Aetherius Society, showing that, while in many ways it can be regarded as being a product of its time, it has also been able evolve in ways that were pioneering for a spiritual movement. I shall also discuss how the movement has dealt with scientific developments that potentially render its beliefs obsolete, but will suggest that the continued existence of the Aetherius Society cannot just be accounted for by a dogged determination to overcome these problems; rather, there is something in its core beliefs that continues to attract people, albeit in relatively small numbers. Finally, and perhaps most importantly, I shall look at the religious development of the movement, discussing the central role of George King, examining in particular the extent to which the principal changes it has undergone have been a direct result of King's own evolving status.

The origins and emergence of the Aetherius Society

The history of the Aetherius Society is in many ways a history of it's founder and leader, George King.[3] Little is known of King's early life other than he was born on 23 January 1919 in Wellington, Shropshire, into what Wallis describes as 'a family imbued with occult inclinations';[4] his mother, in particular, was involved in 'psychic' activities.[5] According to the biographical details provided by the Aetherius Society,[6] King maintained 'deep spiritual interests' from an early age. These were expressed initially through 'traditional Christianity', but, realising that orthodox religion did not possess the answers that he was seeking, he turned to psychic phenomena and then to yoga in order to address his spiritual questions.[7] King seems to have immersed himself in a world occupied by non-orthodox and metaphysical religious groups that were a marginal, though not insignificant, part of the religious scene in London between the two world wars. Whilst these groups were often markedly diverse in their beliefs and practices, arguably to some extent they all had roots in Theosophy. It was not until after the Second World War,[8] however, in 1954, that he appeared as a public speaker for the first time. This period was one of great uncertainty as the Cold War developed, and many in the West, especially those who felt alienated from the political process, 'looked instead for signs and clues of some higher order explanation'.[9] It was into this situation that the first sightings of flying saucers had been reported in the United States in 1947,[10] and subsequently in Europe by the early 1950s.

King's movement into the public arena seems to have coincided with what he claims to be the first encounter with Cosmic Master Aetherius, an extraterrestrial living on the planet Venus. This was the first of many encounters with extraterrestrial beings, including those he identified as Buddha, Jesus and Krishna. King believed these beings to be members of the Great White Brotherhood,[11] a group whose existence had originally been disclosed by the founder of the Theosophical Society, Madame Helena Blavatsky. Blavatsky was in regular spiritual contact with these beings, considering them to be the source of a great deal of her own 'wisdom'.[12] It is arguable, therefore, that, while the beings King contacted were novel in terms of their location – in that, for Blavatsky, they were her *Tibetan* Masters – they may be regarded as a development of theosophical ideas.

During his first encounter with Aetherius, on 8 May 1954,[13] King was told: 'Prepare yourself! You are to become the voice of the Interplanetary Parliament.'[14] King is said to have been initially shocked at the implications of what he was told, but that his previous practice of yoga and meditation assured him that what he had heard was genuine.[15] This was further confirmed for King when, while in a deep meditative trance,[16] he was visited by an Indian Yoga Master (who is said to have arrived through King's locked door). The Master provided a number of special practices and instructions that would enable King to fulfil his calling. It was at this point that he is said to have revealed to King that the Cosmic Intelligences with whom he had come into contact were able to travel to Earth in spacecraft.

King first introduced the public to his powers and revelations in January 1955, at a meeting in Caxton Hall, London. Going into a trance, he relayed a message from 'Master Aetherius'.[17] Perhaps unsurprisingly, this met with a considerable amount of disbelief, even from an audience that was used to hearing unconventional spiritual ideas. Nevertheless, a small but increasing number of people did begin to attend his lectures, during which he made further contacts with other extraterrestrial beings,[18] usually from planets within our solar system. Indeed, attendances had increased to such a level by August 1956 that he felt able to form the Aetherius Society and to give up his job as a taxi driver in order to devote himself to his mission on a full-time basis.[19]

King's experiences of contact while in a 'yogic trance' were not dissimilar to many claimed contacts with extraterrestrial beings during the nineteenth and early twentieth century. Such contacts, according to J. Gordon Melton, usually followed a pattern in which five elements were commonly present: first, they occurred in a spiritualist context, usually a séance; second, they were achieved by some psychic or occult means; third, communication was by telepathy; fourth, the message was normally of a metaphysical nature; and fifth, a religious context was usually assumed.[20] As Melton observes:

> By means of their space contact, contactees could replace the authority of the religious tradition they had cast away. They invoked the momentary authority of science … which they bolstered with the additional information of direct contact with a new and equally authoritative source of information. Each provided a launching pad for the 'religious' speculation they really desired.[21]

King's encounters likewise seem to meet the criteria suggested by Melton. In particular, they 'invoked the momentary authority of science'. Indeed, it is here where King differs from those who had claimed extraterrestrial contact before him. Here we see references to greater scientific knowledge in a milieu where stories of contact and UFO sightings were becoming increasingly prevalent. King was certainly well-versed in the earlier encounters, normally said to have been achieved by means of 'astral travel',[22] but was also greatly influenced by his study of 'radionics' (a form of 'distance healing'[23]), which had a marked influence on the ritual and practice of the Aetherius Society.

King's experiences can also be seen as a reflection of changing attitudes towards extraterrestrials in the 1950s and 1960s, which were usually informed by the aforementioned prevailing political and social attitudes. This, to some extent, is also reflected in the science fiction of the time. As early as 1938, Orson Welles's radio broadcast of H. G. Wells's *War of the Worlds* (first published in 1898) caused hysteria in an America suffering from a sense of insecurity, partly the result of growing tensions in Europe. This continued after the Second World War when 'aliens' were, for the most part, portrayed in a negative light. In the film *They Came from Beyond Space* (1967), for instance, aliens were portrayed as taking over the bodies of individuals in order to infiltrate human society. Again, this reflected America's long obsession with the communist enemy within, and was typical of the genre. Emerging parallel to this dominant narrative, there was also a lesser narrative in which extraterrestrials were viewed less negatively. This can be seen in films with a Cold War theme, such as *The Day the Earth*

Stood Still (1951), influenced by concerns over the nuclear arms race and the sense of humanity's increasing ability to destroy itself. Only through the intervention of an alien being can the leaders of the world be brought together to discuss peace. In *Forbidden Planet* (1956)[24] the principal danger, although initially thought to come from an alien force, actually comes from within the individual in the form of Dr Moribus's *id*. Analysis of these and other films provides some indication of influential views about extraterrestrials within popular culture at the time when King was in the process of founding the Aetherius Society. The more positive portrayals were themselves, although in the minority, a reflection of wider and growing concerns that found their voice in the 1960s peace movement.

We can now begin to contextualise King's encounters with the Cosmic Masters. On the one hand, they can be seen as a clear development of Blavatsky's encounters with her Tibetan Masters, whilst, on the other hand, they can be seen as a reflection of King's own political, social and cultural context. Further evidence for the latter emerges when one compares King's experiences with what Melton regards as being the four principal characteristics of claimed contact with extraterrestrials in the 1950s. These are as follows:

1   contact was usually with beings from within the solar system;
2   UFOs were the only new element in the accounts of contact – although a mystical or paranormal aspect was usually maintained;
3   there remained an emphasis on moral, metaphysical and spiritual messages;
4   most contactees seemed to be operating within a religious context, over half either founding their own occult religion or joining an existing organisation.[25]

Hence, again, it would seem that King's experiences and his founding of the Aetherius Society were very much a product of his time. This in itself is not a particularly bold or novel statement since, as Melton suggests, many other extraterrestrial contactees used their experiences to found new religious movements.[26] What is more interesting is that, while a few of these movements have persisted for nearly half a century and survived the death of their founder, they are very much in the minority. The Aetherius Society is the most important and successful of these. What are the reasons for this?

One of the principal reasons for this longevity may be that, as Ellwood and Partin have suggested, the Aetherius Society 'has by far the tightest organisation and the most explicitly religious structure' of any of the flying saucer religions.[27] This was not immediately apparent during the first few years of the movement's existence. At this time the messages that King received from the Cosmic Masters were a mixture of instructions for health and healing techniques, assurances of the friendliness of extraterrestrials (an important consideration considering the increasing paranoia towards the outsider – especially in McCarthyite America), the potential dangers of atomic science, and the metaphysical activities of the Cosmic Masters.[28] During this time King developed the primary means of contact with the Cosmic Masters that was to become an integral part of the Aetherius Society's ritual routine. This usually occurred when a satellite, known as Satellite No. 3,[29] travelled to the Earth, usually from Mars, to increase the amount of spiritual energy that could be made available to human beings as a defence against evil and outside spiritual influences. As the Cosmic Masters existed at a higher spiritual level, these satellites were undetectable to human beings, information as to their presence being channelled to King by the Cosmic Masters. Arguably the most important such occasion was when contact was established between King and Master Jesus on the top of Holdstone Down in Devon in July 1958. Following this meeting, King was given Jesus's 'Aquarian Age Bible to this Earth', otherwise known as *The Twelve Blessings*. As Wallis comments:

> This meeting produced a considerable change in the Society's activities, for King was commissioned to 'act as an essential link between Earth and the Higher Forces'[30] in the 'charging' of a number of Holy Mountains throughout the world with Cosmic Energy which could be released through prayer for the good of mankind.[31]

Known as *Operation Starlight*,[32] it marked the true beginning of the development of the Aetherius Society into a religious movement. The timing of this intervention by the Cosmic Masters was also significant for the Aetherius Society because it came at the point at which humanity had reached a stage, with the development of the atomic bomb, where it could not only destroy the entire human race, but also the Earth as well. This would have repercussions, not only for this planet, but also for the whole solar system. Hence, those living on other planets decided that it was time to become more proactive. Humanity was perceived by the Cosmic Masters as being at something of a crossroads:

One road leads to disaster, self-inflicted by his own science and materialism. The second leads to a new age, where mankind, through the development of his higher self and abiding by the Law of God, can safely harness his scientific discoveries.[33]

This is why 'the karmic imbalance' needs to be addressed – hence the increased and more visible intervention by the Cosmic Masters 'who wish to help and guide humanity towards a new age'.[34]

It was at this point that King began to formulate a coherent set of beliefs and aims. *Operation Starlight* itself lasted until 1961, by which time all nineteen holy mountains had been 'magnetised'.[35] This is a process that is repeated on regular occasions, usually around twice a year, when it is believed that Satellite No. 3 comes close enough to the Earth to transmit 'spiritual energy' – this follow-up ritual is known as *Operation Space Power*. During these rituals, spiritual energy is also collected by adherents of the Society in specially made receptors (or batteries), and can be released later during Aetherius Society rituals for the benefit of humanity and the planet.[36] According to the Society, 'the most potent form of spiritual practice ... is to perform *The Twelve Blessings* on any of these Holy Mountains during a Magnetization Period'.[37]

It was also during this early period that King formally set out the aims of the Society in the *Cosmic Voice*:[38]

1   to spread the teachings of Master Aetherius, Jesus and other Cosmic Masters;
2   to administer spiritual healing;
3   to prepare the way for the coming of the next master;
4   to organise the Society so as to create favourable conditions for closer contact and, ultimately, meetings with people from other planets;
5   to tune in and irradiate the Power transmitted during a Holy Time or Spiritual Push, in order to balance spiritual practices, irrespective of one's beliefs;
6   to form a brotherhood based on the teachings and knowledge of the Cosmic Masters;
7   to spread the spiritual operation known as Operation Starlight throughout the world, as directed by the Space People.[39]

In 1959, King left England and embarked on an exhaustive lecture tour, often living on very little money, in order to expand *Operation*

Starlight. After a great deal of travelling in America and other mainly English-speaking countries, King was gradually able to build up sufficient popular and financial support to set up a small network of centres. At this time, it is worth noting, he moved to North America, where he perhaps felt that he would find a more ready audience for his ideas. Certainly the emerging alternative religious scene developing in the United States during the late 1950s and early 1960s seemed to reflect many of the monist and pacifist beliefs that formed the basis of the Aetherius Society. King makes the following comment:

> In the Age of Aquarius we will see the merging of science and religion; a breaking down of the barriers between different religions and cultural and racial groups; the introduction of mysticism into orthodox thinking to bring deeper realization about the meaning of life in all aspects; and, above all, a much clearer realization and recognition of the importance of Service to humanity.

Over the following years King travelled widely (again, usually around the English-speaking world) and increased his network of centres whose geographical locations can be seen broadly to reflect the positions of the nineteen holy mountains.[40] These centres seem to operate with relative freedom, although there are plenty of official resources available that encourage centres both to adhere to and spread King's message. For example, in more recent times, the website of the Aetherius Society (http://www.aetherius.org) seems to be used both as an important international point of contact for those interested in UFO spirituality and as a source of information for members – the basic tenets of belief can be found there. This is supplemented by a huge body of literature (usually channelled literature) written by King, as well as around 600 recordings of him channelling messages from the Cosmic Masters, all of which provides a great deal of material from which members worldwide can draw inspiration. Figures for membership of the movement are difficult to come by. That said, a recent report in *UFO News UK* suggested that it had around 10,000 people on its mailing list in the UK alone.[41] Whilst the number of actual members will be somewhat lower than this figure, it does provide some indication of a relatively significant and continuing level of interest in the movement.

The principal beliefs and activities of the Aetherius Society

King developed a fairly sophisticated and mature belief system. This has been neatly summarised in the 'Frequently Asked Questions' section at the Society's website:

1   service to mankind is the most essential yoga or religion in these days;
2   Jesus, Buddha, Krishna and other religious leaders were of extraterrestrial origin and came to Earth to help mankind;
3   the essential teachings of all major religions are similar in nature and all religious people should cooperate with each other;
4   karma and reincarnation are two natural, all pervasive laws of God;
5   there is advanced, intelligent life on other planets in our Solar System existing on a higher vibrational framework than life on the physical plane of Earth;
6   some UFOs are intelligently controlled extraterrestrial spacecraft visiting this Earth. Unlike many UFO groups we believe that extraterrestrials are friendly and here to help humanity in our development;
7   Man, as with all life, is a divine spark of the Creator, or God, and Earth is a classroom on the evolutionary ladder of life back to the source from which we all came;
8   the Mother Earth is a living, breathing entity which is thousands of lives more involved than we are.[42]

As one might expect from a movement that is strongly influenced by theosophical ideas, karma is a significant element of their belief system. As Wallis has shown, for the Aetherius Society karmic law governs everything: 'The karma of individuals and races is … constantly in the process of being "balanced" as they progress through reincarnation towards higher spiritual development, or regress to a lower plane.'[43] As human beings we are perceived as having regressed to a lower plane through our choosing of 'free-will' over 'freedom under karmic law'. Indeed, we are considered to be among the least evolved in our Solar System.[44] Interestingly, the scale of spiritual evolution includes planet Earth, which is itself regarded as a living entity at a much higher state of evolution than those who inhabit it. For the Aetherius Society, it is because of our backward evolution that the Earth has been under frequent attack from evil forces from other parts of the universe, attacks that the Cosmic Masters have sought to repel. In addition, human beings are becoming more able to damage or even destroy the Earth. Consequently, there is a need both to protect the Earth and it inhabitants, and to ensure that the latter reaches a higher state of evolution as soon as possible. King was chosen by the Cosmic Masters to act as a channel through which they could communicate with humanity and deliver the plan according to which higher evolution might be achieved.

We have already seen how the Cosmic Masters are seeking to redress the karmic imbalance through *Operation Starlight*. This was the first of a series of 'operations' that are based on the idea that spiritual energy, and therefore karma, can be manipulated like electricity. *Operation Bluewater* (July 1963 to November 1964), for instance, sought to remove a 'warp' in the Earth's magnetic field that had occurred as a result of both atomic experiments and 'the thought and actions of human beings that interfere with the natural flow of spiritual energies to Earth'.[45] It took place off the coast of southern California in an area believed to be one of planet Earth's psychic centres. Members of the Society were specially trained and directed by King, who remained in touch with the Cosmic Masters during the time of operation. Spiritual energy was collected, intensified and transferred to the psychic centre using equipment developed by King under the direction of the Cosmic Masters.[46]

One of the principal reasons for *Operation Bluewater* was that it paved the way for the longer and more important *Operation Sunbeam*. This began in September 1966 and is still going on. The Cosmic Masters told King that for many years human beings have been using up the Earth's resources: as we increase our knowledge 'we find new ways to abuse our home planet'.[47] *Operation Sunbeam* seeks to redress this imbalance. As the Society states: 'Its general modus operandi is to take Spiritual Energy earmarked for mankind and instead return it to the Mother Earth.'[48] Again, using equipment designed by King, spiritual energy stored in the nineteen holy mountains is extracted and placed in special capacitors where it is intensified and then released at one of the Earth's psychic centres.

Whilst it was claimed that these operations relied on spiritual energy provided by Satellite No. 3, King also formulated a practice that used spiritual energy created by those who took part in the Aetherius Society's rituals. Begun in 1973, this was known as *Operation Prayer Power*. According to the Aetherius Society, *Operation Prayer Power* 'combines dynamic prayer power, Tibetan mantra and the science of radionics to form a potent new tool against disease and suffering on earth'.[49] 'Spiritual Workers' (the sessions are open to anyone who wishes to attend) meet to pray and chant, invoking energy that is collected in similar 'prayer batteries' to those used in *Operation Sunbeam*. Again, this energy is then released in concentrated form:

> Whenever there is a disaster on Earth in need of Spiritual Energy, such as hurricane, earthquake or war, this store of uplifting healing energy can be released almost immediately through a Spiritual Energy Radiator ... This concentrated Prayer Energy is then manipulated by cooperating Masters to the area in need.[50]

These operations again underline the importance of the concept of karma for the Aetherius Society, and also demonstrate how, through *Operation Prayer Power*, a participatory element was included into its practice that not only testifies to the type of movement it is, but also to the sort of person that it attracts:

> At least part of the motivation for membership in the Aetherius Society ... would seem to lie in cognitive insecurity resulting from an awareness of forces at play in the world beyond man's control ... It also seems plausible that a sense of personal insignificance and inadequacy is a prerequisite for the acceptance of ritual rather than empirical means of self-improvement.[51]

This, argues Wallis, may well be one of the reasons why the Aetherius Society did not become as successful as much larger new religious movements such as Scientology, inasmuch that it did not offer a means for individuals directly to enhance their immediate destinies, but rather simply sought to improve their karma. Hence, while the Aetherius Society has persisted for nearly half a century and is, as far as UFO religions are concerned, very successful, it has never been a particularly large organisation. A further reason for this lack of growth in comparison to other new religious organisations is that, whilst on the one hand it provides followers with a well-structured belief system, on the other hand it has to bridge a number of credibility gaps that have been exacerbated by both scientific and technological advances and also the popularisation and public understanding of science. This is clearly a concern for the Society, which devotes much of its website to such problems.

There are, however, still some seemingly insurmountable problems facing the Aetherius Society worldview. For example, although the Society is very clear that the Cosmic Masters primarily originate within our own Solar System, notably from Venus, Mars, Jupiter and Saturn, and that they have been visiting the Earth for thousands of years (e.g. it refers to the *vimanas* found in Vedic and Hindu texts, and to the Star of Bethlehem, as examples of visiting UFOs), it has recently been proved that, with the possible exception of Mars, even the most basic form of life cannot exist on any of these planets, let alone a species that is capable of interplanetary travel. There also seems to be little objective, scientific evidence of spacecraft visiting Earth. This begs a number of questions, many of which are recognised by the Society and summarised as follows: Why has mainstream science not detected this life? Why can we not see their spacecraft? Why do extraterrestrials not land openly on Earth? The basic response is simply that mainstream science is often years behind metaphysical knowledge. '[E]xpert occultists over the centuries have known life on other Planets living on higher spheres of existence'.[52] The literature of the Society also cites the success of mediums contacting the dead and near-death experiences as evidence of the existence of higher planes. More specifically, the ability of the Cosmic Masters to manipulate karma and spiritual energy means that they can alter their 'vibratory rate' and choose to live permanently at this higher level.[53] The same argument is also used to explain why the majority of humanity cannot see the Masters' spacecraft. That said, some do have sightings of UFOs. Is this because they are more spiritually advanced? Not necessarily.

> The Cosmic Masters are able to lower the vibrations of Themselves and Their spacecraft down to the physical level at will. This is why UFO's [sic] are often seen to blink in and out. They have chosen to be seen occasionally, to give mankind a sign that there is more life in the Universe than that on Earth. Occasionally certain Missions they perform on Earth require Their presence on the physical plane.[54]

So, if they occasionally appear, why do they not land more openly? This is because the karmic position of human beings is too lowly to warrant this.[55] Hence, according to the Aetherius Society, humanity's inability to detect, contact or even conceive of these extraterrestrials is the result of general karmic deficiencies that can only be corrected by following the teachings of King, channelled from the Cosmic Masters themselves.

The religious development of the Aetherius Society

As we have seen, the origins of the Aetherius Society can be found in Theosophy. In adapting Blavatsky's ideas, it seems that King was able to develop the movement relatively quickly and to map out a coherent set of beliefs and practices. In particular, the role of the Theosophical Society was important in the development of the type of spiritualism that King espoused:

> The Theosophical Society was founded as a reaction to the inability of spiritualism to develop beyond its limited ideological rationale seeking to investigate the common mystical foundations of world religions and to realise a wider framework of meaning and metaphysics which would provide an explanation of spiritualist and other occult phenomena.[56]

While the Theosophical Society placed spiritualism in a wider religious context, it cannot really be said that it institutionalised it. King, however, was able to build a cohesive and coherent movement by actually increasing the stress on spiritualist activity. This can be seen in a development of the Aetherius Society's theosophical origins towards what Ellwood refers to as a more spiritualistic practice through 'mediumistic nodes of operation',[57] where the greater influence of spiritualism was marked by King's growing importance as a channel for the Cosmic Masters. Through his position as the sole channel of revelation from the Cosmic Masters, King was able to monopolise the 'charismatic legitimation'[58] within the Aetherius Society and thereby 'overcome the constraints on institutionalisation which typically face movements founded on the systematic manifestation of charismatic gifts'.[59] This, in addition to his appropriation of the Theosophical Society's use of karma to explain the current predicament that human beings find themselves in, enabled him to establish a broader framework of meaning than that normally found within spiritualism. Furthermore, by instituting the various 'operations' that underpin the continuation of the Aetherius Society's ritual activity, he provided a context within which he could legitimately expect a high degree of participation from his followers.[60]

In addition to this, King's role in the movement also began to change from that of essentially a medium for the Cosmic Masters to being much more proactive in their Earth-saving activities. As Wallis suggests: 'From being an "unworthy and ignorant servant", he progressed to colleague, confidante and even advisor of his erstwhile superiors. From harbinger of the coming new Master, the equal of Jesus, Buddha, and Krishna, it was clear from around 1958 that ... King himself was destined for a greater role.'[61] This was seemingly confirmed in a transmission received by King in April 1959, in which Master Jesus told him, 'My Son you are now one of Us, and We now declare this to all men.'[62]

This shift of status and role for King had a great impact, not only on his position within the movement, but also on the religious development of the movement itself. This can be seen in the way that the eschatological claims of the movement evolved in order to accommodate King's enhanced function. Indeed, some scholars (most notably Ellwood[63]) consider the movement to display characteristics that could be described as a form of 'apocalyptic theosophy'.[64] In particular, Ellwood discusses a literature within the Society that predicts an apocalypse triggered by the coming of 'the next Master'. This was communicated to King by the Lord of Karma in 1958: 'There will shortly come another among you ... Go ye forth and spread My Word throughout the World, so that all men of pure heart may prepare for His coming.'[65] Whilst this apocalyptic dimension is certainly evident in King's writings, it would seem that it is something that has been played down as part of the process of making King's role within the movement more important. That is to say, while in the very early days of the movement the coming of the Lord of Karma seemed imminent, gradually the stress shifted to the idea that this could only occur at a time when enough of humanity has evolved to a certain karmic level and, moreover, that this time was some way off.[66] This interpretation was further encouraged by the fact that King had already been given the dates of Satellite No. 3's visits to Earth for the next 1,000 years – thereby casting doubt on either the dates or the likelihood of an *immediate* apocalyptic eschatalogical event.[67] Hence, concerning the contemporary Aetherius Society, whilst there is little doubt that it has an eschatological dimension, it is arguable whether it can, strictly speaking, be regarded as apocalyptic in the sense of 'a scenario that foretells the imminent end of the world'.[68] 'Nor', says John Saliba, 'can it be called apocalyptic if this implies that a specific time for landing of the aliens has been foretold. Unlike leaders of some UFO religions ... George King has never announced a particular date for the arrival on earth of alien beings in flying saucers. Much less has he attempted to prophesy the precise time for the advent of a millennium or for the end of the world.'[69] Indeed, the Society's reaction to the mass suicide by members of Heaven's Gate in San Diego in 1997 is instructive. They published a special report on their website decrying the events, explaining them in the following statement: 'In these days of rapid technological growth, especially in the West, we see a technology advancing faster than spiritual growth. This is creating a very dangerous imbalance.'[70] In many ways, this is a remarkable statement from a movement which claims to invoke the 'momentary authority of science'.[71] Yet it provides a good example of a tension that has always existed within the Aetherius Society. Whilst much within the movement has evolved, the technological elements, that were initially so important to it, have remained somewhat fixed and now seem peculiarly outdated. In other words, although the understanding of spiritualism changed and adapted, the attention paid to secular scientific and technological developments failed to keep pace. As a result, while the movement is clearly concerned with explaining these inconsistencies between its ideas and those of contemporary science,[72] it became increasingly unnecessary to qualify and explain them to adherents of the movement because of their growing acceptance of King's charismatic authority.[73]

Consequently, while the extraterrestrial dimension of the movement remains important, inasmuch as it is still the Cosmic Masters who provide much of the spiritual energy to support its spiritual and ritual activities, there has been something of a disjunction between the extraterrestrials and the membership of the Aetherius Society. As we have seen, this has occurred in two stages: first, through King's assumption of many of the Cosmic Masters' roles; and second, through the loss of the movement's direct channel to the Masters following King's death. This has meant that, while many of the Society's operations are able to continue by following the instructions given by King before his death, others cannot be followed unless some form of divination can be found that will enable members to contact the Masters directly.[74] Up to now, five years after King's death, this does not seem to have been a particular problem for the movement, and only time will tell whether or not it can survive without its founder and principal source of religious authority.

Conclusion

Like many new religious movements, the Aetherius Society has focused on its founder for leadership and inspiration. Tapes of King's utterances and his writings are respectively played and read at services, and his position amongst the Cosmic Masters acts as an archetype for others to follow. Such is his centrality to the movement that his death, in 1997, could have been heralded as the end for the Aetherius

Society. This does not seem to be the case, with numbers seemingly remaining small but constant. We have seen that there are a number of reasons for this continuation.

1   King had initially developed a series of strong and coherent beliefs early in the life of the movement, creating a basis for its stability and continuity.
2   He quickly assumed a charismatic presence within the Aetherius Society by monopolising religious power through his claims to contact with the Cosmic Masters.
3   He stressed the importance of karma in the spiritual and ritual activity of the movement. This not only helped him to establish his own authority, operating on a higher spiritual level than anyone else, but also set out a path for members of the movement to follow, thereby encouraging their participation to a level beyond that usually seen in spiritualism.
4   This was further encouraged through the introduction of *Operation Prayer Power*, which empowered ordinary members of the movement to create their own spiritual energy and thereby offered an additional evolutionary route to the attainment of karma.
5   Like a number of other founders of religious movements in the twentieth century, King made provision for the leadership of the movement after his death, stating that another single leader would not replace him.[75] Instead, he appointed of a Board of Directors to take over. This had two effects. On the one hand, it lessened the impact of his death on the movement. On the other hand, it actually enhanced his stature within the movement, ensuring his unique position in its history.
6   Finally, in addition to this, King claimed to have received the times when Satellite No. 3 would be visiting Earth for the next 1000 years, thereby encouraging adherents to collect prayer energy for the future. However, as Saliba suggests, adherents have not, thus far, established ways of divining when the Satellite comes to deliver energy for 'the Emergency Period' when the Earth is particularly in danger, since only King was able to receive this information.[76]

Although it is too early to say whether the Aetherius Society has a long-term future without its charismatic founder, it certainly seems able to continue without direct channelled contact with the Cosmic Masters. Indeed, bearing in mind that this is a movement that has always been on the periphery of new religious life, founded by a man

who was himself never attracted to mainstream ideas, it is conceivable
that it will continue at a stable, if limited, level for some time to come.

NOTES

1 http://www.aetherius.org
2 The Unarius group, founded by Earnest L. Norman in 1954, is another
   notable example. See R. S. Ellwood, 'UFO Religious Movements', in T.
   Miller (ed.), *America's Alternative Religions*, Albany, Suny Press, 1995, p. 393.
3 R. Wallis, 'The Aetherius Society: A Case Study in the Formation of a
   Mystagogic Congregation', *Sociological Review* 22, 1974, p. 27.
4 *Ibid.*
5 *Ibid.*, p. 28.
6 http://www.aetherius.org
7 Aetherius Society, *George King, Our Founder*. Available online:http://www.
   aetherius.org/NewFiles/Dr_George_King.html (19/03/01).
8 He was a conscientious objector (Wallis, 'The Aetherius Society', p. 28).
9 *Ibid.*, p. 36.
10 The first recorded sighting of a UFO was on 24 June 1947, when a pilot
    recorded seeing something that 'flew like a saucer would if you skipped it
    across the water'. The media jumped on this description, coining the term
    'flying saucer' (See Ellwood, 'UFO Religious Movements', p. 393). For a
    discussion of the emergence of the modern UFO movement, see the
    Introduction to this volume.
11 S. Perdue, *The Aetherius Society*. Available online: http://religiousmove-
    ments.lib.virginia.edu/nrms/aetherius.html (19/03/01).
12 Wallis, 'The Aetherius Society', p. 28.
13 Aetherius Society, *George King, Our Founder*.
14 *Ibid.*
15 Wallis, 'The Aetherius Society', p. 29; *ibid.*
16 According to the Aetherius Society website, King had spent the previous
    ten years becoming a master of many forms of yoga, and was able to attain
    Samadhi. This is why he was chosen by the Cosmic Masters
    (http://www.aetherius.org).
17 Wallis, 'The Aetherius Society', p. 28.
18 According to Wallis these included Saint Goo-Ling (a member of the
    Great White Brotherhood living on Earth), Mars Sector 6, Mars Sector 8,
    and Jupiter Sector 92 (*ibid.*, p. 30).
19 *Ibid.*, p. 30.
20 J. G. Melton, 'The Contactees: a Survey', in J. R. Lewis (ed.), *The Gods
    Have Landed: New Religions From Other Worlds*, Albany, SUNY Press,
    1995, pp. 4–6.
21 *Ibid.*, p. 5.
22 *Ibid.*, p. 4. During 'astral travel' an individual senses his/her body and
    consciousness separately; the body, it is believed, remains in one place,
    whilst the consciousness travels outside it.
23 For example, dowsing is sometimes used as a method of medical diagnosis.
24 Based on William Shakespeare's play *The Tempest*.
25 Melton, 'The Contactees', pp. 7–8.
26 *Ibid.*

27 R. S. Ellwood and H. B. Partin, *Religious and Spiritual Groups in Modern America*, Englewood Cliffs, Prentice Hall, 1988, p. 126.
28 Wallis, 'The Aetherius Society', p. 30.
29 There are a number of stories of King travelling on such craft.
30 Taken from the anonymously published *The Story of the Aetherius Society*, n.d., p. 4.
31 Wallis, 'The Aetherius Society', p. 31.
32 This was the first of a series of military-sounding operations that continue to be enacted. For a full list, see J. A. Saliba, 'The Earth is a Dangerous Place – The World View of the Aetherius Society', *Marburg Journal of Religion* 4, 1999. Available online: http://www.uni-marburg.de/religionswissenschaft/journal/mjr/saliba_main.html (6/11/02)
33 Available online:http://wwwaetherius.org./NewFiles/.About_Us_FAQs. html (19/03/01)
34 *Ibid.*
35 According to the Aetherius Society there are a total of nineteen holy mountains. These can be found in Britain (9), the USA (4), Australia (2), France, New Zealand, Switzerland and Tanzania (1 each). See *The Aetherius Society, A Cosmic Concept*. Available online: http://www.spiritweb.org/Spirit/aetherius-society.html (19/03/01).
36 A typical Aetherius Society congregation gets together for a series of weekly services:

> a prayer meeting that includes meditation, recitation
> of some of the Twelve Blessings and petitions for healing;
> a service dedicated to Operation Prayer Power;
> private healing services; a regular Sunday service, at
> which recordings of King or planetary beings may be played

> (Saliba, 'The Earth is a Dangerous Place', p. 9)

37 *The Aetherius Society, A Cosmic Concept*.
38 The official *Journal of the Aetherius Society* June/July 1958, vol. 16, p. 31.
39 Saliba, 'The Earth is a Dangerous Place', p. 3.
40 There are 11 branches of the Society in Britain, 5 in the USA, 2 in Australia and one each in Canada and New Zealand. The Society is particularly active in sub-Saharan Africa, however, with a total of 20 branches, 5 of which are in Ghana. For further details see:http://www. aetherius.org/NewFiles/World_Locations.html#amer
41 A. James, 'The Aetherius Society Meeting', *UFO News UK*, 2001, vol.1:8. Available online: http://www.ufoinfo.com/infonewsuk/v01/0108.shtml.
42 http://www.aetherius.org/NewFiles/About_Us_FAQs.html (19/03/01).
43 Wallis, 'The Aetherius Society', p. 33.
44 *Ibid.*
45 Saliba, 'The Earth is a Dangerous Place', p. 8.
46 *Ibid.*
47 *The Aetherius Society, A Cosmic Concept*.
48 *Ibid.*
49 *Ibid.*
50 *Ibid.*
51 Wallis, 'The Aetherius Society', p. 38.
52 http://www.aetherius.org/NewFiles/About_Us_FAQs.html (19/03/01).

53 *Ibid.*

54 *Ibid.*

55 The Society's website suggests that human beings have all but destroyed the Earth on previous occasions, citing the mythical civilisations of Lemuria/Mu and Atlantis as examples, also stating that humans used to live on a planet between Mars and Jupiter known as Maldek. This was destroyed and the asteroid belt is all that remains of it today – http://www.aetherius.org/NewFiles/About_Us_FAQs.html (19/03/01).

56 Wallis, 'The Aetherius Society', p 40.

57 Ellwood, 'UFO Religious Movements', p. 396.

58 Wallis, 'The Aetherius Society', p. 40.

59 *Ibid.*, p. 27.

60 *Ibid.*, p. 40.

61 *Ibid.*, p. 32.

62 *Ibid.*

63 R. S. Ellwood, *Islands of the Dawn: The Story of Alternative Spirituality in New Zealand*, Honolulu, University of Hawaii Press, 1993.

64 Saliba, 'The Earth is a Dangerous Place', p. 5.

65 *The Next Master.* Available online:http://www.aetherius.org/NewFiles/Next_Master.html (31/03/02).

66 *Ibid.*

67 King, G. *The Five Temples of God*, Hollywood, Aetherius Society, 1975; Saliba, 'The Earth is a Dangerous Place', p. 5.

68 Saliba, 'The Earth is a Dangerous Place', p. 5.

69 *Ibid.*

70 http://www.aetherius.org/hale.htm; Saliba, 'The Earth is a Dangerous Place', p. 5.

71 Melton, 'The Contactees', p. 5.

72 http://www.aetherius.org/NewFiles/About_Us_FAQs.html (19/03/01).

73 An example of this insider/outsider difference can be found in A. James, 'The Aetherius Society Meeting'.

74 Saliba, 'The Earth is a Dangerous Place', p. 10.

75 King, *The Five Temples*, p. 7; Saliba, 'The Earth is a Dangerous Place', p. 10.

76 Saliba, 'The Earth is a Dangerous Place', p. 10.

5

LEGITIMATING SUICIDE
Heaven's Gate and New Age ideology

James R. Lewis

> Earthlings will awaken to ... the lake seething and the great
> destruction of tall buildings ... The scenes of that day will be
> as mad ... the event will begin at dawn and end swiftly as a
> passing cloud ... When the resurrected have been taken up ...
> it will be as a great burst of light ... In the midst of this it is to
> be recorded that a great wave rushes into the mountains ...
> The slopes of the side to the east will be the beginning of a
> new civilization upon which will be the new order, in light ...

In this prophecy one finds many familiar apocalyptic elements, from
the theme of universal destruction to the post-apocalypse vision of a
dawning new order. One can well imagine that these words spilled
unbidden from the trembling lips of an ecstatic Middle Eastern
prophet. Alternately, perhaps they were uttered by a fiery preacher in
harsh, dramatic tones from the pulpit of some backwoods church.
Instead, however, this prediction was one of the central transmissions
of Space Brother Sananda (aka Jesus) to Marian Keech, a middle-aged,
middle-class suburbanite who transcribed them via the medium of
automatic writing in the comfort of her own living room. In other
messages, Sananda assured Mrs Keech that she and a select group of
followers would be taken up by a flying saucer in a kind of *technological
rapture* before the destruction commenced on 21 December 1954.
Needless to say, neither the rapture nor the predicted apocalypse
occurred – a dramatic non-event, the significance of which was
captured in the title of the first and only study of the group, *When
Prophecy Fails*.[1] The scenario predicted in Mrs Keech's prophecy is
eerily similar to that of Heaven's Gate.

On 26 March 1997 the bodies of thirty-nine men and women were
found in a well-appointed mansion outside San Diego, victims of a
mass suicide. Messages left by the group indicate that they believed
they were stepping out of their 'physical containers' in order to ascend

to a UFO that was arriving in the wake of the Hale – Bopp comet. They also asserted that this comet, or parts of it, would subsequently crash into the Earth and cause widespread destruction. In a taped message, their leader further noted that our calendars were inaccurate – that the year 1997 was really the year 2000, as if everyone was in agreement that the world would end precisely two millennia after the time of Jesus.[2]

Heaven's Gate – formerly known as Human Individual Metamorphosis – originally made headlines in September 1975 when, following a public lecture in Waldport, Oregon, over thirty people vanished overnight. This disappearance became the occasion for a media event. For the next several months, reporters generated story after story about brainwashed cult groupies abandoning their everyday lives to follow the strange couple who alternately referred to themselves as 'Bo and Peep', 'the Two', 'Do and Ti' and other bizarre names.

Bo (Marshall Herff Applewhite) and Peep (Bonnie Lu Nettles) met in 1972, and founded one of the most unusual flying saucer religions ever to emerge out of the occult/metaphysical/New Age subculture. Preaching an unusual synthesis of occult spirituality and UFO soteriology, they began recruiting in New Age circles in the spring of 1975. Followers were required to abandon friends and family, detach themselves completely from human emotions as well as material possessions, and focus exclusively on perfecting themselves in preparation for a physical transition (a type of a 'beaming up') to the next kingdom (in the form of a flying saucer) – a metamorphosis that would be facilitated by ufonauts.

Bo and Peep were surprisingly effective at recruiting people to their strange gospel, though their activities did not attract much attention until the Waldport, Oregon, meeting. Six weeks later, the group was infiltrated by University of Montana sociologist Robert Balch and a research assistant, David Taylor. Balch and Taylor represented themselves as interested seekers, and became pseudo-followers in order to conduct clandestine field research. As they would later report in subsequent papers, the great majority of the people who became involved with Bo and Peep were either marginal individuals living on the fringes of society or people who had been deeply involved with occult spirituality for some time before their affiliation with the Two.[3]

However, as useful as this particular insight into the Two's recruits might be, our minds still recoil in incomprehension at the transparent absurdity of Bo and Peep's teachings. How could any sane human being buy into such silliness? And how could a 'prophet' who looked like Mickey Mouse and sounded like Mr Rogers lead a group of over three dozen people to their deaths? Mind control notions that portray 'cultists' as suffering from damaged powers of reasoning are little more than expressions of social disapproval that substitute disparaging labels for real understanding, and hence are barren of insight. Given that Heaven's Gate chose to exit as a group, perhaps a sociological approach would yield more insight than a psychological/psychiatric approach.

Issues of power and obedience were at the very core of the classic sociologist Max Weber's thinking about the legitimation of authority. Weber proposed a tripartite schema of traditional, rational–legal and charismatic legitimations of authority. The dynamics (in the sense of upsetting rather than reinforcing established authority structures) of this schema were largely confined to the factor of charisma, a form of legitimation Weber viewed as particularly – though not exclusively – characteristic of new religious movements.

The discussion of the strategies power élites deploy to maintain their position has consumed a small lake of scholarly ink, not to mention a small forest of trees that sacrificed their lives to the paper industry. In sharp contrast, the analysis of the legitimation strategies deployed by new religions has not moved forward substantially since Weber. While other, more recent, researchers have touched on the subject in passing, no one has published a single article (much less a book) focused on this issue – despite the fact that legitimacy is a core issue for emergent religious movements. The rudimentary state of this topic means that any attempt to extend Weber's discussion in this arena must necessarily be preliminary and exploratory.

Weber's work on the legitimation of authority provides a useful starting point for understanding the legitimation strategies deployed by new religions, but it should immediately be noted that his analysis is also inadequate. For example, in contrast to what one might anticipate from the discussion of charismatic authority in Weber's *Economy and Society*,[4] one often finds new religions appealing to tradition – though the explicit nature of such appeals means that they constitute a variation from what Weber had in mind by the traditional legitimation of authority (which he viewed as largely implicit). Also, when nascent movements attempt to justify a new idea, practice or social arrangement by attributing it to the authority of tradition, it is usually through a reinterpretation of the past that they are able to portray themselves as the true embodiment of tradition. Such modifications of his schema indicate that Weber did not have the last word on this issue. In fact, upon closer examination one finds that contemporary new religions rely upon a wide range of different legitimation strategies.

Charisma – which, in Weber's use of the term, includes direct reve-lations from divinity as well as the leader's ability to provide both mundane and supernatural benefits to followers – may be the keystone in a new movement's attractiveness, but charismatic leaders typically appeal to a variety of other sources of legitimacy. For instance, as I have already mentioned, founders of new religions often appeal to the authority of tradition. Many modern movements also appeal to the authority of reason and science. Yet another strategy is to appeal to an ancient wisdom or a primordial religiosity that antedates current reli-gions.

In the case of Heaven's Gate, Applewhite and Nettles appealed to a wide variety of sources – particularly to a number of facets of New Age ideology, but also to certain aspects of the Christian tradition – to legitimate their authority and their unusual religious vision. This mix of sources is evident in their claims to be Jesus (Applewhite) and God the Father (Nettles) returned, while simultaneously asserting that they were extraterrestrial 'walk-ins' (a New Age notion). A number of observers have emphasised Heaven's Gate's Christian component, to the point of characterising the Two's teaching as 'space-age neo-Christian'.[5] However, though I do not want to downplay the Christian component of their ideological synthesis, it seems clear that the Christian elements were grafted on to a basically New Age matrix. The simple fact that Heaven's Gate attracted seekers from the New Age subculture rather than from the Christian subculture – that 'new agers' rather than Christians could entertain the Two's ideology as a viable, appealing teaching – underscores this point.

In the midst of a society in which the belief system propagated by the Two seems absurd, it is also appropriate to ask how they legitimated their unusual worldview to followers. And finally, after Nettles had died from cancer, which elements of their belief system were Applewhite able to draw upon to legitimate a group suicide? In view of the dramatic end of Heaven's Gate, it might well repay our efforts if we examined the larger spiritual subculture within which such teachings might sound plausible rather than absurd. Though not all aspects of Applewhite's theological synthesis were drawn from New Age thinking, most components of the group's overarching worldview were characteristically New Age, as shall be demonstrated.

Ascended masters and UFOs

Since at least the nineteenth century, the industrialised West has been home to a strand of alternative religiosity that has been variously referred to as 'occult', 'metaphysical' or, more recently, 'New Age'. This non-traditional spiritual subculture has given birth to a variety of distinct organisations and churches, from the various theosophical organisations and New Thought churches to spiritualist denominations and less formally organised 'light centres'.[6]

Despite the existence of formal organisational structures, the core of this ambiguous subculture is constituted by a largely unaffiliated population of 'seekers' who drift promiscuously from one spiritual group to another, never committing themselves to any single vision of truth. One result of the general weakness of doctrinally-oriented organisations is that this subculture can be infiltrated by almost any interesting new idea not overtly antagonistic to the basic tenets of New Age ideology.[7]

As an unusually fascinating form of rejected knowledge that mainstream scientists tend to classify as paranormal, UFOs have always attracted considerable interest within the occult/metaphysical/New Age subculture. Almost from the beginning, however, this subculture transformed flying saucers and their presumed extraterrestrial pilots into spiritual beings who had come to Earth to help us along the spiritual path. To accomplish the transformation of extraterrestrials into wise, esoteric beings, 'ufonauts' were assimilated into earlier models of spiritual sages, particularly the so-called Ascended Masters.

The concept of Ascended Masters, or the Great White Brotherhood, was codified within theosophy by Helena Petrovna Blavatsky in the 1880s, and from there it has been derived by various religious groups that descend from the Theosophical Society. Many people in the New Age movement believe that such Masters guide the spiritual progress of humanity. The equation of Ascended Masters with ufonauts seems to have developed out of an earlier idea, which was that at least some of the Masters were from other planets in our solar system, such as Venus.

In contrast to the modern UFO era, which began with Kenneth Arnold's sightings on 24 June 1947, the theosophical claim of extraterrestrial contact goes back to the late nineteenth century. A useful, somewhat later example of such contact claims can be found in the story of 'I AM'. The I AM Religious Activity is a popularised form of theosophy, reformulated to appeal to a broader audience than earlier theosophical organisations. The founder of the movement was Guy Ballard, who had long been interested in occultism and had studied theosophical teachings.

Ballard was engaged in mining exploration and promotion. In 1930, while he was working near Mount Shasta – a giant volcanic cone in northern California where strange occult events had been said to occur – he had his first substantive contact with another world. While hiking in the woods around the mountain, Ballard reports that he encountered a hiker who introduced himself as the Ascended Master Saint-Germain. Saint-Germain was one of the most famous occultists of modern times. Ballard was, he related, chosen as a messenger to restore the truths of re-embodiment to humankind. Saint-Germain imparted information about karma, the inner reality of the divine – which he referred to as the 'Mighty I AM Presence' – occult world history, and the creative power of thought.

One New Year's Eve, the Master and Ballard joined a gathering inside a cavern in Royal Teton Mountain. The individuals at this assembly played host to twelve Venusians who appeared in their midst in a dazzling display of light, not unlike a *Star Trek* beam-in. These Venusian 'Lords of the Flame' played harp and violin music, and showed the gathered terrestrials scenes of advanced technological achievements from their home world on a great mirror. These events from the early 1930s were reported in Ballard's *Unveiled Mysteries*, which was published a dozen years before Kenneth Arnold's celebrated encounter.[8]

The first noteworthy prophet to emerge in the wake of post-war flying saucer sightings was George Adamski. In the early 1940s he became intrigued with Unidentified Flying Objects, long before they were much discussed by the public. Adamski reported that, on 20 November 1952, he experienced telepathic contact with a humanoid Venusian, and the following month reported another contact in which a hieroglyphic message was given. These encounters were reported in *Flying Saucers Have Landed*,[9] one of the most popular flying saucer books ever written. Adamski gained a broad following and was a much sought-after lecturer.

As we can see from Ballard's report of the Royal Teton gathering, religious and other revelations from Venusians were nothing new. Adamski was thus not an innovator in this regard. Rather, Adamski's contribution was to connect the earlier notion of receiving information from extraterrestrials with the emergent interest in flying saucers. The Ballard example of 'Venusian Masters' also allows us to see that the human imagination has a predisposition to respond to flying saucers – viewed as alien spacecraft – in religious terms.[10]

Even much 'secular' thinking about UFOs embodies quasi-religious themes, such as the crypto-religious notion that the world is on the verge of destruction and that ufonauts are somehow going to rescue humanity – either by forcibly preventing a nuclear Armageddon or by taking select members of the human race to another planet to preserve the species. The psychologist Carl Jung was referring to the latter portrayal of ufonauts when he called them 'technological angels'. The idea of positive, helpful extraterrestrials has been a common theme of much science fiction, from *Superman* (who, it will be remembered, was from another planet) to the friendly alien of Steven Spielberg's *E.T.: The Extraterrestrial* (1982).

Jung postulated a drive towards self-realisation and self-integration which he referred to as the individuation process. The goal of this process is represented by the Self archetype, an archetype characterised by wholeness and completeness. One of the concrete manifestations of this archetype is as a circle symbol, and it was various forms of the circle that Jung referred to as mandalas. According to Jung, mandala symbols emerge in dreams when the individual is seeking harmony and wholeness – seeking which frequently occurs during periods of crisis and insecurity. Jung interpreted the phenomenon of flying saucers – which often appear in the form of circular disks – as mandala symbols, reflecting the human mind's desire for stability in a confused world. From a depth psychological point of view, it is thus no coincidence that the chariots of the gods should manifest in the form of flying saucers.[11]

But if UFOs are the chariots of the gods, then why do the Space Brothers not just land and communicate their ideas to humanity in person? The same question has sometimes been asked with respect to the Great White Brotherhood. One of the salient characteristics of the Ascended Masters was that they preferred to communicate their occult teachings through the medium of telepathic messages sent to select individuals. These chosen vessels then relayed the Masters' messages to the larger public, either vocally in a form of mediumship that would later be called 'channelling', or in written form via a process usually referred to as automatic writing. Because the Ascended Masters are the primary model for the Space Brothers, it comes as no surprise that latter-day UFO prophets should employ the same methods for communicating the wisdom of the ufonauts to the larger public.

George King, founder of the Aetherius Society, proposed that these Masters were actually extraterrestrials who were members of a 'space command' managing the affairs of the solar system.[12] This concept has been built upon by other channellers and groups, such as Michael and Aurora El-Legion, who channel the 'Ashtar Command'. It was from this tradition that Applewhite and Nettles took the basic idea of spiritually advanced ufonauts. And it is easy to connect the Two directly to the theosophical tradition: before meeting Applewhite, Nettles had belonged to the Theosophical Society and had attended New Age channelling sessions at which extraterrestrial beings may have been channelled.

The journey of Bo and Peep

In addition to teaching that ufonauts were spiritually advanced beings, Applewhite and Nettles also taught that aliens had come to pick up spiritually evolved human beings who would join the ranks of flying saucer crews. Only a select few members of humanity would be chosen to advance to this transhuman state. The rest would be left to wallow in the spiritually poisoned atmosphere of a corrupt world. Applewhite would later teach that, after the elect had been picked up by the space brothers, the planet would be engulfed in cataclysmic destruction. When, in 1993, under the name of Total Overcomers Anonymous, the group ran an advertisement in *USA Today*, their portrayal of the post-rapture world was far more apocalyptic than Applewhite and Nettles had taught in the 1970s:

The Earth's present 'civilization' is about to be recycled – 'spaded under.' Its inhabitants are refusing to evolve. The 'weeds' have taken over the garden and disturbed its useful-ness beyond repair.[13]

For followers of the Two, the focus of day-to-day existence was to follow a disciplined regime referred to as the overcoming process or, simply, the process. The goal of this process was to overcome human weaknesses – a goal not dissimilar to the goal of some of the spiritual practices followed by more mainstream monastic communities. For Applewhite, however, it appears that stamping out one's sexuality was the core issue. Furthermore, it is clear that his focus on sexual issues was tied to the problems he had experienced in the past as a direct result of his own sexuality.

Despite the outward success of Applewhite's early academic and musical career, he had been deeply troubled. Married and the father of two children, he secretly carried on a double life as a homosexual. Guilty and confused, he is said to have longed for a platonic relation-ship within which he could develop his full potential without being troubled by his sexual urges. He eventually divorced his wife and, in 1970, was fired by St.Thomas University. Devastated, Applewhite became bitter and depressed.

He met Nettles at a hospital where he was seeking help for his sexual and psychological problems. Nettles and Applewhite quickly became inseparable. For a short while they together operated a metaphysical centre. After the centre folded, they continued holding classes in a house they called *Knowplace*. In 1973 they began travelling in search of a higher purpose. They eventually camped out in an isolated spot near the Oregon coast and, after six weeks, came to the realisation that they were the two witnesses prophesied in Revelation 11.

In the spring of 1975 they recruited their first followers, beginning with a teacher of metaphysics named Clarence Klug and twenty-three of his students. As the first step in the transformational process taught by the Two, their followers abandoned everything that tied them to their everyday lives, including their jobs, families and most of their possessions except for cars and camping supplies (necessary for leading a quasi-nomadic lifestyle). Mirroring their own process, the Two placed males and females together in non-sexual partnerships in which each was instructed to assist their partner in the overcoming process. They also attempted to tune in to the next level, again reflecting the process that Applewhite and Nettles had experienced during their six-week retreat.

The group developed quietly until the media interest that was evoked in the wake of the Waldport, Oregon meeting put them in the spotlight. This new attention awakened fears that Bo and Peep might be assassinated before they could fulfill their mission. They subsequently cancelled a planned meeting in Chicago, and split the group into a number of autonomous 'families' consisting of a dozen or more individuals. These families were then sent on their way, travelling, camping out, begging food and occasionally recruiting new members. Many of the faithful fell away during this period. Around the end of 1975 or the beginning of 1976, the Two re-emerged, gathered together the remnants of their following, and eventually began a new round of recruiting activities.

In the face of strong ridicule, however, Nettles abruptly announced that 'the doors to the next level are closed', and their missionary activity ceased. The harvest had ended, with less than a hundred individuals engaged in the process. Another change was the subsequent announcement that the *Demonstration* had been cancelled because their followers had not been making rapid enough progress in the overcoming process. Rather than focusing on the time when they would be taken up by the saucers, they must concentrate on their own development.

To this end, the Two developed more practices and disciplines to help their followers overcome their human weaknesses. For example, in one exercise known as 'tomb time', followers would go for days without saying anything except 'yes', 'no' or 'I don't know' (other communications took place via written notes). Followers also began to wear uniform clothing.

The semi-nomadic period ended within a few years when two followers inherited a total of approximately $300,000. They then rented houses, initially in Denver and later in the Dallas–Fort Worth area. Each house, which they called a 'craft', had the windows covered to prevent neighbours from watching their activities. Followers adhered to a strict routine. Immersed in the intensity of their structured lifestyle, the teachings of the Two became more and more real to members.

Experiences that seemed to disconfirm the Heaven's Gate worldview were addressed by attributing them to the machinations of evil aliens, who were referred to as 'Luciferians' by the Two. For this aspect of their teaching, Applewhite and Nettles adopted a strategy deployed within certain ultra-conservative Christian groups, which dismisses any challenge to their theology as motivated by demons. However, their vision of a world under assault by evil aliens who keep human beings bound to continuous reincarnations on the Earth plane through delusion and through the distraction of physical pleasures is more clearly related to certain strands of traditional Gnosticism than Christian demonology – though it should immediately be added that Bo and Peep's group did not otherwise exhibit enough relevant traits to be classified as a Gnostic group.[14]

The group's strict segregation from society was suddenly altered in 1983, when many followers visited their families on Mother's Day. However, these members dropped out of contact as soon as they left. It was during these visits that they communicated to their families that they were learning computer technology. Another change took place in 1985 when Nettles died of cancer. The group surfaced again in 1994 when, thinking the lift-off would begin in a year or two, they held another series of public meetings. It was as part of this new cycle of missionary activity that the USA Today advertisement appeared.

Details about how the group came to attach apocalyptic significance to the Hale–Bopp comet are tantalisingly scanty. For whatever reason, someone outside the group had come to the conclusion that a giant UFO was coming to Earth, 'hidden' in the wake of Hale–Bopp. When Heaven's Gate heard this information, Applewhite took it as an indication that the long awaited pick-up of his group by aliens was finally about to take place. The decision that the time had come to make their final exit could not have been made more than a few weeks before the mass suicide. Applewhite had rethought his theology after his beloved partner died because, in order to be reunited with Nettles, her spirit would have to acquire a new body aboard the spacecraft. The death of Nettles seems to have been the decisive influence leading him later to adopt the view that the group would ascend together spiritually rather than physically.[15]

Applewhite may have chosen the option of a group suicide because there seemed to be no other viable solution to the problem of what followers would do after he passed away. This quandary relates Heaven's Gate to one of the more well-known themes in Weber's analysis of religion, namely that the death of the founder of a religion represents a crisis typically addressed via the routinisation of the prophet's charisma – by which Weber meant the transmission and regularisation of her/his charisma in the form of new institutions. Heaven's Gate, however, was never large enough to prompt the Two to consider setting up anything like an institution. And the teaching that the Space Brothers would pick them up within their lifetime effectively prevented Applewhite from considering the option of appointing a successor.[16] So in the end, getting older and failing in health,[17] Applewhite – having already decided some years before that they would make their exit via a group suicide – seems to have been predisposed to interpret any indication that the Space Brothers were coming as a sign it was time to leave. Thus the rumour that a large UFO was approaching Earth in the wake of Hale – Bopp – a rumour widely repeated among UFO enthusiasts on the Internet and discussed in such popular forums as the Art Bell radio show[18] – provided Applewhite with the sign he was waiting for to set in motion the final solution to his quandary.

Graduating to the next level

The idea that the group might depart via suicide had emerged in Applewhite's thinking only within the prior few years. The Two's earlier idea – an idea that had set Heaven's Gate apart from everyone else – was that a group of individuals selected to move to the next level would bodily ascend to the saucers in a kind of 'technological rapture'. Applewhite and Nettles had originally taught that the goal of the process they were teaching their followers was to prepare them to be physically taken aboard the spacecraft, where they would enter a cocoon-like state, eventually being reborn in transformed physical bodies.

Christianity's view of resurrection reflects the influence of the cultures in which it originated and spread during its first centuries in the Mediterranean basin. The idea of resurrection, which was originally formulated within Zoroastrianism, was introduced to Christianity from Judaism. This idea developed in tandem with an apocalyptic vision of history that entailed the end of the world as we know it, and which would result in the defeat of death and evil.[19]

The notion of resurrection is also central to Chapter 11 of the Book of Revelation, the biblical passage Applewhite and Nettles came to view as describing their particular ministry. This chapter recounts the story of two prophets who will be slain. Then, three-and-a-half days later, they will be resurrected and taken up in a cloud:

> At the end of the three days and a half the breath of life from God came into them; and they stood up on their feet to the terror of all who saw it. Then a loud voice was heard speaking to them from heaven, which said, 'Come up here!' And they went up to heaven in a cloud, in full view of their enemies. At that same moment there was a violent earthquake ...
>
> (Rev. 11:11–13)

In the early phase of their movement, Applewhite and Nettles prophesied that they would soon be assassinated. Using the above passage as a script for future events, they further predicted that they would be resurrected three-and-a-half days later and taken up into a flying saucer. The Two asserted that this event would prove the truth of their teachings. As for their followers, they taught that Heaven was the literal, physical heavens, and those few people chosen to depart with the Two would, after their physical transformation, become crew members aboard UFOs.

While the basic teachings seem to have remained constant, the details of their ideology were flexible enough to undergo modification over time. For example, in the early days, Applewhite and Nettles told their followers that they were extraterrestrial beings. However, after the notion of walk-ins became popular within the New Age subculture, the Two changed their tune and began describing themselves as extraterrestrial walk-ins.

A walk-in is an entity that occupies a body that has been vacated by its original soul. An *extraterrestrial* walk-in is a walk-in who is supposedly from another planet. The walk-in situation is somewhat similar to possession, although in possession the original soul is merely overshadowed – rather than completely supplanted – by the possessing entity. The contemporary notion of walk-ins was popularised by Ruth

Montgomery, who developed the idea in her 1979 book, *Strangers Among Us*.[20] According to Montgomery, walk-ins are usually highly evolved souls who are here to help humanity. In order to avoid the delay of incarnating as a baby, and thus having to spend two decades maturing to adulthood, they contact living people who, because of the frustrating circumstances of life or for some other reason, no longer desire to remain in the body. Discarnate entities find such people, persuade them to hand over their bodies, and then begin lives as walk-ins.

The walk-in concept seems to be related to certain traditional South Asian tales about ageing yoga masters taking over the bodies of young people who die prematurely. Another possible source for the contemporary walk-in notion is the well-known (in theosophical circles) teaching that Jesus and Christ were separate souls. According to this teaching, Jesus prepared his physical body to receive Christ and, at a certain point in his career, vacated his body and allowed Christ to take it over. An underlying notion here is that Christ was such a highly evolved soul that it would have been difficult, if not impossible, for him to have incarnated as a baby – and, even if he could have done so, it would have been a waste of precious time for such a highly developed soul to have to go through childhood.

Ruth Montgomery describes the walk-in phenomenon rather dramatically:

> There are Walk-ins on this planet. Tens of thousands of them. Enlightened beings, who, after successfully completing numerous incarnations, have attained sufficient awareness of the meaning of life that they can forego the time-consuming process of birth and childhood, returning directly into adult bodies. A Walk-in is a high-minded entity who is permitted to take over the body of another human being who wishes to depart ... The motivation of a Walk-in is humanitarian. He returns to physical being in order to help others help themselves, planting seed-concepts that will grow and flourish for the benefit of mankind.[21]

In 1983 Montgomery published another book, *Threshold to Tomorrow*, containing case histories of seventeen walk-ins. According to Montgomery, history is full of walk-ins, including such famous historical figures as Moses, Jesus, Muhammad, Christopher Columbus, Abraham Lincoln, Mary Baker Eddy, Gandhi, George Washington, Benjamin Franklin, Thomas Jefferson, Alexander Hamilton and James

Madison. In fact, it seems that Montgomery would identify almost everyone manifesting exceptional creativity and leadership as a walk-in. In her words, 'Some of the world's greatest spiritual and political leaders, scientists, and philosophers in ages past are said to have been Walk-ins.'[22]

In a later book, *Aliens Among Us*,[23] Montgomery developed the notion of extraterrestrial walk-ins – the idea that souls from other planets have come to Earth to take over the bodies of human beings. This notion dovetailed nicely with popular interest in UFOs, which had already been incorporated into New Age spirituality. Following Montgomery, the New Age movement came to view extraterrestrial walk-ins as part of the larger community of advanced souls that had come to Earth to help humanity through a period of transition and crisis. It is easy to see how this basic notion would fit into the Two's ideology, explaining away their human personal histories as the histories of the souls who formerly occupied the bodies of Applewhite and Nettles.

It should be noted that the walk-in idea – a notion implying a radical disjunction between soul and body – also provided Applewhite with an essential ideological component in his rethinking of the ascension scenario, and ultimately helped legitimate their radical departure. In other words, after the death of Nettles, Applewhite had to come to grips with the fact that – under the physical ascension scenario which had been a cornerstone of their teachings for almost two decades – his spiritual partner would miss the chance to escape the planet with the rest of the group. This option was, however, unimaginable to Applewhite. Hence, by the time of the suicides, Applewhite had reconceptualised the ascension as an event in which Heaven's Gate members would let go of their physical 'containers' and ascend *spiritually* to the waiting saucers. Once on board, they would then consciously 'walk-into' a new physical body and join the crew of the Next Level spacecraft. This scenario is related in one of the group's Internet statements:

> Their final separation is the willful separation from their human body, when they have changed enough to identify as the spirit/mind/soul – ready to put on a biological body belonging to the Kingdom of Heaven. (This entering into

their 'glorified' or heavenly body takes place aboard a Next
Level spacecraft, above the Earth's surface.)[24]

Presumably, these new physical bodies would be supplied to Heaven's
Gate members out of some sort of 'cloning bank' kept aboard the
spaceships.

Ancient astronauts and Earth changes

Another notion the Two picked up from the metaphysical subculture
of their day was the ancient astronaut hypothesis. The expression
'ancient astronauts' is used to refer to various forms of the concept that
ufonauts visited our planet in the distant past. The basic idea that
many, if not all, of the powerful sky gods of traditional religions were
really extraterrestrial visitors intervening in human history had been
around for many decades. However, it was not until Erich von
Däniken's 1969 book *The Chariots of the Gods?* (originally published in
German in 1968) that this notion was popularised. While later writers
such as Zecharia Sitchin[25] have developed the notion with greater
sophistication, none have been as influential as von Däniken.

This view, which seems to call into question the validity of religion,
has been adopted by large segments of the New Age culture in a way
that is not seen as contradicting metaphysical spirituality. Instead,
believers view the 'Space Brothers' as working in cooperation with
spiritual forces to stimulate the spiritual evolution of this planet. One
aspect of the ancient astronaut hypothesis is the idea that the contemporary human race is the offspring of a union between aliens and
native terrestrials. Some even believe that a distorted record of this
event can be found in a few enigmatic verses in the book of Genesis
about the sons of God copulating with the daughters of men. This
union produced an intermediate species referred to in Genesis as the
'Nephilim'. In a different version of the same idea, ancient ufonauts
stimulated the evolution of our ape-like forebears to produce present-
day humanity. Our space 'fathers' have subsequently been watching
over us, and will, according to some New Age notions, return to
mingle with their distant offspring during the imminent New Age.[26]

Applewhite and Nettles taught a slightly modified version of the
ancient astronaut hypothesis: aliens planted the seeds of current
humanity millions of years ago, and have come to reap the harvest of
their work in the form of spiritually- evolved individuals who will join
the ranks of flying saucer crews. Only a select few members of
humanity will be chosen to advance to this transhuman state. The rest

will be left to wallow in the spiritually poisoned atmosphere of a corrupt world.

Applewhite would later teach that, after the elect had been picked up by the Space Brothers, the planet would be engulfed in cataclysmic destruction. Though Applewhite's apocalyptic teachings might at first appear to be derived entirely from his biblical background, his decidedly 'this-worldly' vision of our planet's end suggests that his ideology was decisively influenced by the New Age subculture and by the more recent discussion of colliding asteroids found in contemporary popular culture.[27]

Particularly in the teachings of New Age channels, one often finds the theme of apocalyptic 'Earth changes' that were supposed to have taken place around the end of the last millennium. This notion appears to have originally been introduced into the metaphysical subculture via the teachings of Edgar Cayce, as published by his son Hugh Lynn Cayce.[28] Furthermore, these upheavals in the Earth's crust are often thought of as coming about as a direct result of a planetary 'pole shift', a subsidiary notion that was popularised by Ruth Montgomery.[29] (Though, in sharp contrast to Applewhite, New Age thinkers postulate that these dramatic Earth changes will herald a terrestrial Golden Age.) The idea that global destruction would come about as the result of a wandering asteroid is a more recent notion that has been discussed in popular magazine articles and television specials only within the last half-dozen years or so.

Because these notions about walk-ins and Earth changes would have been familiar to the seekers attracted by Bo and Peep to Heaven's Gate, there would have been no need to legitimate or even explain them to new recruits. As hard as it may be for most non-new agers to grasp, such ideas were not only familiar, they were also plausible to members of the New Age subculture. The same observation applies to most of the other key beliefs of the Two's ideological synthesis, such as the notion that the Earth is a schoolroom for spiritual development.

Our terrestrial classroom

Another theme Applewhite and Nettles absorbed from the metaphysical subculture was the view that the spiritual life is a series of learning experiences culminating – in the case of Heaven's Gate – in a 'graduation' to the next evolutionary kingdom. Members of the group thought of themselves as 'students', their fellows as 'classmates', and Applewhite as their 'tutor'.[30] These educational metaphors would have been particularly comfortable and natural for a man who had been a popular university teacher during the first part of his adult life.

Like other religious and cultural systems, the worldview of the contemporary New Age movement is held together by a shared set of symbols and metaphors – shared images of life reflected in the discourse of participants as a set of commonly used terms. For example, due partly to a vision of metaphysical unity inherited from theosophy and from Asian religious philosophy – but also due to this subculture's reaction against the perceived fragmentation and alienation of main-stream society – the New Age movement emphasises the values of unity and relatedness. These values find expression in such common terms as 'holistic', 'oneness', 'wholeness' and 'community'. This spiri-tual subculture also values growth and dynamism – an evaluation expressed in discourse about 'evolution', 'transformation', 'process' and so forth.

The image of education is related to the growth metaphor (e.g. one of our linguistic conventions is that education allows a person to 'grow'). If we examine the metaphysical subculture through the lens of the education theme, we discover that, in contrast to many other reli-gious movements, the dominant New Age 'ceremonies' are workshops, lectures and classes rather than worship ceremonies. Even large New Age gatherings such as the 'Whole Life Expo' resemble academic conferences more than they do camp meetings.[31]

It is also interesting to note the extent to which educational metaphors inform New Age thought. In terms of the way the Western metaphysical tradition has interpreted the ongoing process of reincarnation, spiritual growth and even life itself are learning experiences. The following are some examples of this: Katar, a New Age medium, channels such messages as 'Here on Earth, you *are* your teacher, your books, your lessons and the classroom as well as the student.'[32] This message is amplified by J. L. Simmons, a sociol-ogist, who, in his *The Emerging New Age*, describes life on the physical plane as the 'Earth School',[33] and asserts that 'we are here to learn ... and will continue to return until we do the course' and 'graduate'.[34] Similar images are reflected in an essay on 'The Role of the Esoteric in Planetary Culture', where David Spangler argues that spiritual wisdom is esoteric 'only because so few people expend the time, the energy, the effort, the openness and the love to gain it, just as only a few are willing to invest what is required to become a nuclear physicist or a neurosurgeon'.[35] It would not be going too far to assert that, in the New Age vision of things, the image of the whole of human life – particularly when that life is

119

directed towards spiritual goals – can be summed up as a learning experience:

> Each of us has an Inner Teacher, a part of ourselves which knows exactly what we need to learn, and constantly creates the opportunity for us to learn just that. We have the choice either to cooperate with this part of ourselves or to ignore it. If we decide to cooperate, we can see lessons constantly in front of us; every challenge is a chance to grow and develop. If, on the other hand, we try to ignore this Inner Teacher, we can find ourselves hitting the same problem again and again, because we are not perceiving and responding to the lesson we have created for ourselves. [It] is, however, the daily awareness of and cooperation with spirit [that] pulls humanity upwards on the evolutionary spiral, and the constant invocation and evocation of spirit enables a rapid unfolding of human potential. When the Inner Teacher and the evolutionary force of the Universe are able to work together with our full cooperation, wonders unfold.[36]

In this passage we see, not only the decisive role of the education metaphor, but also how this metaphor has itself been reshaped by the spiritual subculture's emphasis on holism and growth. In other words, the kind of education this subculture values is the education of 'the whole person', sometimes termed 'holistic education', and this form of education is an expression of the 'evolutionary force of the Universe' (a parallel to what, in more traditional language, might be called the redemptive activity of the Holy Spirit). Thus, despite the marked tendency to deploy images drawn from the sphere of formal education – a tendency that has created a realm of discourse saturated with metaphors of 'classrooms', 'graduations' and the like – the metaphysical subculture's sense of the educational process has tended to be more informal (more or less equivalent to learning in the general sense), as well as more continuous – a process from which there may be periodic graduations, but from which there is never a *final* graduation after which the learning process ceases. Even for Heaven's Gate members, graduation from the Earth plane represented entering a new sphere of never-ending personal evolution – The Evolutionary Kingdom Level Above Human.

Though some aspects of this view of the spiritual life as a learning experience are based on tradition (e.g. the Pythagorean 'school'), the widespread appeal of this image of spirituality is a more or less direct result of the manner in which modern society's emphasis on education informs our consciousness. The various social, economic and historical forces that have led to the increased stress on education in the contemporary world are too complex to develop here. Obvious factors are such things as the increasing complexity of technology and of the socio-economic system. Less obvious factors are such considerations as the need to delay the entry of new workers into the economy. But whatever the forces at work in the larger society, by the time the baby boom generation began attending college in the 1960s, formal educational institutions had come to assume their present role as major socialising forces in Western societies. Being a college graduate and achieving higher, and especially professional degrees became associated with increased prestige and the potential for increased levels of income. In other words, to a greater extent than previously, education and educational accomplishments had become symbols of wealth and status.

Because the generation from which the majority of participants in the spiritual subculture have been recruited is the baby boom generation, the majority of participants in that subculture have been socialised to place a high value on education. Baby-boomers, however, also tend to have been participants in the counterculture of the 1960s, which means that they come from a generation that was highly critical of traditional, formal education.

Though some members of that generation revolted against the educational establishment by denying the value of education altogether, other college students of the time reacted against what they saw as an irrelevant education by setting up alternative educational structures such as the so-called 'free schools'. These educational enterprises, which could offer students nothing in terms of degrees or certification, were viable, at least for a time, because they offered courses on subjects people found intrinsically interesting – including such metaphysical topics as yoga, meditation and so forth. The free school movement, in combination with the adult education programmes that emerged in the 1970s, provided the paradigms for the independent, metaphysical educational programmes that would eventually emerge.

As is evident from even the most casual perusal of the group's writings, Heaven's Gate was dominated by the educational imagery found in the contemporaneous New Age subculture. As has already been noted, Applewhite viewed himself as a teacher, his followers were students, their spiritual process was likened to an educational process (in their 'metamorphic classroom'), and their goal was referred to as a graduation. In the group's writings published on the Internet, they discussed how their 'Teachers' on the Next Level had an 'extremely detailed lesson plan' designed for their personal growth. Then, towards the end, they received signals that their 'classroom time was over' and that they were ready to graduate to the next level.[37]

The same basic images can be found in the teachings of innumerable contemporary spiritual teachers. For example, John-Roger, the founder of the Movement of Spiritual Inner Awareness (MSIA), asserts that:

> The Earth has been designated as the classroom where you learn lessons. [Y]ou're ... in a continual learning process, which will bring forth that which is for your highest good. When you have finished your lessons, you graduate to other levels of consciousness.[38]

This is not, of course, to imply that MSIA is another potential Heaven's Gate, but rather that the basic images at work in Applewhite's teachings were derived more or less directly out of the same metaphysical subculture that shaped MSIA and certain other emergent religions.

Thus, with the exceptions, first, of suicide being the means by which the transition to the next evolutionary sphere is to take place, and second, of the next sphere being a literal, physical realm (a spacecraft), the basic concepts informing Heaven's Gate's thought world would have been recognisable to any serious metaphysical seeker. However, even the notion of a physical spaceship being a quasi-heavenly realm is already implicit in the marked tendency of the New Age movement to portray ufonauts as spiritual beings. Furthermore, the widely accepted walk-in notion provides a readily understandable mechanism by which such a transition could be accomplished.

Death in the New Age

This leaves only suicide as the one anomalous component of Applewhite's synthesis. We should note, however, that there are many phases of the New Age movement that portray death – if not suicide – in a positive light. For example, the basic metaphysical/New Age afterlife notion is reincarnation, though this process is regarded somewhat differently by the New Age than by the Asian religions from which the notion is derived. Whereas in a tradition like Buddhism reincarnation is viewed negatively, as a process that brings one back into the world to suffer, in the metaphysical subculture reincarnation is viewed as part of an extended education programme stretched across many lifetimes, and is thus part of a positive process. In the same vein, the interest many participants in occult/metaphysical spirituality have displayed in learning about their past lifetimes in the hope of discovering that they had been some famous or otherwise exalted personality would be anathema to a traditional Buddhist.

The New Age movement is also home to advocates of conscious dying. The expression 'conscious dying' refers to an approach to dying in which death is regarded as a means of liberation of one's own consciousness – in other words, as a means of achieving enlightenment. This approach, ultimately inspired by Tibetan Buddhism, was popularised in the New Age subculture through the work of Baba Ram Das and Stephen Levine. In line with the New Age emphasis on spiritual-unfoldment-as-education, dying thus acquires a positive valence as part of the larger learning process.[39]

Finally, it is within the metaphysical subculture that one finds the most interest in the near death experience. The expression near death experience (NDE), sometimes also called the 'pseudo-death' experience, refers to the seemingly supernatural experiences often encountered by individuals who have suffered apparent death, and have then been restored to life. The principal impetus for modern studies on NDEs was the publication in 1975 of the book *Life After Life*, by psychiatrist Raymond A. Moody,[40] which followed earlier researches on this topic by other physicians such as Elizabeth Kubler-Ross and Russell Noyes.

Moody's work describes the results of more than eleven years of inquiry into NDEs and is based on a sample of about 150 cases. He outlines nine elements that seem to occur generally (but not universally) in the NDE experiences.

1   Hearing a buzzing or ringing noise, while having a sense of being dead.
    At this initial stage of the NDE, the experiencers are confused and try, unsuccessfully, to communicate with other people at the scene of their death.
2   Peace and painlessness.
    While people are dying they may be in intense pain, but, as soon as they leave the body, the pain vanishes and they experience peace.
3   Out-of-body experience.
    NDEers often have the experience of rising up and floating above their own body surrounded by a medical team, and watching it

there down below, while feeling very detached and comfortable. They experience the feeling of being in a spiritual body that looks like a sort of living energy field.

4   The tunnel experience.
     The NDEers then experience being drawn into darkness through a tunnel, at an extremely high speed, or going up a stairway (or some other symbol of crossing a threshold) until they enter a realm of radiant golden-white light.

5   Rising rapidly into the heavens.
     Instead of a tunnel, some NDEers report an experience of rising suddenly into the heavens, and seeing the Earth and the celestial sphere as if they were astronauts in space.

6   People of light.
     Once on the other side of the tunnel, or after they have risen into the heavens, NDEers meet people who glow with an inner light. Often they find that friends and relatives who have already died are there to greet them.

7   The Being of light.
     After connecting with these beings, NDEers meet a powerful, spiritual Being who some have called an angel, God, or Jesus.

8   The life review.
     This higher being presents NDEers with a panoramic review of everything they have done. In particular, they experience the effects of every act they have ever done to other people, and come away feeling that love is the most important thing in life.

9   Reluctance to return.
     The higher being sometimes says that the NDEer must return to life. In other experiences, the NDEer is given a choice of staying or returning. In either case, NDEers experience a reluctance to return. The people who choose to return do so only because of loved ones they do not wish to leave behind.

The NDE has attracted extensive public interest because of its seeming support for the notion of life after death. As reflected in the above list of characteristics, it is clear that the overall picture of the dying process to emerge from NDE studies is quite positive, even attractive. Furthermore, with respect to our larger discussion, it should also be noted that trait number five sounds like it could have been (though I actually doubt that it was) the immediate source of Applewhite's idea that his group could die and ascend to a waiting spacecraft.

In this regard, in another one of his books, Moody mentions an ecstatic vision Carl Jung experienced during an apparent NDE.[41] Following a heart attack, Jung found himself a thousand miles above the surface of the Earth, on the threshold of entering a floating temple in a giant rock where he would finally discover the answers to all of his questions. In this vision, Jung vividly describes the terrestrial globe, his sense of letting go of everything associated with earthly life, and his sense of anticipation of the glories awaiting him upon his entrance into the temple:

> It seemed to me that I was high up in space. Far below I saw the globe of the Earth, bathed in a gloriously blue light. I saw the deep blue sea and the continents ... A short distance away I saw in space a tremendous dark block of stone, like a meteorite ... As I approached the steps leading up to the entrance into the rock, a strange thing happened: I had the feeling that everything was being sloughed away; everything I aimed at or wished for or thought, the whole phantasmagoria of earthly existence, fell away ... I had the certainty that I was about to enter an illuminated room and would meet there all those people to whom I belong in reality ... There I would at last understand ... what historical nexus I or my life fitted into.[42]

Finally, Jung notes his profound disappointment when his doctor brings him back to his body before he had a chance to cross the threshold.

Again, with only a little interpretation (e.g. floating rock = space-craft), the whole experience could be taken as almost a blueprint for what Heaven's Gate members believed would happened after their deaths. This is not, of course, to assert that either NDE research or the writings of Carl Jung encourage people to take their own lives. It is, however, clear that, if taken seriously, reports of near death experiences paint a positive enough portrait of dying to take the sting out of death. Thus, far from being crazy or irrational, even the final dramatic exit of Heaven's Gate becomes understandable in terms of the thought world of the metaphysical subculture from which Applewhite drew his theological synthesis.

Conclusion

A factor in failing to understand movements like Heaven's Gate is a mistaken theoretical perspective – derived ultimately from Weber –

that portrays the personal charisma of the founder as the 'glue' holding together alternate views of reality. Such a perspective misconstrues the role of charisma. In the first place, no matter how charismatic the prophet, his/her message must somehow address the concerns of potential recruits in a satisfactory manner if he/she is to convince more than a handful of close associates. In other words, a new vision has to have more going for it than merely the personality of the revealer.

In the second place, although the prophet's charisma may be necessary in giving life to the vision during the nascent stages of the new movement, the actual adoption of an emergent religion by a group of followers recruits the forces of social consensus to the side of the new revelation – forces that tend to maintain the alternate vision of reality independently of the charisma of the founder. To think of this in terms of the micro-sociology of knowledge,[43] the plausibility of a particular worldview and its accompanying lifestyle is maintained by the ongoing 'conversation' that takes place among the members of a particular community. Thus, as long as a new religion continues satisfactorily to address the concerns of followers, even things like a failed prophecy or a leader's blatant hypocrisy will not induce a crisis of faith.

Finally, prophets themselves do not rely upon their personal charisma as their sole source of legitimation. Instead, they plant their new visions on the familiar foundations of pre-existing religious ideas, which allows their new teachings to appear plausible to potential recruits. In other words, despite what critics sometimes allege, founders of new religious movements do not invent their religious systems *ex nihilo*. With respect to Heaven's Gate – and although it may seem counterintuitive to anyone not familiar with the many exotic ideas floating around the New Age subculture – the Two's message was really not all that 'weird' to the people who became their followers. Similarly, the notions that death is a potentially positive experience and that one can exit one's body to consciously re-emerge in another realm are simply not odd or irrational within religious communities, New Age or otherwise. It was thus a relatively small step for Applewhite to legitimate a group suicide, meaning that the group's dramatic exit was a completely plausible scenario undertaken willingly – not the exceptional act of a mesmeric cult leader pushing his blind sheep over the edge of an abyss.

NOTES

1   L. Festinger, H. W. Riecken and S. Schachter, *When Prophecy Fails*, Minneapolis, University of Minnesota Press, 1956.
2   E. Thomas, 'The Next Level', *Newsweek Magazine*, 7 April 1997.

3   R. W. Balch, 'Waiting for the Ships: Disillusionment and the Revitalization of Faith in Bo and Peep's UFO Cult', in J. R. Lewis (ed.), *The Gods Have Landed: New Religions from Other Worlds*, Albany, State University of New York Press, 1995, pp. 137–66.

4   M. Weber, *Economy and Society: An Outline of Interpretive Sociology*, G. Roth and C. Wittich (eds), E. Fischoff (trans.), New York, Bedminster Press, 1968.

5   J. R. Hall, *Apocalypse Observed: Religious Movements and Violence in North America, Europe and Japan*, London, Routledge, 2000, p. 178.

6   J. G. Melton, J. Clark and A. A. Kelly, *New Age Encyclopedia*, Detroit, Gale Research, 1990.

7   J. R. Lewis, 'Approaches to the Study of the New Age', in J. R. Lewis and J. G. Melton (eds), *Perspectives on the New Age*, Albany, State University of New York Press, 1992, pp. 1–12.

8   J. G. Melton, 'Church Universal and Triumphant: Its Heritage and Thoughtworld', in J. R. Lewis and J. G. Melton (eds), *Church Universal and Triumphant in Scholarly Perspective*, Stanford, Center for Academic Publication, 1994, pp. 1–20.

9   D. Leslie and G. Adamski, *Flying Saucers Have Landed*, New York, The British Book Centre, 1953; 2nd edn, London, Futura Publications, 1977.

10 J. R. Lewis (ed.), *UFOs and Popular Culture: An Encyclopedia of Contemporary Myth*, Santa Barbara, ABC-Clio, 2000.

11 C. G. Jung, *Symbols of Transformation*, Collected Works of C. G. Jung, Sir Herbert Read *et al.* (eds), R. F. C. Hull (trans.), vol. 9, pt. 1, 2nd edn, Princeton, Princeton University Press, 1967 [1956]; C. G. Jung, *Flying Saucers: A Modern Myth of Things Seen in the Skies*, R. F. C. Hull (trans.), New York, Signet Books/New American Library, 1969 [1959].

12 J. A. Saliba, 'The Aetherius Society', in Lewis, *UFOs and Popular Culture*, pp. 7–10.

13 Cited in Balch, 'Waiting for the Ships', p. 163.

14 J. R. Hall, *Apocalypse Observed: Religious Movements and Violence in North America, Europe, and Japan*, London, Routledge, 2000, p. 177.

15 C. Wessinger, *How the Millennium Comes Violently: From Jonestown to Heaven's Gate*, New York, Seven Bridges, 2000, pp. 237–9.

16 *Ibid.*, p. 244.

17 R. Perkins and F. Jackson, *Cosmic Suicide: The Tragedy and Transcendence of Heaven's Gate*, Dallas, Pentaradial Press, 1997, p. 81.

18 *Ibid.*, pp. 76–9.

19 J. R. Lewis, *Encyclopedia of Afterlife Beliefs and Phenomena*, Detroit, Gale Research, 1994.

20 R. Montgomery, *Strangers Among Us: Enlightened Beings from a World to Come*, New York, Coward, McCann & Geoghegan, 1979.

21 *Ibid.*, pp. 11–12.

22 *Ibid.*, p. 12.

23 R. Montgomery, *Aliens Among Us*, New York, Fawcett Crest, 1985.

24 Heaven's Gate, 'Time to Die for God? – The Imminent "Holy War" – Which Side are You On?' Available onlinehttp://:www.heavensgatetoo.com (24/09/96).

25 Z. Sitchin, *The Twelfth Planet*, New York, Avon, 1976; *Divine Encounters: A Guide to Visions, Angels, and Other Emissaries*, New York, Avon, 1995.

26 J. R. Lewis and E. D. Oliver, *Angels A to Z*, Detroit, Gale Research, 1995.

27 E. Thomas, 'The Next Level', *Newsweek Magazine*, 7 April 1997.
28 E.g. H. L. Cayce, *Earth Changes Update*, Virginia Beach, A.R.E. Press, 1980.
29 Montgomery, *Aliens Among Us*.
30 Heaven's Gate, 'Time to Die for God?'
31 J. R. Lewis, *Seeking the Light: Uncovering the Truth About the Movement for Spiritual Inner Awareness*, Los Angeles, Mandeville Press, 1997.
32 Clark (channelled by Katar), 'Back to School – Earth Revisited', *Open Channel: A Journal with Spirit* 2, November–December, 1988, p. 7.
33 J. L. Simmons, *The Emerging New Age*, Santa Fe, Bear & Co., 1990, p. 91.
34 *Ibid.*, p. 73.
35 D. Spangler, 'The Role of the Esoteric in Planetary Culture', in M. Katz, W. P. Marsh and G. G. Thompson (eds), *Earth's Answer: Explorations of Planetary Culture at the Lindisfarne Conferences*, New York, Harper & Row, 1977, pp. 193–4.
36 Findhorn Foundation, *Catalogue*, Autumn/Winter, 1986–87.
37 Jwnody, 'Overview of Present Mission'. Available online: http://www.heavensgatetoo.com (April 1996).
38 John-Roger, *The Way Out Book*, Los Angeles, Baraka Press, 1980.
39 M. F. Bednaroski, *New Religions and the Theological Imagination in America*, Bloomington, Indiana University Press, 1989.
40 R. A. Moody, *Life After Life*, New York, Bantam, 1975.
41 R. A. Moody, *The Light Beyond*, New York, Bantam, 1989.
42 C. G. Jung, *Memories, Dreams and Reflections*, New York, Vintage, 1965, pp. 289–91.
43 P. L. Berger and T. Luckmann, *The Social Construction of Reality*, Garden City, Anchor Books, 1966.

6

THE URANTIA BOOK

Sarah Lewis

...I am utterly convinced that, circa 1906–55, non-material
beings of super-human intelligence and maturity interfaced
regularly with a group of (eventually) six mortals for the
purpose of providing a religious revelation of epochal significance.[1]

The URANTIA[2] Book[3] presents its readers with a vast spectrum of new
ideas. These include 'new concepts of a far-flung cosmos' and the
notion of 'millions of other inhabited planets'. It introduces the reader
to 'scores of different and varied echelons of celestial personalities'. It
gives 'confirmation of the evolutionary origin of humankind – even of
an evolutionary cosmos'. Further, *The URANTIA Book* provides an
'intimation of multiple Creator Deities'.[4]

The Aim

The URANTIA Book aims to unite science, religion and philosophy,
noting that, when viewed separately, these three disciplines are unable
to answer the fundamental questions of existence.[5] 'The result is an
uplifting vision for humankind that is without parallel or precedent in
literature'.[6] David Bradley makes the following point:

> God is love, the creator, sustainer, and upholder of all
> creation. *The URANTIA Book* is a great revelation, a presen-
> tation of universal facts and truths to us, about the creator
> and about creation. It greatly expands our views and under-
> standings of the creator and the cosmos, and with this bigger
> picture, science, religion and philosophy become integrated.
> We are not alone in the universe, quite the contrary. *The
> URANTIA Book* was written by love-respecting, civilized
> inhabitants of the universe. It was written by a revelatory
> committee, through a contact human, for the betterment of

our planet. The identity of the contact human is unknown and unimportant.[7]

Similarly, E. P. Moyer argues that, because we are currently experiencing a planetary crisis, a crisis on all levels,[8] *The URANTIA Book* was provided to give guidance to humanity, and followers of *The URANTIA Book* are to serve the rest of humanity through administering this guidance. Further, that without *The URANTIA Book*, humanity cannot understand its situation or salvage it.

> *The URANTIA Book* has the capacity to make a significant contribution to the religious and philosophical thinking of all peoples; it truly has the potential to shape world destiny ... Over and over, people from around the world have discovered that the book has profoundly impressed and changed their lives – inspired and stimulated them to reach new levels of spiritual growth and enhanced living.[9]

Content

The URANTIA Papers were published in 1955 as *The URANTIA Book*. The book is 2,097 pages in length, and contains 196 chapters, divided into four sections. It is said to contain the Earth's fifth revelation from God and is seen as the most complete revelation so far available to humanity. It outlines the nature of God, creation and humanity and aims to dispel any conflict that might be perceived to exist between science and religion.

The URANTIA Papers teach that URANTIA has been given five revelations from God.[10] These revelations are to aid the evolutionary process from 'low life' to 'light and life'. Light and life is the ultimate level that humanity strives to reach. The first revelation was the Planetary Prince of URANTIA, Caligastia, who was the spiritual planetary administrator[11] but joined the rebellion against God. The second revelation was Adam and Eve, who disobeyed God's mission for them. Third was Machiventa Melchizedek, described in the Bible as Melchizedek, a Son of God of a special order of Sons engaged to do emergency services.[12] The fourth revelation was Jesus Christ, and the final revelation is the *URANTIA Book*.

The first section of *The URANTIA Book*, containing thirty-one chapters, is titled 'The Central and Superuniverses',[13] sponsored by a Uversa[14] corps of twenty-four superuniverse personalities acting by authority of the Orvonton Ancients of Days.[15] This first section outlines the nature of God (including the notions of eternal son and infinite spirit) and God's relationship with creation, and it also discusses the structure of the wider cosmos and its inhabitants.

The second section of *The URANTIA Book*, comprising twenty-five chapters, is entitled 'The Local Universe', sponsored by a Nebadon[16] corps of local universe[17] personalities acting by authority of Gabriel[18] of Salvington.[19] This section outlines that part of the cosmos in which humanity resides. It deals with issues such as the evolution and administration of the local universes, their personalities and ministering spirits. This section also highlights the physical aspects of the local universe, planetary Adams, the Lucifer Rebellion and Universal Unity.

The sixty-three chapters of section three give the 'History of URANTIA', sponsored by a corps of local universe personalities acting by authority of Gabriel of Salvington. This section on the origins of URANTIA provides an overview of various evolutionary stages, and includes a discussion of marine life, early humanity, the creation of different races, Eden, Adam and Eve, and the development of modern civilisations. It also discusses the evolution of social practices, from marriage and family life to ghosts, magic and shamanism, sin, sacrifice and atonement, and prayer. The latter part of this section highlights the 'real nature of religion', religious experience and the Trinity.

The final section, of seventy-seven chapters, discusses the 'Life and Teachings of Jesus', sponsored by a commission of twelve URANTIA midwayers[20] acting under the supervision of Melchizedek,[21] the revelatory director. The basis of this narrative was supplied by a secondary midwayer who was at one time assigned to the superhuman 'watchcare' of the Apostle Andrew.[22] It includes chapters on the birth, childhood and adolescence of Jesus, his baptism, ministry, crucifixion and resurrection.

The Papers that precede the Jesus Papers embrace 400 billion years of history. That the Jesus Papers span 773 pages, and deal with the thirty-three or so years of Jesus's life, indicates just how important Jesus is within *The URANTIA Book*. The Jesus Papers were not given as a result of questions posed by 'the Forum' (see page 000), as were most of the Papers, but as an unexpected revelation appearing to be the 'intended ... final masterpiece'.[23] Consequently, this would appear to place the URANTIA Papers within Christianity. 'The papers are essentially an exposition and expansion of the life and teachings of Jesus of Nazareth placed in a splendid cosmological context – in a scale that has never before been attempted on this planet.'[24] *The URANTIA Book* notes that 'The great hope of URANTIA lies in the possibility of a new revelation of Jesus with a new and enlarged presentation of his saving message which would spiritually unite in loving service the numerous families of his present day professed followers'.[25]

The emergence of the URANTIA Papers

The URANTIA Papers were received through an unnamed person, known as the 'sleeping subject' or 'contact personality'. Moyer notes that the 'sleeping subject' was the link between the material world and the spirit world.[26] All that is known of this person is that it was a male patient of the psychiatrist Dr William Sadler. Those who witnessed the events insist that the 'sleeping subject' was not a medium nor did he 'channel' or 'automatically write' the URANTIA Papers.[27]

The early contacts between 1906 and 1911 were William Sadler, his wife Dr Lena Sadler, the 'sleeping subject' and the subject's wife. The wife of the sleeping subject had become concerned about the deep sleeping patterns of her husband and had called on the advice of William Sadler. 'The peculiar sleep',[28] during which the sleeping subject suffered from 'abnormal movements', was observed. Gradually the sleep became, as Larry Mullins notes, 'more remarkable and perplexing'.[29] Mullins describes 'the first contact': [30]'... the subject was moistening his lips ... Perhaps we should ask a question ... "How are you feeling?" ... To the great astonishment of everyone, the subject spoke! But the voice was peculiar, not his normal voice. The voice identified itself as a student visitor on an observation mission from another planet.'[31] This 'being' apparently was conversing through the 'sleeping subject' by some means, and this then became a common occurrence. Later, two other people were admitted to witness the events, one of whom became the secretary. Together, the six people involved became known as the 'Contact Commission', although it was only ever the 'sleeping subject' who was used as the actual contact.

William Sadler's initial explanation for the event was that it was being generated by the mind of the individual.[32] However, he abandoned this initial diagnosis of 'automatic speaking' after examining the 'sleeping subject' under hypnosis. Similarly, further attempts to find 'another scientific answer' failed. The 'sleeping subject' was also viewed by Sadler as being in good health, and any notion of him suffering from any form of psychiatric ailment was refuted by Sadler.

Initially, the 'student visitors' that appeared to work through the 'sleeping subject' made their presence known solely through voiced means. However, this was to change in early 1925 with the appearance of 'a voluminous handwritten document'[33] in the house of the 'sleeping subject'. As with the initial assumption that the early contacts were the result of automatic speaking, Sadler felt the recent episode could be explained as automatic writing. Yet, after carrying out some tests (including handwriting analysis), the notion of automatic writing was likewise dismissed. The manuscript was typed and that was to become the regular method of receiving information.

The Forum

In 1923 the Forum was established. It consisted of a group of people, organised by the Sadlers in their home, whose initial aim was to discuss philosophical issues. Needless to say, the 'sleeping subject' soon became the principal topic of discussion. The Forum was used to generate questions that would be put to the 'student visitors' through the Contact Commission. (It should be noted that it was only the members of the Contact Commission who witnessed the activities of the 'sleeping subject', and only they who knew his identity.) In fact, the majority of the URANTIA Papers (with the exception of the Jesus Papers) were the result of questions posed by the Forum over the years. What the 'student visitors' divulged was dependent on the level of knowledge and understanding of the Forum, and therefore revelation was clearly progressive. Once all the papers were received, there were questions posed concerning the 'clarification of concepts' and the 'removal of ambiguities'.[34]

In late 1925 the Forum became a closed group, with members signing a pledge of secrecy. The pledge read as follows: 'We acknowledge our pledge of secrecy, renewing our promise not to discuss the URANTIA Revelations or their subject matter with anyone save active Forum members, and to take no notes of such matter as is read or discussed at the public sessions, or make copies or notes of what we personally read.'[35] The Forum held its last meeting in 1942. *The URANTIA Book* was published in 1955, and 'shortly after the publication of *The URANTIA Book*, a final message from the Midwayers was received by the contact Commission: "You are now on your own." After nearly fifty years, the connection between the mortals of our planet and the unseen Midwayer Commission was severed and went dead.'[36]

Secrecy

The exact circumstances surrounding the receipt of the Papers has been a well-guarded secret. 'There are only a few of us still living who were in touch with this phenomenon in the beginning, and when we die, the knowledge of it will die with us. Then the book will exist as a great spiritual mystery, and no human will know the manner in which it came about.'[37] And there has been much debate and speculation on exactly how the URANTIA Papers were received. Mullins notes that 'In an ideal world, these questions would not arise, the message of the Papers alone should speak for their authenticity. This was the original hope of Dr Sadler.'[38] He continues:

> Any thinking person must wonder if the events just described could have really happened. Possibly only a long-time reader of the URANTIA Papers could be quickly convinced that the events that I have pieced together and depicted here actually occurred. The URANTIA Papers are the best testimony of their own validity. Virtually anyone who studies them with care and an open mind must be persuaded that they are, at the very least, a unique presentation of who we are, where we came from, and where we are going.[39]

Sadler gave two main reasons why the Forum was instructed not to divulge the exact events surrounding the revelation that would emerge as *The URANTIA Book*.[40] First, there are too many 'missing links'; no one really understands how the revelations were received. Second, revealing the name of the 'contact personality' would lead to a human individual being identified with *The URANTIA Book*. This would be unacceptable because the aim is for *The URANTIA Book* to stand alone, without 'mortal connections'. If an association were to be made between a human being and the Papers, this person could then be ascribed a status that is wholly inappropriate. *The URANTIA Book* is to stand on its own as a great text, without leading to the veneration of any human beings involved in it. Mullins notes: 'The risk is one of developing a cult around *The URANTIA Book* itself, a virtual "religion" about the Book – to the exclusion of its message and teachings. Perhaps the most unsavoury idea that has come forward is that the contact Commissioners had secret powers and special spiritual status. People love stories of this nature.'[41]

Naming the 'sleeping subject' might also have allowed critics to search for events in his life that would arguably make him an unsuitable object for such revelation, thus discrediting the Papers. There might also have been a desire to protect the 'sleeping subject' and his family from intrusion. Yet Moyer notes that, 'While technically obeying the instructions [to never reveal the identity of the 'sleeping subject'] I feel that he [Sadler] wanted the world to know what had happened, and left it to later investigators to piece together his various clues.'[42]

Assessing how successful the secrecy motif has been in terms of gaining interest in the Papers is difficult. The secrecy surrounding the origins of the Papers has proven attractive to many people, but deterred others. That is to say, whilst some people would certainly have been deterred, others have been attracted by the myth and the mystery evoked and, arguably, this has been a great inducement to investigate The URANTIA Book further. Moyer notes the importance of 'faith decision', that 'we must all make up our own minds about revelation. We cannot do that if revelation comes to us with absolute sureness.'[43]

Channelling?

The URANTIA Foundation freely clarifies how the URANTIA Papers were *not* received. It states that they were *not* received through hypnotism, automatic writing, clairvoyance, trances, spirit mediumship, telepathy or double personality, or through séances. Clearly, URANTIAns understand the revelation to have been delivered in a way that is not comparable with other revelations. The receipt of The URANTIA Book is to be viewed as a unique experience and a unique revelation.

The URANTIA Foundation notes how those involved in the early events leading to the formation of the URANTIA Papers had considerable experience in the investigation of psychic phenomena, and how these people concluded that the personality associated with the URANTIA Papers was unlike any other type of known psychic phenomena.[44] The URANTIA Foundation also urges that those involved with the emergence of the early papers were in no way connected with spiritualism, the terminology of the URANTIA Foundation showing clearly that spiritualism does not gain any support from URANTIA. URANTIAns are adamant that the URANTIA Papers were *not* channelled, but rather that a 'blending' of the 'sleeping subject' and the 'student visitors' occurred. Both Mullins and Moyer are eager to refute any ideas that the Papers were channelled through the 'sleeping subject', noting William Sadler's condemnation of matters of those kinds.

Moyer notes that:

> From this evidence we can now come to grips with the process of SS [the 'sleeping subject']. He was mechanically manipulated by the midwayers. They could control his voice, and

move his arms. Thus they were able to communicate either orally or manually. They engaged in these activities only when the man was fully asleep because they did not want to violate his conscious mind, or his personal will. They never entered his mind, they had no need to do so.[45]

For Moyer, it is important to distinguish between the events surrounding the emergence of the Papers and those surrounding the work of people such as Edgar Cayce,[46] who, says Moyer, would have been aware of entering into a psychic state. Channelling, for Moyer, means that the human mind has invited 'invasion', and this means that evil spirits could be unintentionally summoned. If, however, the mind knows nothing of the act, it cannot be invaded by evil. He notes: 'The Devil cannot influence the normal mind against its free and natural choosing.'[47] The 'sleeping subject', therefore, was safe, as he knew nothing of the events in which he was involved and could therefore not have been inviting evil spirits. Mullins goes on to note that, although the mind of the 'sleeping subject' or 'contact personality' was not used, it is likely that the divine fragment ('Thought Adjuster'[48]) within him was used.[49]

Whilst there is, for understandable reasons, an antipathy to channelling, it is important to note that channelling is not always concerned with possession and could be described as 'blending'. Arguably there exist different types and degrees of channelling, and Moyer and his predecessors ignore this. This is likely to be a response to the controversy surrounding spiritualism and the later 'New Age' channelling. If Sadler insisted that the papers were received through means other than those connected with spiritualism, he might have hoped to divert the kind of negative response common towards spiritualism at that time from being levelled against the URANTIA Revelation. It should also be remembered that Sadler was a former Seventh-Day Adventist and, although he disagreed with much of the belief system of that sect, he clearly retained the suspicion and condemnatory feelings towards spiritualism that were common within the sect. Sadler further wanted to have the URANTIA Revelation stand as a unique revelation, imparted through a method never before experienced. He did not want the Revelation to be explicable through known means, as this would have detracted from its uniqueness. The result was that Sadler went to great lengths to comment on how the Papers were *not* received, even though he could not (or would not) give any accurate explanation of how there *were* received. Descriptions of channelling, particularly more recent ones, tend to be quite graphic, with those involved being aware of the situation at some point. In contrast, the Contact Commission insisted that the 'sleeping subject' was never aware of the use the 'student visitors' made of him. Followers of the Papers make much of the idea that channelling is about possession, not blending, but this fails to take into account the numerous types and degrees of channelling described by others.[50]

The preparation of Sadler

Despite the desire not to associate any human being with the URANTIA Papers, it is clear that William Sadler is accorded a high status within the URANTIA Foundation. 'Both Sadler and Christy [the secretary] have been held up as idols in the work of the Revelation. Without question the Revelation would not have appeared without Sadler. He was the key personality'.[51] This terminology suggests charismatic qualities and could arguably be placing Sadler into the category of 'the chosen'. Moyer argues that Sadler was the ideal person to receive the Papers, since he was a doctor and a person highly sceptical of psychic phenomena, believing such things to be an abnormal act within the human mind.[52] He also notes the psychological preparation of Sadler, including his disillusionment with some figures within Seventh - Day Adventism, his former church.

> They [the celestial agencies] removed him [Sadler] from allegiance to church bodies, and to human organizational structure. Little was Sadler aware how he was being prepared for more important service to God and to his fellow man. Disillusionment with the world produces alterations in attitude which prepares a human mortal for more profound insights into spiritual realities. For those who can benefit, it reduces naïveté and strengthens character, while it molds the mind to more rigorous assessments and firm decisions.[53]

Language

The URANTIA Book introduces the reader not only to new concepts but also to a new 'language'. The Anti-Cult Movement often highlights this 'new language' element as a method used by 'cults' to bond members to the movement and to exclude outsiders. Hence, it is sometimes used to support 'brainwashing' allegations, viewed as an attempt to encourage a break with 'reality'. However, most groups, whether religious or secular, have their own 'language' to varying degrees; there will always be phrases, 'buzz-words' and group-specific terminology. Moreover, concerning *The Book of URANTIA*, the explanations given of the 'language' are readily available. Indeed, according to Sadler, the use of URANTIAn-specific terminology crosses the boundaries of language, thereby increasing, rather than diminishing, its accessibility.[54]

The Foreword to *The URANTIA Book*, authored by the Divine Counsellor, notes the following:

> In the minds of the mortals of URANTIA – that being the name of your world – there exists great confusion respecting the meaning of such terms as God, divinity, and deity. Human beings are still more confused and uncertain about the relationships of the divine personalities designated by these numerous appellations. Because of this conceptual poverty associated with so much ideational confusion, I have been directed to formulate this introductory statement in explanation of the meanings which should be attached to certain word symbols as they may be hereinafter used in those papers which the Orvonton[55] corps of truth revealers have been authorized to translate into the English language of URANTIA.[56]

Moyer argues that 'many names were chosen to cause us to reach beyond the habits of our current religious attitudes and social views ... We should also keep clearly in mind that names are not the things they represent. They are symbols of reality but they are symbols only ... They are useful tools for us to make those realities accessible to thought and for communication.'[57]

The URANTIA Book states that:

> It is exceedingly difficult to present enlarged concepts and advanced truth, in our endeavour to expand cosmic consciousness and enhance spiritual perception, when we are restricted to the use of a circumscribed language of the realm. But our mandate admonishes us to make every effort to convey our meanings by using the word symbols of the English tongue. We have been instructed to introduce new terms only when the concept to be portrayed finds no terminology in English which can be employed to convey such a

new concept partially or even with more or less distortion of meaning.[58]

New language: God

The URANTIA Papers present an interpretation of God which, whilst having some continuity with traditional Christian orthodoxy, largely departs from it. *The URANTIA Book* notes, 'The Universal Father is the God of all creation, the First Source and Center of all things and beings'; God creates, controls and upholds.[59] Furthermore, 'DEITY is personalizable as God, is prepersonal and superpersonal in ways not altogether comprehensible by man. Deity is characterized by the quality of unity – actual or potential – on all supermaterial levels of reality; and this unifying quality is best comprehended by creatures as divinity.'[60]

For followers of the Papers, God does not inhabit or manifest himself personally in the local universes, but through his Creator Sons. The local universes are fathered by the Creator Sons, 'but the Universal Father is in every way *divinely* present in the Creator Sons'.[61] The Universal Father shares his nature with the Eternal Son of Paradise and the Infinite Spirit,[62] becoming the Eternal Paradise Trinity, and it is through them that humanity has a 'relationship' with God. The Papers state 'God can be realized only in the realms of human experience ... '[63]

To summarise, the Papers acknowledge that, whilst God is often thought of as the creator, and whilst he did create Paradise and the central universe of perfection, he did *not* create the universes of time and space; these were created by the Paradise corps of the Creator Sons.[64] The Universal Father did not personally create Nebadon (the local universe of which URANTIA is one planet); Nebadon was created by his Son Michael.[65]

New language: the universe

The Eternal Paradise Trinity dwells in the Isle of Paradise, the 'gravity centre of creation'...[66] This central area is part of a planetary family[67] known as Havona. Havona 'is of enormous dimensions and almost unbelievable mass and consists of one billion spheres of unimagined beauty and superb grandeur ... '[68] The URANTIA Papers distinguished between Havona and other worlds, including URANTIA.

[Havona] is the one and only settled, perfect, and established aggregation of worlds. This is a wholly created and perfect universe; it is not an evolutionary development. This is the eternal core of perfection, about which swirls that endless procession of universes which constitute the tremendous evolutionary experiment, the audacious adventure of the Creator Sons of God, who aspire to duplicate in time and to reproduce in space the pattern universe, the ideal of divine completeness, supreme finality, ultimate reality, and eternal perfection.[69]

Havona, therefore, is the style of existence that all other worlds aspire too, including the Earth (i.e. URANTIA). All that stands outside Havona is evolutionary and aspires to that perfection. The URANTIA Papers, although finding support within common theories of evolution, espouse the idea that evolution need not be the gradual and slow process that is usually identified as symbolic of evolutionary theories. For example, it is stated that the first two humans on URANTIA were a brother and sister, born to primates, but who represented an evolutionary leap from their ancestors,[70] and from whom would emerge the entire human race.[71]

Orbiting around Havona are seven huge, evolutionary and inhabited universes, each comprised of approximately one trillion inhabited worlds.[72] Bradley notes:

For administration, each 1,000 inhabited planets comprise a system, and 100 systems comprise a constellation. One hundred constellations comprise a local universe, 100 local universes comprise a minor sector, 100 minor sectors comprise a major sector, and 10 major sectors comprise one of the seven superuniverses.[73]

The local system of which URANTIA is a part is known as Satania and the local universe is Nebadon. URANTIA stands apart from other planets. Other planets had life carried to them by 'Life Carriers', 'but we brought no life to URANTIA. URANTIA life is unique, original with the planet. This sphere is a life-modification world; all life appearing hereon was formulated by us right here on the planet; and there is no other world in all Satania, even in all Nebadon, that has a life existence just like that of URANTIA.'[74]

URANTIA has distinct problems: 'Your world is out of step in the planetary procession.'[75] URANTIA became isolated as a result of the

Lucifer rebellion and 'on a confused and disordered planet like URANTIA such an achievement [peace] requires a much longer time and necessitates far greater effort.'[76] URANTIA has become a 'backward and confused world'.[77] Lucifer was a local universe son of God but, with his assistant Satan, turned his back on the Divine, instead advocating 'self-assertion and liberty'; their ideas culminated in the Lucifer Declaration of Liberty.[78] It was Satan who furthered the Lucifer rebellion on URANTIA.

New language: Adam and Eve

'Adam and Eve, a ... Son and Daughter of the local system, arrived and began the difficult task of attempting to untangle the confused affairs of a planet retarded by rebellion and resting under the ban of spiritual isolation.'[79] According to the URANTIA Papers, Adam and Eve were too impatient with the mission and wanted immediate results, 'but the results thus secured proved most disastrous both to themselves and to their world'.[80] That is, they failed to adhere to the mission God set out for them. However, there is no notion of a 'fall of humanity'. The Papers state that, although Adam and Eve were finally degraded in status, they did contribute to the advancement of civilisation on URANTIA.[81] The Papers argue that there can be no 'fall', as that would contradict evolutionary theory. Later, the Lucifer rebellion aimed to ruin the mission of Jesus Christ but failed, and Lucifer was imprisoned, although humans were left free to do evil should they choose. The death of Jesus is described as '... the enrichment of human experience and the enlargement of the way of salvation ... [it] is not the *fact* of his death but rather the superb manner and the matchless spirit in which he met death'.[82]

New language: Jesus

The Eternal Father and Eternal Son produce Creator Sons. Creator Sons are educated in the central universe, and then they join with a daughter of the Infinite Spirit and are able to create evolutionary solar and planetary systems, i.e. a local universe.[83] Jesus Christ is our local universe Creator Son. 'Creator Sons are of the Order of Michaels, our local universe is named Nebadon; therefore, our local universe Creator Son is called Michael of Nebadon ... our Creator Son incarnated here as Jesus Christ.'[84]

Jesus is viewed as a 'perfect demonstration of ... realization and revelation of the personality of God in a truly human experience',[85] and as humanity's best example of the personality of God. Jesus was both man and God, and 'the supreme purpose of the Michael bestowal was to enhance the *revelation of God*'. Jesus was a Creator Son and representative of the Isle of Paradise. He was the incarnation of our local universe Creator Son, Michael of Nebadon.[86] Creator Sons are necessary for the entry of Thought Adjusters (fragments of the Divine) into the human mind. Creator Sons '... live ordinary lives ... [and] ... labor in various capacities [Jesus was a carpenter], with just one exception: They do not beget offspring'.[87] Jesus came as an ordinary man so that the common people might understand him and receive him.[88] Creator Sons are ultimately teachers, 'exclusively devoted to the spiritual enlightenment of the mortal races on the world of their sojourn'.[89]

Michael chose URANTIA as the planet whereon to enact his final bestowal.[90] The Papers explain that it cannot be fully understood why he chose to reside in Palestine and, further, why Mary and Joseph were chosen to receive Michael (i.e. Jesus Christ). Nevertheless, they do note that Gabriel simply decided that '... the Hebrews possessed those relative advantages which warranted their selection as the bestowal race',[91] and Mary and Joseph '... possessed the most ideal combination of widespread racial connections and superior average of personality endowments'.[92]

New language: humanity

'The myriads of planetary systems were all made to be eventually inhabited by many different types of intelligent creatures, beings who could know God, receive the divine affection, and love him in return.'[93] URANTIA mortals (i.e. humans) cannot become perfect in the infinite sense, but they can strive to achieve this in a finite way.[94] God has set the task for mortals to strive upwards 'for higher and higher levels of spiritual values and true universe meanings',[95] but this is to be done of their own free will. Mortals must work through their 'materialistic handicaps and limited spiritual endowments'.[96]

A new religion?

Martin Gardner states that the followers of *The URANTIA Book* believe they have founded 'a new religion superior to Christianity'.[97] This claim, however, lacks evidence and is not supported by the Papers themselves: '... *The URANTIA Book* does not advocate a new organized religion. Its viewpoint builds upon the religious heritages of the past and present, encouraging a personal, living religion based on faith and service to one's fellows.'[98] The material presented by the URANTIA Papers is to serve as an explanation of existing material, not a presentation of new material. The URANTIA Foundation does not aim to produce a new religious organisation, but to build on and clarify what already exists.

> The time is ripe to witness the figurative resurrection of the human Jesus from his burial tomb amidst the theological traditions and the religious dogmas of the nineteen centuries … What a transcendent service if, through this revelation, the Son of Man should be recovered from the tomb of traditional theology and be presented as the living Jesus to the church that bears his name, and to all other religions![99]

That said, logically there must be some understanding that *The URANTIA Book* is superior to the Bible in some sense, in that it is believed to be a clarification of and an expansion of Christian belief. However, whilst *The URANTIA Book* may be understood in this way, the followers themselves do not present a negative image of the Bible. Certainly *The URANTIA Book* is not understood to undermine the beliefs of the Christian tradition. Whilst *The URANTIA Book* acknowledges that there is much human corruption within institutional Christianity, this is not understood to be a failing of the religion itself. Also, it is believed that in the past (even during the early Christian period) the time was not right to receive the knowledge that would eventually be revealed in the Papers. The knowledge humanity gains from the Papers is progressive and it is not a weakness of the Bible or Christianity that it was not imparted sooner.

Moyer notes the existence of many interpretations of the Bible and argues that it contains many human corruptions.[100] The teachings of *The URANTIA Book* are opposed to the sectarianism that has existed in Christianity, so the aim is unification through new revelation, not the formation of a new religion.

> [P]aganized and socialized Christianity stands in need of new contact with the uncompromised teachings of Jesus; it languishes for lack of a new vision of the Master's life on earth. A new and fuller revelation of the religion of Jesus is destined to conquer an empire of materialistic secularism and to overthrow a world sway of mechanistic naturalism. URANTIA is now quivering on the very brink of one of its

most amazing and enthralling epochs of social readjustment, moral quickening, and spiritual enlightenment.[101]

Mullins highlights the fear of 'churchification' and organised religion. 'There was even a marked uneasiness in the original [URANTIA Brotherhood] group toward the use of an opening prayer for meetings.'[102] The Brotherhood, as a result, went on to describe itself as 'an educational–social organization with a religious purpose'.[103] The initiation of a 'spiritual renaissance' was the aim for many within the URANTIA Brotherhood.[104]

The URANTIA Foundation

The URANTIA Foundation, an educational foundation focused on the translation, publication and distribution of *The URANTIA Book*, was established in 1950 as the guardian of *The URANTIA Book* and to ensure the promulgation of the revelation. 'Its ultimate mission is to increase and enhance the comfort, the happiness, and the well-being of man, as an individual and as a member of society, through the fostering of a religion, a philosophy, and a cosmology which is in line with man's current intellectual and cultural development.'[105] The URANTIA Foundation oversaw the publication of *The URANTIA Book* in 1955 and upholds strict copyright regulations.

URANTIA Foundation outreach programmes

The URANTIA Foundation places importance on spreading the 'good news' and disseminates *The URANTIA Book* throughout the world. It also holds international conferences that aim to integrate the will of God into the everyday lives of individuals, with songs, music, drama, dance, personal testimonies and study activities for younger participants. A URANTIA Society may be formed if there are ten or more people believing in the teachings of *The URANTIA Book*. Proselytising is usually 'quiet and gradual … Only a few individuals have exhibited some restlessness and craving for aggressive plans for increased distribution … One thing should be made clear: Nothing is done to interfere with the energetic and enthusiastic efforts of any individuals to introduce *The URANTIA Book* to his varied contacts and human associations.'[106]

The URANTIA Foundation asks for support in translating *The URANTIA Book*, either in the form of donations or in the form of actual translation work. The size and terminology of the book clearly means that translating it is a long process. *The URANTIA Book* is currently available in seven languages and is in the process of being translated into fourteen other languages. The URANTIA Foundation aims to have translated *The URANTIA Book* into sixty languages by 2030, therefore ensuring that approximately 84 per cent of the people in the world will be able to read it.[107] The URANTIA Foundation claims that 400,000 people have made contact with *The URANTIA Book*, with 24,743 copies sold in 2000 which was almost twice the number sold in 1999.

Conclusion

The URANTIA Book introduces many new concepts concerning the cosmos, yet it is the material surrounding the life and teachings of Jesus, and the status accorded him, that are likely to find the greatest opposition, particularly from within mainstream Christianity. Harris and Belitsos argue that section four of *The URANTIA Book*, the Jesus Papers, is neither 'gnostic' nor 'New Agey', but 'solidly rooted in the New Testament story'.[108] In declaring that there was no intention to create a new religion, the URANTIA Foundation echoes the claim of the Family Federation for World Peace and Unification,[109] which has always stated that Sun Myung Moon came to fulfil Christianity, not to found a new church.[110] It was only when Moon's message was not accepted within Christianity that a new church emerged. There are many concepts presented within the *Divine Principle* of the Unification Church[111] that would be new to traditional Christians, and would therefore make it less likely that Moon could have had his ideas accepted as a fulfilment of Christianity, as the Completed Testament. The same point could be made of *The URANTIA Book*; an idea that is so new and so different will find it hard to be accepted within the mainstream parent religion that it believes it is clarifying. The development of a new religion might not be the initial aim, but it does seem to be inevitable.

NOTES

1   L. Mullins, *A History of the URANTIA Papers*, Boulder, Penumbra Press, 2000, pp. 4–5.
2   URANTIA is the name for Earth in *The URANTIA Book*. Explanations of terminology are taken from the Glossary provided in D. Bradley, *An Introduction to the URANTIA Revelation*, Arcata, White Egret Publications, 1998.
3   *The URANTIA Book*, Chicago, Uversa Press, 1996; first published in 1955.

4 W. S. Sadler, *A History of the URANTIA Movement*:www.urantia.org/pub/ahotum.html
5 F. Harris and B. Belitsos (eds), *The Center Within*, Novato, Origin Press, 1998.
6 Mullins, *History of the URANTIA Papers*, p. 4.
7 Bradley, *Introduction to the URANTIA Revelation*, p. 1.
8 See *ibid.*, p. 12.
9 Available online: http://www.urantia.org/about.html (4 November 2001), p. 1
10 Bradley, *Introduction to the URANTIA Revelation*, p. 79.
11 *Ibid.*, p. 115.
12 *Ibid.*, pp. 112, 113
13 A 'superuniverse' is one of seven evolutionary universes around the eternal central universe of creation.
14 'Uversa is the headquarters of our superuniverse.'
15 'Ancients of Days' are superuniverse-level judges.
16 Nebadon is the local universe of which the planet URANTIA, 'our world', is a part.
17 A local universe is a universe created by a Creator Son and a Daughter of the Infinite Spirit. It consists of 100 constellations; each constellation consists of 100 systems; each system has about 1,000 inhabited planets when mature.
18 Gabriel is an order of being termed 'Bright and Morning Star' and there is one in each local universe. They act as chief executives for 'Creator Sons' in local universes.
19 Salvington is the headquarters of our local universe.
20 'Midwayers' stand between the realm of mortals and the realm of angels.
21 'Melchizedek Sons' are local universe 'Sons of God' who perform emergency services.
22 *The URANTIA Book*, p. v.
23 Mullins, *History of the URANTIA papers*, p. 127.
24 *Ibid.*, p. 4.
25 *The URANTIA Book*, p. 2086.
26 E. P. Moyer, *The Birth of a Divine Revelation*, Hanover, Moyer Publications, 2000, p. 6.
27 Mullins, *History of the URANTIA Papers*, p. 5.
28 *Ibid.*, p. 149.
29 *Ibid.*, p. 150.
30 See also Moyer, *Birth of a Divine Revelation*, pp. 99–106.
31 H. Sherman, *How to Know What to Believe*, New York, Fawcett, 1976; quoted in Mullins, *History of the URANTIA Papers*, p. 50.
32 Moyer, *Birth of a Divine Revelation*, p. 5.
33 Mullins, *History of the URANTIA Papers*, p. 67.
34 Sadler, *History of the URANTIA Movement*, p. 7.
35 *Ibid.*, p. 4.
36 Mullins, *History of the URANTIA Papers*, p. 183.
37 Sherman, *How to Know What to Believe*; quoted in Mullins, p. 81.
38 Mullins, *History of the URANTIA Papers*, p. 81.
39 *Ibid.*, p. 87.
40 Sadler, *History of the URANTIA Movement*, pp. 6–7.

41 *The URANTIA Book*, p. 82.
42 Moyer, *Birth of a Divine Revelation*, p. 7.
43 *Ibid.*, pp. 9, 82.
44 Sadler, *History of the URANTIA Movement*, pp. 1–12.
45 Moyer, *Birth of a Divine Revelation*, p. 8. See also pp. 82–98.
46 *Ibid.*, p. 8.
47 Moyer, *Spirit Entry into Human Mind*, Hanover, Moyer Publishing, 2000, p. 71.
48 The Thought Adjuster is the fragment of the Heavenly Father that indwells the human mind.
49 Mullins, *History of the URANTIA Papers*, pp. 5, 90–1.
50 See, for example, Suzanne Riordan, 'Channeling: A New Revelation?', in J. R. Lewis and J. G. Melton (eds), *Perspectives on the New Age*, Albany, State University of New York Press, 1992, pp. 105–26.
51 Moyer, *Birth of a Divine Revelation*, p. 8.
52 *Ibid.*, p. 9.
53 *Ibid.*, p. 57.
54 Sadler, *History of the URANTIA Movement*, p. 12.
55 Orvonton is one of seven evolutionary superuniverses comprising Nebadon and others.
56 *The URANTIA Book*, p. 3.
57 Moyer, *Birth of a Divine Revelation*, p. 31.
58 *The URANTIA Book*, p. 3.
59 *Ibid.*, p. 17.
60 *Ibid.*, p. 4.
61 *Ibid.*, p. 23.
62 *Ibid.*, p. 20.
63 *Ibid.*, p. 19.
64 *Ibid.*, pp. 19–20.
65 *Ibid.*, p. 20.
66 Bradley, *History of the URANTIA Papers*, p. 9.
67 *The URANTIA Papers*, p. 133.
68 *Ibid.*
69 *Ibid.*
70 *Ibid.*, p. 589.
71 *Ibid.*, pp. 622–3.
72 Bradley, *History of the URANTIA Papers*, p. 10.
73 *The URANTIA Book*, p. 10.
74 *Ibid.*, p. 587.
75 *Ibid.*, p. 525.
76 *Ibid.*
77 *Ibid.*, p. 526.
78 See *ibid.*, pp. 531–2.
79 *Ibid.*, p. 718.
80 *Ibid.*, p. 735.
81 *Ibid.*, p. 740.
82 *Ibid.*, p. 1775.
83 Bradley, *History of the URANTIA Papers*, p. 11.
84 *Ibid.*, p. 113
85 *The URANTIA Book*, p. 25.
86 Bradley, *History of the URANTIA Papers*, p. 79.

 87 *The URANTIA Book*, p. 201
 88 *Ibid.*, p. 1177.
 89 *Ibid.*, p. 201.
 90 *Ibid.*, p. 1176.
 91 *Ibid.*
 92 *Ibid.*, p. 1177.
 93 *Ibid.*
 94 *Ibid.*, p. 17.
 95 *Ibid.*, p. 18
 96 *Ibid.*, p. 20.
 97 M. Gardner, *On the Wild Side*, Buffalo, Prometheus Books, 1992, p. 106.
 98 Available online: http://www.urantia.org/about.html (4 November 2001),
     p. 1.
 99 *The URANTIA Book*, p. 2090
100 Moyer, *Birth of a Divine Revelation*, pp. 13–14.
101 *The URANTIA Book*, p. 2082.
102 Mullins, *History of the URANTIA Papers*, p. 264.
103 M. J. Sprunger, 'The Future of the Fifth Epochal Revelation', a paper
     dated 10 February 1993, p. 1; quoted in Mullins, *History of the URANTIA
     Papers*, p. 264.
104 *Ibid.*
105 Available online: http://www.urantia.org/foundation.html (4 November
     2001), p. 1.
106 Sadler, *History of the URANTIA Movement*, p. 12.
107 Available online: http://www.urantia.org/foundation.html (4 November
     2001), p. 6.
108 *The URANTIA Book*, p. 7.
109 Formerly the Unification Church.
110 See S. Lewis, 'The Lord of the Second Advent – the Deliverer is Here!',
     in F. Bowie (ed.), *The Coming Deliverer*, Cardiff, University of Wales
     Press, 1997.
111 *Divine Principle*, Thornton Heath, HSA-UWC, 1973.

7

THE UNITED
NUWAUBIAN NATION OF
MOORS

Theodore Gabriel

One of the most interesting developments in modern religious history is the rise of religions which are based on, or have links with, belief in extraterrestrial beings. The Nuwaubian Nation of Moors (herein after called Nuwaubians) is one such community which believes its founder comes from a distant planet and which also has eschatological expectations related to extraterrestrial beliefs.

UFO religions

It is not surprising that UFOs are the basis for some highly colourful new religious movements. UFOs are shrouded in mystery and are the source of incredible happenings beyond the realm of physical possibilities, and of experiences by human beings which are akin to mystical experiences. The UFOs perform that which is beyond normal human experience and capability and which seem to negate common physical laws. They can move at incredible speeds and change and reverse direction without coming to rest or even reducing their velocity. They often emit light and arrive surrounded by burgeoning luminous clouds, reminiscent of, for example, the common representation of the second coming of Christ, and they can have an extraordinary effect on machinery, on electrical currents and even on states of mind. They are believed to be inhabited by beings which, while generally anthropomorphic, have superhuman capabilities and scientific knowledge far beyond what human beings have attained. Supposed abductions are rampant and have a lasting effect on the subjects who experience these extraterrestrial visitations, akin to visions, theophanies and other paranormal religious experience. A whole corpus of narratives has arisen around UFO experiences, both fact and fiction (mythology?), which have a considerable readership. Indeed, it is evident that some new religious movements consider

UFOs to have quasi-supernatural status, though technically they are within the ambit of the material rather than the spiritual world.

The Nuwaubians

The Nuwaubians, mainly composed of African Americans, is an instance of a new religious movement which is totally universal in its ideology, encompassing ideas from most of the important world religions and trying to synthesise these ideas and teachings in order to enhance its appeal for a very wide clientele. Its founder, Dwight York, a Black American, was born in New York in 1935 and is said to be an ex-convict who had spent time in prison in the 1960s for assault, resisting arrest and possession of a dangerous weapon. The different names and titles that York adopts, and the ever-changing appellations of the cult, are a clear enunciation of the ecumenism, shifting ideologies and efforts to universalise the appeal of the cult. York is also known as Malachi Z. York, Isa Abdallah, The Qutb ('Axis of the Universe' – a Sufi term), Neter A'aferti Atum Re, Chief Black Eagle, The Lamb, and al Hajj al Imam Isa Abdallah Muhammad al Mahdi. Similarly, the organisation has adopted names such as the Ansaru Allah (Helpers of Allah), Ansaru Pure Sufi, Nubian Islamic Hebrews, Yamassee Native American Nuwaubians, Ancient Holy Tabernacle of the Most High, and Mystic Order of Melchizedek. The shifting identities – American Indian, African, Sudanese, Nubian, Egyptian, Jewish, Christian and Islamic – that these names presuppose are evident. A cosmological dimension is added by the claim that York is a being from a distant planet in the nineteenth galaxy, Illywun. This challenges the idea that the Nuwaubians are a purely Black phenomenon, but tries to identify with all races, all faiths and all intelligent life forms, terrestrial or extraterrestrial. Ansaru parents are exhorted to breed intelligently with the help of extraterrestrials, so as to give rise to 144,000 pure Nubian children who will be raptured to Planet Rizq in the galaxy Illywun in the year 2003.[1]

The origins of the Nuwaubians

The Nuwaubians started out essentially as one of the many Black Nationalist movements in the United States in the latter half of the twentieth century. These movements are no doubt prompted by the continued discrimination and oppression of African-Americans in society after their emancipation from slavery in 1865. The economic deprivation, social isolation and ghettoisation of the Blacks led to movements such as the Nation of Islam, Black Hebrew, Five Percenters and Rastafarians, which sought to strengthen Black consciousness, improve their self-esteem and morale, and provide a forum for combating racism and economic oppression.

Rather than Socialism, Marxism or other such ideologies, the move-ments attempted to use religious motifs, which had more emotional appeal and provided a more powerful source of hope as being supported by God instead of purely materialistic forces. Most of these movements seem to have rejected Christianity since their apparent oppressors were at least nominally Christian and, like the Ku Klux Klan, used Christian religious symbols and language in their anti-Negro rhetoric. Islam was an obvious choice with its dominant themes of egalitarianism and soli-darity, one of Muhammad's initial acts being to set slaves free. 'Those foremost in faith will be the foremost. These will be those nearest to God', says the Qur'an, thus recognising no social gradations except that based on faith.[2] But Islam was by no means the only religious ideology resorted to in the campaign for enhancement of Black morale in American society. Judaism, African religions, Hinduism and even Black Christian cults such as Rastafarianism were adapted to this purpose.[3]

Dwight York – a religious and cultural *bricoleur*

York seems to be constantly changing the affiliations of his group to different religions and cultures. Beginning with his own brand of Islam, emphasising the mystical path of Sufism, during which time the community adopted the term 'Ansaru Pure Sufi', he later tried to assume a Jewish identity. He had earlier branded Jacob as the 'Father of Judaism and Christianity, the religions of the Devil'.[4] Even during the Sufi phase, York had adopted the Star of David as the cult's symbol, with a Tau cross inside.[5] However, in 1969 he changed the name of the cult to 'the Nubian Islamic Hebrews', and his title to Rabboni Yeshua Bar el Haady, which has both Jewish and Christian connotations. Though adopting Jewish symbols and titles, he defined his followers as the true Jews and condemned the 'so called Jews' of Israel as the 'cursed seed from Canaan'.[6] These shifting religious affiliations, accompanied by condemnation of the recognised followers of the religion of his adoption of the moment, are a constant feature of York's *modus operandi*. Abu Ameenah Bilal Philips, in his monograph on the Nuwaubians takes great pains in analysing York's Islamic teachings and exposes most of them as highly heretical with respect to Islamic beliefs. Concepts postulated by York, such as, for example, incarnation and astrology, are obviously incompatible with Islam. Moreover, he points out that York denies his followers access to the Qur'an, alleging that present translations are flawed but at the same time denying them training in Arabic.[7] The motivation is evidently to keep his followers from challenging his own heterodox teachings on Islam, as a result of their perusal of the Qur'an. Philips further notes various inconsistencies in York's own translation of the Qur'an, though York claims his translation to be the most authentic. He alleges that the Yusuf Ali translation, a popular translation to English, is directed towards a Christian interpretation of Islam.[8] York denies totally the validity of the Hadith (Sayings of the Prophet). It is also strange that, while extolling the virtues and importance of family life and the conjugal relationship, he denies such relationships to his followers except at strictly controlled intervals. He urges his female followers to pattern themselves on the Islamic paradigms of the wife and the mother, apparently desiring the creation of stable family units. But in reality the husbands and wives are segregated in dormitories, separated also from their children. York permits spouses to cohabit only once every three months. They are permitted to meet in the 'Green Room' by prior appointment only. This, according to Palmer and Luxton, smacks of eugenics rather than encouraging stable and loving family relationships.[9] Initially advocating a typically patriarchal Islamic approach to womanhood, York suddenly cast himself in the role of a liberator of women, urging them to cast off the veil and condemning the Arab world for its double standards in male and female attire. These are clear examples of York's startling methodology of adhering to diverse religions and later rejecting their tenets.[10]

York's cultural divagations

Similarly, in the cult's history you could find numerous cultural shifts – African, Sudanese, Ethiopian and currently Egyptian. The cult's costumes and symbols change in phase with York's divagations. During his Mahdist phase, York travelled to the Sudan and took great pains to cultivate the descendants of the Sudanese Mahdi who staged a rebellion against the British colonialist power in the latter half of the nineteenth century. A famous contemporary figure of the Mahdi's family, Saadiq al Mahdi, came to the USA and took part in the cult's celebrations in 1978. York even changed his date of birth to 1945 from 1935 so that he could claim to be the *mujaddid* (reformer) of the century who was predicted to be born one hundred years after the birth of the original Mahdi of the Sudan in 1845. York claimed to be the

Mahdi's grandson, took photographs of himself standing at the conflu-
ence of the White Nile and the Blue Nile, and adopted the Mahdist
crescent and spear as the cult's symbol. The Sudanese *jalabeeyah* and
white cap became the group's standard costume.

In 1980 the Mahdist phase passed and York claimed to be the
Messiah, the Christ. This claim was especially convenient, since the
return of Christ is expected by both Christians and Muslims.

The Nuwaubians and extraterrestrials

Thus the Nuwaubians is distinctive in that they use motifs and ideas
from many religions, including Christianity, one after the other to
affirm Black identity and strengthen Blacks' self-esteem and sense of
achievement. This is obviously an effort to make Nuwaubian's appeal
universal. The climax of this comes in identifying themselves as
extraterrestrials so as to gain a cosmological significance beyond the
confines of earthly identities. As manifested in their propagandist literature, they also try to bestow a quasi-scientific character to their
ideology by using psychological or parapsychological scientific terminology. Psychometry and telepathy are some of the terms used.[11] There
is mention of Quantum Physics, personal triads and similar scientific
terms in their literature.[12] York sometimes attempts a pseudo-scientific
explanation of Qur'anic verses, as in his interpretation of angels,
humans and *djinn*.[13] He writes:

> Angels are simple electro-magnetism like the *Haalat*. What is
> *al Haalat*? In man, there is a voltage and current between his
> Crown seat and Root seat. This flow gives rise to a magnetic
> field which surrounds him. This magnetic force field of nega-
> tive and positive charges is called man's Aura or *Haalat*. This
> magnetic force field contains the Ether Particles of Green
> Light which are waiting to be drawn into the body by the
> Seats.[14]

York's writings are full of such pseudo-scientific terminology. It is as
though he seems fettered by orthodox religious beliefs and would like
to liberate himself and take on a more rational and universal identity.
This is in resonance with Nuwaubian's claims to be extraterrestrials
with superior scientific knowledge and mental and psychic abilities. In
a similar way to the Unarius Academy of Science,[15] The Nuwaubians
seek to dissociate themselves from the identity of being a religion:
'Unarius is not a religion because it is the prescription for healing

oneself from the rituals of dogmatic teachings. The teaching of this organisation is to set the person free from old belief.'[16] In popular lore, extraterrestrials have highly advanced scientific knowledge and uncommon gifts of the mind such as telekinesis. The Nuwaubian cult's literature states: 'The third approach is to achieve unity between your inner forces and outer forces which link you to a cosmic or universal flow the all which flow through nature [sic]. It is in fact all nature and all other existence.'[17]

The attempt to rationalise religion and impart a scientific character to religious beliefs is evident, as mentioned previously, in his exegesis of some Qur'anic verses. The need for spiritual growth in consonance with technological advancement is also postulated by another UFO cult, the Aetherius Society,[18] founded by George King in 1954.[19] The Aetherius Society predict the ending of human civilisation on Earth as a result of increased materialism. They state that the only hope for the human race is the development of the higher selves as we advance scientifically. This is also emphasised by York when he tries to integrate scientific terminology and ideas with development of higher faculties of the mind.

York and racism

The Nuwaubians have now distanced themselves from the racist ideologies of many Black Nationalist movements such as the Nation of Islam, though initially they also subscribed to such ideas. Racist ideologies in such communities are inevitable since there is an attempt to recover a sense of humanity and self-esteem after being subjected to centuries of racial abuse, degradation and marginalisation. Even in contemporary times the separatist and arrogant attitudes of some White supremacists provoke this kind of response. In a kind of *quid pro quo* response, Black Nationalists sought to make the Black person superior to the White by ascribing an earlier origin to their race, as being the first of the human species, and the Whites as the creation of a Black Muslim geneticist rather than of God.[20] They categorise God as a Black person, and it is noteworthy that eventually York designated himself as an incarnation of God, an idea highly heretical from an Islamic perspective. In their disputes with Putnam County officials who accused the Nuwaubians of being Black separatists, McDade, a Nuwaubian spokesman, vehemently denies that they are racists. He points out that, while the members are predominantly Black, they also have White and Asian members in their midst.[21] Like the issue of religion, York's theses on race are constantly undergoing revision.

Concurring initially with Elijah Muhammad (Nation of Islam) that the Whites are a race of devils and the white skin is associated with the disease of leprosy as mentioned in Leviticus, and proscribing intermarriage with Whites, later on he abandoned this stance and exhorted the members to embrace people of all colours, 'black white, purple, green or aquamarine', as long as they believed in the Islamic *shahada or creed*.[22]

Later on, in 1992, he again moved on from this ideology, describing people of brown colour as the original humans.[23] As with the issues of religion and ethnicity, York's ideas on race display a trend towards universalism culminating perhaps in his claim that the Nuwaubians are extraterrestrials.

The Egyptian connection

The most recent stance that York has taken is that the Nuwaubians are Egyptians. To this end he has incorporated Egyptian motifs not only into the external symbols and paraphernalia of his cult, but also in its teaching. In their present headquarters in Eatonton, Putnam County, Georgia, the community has built pyramids, a Sphinx and obelisks and gateways featuring hieroglyphics and figures of Egyptian gods and rulers. The palace is called Tama-Re, Egypt of the West. Teachings claimed to be from Neteru, an ancient Egyptian deity, are propagated. York and his followers dress in Egyptian costumes. Egyptian-sounding chants resound throughout the campus.

The incorporation of Neteru, an ancient Egyptian deity (properly spelt Ntr) is highly interesting, since this deity predates the gods of the Osiris cycle, Horus and even the sun god Ra in the Egyptian pantheon. The concept of Ntr is indicative of a deep undercurrent of monotheism in Egyptian religion and is very similar to the henotheism of Hinduism in which the polytheism of the numerous gods and goddesses are overshadowed by the monotheistic and monistic conception of one deity underlying them all, the Brahman. It is also comparable to the unity of God in the Western monotheisms of Judaism, Christianity and Islam. By adopting Ntr as the focus of his attention, York is again broadening the religious identity of the Nuwaubians to encompass many of the major living religious traditions.

In a proclamation, York claims the Nuwaubians to be descended from the most ancient race in the Americas who had migrated to the two continents from Egypt before the continental drift, having traversed vast distances on foot to set up colonies noted for their affluence and prosperity. York denies that African-Americans were brought to the USA from Africa in slave ships. He claims that they are the descendants of the ancient Atlanteans, whose dominion extended 'from North-East and South-West Africa, across the great Atlantis even unto the present North, South and Central America and also Mexico and the Atlantis Islands (the Caribbean)'.[24] They are also children of the original Egyptians who are properly called Tahitas or T'uaf, descendants of a personage known as Tah, 'The Opener'. Egypt is word of Greek origin, Aheegooptos, meaning 'burnt faces'. The term 'Nuwaubian' preceded both 'Egypt' and 'Kemet' – which means the sons of Kham or Ham, the son of Noah.[25] York assumes the title 'Supreme Grand Hierophant of the Ancient Egyptian Order'. (It is apparent that York assigns numerous followers to research in various fields and presumably gets his information and terminology from the labour of these devoted followers.[26]) York seems to think that the Nuwaubians are the only true Egyptians remaining in the world: 'The natives living in the land of Egypt today bear little resemblance to these noble Nuwbuns [sic], the masters of Architecture, Science and Mathematics of thousands of years ago. Today you have Turks, Greeks, Romans, Canaanites mixed with Arabs. Very few Egyptians of the pure Negroid seed can be found there, but in the Western world you find this lost tribe.'[27]

The attempt to link his organisation with Egypt is again a move in the direction of freeing the sect from being restricted to particular contemporary religions or ideologies, and part of the trend to universalise the sect. The Egyptian civilisation is one of the most ancient and acclaimed of all civilisations, and the association with a religion or culture which is no longer extant would give this sect a more universal identity than would be achieved by affiliation to Islam, Judaism or Christianity. The teachings selected from Egyptian religions are mainly intended to improve the faculties of the mind rather than based on any particular theological formulations or doctrinal dogma. York states:

> You say I was born a Christian or a Muslim, and that is not true. You were not born with a religion or belief … For it is Right Knowledge, the Right Wisdom and the Right Overstanding [sic] that makes success in life. A special kind of Outformation [sic] received as information, the mere existence of a special kind of facts, the mere existence of which is unknown to many people.[28]

York therefore claims to restore and communicate Egyptian knowledge, which has been lost or neglected for centuries. He claims to reveal the 'facts of Universal life of the ancient Neteru taught by the ancient Egyptian Order, in the higher degrees of the order of Imhotep and the Sisters of Aset.'[29] As mentioned above, these are not in the main religious creeds or doctrines, but are rather Egyptian teachings on how to improve one's mental faculties and how to attain happiness, peace and harmony of mind. In the movement's literature York gives various such objectives:

How to overcome many obstacles that are holding you back.
(a) Unlocking the power of the imagination.
(b) Putting intuition to work.
(c) Using suggestion instead of medicine.
(d) How to overcome worry.
(e) Making your subconscious to work for you.
(f) How to conquer nervousness and fear.
(g) Experiments with mental telepathy.
(h) The source of human energy.[30]

Some more esoteric attainments are also mentioned:

(a) Creating material things from abstract thought.
(b) A discourse on the dead returning to life.
(c) Proofs of the immortality of the soul.
(d) Underrating the wheel of life.
(e) Using cosmic forces in our everyday life.

Egyptians and extraterrestrials

Nuwaubian literature claims the Egyptians were extraterrestrials who came from the planet Rizq to escape its imminent destruction by powerful rays from their three suns – Utu, Apsu and Shamash. They came in planet-sized spacecraft that travelled at the speed of light. The 'Annunaqi Eloheem' (usually spelled Elohim), as the Nuwaubian cult call these ancient Egyptians, were so morally enlightened that 'if you confronted one of them with a weapon they would let you shoot them rather than hurt you'.[31] York claims to be one of them, and the Ansaru now believe the Negro race to have originated from the Annunaqi Eloheem.

It appears that the Egyptian phase is a step closer to the culmination of the cult's ultimate universalisation which is set *not* in the supernatural or spiritual realms, but in an extraterrestrial world which, however extraordinary or unknown, is still a part of the material universe. By identifying with the Egyptian civilisation, York effectively casts off the mantle of being restricted by one of the contemporary and, in a sense, limiting religious identities. The belief is that the Egyptian religion is the ideological basis of most prominent contemporary religions, including Semitic, Indian and the Eastern faiths. The emphasis here is not on theological or doctrinal matters, but on the intrinsic potential and greatness of the human personality. According to York, human beings lost many of their innate faculties due to genetic tampering by extraterrestrials. The removal of the 'barathary gland', he says, led to the loss of psychometry, telepathy, clairvoyance and intuition, which human beings initially possessed: extraterrestrials took away 'the senses necessary for random access throughout the boundless universe, and trapped you in a state of cause and effect. You were to be named human, given the lesser knowledge which controls you.'[32]

York seems to claim that the human being in its present state is much diminished with respect to mental faculties. Again, Unarians also believe that human society has been regressing for hundreds of thousands of years. They believe that, over time, humanity lost its connection with the rest of the universe. Hence, they await the arrival of Pleiadeans (extraterrestrials from the constellation Pleiades) who will initiate a spiritual renaissance of humankind.[33] Similarly, York asserts that the eschatological 'rapturing' to the planet Rizq will restore these lost faculties to humanity and thereby restore the race to its former glory. In one brochure, York mentions seven planes of mental and spiritual attainments. These are as follows:

1st Material (Governor of carnal desire, material not spiritual);
2nd Plane of Force (The force between voluntary and involuntary actions which is life substance);
3rd Spiritual Plane (Emotions are manifested);
4th Mental Plane (Guardian Angels; thoughts are formed);
5th Divine Truth (Spark of Life; 'Hayah');
6th Divine Reality (Crown Chakra, and Mental Force Field; Peanal Chakra);
7th Union with Allah (Eternal Bliss).[34]

A scrutiny of these stages of attainment will show that there is a gradual progression from the purely material to the wholly spiritual, culminating with Union with Allah – a highly heretical notion in mainstream Islam, but one that is prevalent in Sufi Islam.[35] It is also noteworthy that these concepts use Christian, Islamic and Hindu ideas. The idea of the 'crown chakra' is part of Kundalini Yoga, and belief in guardian angels is popular in Christianity.

Since York is believed to be an extraterrestrial from the planet Rizq, he presumably possesses these faculties of telepathy, etc., to the full. This is certainly a claim to superhuman power and greatness for the founder of the Nuwaubian cult, and one which will substantiate and enhance his leadership and influence over others.

There is much in the Nuwaubian literature to demonstrate their strong belief in extraterrestrials. They claim that there are extraterrestrials among humans hidden away in subterranean regions and who occasionally interbreed with humans. For example, the Deros who live in caves are exceptionally obese. Hence, it is claimed that particularly obese persons might be offspring of the union between the Deros and humans. Glandular dysfunction is a trait of the Deros, Nuwaubian say. The Teros are another race of subsurface extraterrestrials. Their chromosomal structure is different from that of humans, and if they interbreed with humans, the result is Down's syndrome.

As with other UFO groups, notably the Raëlians,[36] ultimately York attributes the origins of the human race to extraterrestrials. Indeed, the creation of the human species by extraterrestrials seems to be a common theme in UFO religions. Perhaps this is not surprising, in that there seems to be such a vast gulf of difference between human intelligence and capabilities and those of the rest of the animal kingdom. Thus, for some, such as certain Christian creationists and UFO believers, some form of special creation, whether of extraterrestrial genesis or otherwise, seems a preferable explanation to Darwinian evolution. Certainly, an extraterrestrial origin will easily explain the tremendous superiority of the human species.

Evidently York's thesis is that the human race is a subspecies of extraterrestrials. As we have seen, human beings have been deliberately subjected to genetic modification by extraterrestrials from whom they descended, to make them mentally inferior, by removing what York terms the 'barathary gland', dispossessing the human species of extrasensory powers such as telepathy and telekinesis. It is also interesting to note that York considers Earthly life to somehow diminish the powers of extraterrestrial beings. This is clear in his descriptions of the Deros as having degenerated so much that they have lost much of their intelligence and have become extremely obese.[37] Similarly, the Teros are said to be prone to leukaemia and Down's syndrome.[38] Indeed, they are said to have bored very deep into the Earth in order to preserve their sanity. The need to transport the Nuwaubian community to their planet of origin, Rizq, to undergo a rebirth, a revitalisation, is therefore clear, since they cannot hope to achieve this on the Earth.

Conclusion

Were York's shifting ideologies and ethnic and religious identities merely pragmatic, self-serving and opportunistic devices for acquiring power, wealth and domination over the Black community of the USA? Did he just latch on to the popular Black nationalist ideological trend of the moment? Was his eclecticism, as one of Philips's interviewees suggests, just a clever psychological ploy to attract members to his cult and replace those who leave?[39] Or, as Palmer and Luxton opine, was the Nuwaubian Nation of Moors a laboratory for racial, social and religious experimentation?[40] I feel that York's bricolage of clashing traditions and cultural affiliations is the story of an exploration, a quest to find a meaningful identity for the Blacks of America. It is no doubt a product of the Black cultic milieu of Harlem, where occultism, Christianity, Judaism and Islam coexisted and blended in the quest for the restoration of Black self-esteem and liberation from racial oppression. But, unlike other Black leaders, York seems to be continually liberating himself from conventional religious and ethnic attachments and aspiring for a universalism which he tries to achieve through ever more fanciful ideologies. He creates for himself and his followers new identities based on ancient extinct cultures and, finally, on extraterrestrial mythology. His final choice of an identity transcending earthly identities is appropriate to a modern age in which space exploration and cosmology have made great strides. I agree with Palmer and Luxton when they state that York and his followers are avant-garde explorers of postmodern Blackness.[41] Their ideological explorations display all the hallmarks of the iconoclastic and indefinable nature of the postmodern age.

NOTES

1 Mentioned in S. J. Palmer and S. Luxton, 'The Ansaru Allah Community: Postmodernist Narration and the Black Jeremiad', in P. B. Clarke (ed.), *New Trends and Developments in the World of Islam*, London, Luzac Oriental, 1998, p. 361.
2 Qur'an 56: 11–12 (trans. by A. Yusuf Ali).
3 The idea of the 'Wheel of Life' that Nuwaubian literature often uses is a key concept in Hinduism.
4 A. A. B. Philips, *The Ansaru Cult in America*, Riyadh, Tawheed Publications, 1988, p. 2.
5 A cross with a loop at the top.
6 Palmer and Luxton, 'Ansaru Allah Community', p. 357.

7 *Ibid.*, p. 56.
8 Mentioned in Philips, *The Ansaru Cult*, p. 57.
9 Palmer and Luxton, 'The Ansaru Allah Community', p. 361.
10 *Ibid.*
11 'The Egyptian Mysteries'. Available online: http://www.Ansaru/2017.htm (January 2002).
12 E.g. in 'The Egyptian Mysteries'. Available online:http://www.Ansaru/6205.htm (January 2002), p. 1.
13 *Ibid.*, p. 82–85.
14 Quoted in Philips, *The Ansaru Cult*, p. 3.
15 For a discussion of Unarius, see Chapter 3 above.
16 Available.religiousmovements.lib.virginia.edu/nrms/unariushtonline:http://ww wml (July 2002), p. 6.
17 Available online: http://www.Ansaru/6205.htm (January 2002), p. 1.
18 For a discussion of the Aetherius Society see Chapter 4 above.
19 Available online:http://www.religiousmovements.lib.Virginia.edu/nrms/aeth erius .html (July 2002), p. 4.
20 The Nation of Islam states that the Whites are devils, the product of genetic experiments conducted by a Black scientist, Yacoub, on the island of Patmos.
21 *The Macon Telegraph*, 8 August 1999.
22 Palmer and Luxton, 'The Ansaru Allah Community', p. 362.
23 *Ibid.*, p. 363.
24 Available online: http://www.therighttrack.com/htmweb.html (July 2002).
25 Office of the Mayor, the City of Augusta, Proclamation. Available online: http://www.Ansaru/2026.htm (July 2002), p. 1.
26 Philips, *The Ansaru Cult*, p. 136.
27 'A Depiction of the Mississippi Community of Caholka, Illinois; Not the Pyramidal Mounds.' Available online: http://www.Ansaru/2010.htm (July 2002), p.1.
28 'The Egyptian Mysteries. How One Amazing Night Could Change Your Life.' Available online: http://www.Ansaru/201.htm (July 2002), pp. 1, 2
29 *Ibid.*
30 *Ibid.*
31 'Extra-Terra-Astrals in our midst.' Available online:http://usersnetropolis.net /moorish/page14.htm (July 2002), p. 1.
32 D. York, Z. Malachi, El Hayy 'The Living Soul, The Holy Tablets', Chapter Seven, Tablet 1, verses 1:20–1:34. Available online: http://www.the right-track.com/htmweb.html (July 2002).
33 Available online:http://www.religiousmovements.lib.virginia.edu/nrms/unar ius.html (July 2002), p.3.
34 'Behold the Seven Planes'. Available online:http://www.therighttrack.com/ htmweb.html (July 2002).
35 The Sufi identity is one of the earliest that the cult embraced.
36 See: http://religiousmovements.lib.virginia.edu/nrms/rael.html (July 2002), p. 8.
37 Available online: http://users.netropolis.net/moorish/page12.htm (July 2002) p. 1.
38 Available online: http://users.netropolis.net/moorish/page13.htm (July 2002) p. 1.
39 Philips, *The Ansaru Cult*, pp. 165–6.
40 Palmer and Luxton, 'The Ansaru Allah Community', p. 367.
41 *Ibid.*, p. 369.

8

FROM EXTRATERRESTRIALS TO ULTRATERRESTRIALS

The evolution of the concept of Ashtar

Christopher Helland

Introduction: the Ministry of Universal Wisdom

By the late 1940s and early 1950s dramatic increases of interest in extraterrestrials and UFOs would create enough enthusiasm for this phenomenon to establish several high-profile UFO groups in the United States. Among these were the Aetherius Society, the Adamski group, and the Unarius Academy of Science. Although not as influential or as well-know now, in the 1950s George Van Tassel (1910–78) created arguably the most prominent of them all, the 'Ministry of Universal Wisdom'.

Prior to this, Van Tassel had an established career as a flight inspector and engineer for Douglas Aircraft, Howard Hughes and, finally, Lockheed. In 1947 he moved with his family to Giant Rock, an area near Yucca Valley, California, where he eventually instituted the most successful and well-known UFO meeting centre of the time, the Ministry of Universal Wisdom. This group, founded in 1953, had its origins in the late 1940s with the establishment of 'The Brotherhood of Cosmic Christ'. This organisation led, in 1950, to the formation of a scientific research ensemble called 'The College of Universal Wisdom', which eventually became, in 1953, 'a science philosophy organization' called the Ministry of Universal Wisdom.

The Ministry of Universal Wisdom promoted itself as a scientific research consortium interested in 'the UFO experience'. Although its research also included investigating and encouraging 'the healing arts', the primary focus was the collecting and analysing of all information relating to the UFO phenomenon. This included a significant number of interviews with individuals who claimed to have been contacted by extraterrestrials. As a result of the great popular interest in his ideas, particularly the interest of radio and television stations, Van Tassel became the most well-known promoter of contactee experiences, making him something of a celebrity in the 1950s. He lectured widely about UFO activity, and promoted his own encounters in his 1952 book *I Rode a Flying Saucer! The Mystery of the Flying Saucers Revealed*[1] – which is a deceptive title, since here he does not claim actually to have ridden in a flying saucer. Having said that, in the following year, 1953, he did claim to have finally experienced flight in a flying saucer. Nevertheless, the experiences he reported in 1952 would set the stage for a large contactee movement based at his property at Giant Rock.

It was also in 1952 that Van Tassel began to receive extraterrestrial messages via a telepathic connection which introduced to the UFO and metaphysical communities a being called Ashtar.[2] Thus it was not a traditional form of UFO contact that was being claimed, but rather a much more esoteric form of communication, similar to 'channelling' which claims that spirit entities communicate through specially sensitive individuals (mediums/channels). Having said that, Van Tassel played down the mystical nature of his communications, believing that he was presenting, rather than some new form of religion or science, an expansion of 'those things already accepted'. He claimed that he was telepathically receiving transmissions from advanced extraterrestrial devices. Consequently, he argued, this is a case of technology at its finest, rather than metaphysical or paranormal activity. As to his ability to receive these messages, he argued that extra-sensory perception (ESP) is a normal human ability. That he, rather than anyone else, received these messages was simply because he was 'in resonance' with the messages being sent. Indeed, he was psychologically attuned to be a channel for intergalactic beings. That said, he taught that, not only did he need to practise meditation techniques (which he had developed) in order to maintain and improve this contact, but he also believed that his techniques could be taught to others. Consequently, people would travel to Giant Rock for training sessions and retreats at the 'Ministry of Universal Wisdom'. Also at the Ministry, he held weekly channelling sessions, during which those assembled would ask questions, channel answers, and give detailed accounts of life on other planets and in other star systems. Almost inevitably, the gatherings led, in spring 1953, to the organisation of the first of many Giant Rock Spacecraft Conventions. These conventions, which were extremely successful (at one point having as many as 10,000 attendees), would continue on a regular basis for the following 30 years. During these conventions, most of the well-known UFO contactees attended as speakers, giving their accounts of extraterrestrial contact and even channelling messages from outer space for those gathered. Indeed, it was during these first channelling sessions that the figure of Ashtar gained prominence.

In Van Tassel's early messages, Ashtar spoke with a great deal of apocalyptic concern over the development and testing of the hydrogen bomb. According to the messages, detonation of this device would trigger catastrophic destruction – destruction which would have implications not just for Earth, but also for this section of the galaxy! Indeed, he claimed that it was principally to prevent this from occurring that he was contacted by Ashtar. Furthermore, he wasn't simply to convey an apocalyptic warning, but he was also given instructions and information to pass on to the American government. The first of these messages from Ashtar was channelled on 18 July 1952:

> Hail to you, beings of Shan [Earth]. I greet you in love and peace. My Identity is Ashtar, Commandant Quadra sector, patrol station Schare, all projects, all waves ... When they explode the hydrogen atom, they shall extinguish life on this planet. They are tinkering with a formula they do not comprehend. ...They are destroying a Life-giving element of the Creative Intelligence. Our message to you is this: You shall advance to your government all information we have transmitted to you ... We are not concerned with man's desire to continue war on this planet, Shan. We are concerned with their deliberate determination to extinguish humanity and turn this planet into a cinder.

Needless to say, Van Tassel's attempts to influence the US government and the scientific community did not progress well. Consequently, further messages reflected this tension. Quite early in the channelling sessions, the teachings from Ashtar began to develop into a complicated mythic narrative that recognised Earth governments as negative or dark organisations bent on controlling humankind. As the story unfolds, Ashtar is viewed as a liberating physical force in conflict with negative space beings that are influencing the Earth and its inhabitants. Despite this conflict, the Ashtar forces are presented as being obviously superior in battle capabilities and relatively impervious to attempts to thwart their mission. On 3 August 1952, the message from Van Tassel began as follows:

> Our efforts are in the cause of peace, true peace. Many of your higher authorities throughout the nations of the planet Shan

have lost all comprehension of the word 'peace', for they are under the influence of the forces of darkness. The first thought that enters the minds of those in this darkness is not to find out what the other object of our visitation is, but rather to destroy us, to find out what we are made of. We can assure you that all their efforts, made with the objects of destruction, will avail them naught ... We are not desirous of staging a show but I will inform you that if opposition forces, mortal or otherwise, persist in their efforts we can put 100,000 units a second in operation.

These early messages also reflect the secular manner in which Van Tassel and the Ministry of Universal Wisdom viewed extraterrestrials. Messages are replete with technical jargon and pseudoscientific information. Ashtar and the forces that have accompanied him to Earth were presented, not just as warriors, but also as advanced scientists willing to share information with all who are willing to listen. The following message of 15 August 1952 reflects this position:

This release of free hydrogen into the atmosphere of this planet, will cause flames to engulf many portions of this planet momentarily. Those in authority, in the governments, are assuming direct responsibility, not only for the people inhabiting this planet, but their own immediate families, wives, children, parents and relatives are also their responsibility, for these dear ones shall not escape. You in authority, of the governments of the planet Shan, think twice if you would have your loved ones with you. Consult your physicists, ask them about the parallel condition of frozen equilibrium. They will inform you, if they speak the truth and are not influenced otherwise, by the forces of darkness, that this is truth. Wake up, you who would believe only those who direct you. Stand before the people. Tell those who influence your mental decisions, that they too are involved. In the light of love, I transmit you a continuous beam here, through a *ventla* which has been stationed in this cone of receptivity at a level 72,000 miles above you, beyond reach of any traps. I shall return, my love, I am Ashtar.

Despite the efforts and obvious concerns of Van Tassel and the Ministry, the first hydrogen bomb was exploded by the United States government at Enewetak in the South Pacific on 1 November 1952.

Russia followed with a similar test in Siberia during 1953. Despite Ashtar's failed prophecy concerning the wholesale destruction of life on Earth following the detonation of the bomb, the channelled messages continued. However, perhaps inevitably, there was a shift *from* concern with the hydrogen bomb tests and extraterrestrial intervention to prevent the destruction of Earth *to* details regarding the way Ashtar's forces had been able to assist the planet in surviving the crisis. In fact, according to messages channelled after the test, a great effort was now under way to repair any of the damage caused by the bomb. On 13 February 1953 Van Tassel communicated the following message to his group:

> I am Ashtar, Commandant Vela Quadra sector, station Schare. You have just heard the authority granted by Schonling Lord God of the 3rd dimensional sector, for our authority to take corrective measures. We are creating a Light energy vortices near the planet Shan in an effort to stabilize your planet. This effort requires the combined forces of 86 projections, 9100 waves, of 236,000 ventlas. Needless to say this vortices is going to create extensive damage to counteract the unbalance man has created on Shan. Our center extends to you their love and blessings. My Light, I am Ashtar.

One of the most controversial aspects of Van Tassel's teaching was his interpretation of the Bible. Although this manner of interpretation is not particularly novel now, having being made famous by Erich von Däniken in his book *Chariots of the Gods?* (1968)[3] and later promoted by other UFO religious groups such as the Raëlian movement, in the 1950s it did create a stir. Essentially, he believed the Bible to contain true information concerning extraterrestrial activity upon the planet, information that has been misinterpreted and misrepresented by the dominant religious authorities.

Van Tassel frequently referenced biblical narratives and would cite passages he alleged supported his view that advanced beings from other planets had been visiting Earth since ancient times. For example, reflecting on Genesis, he argued that there was evidence within the narrative that humanity had extraterrestrial origins and belonged to a race which had been 'seeded' throughout the cosmos. Humankind was placed upon Earth as part of a continuing cycle of evolution and development. However, the original 'Adamic race' 'fell from grace'. In the following passage he seeks to explain his thesis:

For the first time God is left out of the equation and we have a 'Lord God' (Heb. Jehovah Elohim). This character was one of the Adamic race who was in the colony that had been landed here by spacecraft. The men of the Adamic race did not bring their women with them when they first landed on Earth ... The Lord God brings Eve into the picture – not the Creator. The Lord God said that the Adamic men were lonesome (Gen. 2:18) ... Then the Lord God pops Eve out of a rib after one of their people fell into deep sleep (Gen. 2:21–2). God brings about the creation of people through birth everywhere in the Universe, not by making women out of ribs. The race of Eve were the highest form of lower animal life on the planet. They were not apes, but they were also not the race of man, created by God.[4]

His teachings concerning Jesus were, unsurprisingly, equally controversial, in that he viewed Jesus as a being from space that volunteered to help humankind. Van Tassell believed that 'the conditions of Earth require outside intervention'. Consequently, Jesus was viewed as a more evolved being that came to Earth to assist in delivering humankind from the planet. Jesus did not die, but rather was 'taken up on the transistor beam' after he had established the foundation for his cosmic return, which was to occur in conjunction with a fleet of spacecraft in the 1950s. To support this narrative, Mary, as the mother of Jesus, is also understood to be a space being who 'became pregnant and was landed on Earth by the space people'. Similarly, the three wise men who followed 'the spacecraft called the Star of Bethlehem' were higher beings sent to supervise the birth.

By reading carefully Matthew 1:18–25, it is plain that Joseph became the husband of Mary 'before they came together' and after 'she was found with child'. In Matthew 1:25 it is made clear that Joseph 'knew her not'. It is evident that Joseph was the same as a stepfather to Jesus. There was no blood of Joseph in Jesus.

Mary is one of the space people; one of the 'male and female' that God created (Gen. 1:27) before He ended His Work (Gen 2:2), and before the crossbreeding of Adam and Eve took place.

Mary volunteered for the assignment of bringing, through birth, to the Earth, a son of the Adamic race of man. Jesus also accepted the assignment knowing before his Earthly birth what it entailed.[5]

This particular interpretation of Christian belief was based upon Van Tassel's spiritual and religious philosophy. The Ministry of Universal Wisdom taught a form of pantheism informed by a concept of Universal Mind. According to this system of belief, God is interpreted as 'the Mind Force' that expanded out and created all things through the process of his own thought. In Van Tassel's words, 'God is the infinity of an endless *electrical universe* that *thought* atoms, solar systems and galaxies into being. Humans are *thought forms of God's* creation of individual life forms.'[6] After the creation, God entered a period of rest when Universal Mind became neutral, or static, waiting for individuals to activate it. In this way, 'each person is a center of activity in the static mind of God'. Van Tassel taught that all individuals have the ability to tap into this Universal Mind and thereby be in harmony ('resonance') with the creative power of the cosmos, because they are in fact a physical manifestation of this power with the ability to 'command, select to improve, or maintain [their] dominion'. Moreover, this harmonious relationship with the Universal Mind facilitates evolutionary progress. Consequently, according to this cosmology, as a result of a superior relationship with Universal Mind, extraterrestrial life forms such as Ashtar are at an advanced evolutionary stage.

Developing this thesis in a more spiritualistic direction, Van Tassel claimed that he could receive information, not just from extraterrestrials, but also, by accessing the Universal Mind, from humans who had long since passed away. Perhaps the most significant example of such a contact was with the scientist Nikola Tesla, a famous and revolutionary inventor from the turn of the twentieth century. The messages Van Tassel received from Tesla comprised instructions to build a machine that had the ability to 'recharge energy into living cell structure'. He called the machine (a four-storey building, 55 feet in diameter with a domed roof) 'the integratron', and claimed that, not only would it rejuvenate a human and add decades to a lifespan, but also it could act as a time machine.

Ashtar Command: attempts to initiate a movement

While the weekly channelling sessions were occurring at Giant Rock, a division developed within the group over the messages being received from Ashtar. The concept of 'the Ashtar Command' had quickly become popular among many prominent contactees and channellers, and a number of people began presenting information based upon the figure Van Tassel had first promoted. Robert Short (also known as Bill Rose), an editor of the 1950s UFO magazine *Interplanetary News Digest* and a member of the group, believed that Van Tassel should make the Ashtar message more commercial or mainstream by promoting Ashtar's channellings to a greater degree. Van Tassel disagreed and, as a result, Robert Short eventually broke away from the Ministry of Universal Wisdom and started his own group called 'Ashtar Command'.

By the mid-1950s Ashtar and the concept of a galactic law enforcement organisation preparing to rescue humanity had become well-established within UFO religious circles. Many respected individuals from the esoteric channelling milieu began reporting contact with the Ashtar figure, promoting a message of the imminent landing of UFOs and widespread contact. In 1955, Elouise Moeller channelled a question-and-answer session from the Ashtar Command concerning their ships, space travel, life after death and life on Venus. She believed, apparently quite sincerely, that a fleet of spacecraft from the Ashtar Command would be arriving in the near future:

> Questions have been asked why there are not more of the spaceship seen in the skies. We would like to answer that by saying that they are there. It is not necessary for them to be seen in such great numbers at this time for the work. The learning that was occasioned by the sight of our brethren of Earth beholding these shining vessels of love and service to you of Earth in the skies has served its purpose, and they are now on other missions. However, the time will come when great fleets of them, vast armadas, will be seen in the skies, and that will tell you who are drawn so close to our hearts that another phase of our work has begun. At that time we expect the conditions to be propitious for the taking of those who are inwardly prepared on shorter or longer journeys.[7]

This widespread contact reported between the Ashtar Command and humanity led to a great deal of speculation concerning life on the other planets in our solar system, since a number of individuals (including Van Tassel) claimed to have been taken by Venusians aboard their spacecraft. Adelaide J. Brown channelled a number of messages concerning the appearance of spaceships in Earth's atmosphere and life throughout the solar system:

The truth is that almost every planet is inhabited by beings very similar to man. There also is vegetable and animal life. In fact, few of the planets are barren and uninhabitable.

Besides this, many of them have civilizations which far surpass that of any nation on the Earth. It is known by your historians that there have been civilizations on Earth that have fallen and disappeared. Archaeologists are now making discoveries which show that there were marvelously advanced civilizations on the Earth, which for one reason or another were destroyed, and disappeared from the face of the Earth. Their marvelous cities are being uncovered, and much is being learned about the lives of those ancient peoples. Wonderful civilizations like these are now flourishing on many of the planets in this solar system.[8]

This form of focused, topic-specific channelling, however, presents a twofold difficulty. First, as scientific knowledge of the solar system progressed, it became increasingly evident that there was no life, let alone complex and advanced civilisations, flourishing on Venus, Mars or any of the other planets where life had been reported. Second, there was the continued problem of failed prophecy. It seemed clear that messages indicating the imminent arrival of the Ashtar Command forces had been, to say the least, exaggerated. Despite further messages detailing widespread mass landing scenarios, no spacecraft appeared to transport the faithful to higher worlds and higher realms.

These failings took an enormous toll on the Ashtar Command movement, principally because there was no central authority to filter the messages or present a clear response to alleviate the confusion and distress caused by the failed prophecy. Although Robert Short had devoted a significant amount of time and energy to promoting the Ashtar message, he was, strictly speaking, neither the leader nor the only interpreter. Dozens of people were claiming contact with Ashtar (and therefore authority) and presenting conflicting messages.

Tuella keeps the faith

With the continued problems pertaining to the content of messages, the lack of any centralised authority, and even the consolidation of the movement, channelling Ashtar began to wane in popularity. Indeed, the entire concept of the Ashtar Command may have been lost had it not been for the work done by a charismatic channeller named Tuella (the pseudonym of Thelma B. Terrill) in the 1970s and 1980s.

Although she channelled information from traditional theosophical 'Ascended Masters' (e.g. Kuthumi/Koot Hoomi, Saint Germain, Jesus), she also presented continuous information regarding the undertakings of the Ashtar Command and higher galactic extraterrestrial forces. Her two most popular books, *Project World Evacuation* (1982)[9] and *Ashtar: A Tribute* (1985),[10] presented detailed and complex information concerning the unfolding drama that she believed was playing out in the galaxy. Her work presented an epic narrative of battles between good and evil extraterrestrial forces.

In Tuella's initial messages, Ashtar represents a physical manifestation of an extraterrestrial commander. He is very much a 'flesh and blood being', on his way to Earth to assist the evacuation of selected individuals before the onset of widespread apocalyptic destruction. *Project World Evacuation*, which represented a new version of the Ashtar message, was widely circulated before it was published in 1982. Whereas Van Tassel's communications from Ashtar, reflecting his own scientific background, had focused on the testing of the hydrogen bomb, Tuella, a theosophical channeller, communicated a fundamentally 'New Age' message which focused on the destruction of the Earth by 'disruptions in the magnetic field'. These disruptions were caused by thousands of years of negative energy building up in the atmosphere of the planet.

> The hatred, wars, murder, and atomic experiments have all collectively added extra weight in the form of negative energy to poles of your planet, and very soon it is likely to tilt further on its axis, creating destruction to the surface of your planet through resulting Earthquakes, tidal waves, volcanoes, and windstorms of unprecedented velocities.
>
> Most of the people of Earth would be killed – if it were not for us, your space brothers and sisters who are monitoring force and danger to you every moment of your existence.
>
> There are millions, yes, millions of spaceships invisible to your eyes at your present level of 'vibration.' For years we have been encircling your planet; some of our 'mother ships' anchored high in your atmosphere are 100 miles across: These 'mother ships' contain entire cities with gardens, grass, trees, and accommodations for literally millions of people![11]

Tuella developed the Ashtar narrative to include complicated hierarchies of extraterrestrial forces. Her channelling extended an entire mythos enveloping Ashtar and the Ashtar Command. Within this cosmology, Ashtar was directing a fleet of millions of spacecraft involved in the evacuation of planet Earth. In order to survive the forthcoming catastrophe, the human race had to be removed from the planet. Her teachings are therefore 'pretribulationist', in the sense that faithful humans will be evacuated from the surface of the planet prior to apocalyptic catastrophe – those remaining behind will endure years of tribulation and eventual destruction. Only after this has taken place will the Earth be habitable again. After the Earth had passed through this destructive phase, the planet would be reengineered and developed so that those returning will be able to live in a 'golden era'.

> We are very experienced in the evacuation of populations of planets! This is nothing new for the galactic fleet! We expect to complete the evacuation on Earth of the Souls of Light in 15 minutes – even though they are of a tremendous number.
>
> We shall rescue the souls of light first. On our great galactic computers we have stored every thought, every act you have done in this and previous lifetimes. Our computers are locked onto the coordinates where you Souls of Light are located.
>
> After the evacuation ... the invitation will be extended to all remaining souls on the planet to join us.[12]

Despite her enthusiasm in promoting the immanent arrival of the Ashtar Command forces, Tuella would have to adapt her narrative to account for the failed Earth evacuation. This occurred in several ways, the most notable of which was a shift from *direct physical* intervention by Ashtar to *indirect spiritual* assistance from afar. Tuella's message altered accordingly. She spoke less of physical UFOs and increasingly emphasised the spiritual nature of liberation and the religious teachings of Ashtar. In effect, she transferred the Ashtar movement to mainstream theosophical spirituality. Consequently, Ashtar emerged as 'highly evolved in the upper worlds, very influential ... equal to and often beyond the force-field even of Ascended Masters'. In 1983, Tuella made this shift explicit in her book *Lord Kuthumi: World Messages for the Coming Decade*[13] which focuses very clearly upon the need for spiritual salvation, rather than extraterrestrial intervention.

Shortly before her death, Tuella published her final volume of channelled messages, *A New Book of Revelations* (1995),[14] in which, reinterpreting the biblical Book of Revelation, she presents an apocalyptic vision of the future. However, in accordance with the spiritual direction of her thought, she teaches that the human race must make an ascension or transition to a more spiritual state of existence if it is to survive. The idea of a literal evacuation of the Earth is explicitly downplayed as being 'a most difficult task to carry out in light of all that would be involved'.

Further developments

Despite Tuella's shift from extraterrestrial evacuation of the planet to spiritual ascension of humankind to a higher dimension, several Ashtar channellers continued with a more UFO-based cosmology. This made the formation of a cohesive post-Tuella movement problematic. Indeed, even in the 1980s and early 1990s, when Tuella was alive, the Ashtar Command was a factional organisation. Nevertheless, whilst failed prophecies continued, several prominent channellers persisted with the promotion of Earth evacuation scenarios based upon time-specific prophecies.

Yvonne Cole, who had been channelling Ashtar since 1986, warned her followers that the destruction of the planet would occur in 1994. Her channelling promoted the extraterrestrial component of the Ashtar Message, and she promised followers that they were needed for specific duties after contact occurred. These roles included acting as advisers, ambassadors and peacekeepers between the alien races and humankind. She channelled detailed information about the nature of Ashtar's ships and also about the different types of space beings that humankind would encounter after the mass landing event. Her messages were exciting and enthusiastic – unfortunately, they were also wrong! Despite promoting the coming of the Ashtar Command forces for several years, they failed to arrive.

Notwithstanding this major failed prophecy there were still several individuals actively involved with the Ashtar movement. By the mid-1990s these people began using the Internet and then the World Wide Web to communicate their messages and to form a more unified organisation. It was also at this time that a cohesive response was formulated to account for the continuous failed prophecy concerning the arrival of the Ashtar Command space forces.

By using Internet communication to unite a dispersed group of channellers, Ashtar Command was able to lay groundwork concerning the types of messages considered authoritative. A great deal of effort was put into producing a single Ashtar worldview and getting devotees to sing from the same hymn sheet, so to speak. Messages relating to conspiracies (e.g. alien and/or governmental takeovers), apocalyptic scenarios (particularly Earth's destruction), extraterrestrial mass evacuations and general fear-mongering were declared invalid. However, because it was important not simply to identify those devotees who had channelled such messages as charlatans, which would be damaging to the movement, it was claimed that they had been deceived and given false information by those who opposed Ashtar and the forces of good. Indeed, in an attempt (a) to produce some continuity and consistency with previous messages from Ashtar, and (b) to explain contradictory messages from the past, the movement further developed its demonology. That is to say, messages and practices from a previous generation, which were thought not to be consistent with the current cosmology and communications, were attributed to the interference of negative space beings in the upper atmosphere of the planet. More specifically, it was claimed that several young members of Ashtar's training forces had defected and become evil beings. This occurred decades ago when a group of cadets rebelled from the Ashtar Command and formed their own negative extraterrestrial government. These beings made alliances with 'others of similar rebellious nature' and began operating upon the 'lower planes closest to the Earth'. Any messages that had been channelled in the past that contained overly negative information or erroneous dates for landing events were blamed upon these beings.

More significantly – and this was crucial to the formation of an orthodoxy – contemporary channelers began to insist that no more channels 'would be opened' to receive the Ashtar message, unless they were operating upon the 'level of the soul'.

This new 'orthodox' unified group set twelve guidelines to function as a form of mandate for the Ashtar Command movement, something that had never been attempted in the past forty-five years of channelling Ashtar. These guidelines outlined what the movement stood for and clarified the role Ashtar would play in his interactions with society. Although the mandate is an 'overview of the Command's current tasks as they pertain to your world', there is a definite spiritual focus. For example, the fourth point reads as follows:

> We inspire the spiritual expanding of consciousness which allows for a greater understanding of your multi-dimensional Divinity and Divine Function within this vast and inhabited Cosmos.

Ashtar is now presented as a divine figure on a par with Jesus Christ. Indeed, it is not difficult to see the theosophical influence of Tuella on contemporary Ashtar belief.

Lord Ashtar is an Ascended, Immortal and 'Christed' Master. He is of the race of the Adam Kadmon HU-Man and is a Ray emanation or 'son' of the one know as Lord Sananda [Jesus] and His Divine counterpart or twin-Flame, and the one known as Lord Michael and his twin-Flame ... being formed of the combined blending of their Light Codes and Essences.[15]

This new framework recognised that there are millions of spaceships constantly in the vicinity of the Earth, but that those 'guardianships' would never intervene on the planet's surface, unless there was a serious problem such as a third world war or an 'astrophysical catastrophe'. An analysis of messages reveals that Ashtar's influence is becoming increasingly subtle: e.g. 'encouraging the shift from fossil fuel to free energy, and non-polluting energy sources and transportation'.

Again, to reiterate the point, the group which has emerged is shaped by these new guidelines, noticably more spiritually focused and less concerned with extraterrestrial spaceships and visitors. The primary focus of the group is the liberation of the human race by means of a spiritual ascension. Consequently, the introductory material to the new Ashtar Command reads:

The Ashtar Command is a spiritual network of Lightbeings who differ from the Ascended Masters only in that we perceive them as beings of Light that are linked to other planetary star systems, and hence we may regard them as ETs [extraterrestrials]. Their role is also to assist us on a personal, spiritual level.[16]

In fact, very little distinguishes the new Ashtar Command from other theosophy-influenced groups, since, as is the case with the Aetherius Society, they also teach an extraterrestrial cosmology. However, having said that, in 1994, a distinctive component was incorporated into the Ashtar worldview, namely, 'the lift-off experience'.

The 'Pioneer Voyage'

In 1994, a small group of Ashtar Command members claimed that an extraordinary event had taken place: 'the lift-off experience'. What they communicated through the Ashtar network was that they had been taken off Earth and placed aboard the 'ships of Light' that were circling the planet. According to this communiqué, the 'Galactic Fifth Fleet' coordinated a very difficult event, during which members experienced 'physical vibrational transfer'. This involved the human consciousness (or, sometimes, the 'etheric body') being raised from the physical dimension and transferred to the 'Light ships'. This inspired much enthusiasm among the membership, since it was revealed that the event would be replicated through very specific procedures in December of that year.

Over 250 people participated in the second 'lift-off experience', the successful outcome of which was immediately declared by the leadership: 'In manifesting the 2nd Voyage, we have opened a portal to the AC [Ashtar Command] Ships forever.' By claiming that a portal had been opened, anyone involved with the Ashtar Command could now theoretically 'raise their vibration' in order to be transported to these extraterrestrial vessels. The procedure involved in raising one's vibration is quite simple and involves eight steps: Personal protection; Comfortable position; Mantra; Focus; Request; Consciousness transference; Return; and Recall. The mantra used by the group (which is clearly influenced by theosophical teaching) is as follows: 'I AM a guardian of the Light, I AM Love in action here, Co-operating with the Ashtar Command. I AM dedicated to the Kingdom of God on Earth, Interplanetary fellowship, and universal peace.' The Pioneer Voyage would occur during the period of a devotee's meditative state and would later be revealed to the individual in some form of conscious recall.

After the excitement abated, most individuals within the group began to suspect that they hadn't actually been anywhere or done anything during their special meditation. However, a core group of seven Ashtar Command members meeting in Australia began providing detailed accounts of their time aboard the ships. A great amount of information was provided, detailing designs of spaceship, uniforms, living quarters, and other general data that painted a fairly clear picture concerning the Ashtar environment. These experiences were posted on several websites. This information led other members of the group to relate similar experiences. One particularly helpful piece of information that was received and incorporated into the Ashtar worldview was that time did not function in the same manner upon the spaceship as it did upon Earth. This accounted for the fact that a short meditation session could lead to a voyage involving days or even weeks on a spacecraft. Furthermore, members who could not report any form of recall were encouraged to continue with the practice, since they were told that other members of the group had seen them aboard the spaceship.

The concept of the 'Pioneer Voyage' has been extremely successful within the Ashtar movement. In fact, several websites have been developed to allow members to relate and share their narratives, which often include the names of the spacecraft they board, their rank whilst on the vessels (often the Commanding Officer), and their particular association with Ashtar. Despite the increasingly elaborate complexity of the narratives, the general themes remain in accordance with the experiences reported by the group in Australia. Those involved also claim that these events are occurring upon a spiritual or etheric dimension and not a physical one. Consequently, the concept of an extraterrestrial encounter is understood in terms of a fruitful dialogue between humans and more evolved spiritual beings.

Conclusion

One of the most significant aspects of this belief system is that it is based on faith in an extraterrestrial celebrity. Over a period of fifty years the understanding of Ashtar and his forces has shifted considerably. In this sense, Ashtar as a concept has fared much better than any particular group founded upon the messages which Van Tassel or Tuella claimed to receive. Indeed, whilst the content of the messages has changed, Ashtar has remained central, surviving the various groups that have been founded to propagate his message, and the numerous failed prophecies which have come with them.

Perhaps the most significant shifts to have taken place have been as a result of failed prophecy. That channellers of Ashtar have continued to prepare for mass extraterrestrial contact, only to be disappointed, has led to an evolution of beliefs regarding the significance and nature of Ashtar and the liberation he offers. The understanding of Ashtar as a flesh-and-blood extraterrestrial has now been replaced by an understanding of him as a spiritual being, even an Ascended Master. He is a source of spiritual wisdom and enlightenment. Consequently, the present day organisation has embraced the salvific concept of a spiritual union between the human race and advanced spiritual beings, rather than liberation by means of the physical intervention of a fleet of UFOs. Parallel to this has been an evolution of the self-perception of the channellers of Ashtar, which has shifted from the role of eschatological prophets of impending apocalypse to spiritual guides and teachers similar to those within the theosophical tradition.

This spiritualising shift has allowed the Ashtar movement to flourish despite decades of disappointment regarding the non-landing of physical UFOs and scientific scepticism concerning the existence of physical beings on other planets in our solar system.

NOTES

1 G. Van Tassel, *I Rode a Flying Saucer! The Mystery of the Flying Saucers Revealed*, Los Angeles, New Age Publishing, 1952.
2 An introductory discussion of George Van Tassel and Ashtar Command can be found in C. Helland, 'Ashtar Command', in J. R. Lewis (ed.), *UFOs and Popular Culture: An Encyclopedia of Contemporary Myth*, Santa Barbara, ABC-Clio, 2000, pp. 37–40.
3 E. von Däniken, *Chariots of the Gods? Unsolved Mysteries of the Past*, trans. M. Heron, London, Souvenir Press, 1969; originally published in German by Econ-Verlag Gmbh (1968).
4 G. Van Tassel, *When Stars Look Down*, 2nd edn, La Jolla, Trade Service Publications, 1999, pp. 63–4.
5 *Ibid.*, p140
6 *Ibid.*, p18 (emphasis in the original).
7 Tuella, *Ashtar: Revealing the Secret Identity of the Forces of Light and Their Spiritual Mission on Earth*, New Brunswick, Inner Light Publications, 1994, p. 123.
8 T. Green-Beckley (ed.), *Space Gods Speak: An Ashtar Command Book*, New Brunswick, Inner Light Publications, 1992, p. 4.
9 Tuella, *Project World Evacuation by the Ashtar Command*, Utah, Guardian Action Publications, 1982.
10 Tuella, *Ashtar: A Tribute*, Deming, Guardian Action Publications, 1985.
11 *Ibid.*, p52–3.
12 *Ibid.*, p56
13 Tuella, *Lord Kuthumi: World Messages for the Coming Decade*, Deming, Guardian Action Publications, 1983.
14 Tuella, *A New Book of Revelations*, New Brunswick, Inner Light Publications, 1995.
15 A message channelled by 'Athena'. Originally this message was located at http://www.Ashtar.org. This site is no longer operational.
16 Soltec, primary channeler for Ashtar Command. Available online: http://spiritexpress.org/acc/home/acommand.html.

9

UFO FAITH AND UFOLOGICAL DISCOURSES IN GERMANY

Andreas Grünschloß

The gods of antiquity were alien astronauts, nothing else! –
Thus, I have spoken.

Erich von Däniken

With the help of our Star Brothers and Sisters and with the
newly mastered techniques of materialization, dematerializa-
tion, precipitation, etc. we will create … everything needed
for our life. Telepathy will be the everyday language, and time
as we know it on Earth today will no longer be valid … We
will not only be able to use these supernormal techniques, but
we will also learn how to engage in intergalactic space travel.
We will master the use of free cosmic energies and we will
manifest things, food, etc. by free will. Everything will be
possible when we live and act according to the cosmic-divine
laws.

Walter and Theres Gauch-Keller

In a secular industrialized society, visionary experience has to
stage itself in the garment of a technological legend (alien
abduction), comparable to the rural gown of hobgoblin
encounters in the middle ages … Reports about UFO-contacts
are fairy tales, through which the abductee is communicating
with society.

Ulrich Magin

The three statements quoted above are fairly representative of typical
perspectives on and within ufology[1] and UFO faith[2] in Germany,[3]
although the same could probably be said about most other Western
countries.[4] First, there is the discourse on so-called *Prä-Astronautik* or
Paleo-SETI (i.e. the search for extra-terrestrial intelligence in ancient
times), mainly triggered by Erich von Däniken and his epigenous
followers who focus on the supposed Ancient Astronauts' interventions

on Earth by means of alternative archaeological–historical 'research'.[5] Second, we find a whole series of esoteric ufologies with manifest religious significance: from single authors with more or less enthusiastic 'reading circles' to sociologically well-consolidated new religious movements, most of them reporting visionary or telepathic encounters with alien 'masters' and revelations by benevolent 'Star Beings', sometimes implying very strong apocalyptic expectations. And third, there are critical and sceptical observers of UFO sightings, close encounters, abduction stories and UFO faith generally, who dedicate themselves to a more or less rigorous examination and falsification of alleged 'UFO' phenomena.[6] Needless to say, these three perspectives are ideal-typical, since they sometimes overlap and merge. For example, the modern Ancient Astronaut myths, in the style of von Däniken, can also be appropriated by esoteric/religious ufologies (e.g. as a 'Return of the Ancients'[7]), and, vice versa, Paleo-SETI adherents can also show faith in an alternative esoteric religiosity including alien masters, or they might participate in other discourses on contemporary UFO sightings.[8] However, whilst UFO discourses overlap, they are also fractionated and can appear hostile towards each other (e.g. on the one hand, optimistic, but 'sober' UFO reporters attacking 'crazy' esoteric ufologies, and on the other, hard-headed UFO 'sceptics' attack both; or Paleo-SETI authors argue against UFO religious organisations such as the Raëlians[9]).

As in many other Western countries, UFO topics (broadly conceived) have become very popular and can be found on supermarket bookshelves in Germany[10] (e.g. the Roswell mystery, Ancient Astronauts, UFO encounters and abductions), and a recent year-by-year list of UFO-related publications shows an increasing output during the last decade – after the gradual decline following the first UFO boom. That said, at the same time, many aspects of the UFO phenomenon tend to be ignored or dismissed as fakes or delusions by the majority of the public, and, generally speaking, most Germans are unaware of, or know little about, UFO religions – if they know anything, it is usually the result of media reports of the activities of groups such as Heaven's Gate, the Raëlian Religion, or Germany's most prominent UFO-related group, 'Fiat Lux'. However, such reports are often sensational and generally seem to reaffirm the belief that adherents of UFO religions are 'superstitious' or even 'insane'.

The gradual development of German UFO study groups

Following the North American and international UFO boom in the early 1950s, the Deutsche UFO/IFO–Studiengesellschaft[11] (DUIST) was founded as early as 1956 and operated from Wiesbaden during its major phase under the leadership of Karl L. Veit. Although heavily influenced by alternative religiosity (especially the Jacob Lorber movement) and by theosophic/esoteric ufologies, as well as by contactee faith, à la Adamski (the DUIST emblem, for example, includes the typical Adamski flying saucer 'scout') and Ashtar[12] channellings, DUIST was the first (and only) institutionalised forum for all kinds of ufological discourse in Germany and thus greatly influenced the discussion up to the 1970s. From the outset, DUIST was accompanied by the journal UFO-Nachrichten and the publishing house Ventla Verlag in Wiesbaden, which published German translations of many of the modern 'classics' of the American contactee culture, including the works of George Adamski, Daniel Fry, Orfeo Angelucci, Ethil P. Hill, Howard Menger and Tuella (Thelma B. Terrill). It was typical of DUIST to amalgamate UFO sightings, alleged photographs, reports of personal encounters, Ancient Astronaut theories and esoteric channelings into a web of 'proofs' of the existence and Earthly intervention of interplanetary spacecraft with benevolent numinous personnel.

DUIST has also organised several regional and international 'research congresses', selections of the proceedings of which have been published.[13] They exhibit an enthusiastic appraisal of the UFO faith, including many attempts to defend the key players in the contactee movement in America (e.g. Adamski and Fry) who had already faced severe criticism during the formative period of Western ufology. Erich von Däniken, too, just one year before the publication of his bestseller Erinnerungen an die Zukunft (Chariots of the Gods?), was invited to the 1967 convention in Mainz to speak about the astronaut gods of antiquity (his paper was entitled, 'Did Our Ancestors Receive Visitors from Outer Space?'[14]).

Gradually, however, younger UFO enthusiasts became increasingly dissatisfied with the overly uncritical and esoterically-biased UFO faith of the bourgeois 'old men and ladies' of DUIST and, consequently, started to follow their own interests in new private research circles, which were to become an important source of several more-or-less critical UFO study groups. Although never formally dissolved, because its influence waned and also because Karl Veit became increasingly blind, DUIST ceased operations in the late 1980s. There was also, until 1994, a temporary termination of the journal *UFO-Nachrichten*.[15]

Reflecting on his former experiences with DUIST, Werner Walter of the German CENAP (Centrales Erforschungsnetz für Außergewöhnliche Himmelsphänomene[16]) writes: 'There was an increasing criticism of the naive credulity of UFOlogists', which proved to be 'the foundation stone for a new generation of UFO researchers and UFOlogists'.[17] CENAP, one of the new generation of UFO organisations, originated as a private UFO research group in Mannheim, and started officially in 1975 with the magazine *CENAP Report*. Likewise, the Gesellschaft zur Erfoschung des UFO-Phänomens (GEP)[18] had already been founded in 1972 in more or less the same vein. GEP also runs the critical magazine *Journal für UFO-Forschung*. Members of both groups have been active in recent years in the 'Cröffelbach Conventions', where mostly critical UFO researchers meet annually (in Cröffelbach near Heilbronn). The focus of the conferences is, as one might expect, the critical investigation of UFO phenomena. GEP reports that, after investigating between 500 and 700 cases, only 1 per cent of them can be counted as having 'good UFO' probability, and none can be considered as belonging to the 'best UFO' category (i.e. no other interpretation seems possible). Another newer critical UFO group worth noting is the Gesellschaft zur Wissenschaftlichen Untersuchung von Parawissenschaften (GWUP).[19] The founders and members of all these groups come from a range of – often non-academic – backgrounds.

Much more enthusiastic about the existence of UFOs is the German and European branch of the Mutual UFO Network (MUFON) – in Germany called Gesellschaft zur Untersuchung von Anomalen Atmosphärischen und Radar-Erscheinungen (MUFON-CES).[20] Another prominent and enthusiastic UFO group is von Däniken's former Ancient Astronaut Society (AAS), nowadays calling itself Gesellschaft für Archäologie, Astronautik und SETI,[21] with its well-known focus on extraterrestrial intervention and advanced technologies in ancient human history. The AAS journal *Ancient Skies* was founded in 1976, the current German version being *Sagenhafte Zeiten*.[22] Since many Paleo-SETI authors are publishing in German, it is not surprising that this branch of ufology has become particularly popular in Germany, Switzerland and Austria. There are several smaller and regional branches and an abundance of German Paleo-SETI pages on the Internet[23] – including the official online forum of the German AAS[24] and von Däniken's own homepage.[25] In the last few years, German discussions about Paleo-SETI have been significantly increased by von Däniken's prestige project, the huge theme park 'World Mysteries' in Interlaken, Switzerland, which is supposed to open its doors in late 2002.[26] This will no doubt trigger a new phase of public discussions about the Paleo-SETI hypothesis.

Apart from those mentioned above, there are numerous local groups in Germany which meet on a regular basis, as well as various esoteric circles which focus on the channelled messages from the *Sternengeschwister* (star siblings). Such groups would include, for example, Berlin's Santiner Kreis and the various Ashtar-related groups.[27] *UFO Nachrichten* and the various esoteric magazines such as *Esotera* or *Magazin 2000* (especially the latter) provide regular updates of meeting venues and contacts. On the Internet, the server www.alien.de (a good introduction to German discourses on UFOs and UFO faith) provides a range of ufological postings.

The special case of the Paleo-SETI discourse

The people involved in Paleo-SETI discourses are very clear about their own perspective: they don't want to be understood as 'religious', 'sectarian' or 'cultic', but rather perceive themselves to be the spearhead of truly enlightened and unbiased 'scientific' research into ancient human history. This approach can be traced back to Charles Fort and his iconoclastic *Book of the Damned* (first published in 1919, followed by three further volumes)[28] which propagated the idea that 'we are the property' of some mysterious alien force – an esoteric truth which he sought to establish with reference to various anomalistic traces in the world. The Frenchman Robert Charroux developed a similar thesis in his publications. However, it was von Däniken of Switzerland who finally developed and disseminated the idea that the gods of antiquity were nothing but alien astronauts. The quasi-historical investigation of the past and of protological events, which interpreted human religions, creation myths and archaeological remains in terms of a cargo cult-like reverence for humanoid astronauts from outer space, quickly gained an immediate and fascinated following, von Däniken's first book *Erinnerungen an die Zukunft* (1968) becoming an international bestseller. For von Däniken, ancient myths, archaeological remains and certain scriptures are all interpreted as evidence supporting the ancient astronaut hypothesis: e.g. references to ancient spaceships (*vimanas*) and nuclear weapons can be found in the Vedas, the creation myths of Genesis contain memories of alien genetic engineering,[29] and Mayan remains in the pyramid of Palenque are pictorial references to extraterrestrial space flights.[30]

As already mentioned, the Paleo-SETI discourse has institutionalised itself in local and international 'research associations'. The Ancient Astronaut Society Research Association (AASRA) Internet site states: 'The AASRA is determined to prove, using scientific research methods, but in "layman's terms", as to whether or not extraterrestrials have visited Earth in the remote past.'[31] However, the compatibility with critical interpretative science appears extremely small. Without applying sufficient hermeneutic care to the original contexts, selected religious myths and archaeological artifacts are taken primarily at face value in order to 'prove' the thesis that our ancient ancestors have indeed encountered superior alien visitors and their advanced technologies. From an academic religious studies perspective, such heavily biased interpretations of ancient artifacts and texts can themselves be understood as 'neo-mythic' activity – indeed, as the mythic 'foundation' of a modern worldview. Technological explana-tions, projected back into the past, disenchant traditional mythic narratives (such as those of the creation in Genesis), whilst, at the same time, retaining the myths as essentially factual accounts. Apparent falsifications of Paleo-SETI findings, such as the 'light bulbs' of ancient Egypt, or the Mayan relief of a spacecraft pilot, are usually dismissed as unreliable and ambiguous. Indeed, in an editorial to *Sagenhafte Zeiten*,[32] Ulrich Dopatka stated that even 'discarded' evidence should always be considered in the process of evaluation. Thus, dismissing standard academic procedures of critical falsification, Paleo-SETI research must be understood in terms of *popular ideology* and *mythic theory of religion*.

Whilst there is little convincing evidence to support this modern myth about ancient astronaut gods,[33] it is not only a consistent element in contactee spiritualities and other esoteric reconstructions of humanity's religious history, the most prominent contemporary example for this being the Raëlian Religion,[34] but the theory is regu-larly revived in contemporary science-fiction films and literature (e.g. *Stargate* and *Mission to Mars*).[35]

Religious UFO groups

Whilst, as noted above, the Raëlian Religion is possibly the most prominent of UFO organisations, the German branch is relatively small and appears in public mainly at local esoteric fairs. The group itself reports a membership of around 700 (at most). There is no formal centre in Germany (apart from an information address in Müllheim), and, according to the general rules of this move-ment, there is little ritual/spiritual practice on a regular basis – apart from the regular Raëlian 'holidays' and the yearly meetings and seminars.

In Germany there are other, more prominent UFO organisations, perhaps the most prominent being the Fiat Lux community.

Uriella and the Fiat Lux movement

The popularity of Fiat Lux is principally due to several media reports in the press and on television, which focused, not only on the group's religious beliefs, but also on their questionable usage of alleged natural cures and healing potions, as well as related court trials.[36]

Erika Bertschinger, the founder of the movement, was born in Zürich in 1929, and worked as a secretary and interpreter prior to her career as a spiritual healer and charismatic leader. She adopted the 'spiritual name' Uriella, and in the 1970s claimed to have gained (by God's grace) various paranormal faculties such as clairvoyance, remote hearing and remote healing. But she functions primarily as the 'full trance medium' or 'speaking-tube' for esoteric messages from Jesus Christ and, less often, the Virgin Mary.

The 'religious order' Fiat Lux was founded in 1980, and is now located in the southern Black Forest, with centres in the villages of Ibach and Strittmatt (near Waldshut). The movement is made up of an inner circle of 135 full-time members ('*Ordensträger/-innen*'), a second circle of roughly 800 dedicated followers, and, it is estimated, a further 2000 sympathisers. Fiat Lux life is strictly regulated and monastic. Devotees are given a new spiritual name, they wear white (shining) clothing, they observe set times for prayer, they are both celibate and vegetarian, and seek to follow numerous other rules which are believed to maintain 'pure' conduct. The group runs Adsum, a small humanitarian help project which operates particularly in Eastern Europe. The primary religious event is the Sunday service, central to which are Uriella's public 'full trance-revelations', delivered as long speeches (by Jesus) addressed to the assembly. These addresses form a new body of revelation which is regarded as normative and sacred. The Sunday service is followed by separate sessions of spiritual healing.

The Fiat Lux faith is syncretistic and apocalyptic in outlook,[37] including many facets of today's esoteric groups and UFO movements. As is the case with several UFO groups, humanity is understood to live in the end times, facing imminent and apocalyptic natural and political disasters (earthquakes, volcanic eruptions, flooding, global warfare – central to which will be Nazi UFOs currently hidden in the Antarctic). However, the good news of Fiat Lux is that, under the command of Jesus Christ, benevolent space beings (*Santiner*) will evacuate the chosen one-third of humanity before the final 'three dark days'. The evacuation will take place by means of small spherical space ships descending from giant spherical 'motherships', and access will be granted only to spiritually advanced beings with 'refined vibrations'. Even so, during a three-week period following the evacuation, there will be a grand spiritual awakening and purification of the earthly souls on the motherships. Also during this period, the Earth will be transformed into Amora, a paradisiacal planet of new fauna and flora, on which the sunken continents of Atlantis and Mu have been resurrected. The Earth will then be repopulated by the enlightened ones, Christ will return, *yin* and *yang* will be balanced, angels and other numinous beings will be in constant contact, humans will experience an as yet unknown creativity, and new, solely green technologies will be employed.

These events were originally announced for the summer/autumn of 1998,[38] but, in late 1998, Uriella revealed a 'temporary postponement' granted by God. The postponement, she said, was due to the immense praying energies of the faithful. Since then the group has taught a complex of doctrines which include world–society–matter renunciation, an imminent 'golden age', and purification of the soul. Within the supportive enclave of the chosen few, this serves to give meaning to the life of the devotee and increasingly focuses the mind on the teaching of the charismatic leader.

Other forms of UFO-related spirituality

Another post-Christian movement, Universelles Leben (formerly Heimholungswerk Jesu Christi) serves as an example of how UFO-related beliefs can be incorporated within a principally non-ufological religious organisation without changing the religious outlook of the group on the whole. Whilst the practices and beliefs of this group, which are based on the revelations of Gabriele Wittek (b. 1933),[39] are not fully accessible to outsiders, in the early 1980s it was being claimed that messages of a 'Brother Mairadi' from the planet 'Chuli' were being received, which warned humanity of imminent apocalyptic and eschatological events.[40] However, there was also a message of salvation. Brother Mairadi and his ethereal siblings will, it is claimed, assist Jesus in his salvific work. They will, for example, dispatch a *Strahlungsglocke* (beam-globe), which will protect Earthlings from the harmful side-effects of the eschatological apocalypse. As in the case of Fiat Lux, esoteric teachings and pseudo-Christian apocalyptic beliefs are amalgamated here with elements of ufology. That said, whilst the group does not play down its ufological beliefs, even advertising its 'scriptures' in *UFO-Nachrichten*, the ufological discourse does not appear to play a major role in the faith as a whole.

It would probably be true to say that UFO-related channelling and mediumship has permeated most strands of German esoteric spirituality, as well as the various New Age networks and fairs in Germany. Indeed, during the 1990s, a popular Ashtar-related mission brochure entitled *Aufruf an die Erdbewohner* (*Appeal to the Earth-People*) was distributed throughout German esoteric networks. It included an illustration depicting the typical 'big beam scenario' of the apocalyptic days prior to the 'New Age' of a paradisiacal Earth.[41] Human beings are beamed aboard small, disc-shaped 'lightbeam ships' which descend from large, cigar-shaped motherships approaching the Earth in the formation of giant crosses. Also significant for the propagation of ufological ideas in Germany has been the 'Frankfurter Ring'. An alternative pedagogic institution and forum for all kinds of esoteric spiritualities in the city of Frankfurt, it presents a range of UFO faith-related seminars in its annual programme.[42] Again, as well as the various Ashtar circles and Lightwork/I AM organisations in Germany which teach UFO beliefs, there are numerous small local groups oriented around charismatic individuals (often mediums/channels) which incorporate ufological beliefs: e.g. Metharia in the Eckernförde region, Weltuniversität of Heide Fittkau-Garthe in Hamburg, and Universelles Lichtzentrum Erde in Gütersloh.

Interestingly, there are also some ufological strands in neo-pagan German religiosity[43] which combine a seemingly 'nativistic' quest for an *artgemäße* (racially appropriate) religion and the search for the mythic civilisations of Thule and Atlantis[44] with legends about secret Nazi UFOs from the Third Reich. As we have seen to be the case with Fiat Lux, the claim is often made that there is to a secret Nazi flying-saucer base located in the Antarctic (a belief which is sometimes combined with hollow-Earth theories).[45] Often these 'flying discs' (*Flugscheiben*) resemble the Adamski type of saucer and are called *Haunebu* or *Vril*.[46]

As Mikael Rothstein discusses in his essay in this volume (Chapter 13), there are ufological elements within Scientology's myths, elements that sometimes emerge during their formal auditing sessions. Scientology's German splinter community, Freie Zone,[47] which was formed following the departure of 'Captain' Bill Robertson, formerly a close collaborator of L. Ron Hubbard, still has many explicitly UFO-related teachings on its web pages.[48] These are interesting because they shed some light on the enthusiasm for ufology and science fiction which was cultivated in the formative phase of Scientology. Indeed, even the highly arcane story of the intergalactic ruler Xenu who packed souls ('Thetans') into the Earth's volcanoes (a part of secret Operation Thetan III teachings) is related by Hubbard in the style of a simple science-fiction novel (not officially published, but, until recently, it could be read on unauthorised Internet sites).

Concluding remarks

In many ways German UFO religion is not particularly exceptional compared to that of other Western industrial societies. Most of what can be said about UFO religions elsewhere in the West is also true of German groups. As in much UFO religion from the formative period in the 1950s, German revelations and channelled messages can be traced back to theosophy and spiritualism. Similarly, technological imagery and metaphors are used to reinterpret traditional religious and folkloric beliefs, be they apocalyptic fears, eschatological hopes, revelations from higher spiritual entities, or the search for a theosophical gnosis which will overcome the frustrations, the worries and the impermanence of everyday human existence (i.e. the 'ascension' of the 'spiritual' over the 'material'). Whether one thinks of Scientology's 'religious technology', or the 'prayer batteries' of the Aetherius Society, as in all forms of UFO faith, within German UFO belief there is a synthesis of the modern technological *Weltanschauung* and traditional religious aspirations. Fiat Lux's Uriella, for example, whilst emphasising the spiritual nature of her messages, uses technological metaphors and images (e.g. 'photons of Light' are supposedly being channelled through the Eucharist).

In millenarian versions of UFO faith, angelic alien beings from higher spheres approach mankind, bringing both enlightenment and what might be understood as 'cargo' in the form of superior technologies. Their arrival heralds a new world, a technological utopia understood religiously in terms of paradise – spiritual and technological perfection are finally merged. Indeed, spirituality can, to some extent, progress by technical means ('angelic tools') – and, at the same time, the 'cold' world of the modern scientific worldview is re-enchanted. The celestial beings and mythical heroes[49] return with their fascinating alien cargo.[50] That said, we have seen that ufological re-enchantment does not mean the return of traditionally supernatural beliefs. Apparently numinous beings from outer space are often regarded as humanoid astronauts. Hence, in effect, UFO religion promotes a disenchanting euhemerism[51] founded on a mythic history.[52] However, despite any technological metaphors and anti-supernaturalism, one can easily detect the 'religious' quest for meaning, truth and authentic revelation. UFO faith, therefore, can be understood to oscillate between *disenchantment* and *re-enchantment*.

Furthermore, the prospect of being able to appropriate new power, control and meaning (including paranormal faculties, superior gnosis, membership in the millennial ground crew, etc.) is highly compatible with optimistic fantasies of technological evolution and increasing scientific control. UFO faith can appear highly attractive and even plausible within our modern industrial 'cultures of narcissism', where the individual often struggles for meaning in a thoroughly meaningless and technological world. It is not difficult to understand how, in contexts of economic vulnerability, socio-cultural discomfort and obscurity, the promises of UFO religions can appear very appealing. The individual becomes a 'star seed', a 'light worker', or a Thetan, located 'above' the merely material world with all its complexities; as a new-born being a person enters a new social circle, becoming a member of an enlightened élite. Whilst different groups tend to attract different sorts of people (e.g. in Germany, Fiat Lux's revelations and promises of healing seem to appeal to less affluent and less educated people, whereas more successful and educated individuals are attracted by Scientology's cool technological and efficient image), despite all their differences in detail, religious ufologies express a common theme, namely, the search for an integral vision of reality, in which there is a 'synthesis of science and religion'.

NOTES

1   *A note on terminology.* In this essay, 'ufology', like the adjective 'ufological', is used as a handy umbrella term in the broadest sense, referring to all kinds of discourses – including critical ones – dealing with alleged alien spacecraft, alien astronauts or other extraterrestrial beings from space or other dimensions, even if the groups associated with the discourses hesitate to use the 'ufology' label themselves (e.g. Paleo-SETI believers). 'UFO faith' is used more specifically to indicate a positive affirmation of alien craft or extraterrestrial beings (and related encounters or interventions, including 'channellings' and alien 'revelations'), even if this faith presents itself in the form of an alternative science or research project, rather than a primarily 'religious' endeavour.

2   See A. Grünschloß, *Wenn die Götter landen … Religiöse Dimensionen des UFO-Glaubens*, EZW-Texte 153, Berlin, EZW, 2000, and my contribution to J. R. Lewis (ed.), *The Encyclopedic Sourcebook of UFO Religions*, Amherst, ABC-Clio, 2002. An earlier version of the latter article is accessible through the academic Internet resource *Marburg Journal of Religion*

3:2, 1998 (www.unimarburg.de/religionswissenschaft/journal/mjr/ufogruen .html).

3 UFO faith in Germany has not been treated in a scholarly way so far. That said, there is some relevant discussion in E. Benz, *Außerirdische Welten: Von Kopernikus zu den Ufos*, Freiburg, Aurum, 2000. A non-academic bibliographical survey and useful tool for the study of ufological discourses in Germany is Dieter von Reeken, *Bibliographie der selbständigen deutschsprachigen Literatur über Außerirdisches Leben, UFOs und Prä-Astronautik*, Lüdenscheid, GEP, 1996; see also his website which includes regular updates: http://home.t-online.de/home/dieter.reeken-lg

4 Cf. J. R. Lewis (ed.), *UFOs and Popular Culture: An Encyclopedia of Contemporary Myth*, Santa Barbara, ABC Clio, 2000; J. R. Lewis (ed.), *The Gods Have Landed: New Religions from Other Worlds*, Albany, State University of New York Press, 1995. In the latter volume, see especially the essay by J. A. Saliba, 'Religious Dimensions of UFO Phenomena', pp. 15–64.

5 See P. Andersson, 'Ancient Astronauts', in Lewis (ed.), *UFOs and Popular Culture*, pp20–5.

6 A good orientation is provided in J. Clark, *The UFO Encyclopedia*, 2 vols, Detroit, Apogee Books, 1997, as well as in his more concise *The UFO Book: Encyclopedia of the Extraterrestrial*, Detroit, Apogee Books, 1998.

7 See Norman Paulsen, *Sunburst – Return of the Ancients*, Goleta, Sunburst Farms Publishing Co., 1980. The volume provides interesting insights into the formative phase of his Sunburst community (or Brotherhoood of the Sun) as well as into the Paleo-SETI-like foundation mythology. Later editions of the volume appeared under the title *The Christ-Consciousness*, but without some of the strongly ufological and apocalyptic passages. Cf. G. Trompf, 'The Cargo and the Millennium on Both Sides of the Pacific', in G. Trompf (ed.), *Cargo Cults and Millenarian Movements*, Berlin, Mouton De Gruyter, 1990, pp35–94. See also Trompfs discussion in Chapter 11.

8 In Germany, the publications of Walter-Jörg Langbein function as a bridge between traditional 'hard core' Paleo-SETI speculations and spiritual reflections on contemporary UFO sightings or the quest for a 'cosmic' religiosity. See his *Götter aus dem Kosmos*, Rastatt, Moewig, 1998, and *Am Anfang war die Apokalypse. Warum wir Kinder der Astronauten wurden*, Lübeck, Bohmeier, 2000.

9 L. A. Fischinger and R. M. Horn, *UFO-Sekten*, Rastatt, Verlagsunion Pabel Moewig KG, 1999. Although written from a Paleo-SETI-friendly perspective and including many dismissive statements of faith perspectives, the volume offers a good overview of UFO religions. Including interviews with persons active in the UFO community, it offers a good introduction to the various German ufological perspectives. See also the following website: www.alien.de/fischinger/UFO-Esoterik.html.

10 C. G. Jung provided a psychological interpretation from his particular perspective back in 1958. See C. G. Jung, *Flying Saucers: A Modern Myth of Things Seen in the Skies*, trans. R. F. C. Hull, New York, Signet Books/New American Library, 1969 (German original: *Ein Moderner Mythus: Von Dingen, die am Himmel gesehen werden*, Stuttgart/Zürich, Rascher, 1958). For an overview of Jung's interpretation see Chapter 16 of

this volume.

11 German UFO and IFO Study Society. 'IFO' stands for 'identified flying object' (i.e. 'interplanetary' spacecraft).

12 See e.g. G. Van Tassel, *I Rode a Flying Saucer! The Mystery of the Flying Saucers Revealed*, Los Angeles, New Age Publishing, 1952. The emergence of the Internet has seen an increase in Ashtar channellings; see C. Helland, 'Ashtar Command', in Lewis (ed.), *UFOs and Popular Culture*, pp. 37–40; see also Helland's discussion in Chapter 8 of this volume.

13 Still available through Turmalin-Verlag (Ventla Verlag Wiesbaden Nachfolger) in Gütersloh are: *Dokumentarbericht – 7: Internationaler Weltkongreß der UFO-Forscher in Mainz 1967*, Wiesbaden, Turmalin-Verlag, 1968; *Dokumentarbericht – 10: Internationaler Interner Kongreß der UFO-Forscher, Wiesbaden 1972*, Wiesbaden, Ventla-Verlag, 1973; *Dokumentarbericht – 11: Internationaler Interner Kongreß der UFO-Forscher, Wiesbaden 1975*, Wiesbaden, Ventla-Verlag, 1976.

14 See *Dokumentarbericht – 7: Internationaler Weltkongreß der UFO-Forscher in Mainz 1967*, pp. 94–7.

15 Since 1994 it has been published in Obergünzburg (near Kempten). The publishing house Ventla Verlag in Wiesbaden was transferred to the Turmalin Verlag in Gütersloh and is incorporated there under the name Ventla Verlag Nachfolger.

16 Central Research Web for Extraordinary Aerial Phenomena.

17 See http://www.alien.de/cenap/historisches/historisches1.htm (June 2002).

18 Society for Investigation into the UFO Phenomenon: www.ufo-forschung.de; www.alien.de/gep.

19 Society for Scientific Research into Para-sciences. Available online: http://www.gwup.org.

20 Available online: http://www.mufon.com; www.mufon-ces.org.

21 Research Association for Archaeology, Astronautics and SETI: http://www.aas-fg.org; international website: http://www.aas-ra.org.

22 Paleo-SETI research is also published in *UFO-Nachrichten*.

23 See, e.g.: http://www.mysteria3000.de; http://www.alien.de/fischinger;http://www.alien.de/langbein; or, from a more critical perspective: http://www.alien.de/richter. Most members of the German Giordano Bruno Society are also Paleo-SETI adherents: see http://www.giordano-bruno-gesellschaft.de.

24 http://www.rede-mit.de/aas.

25 http://www.daniken.com.

26 http://www.mysterypark.ch.

27 On Ashtar-related groups, see Chapter 8 of this volume.

28 See C. Fort, *The Book of the Damned*, London, John Brown, 1995.

29 This is one of the beloved standard topics (also appearing in the Raëlian Religion). For a recent exposition see L. A. Fischinger, *Götter der Sterne: Bibel, Mythen und kosmische Besucher*, Weilersbach, Reichel, 1997.

30 There exists a real abundance of books on these topics – by von Däniken himself, as well as by other writers in the Paleo-SETI tradition (e.g. Walter-Jörg Langbein, Lars Fischinger, Ulrich Dopatka), many of them publishing only in German. See Andersson, 'Ancient Astronauts', and, for a good recent critical investigation into von Däniken's research, see M. Pössel, *Phantastische Wissenschaft. Über Erich von Däniken und Johannes von*

Buttlar, Reinbek, Rowohlt, 2000. Ulrich Dopatka has compiled a helpful (non-academic) encyclopedia of Paleo-SETI theories: *Die große Erich von Däniken Enzyklopädie: Das einzigartige Nachschlagewerk zur Prä-Astronautik*, Düsseldorf, Econ, 1997. There was also an interactive CD-ROM published as the 'official reference work of the Ancient Astronaut Society': *Kontakt mit dem Universum. Mysteries of the World*, CD ROM, Taufkirchen, Magellan Entertainment, n.d.

31 See the opening page of http://www.aas-ra.org.

32 *Sagenhafte Zeiten* 2 (2001).

33 See Walter-Jörg Langbein, *Astronautengötter: Versuch einer Chronik unserer phantastischen Vergangenheit*, Berlin, Ullstein Buchverlage GmbH & Co., 1995.

34 The first book by Claude Vorilhon (Raël), *Le livre qui dit la verité* (1974) appeared soon after the first paradigmatic books of Robert Charroux and Erich von Däniken. Raëlian creationism is discussed in detail in Chapter 2 of this volume.

35 As noted above, Paleo-SETI theorists themselves often toy with additional esoteric reconstructions of their *Weltanschauung*. Indeed, Erich von Däniken himself wrote a book propagating a highly esoteric anthropology, where all kinds of religious visions (especially from his own Catholic background), revelations and miracles are interpreted as a basic human capacity (created by aliens, of course) to communicate with higher realms. See *Erscheinungen: Phänomene, die die Welt erregen*, Düsseldorf und Wien, Econ-Verlag, 1974, pp. 273ff; *Miracles of the Gods: A Hard Look at the Supernatural*, London, Souvenir Press, 1975.

36 To my knowledge there exists no academic treatment of this movement. The only book so far available is written from a strongly Christian apologetic perspective: G. Grandt, M. Grandt and K.-M. Bender, *Fiat Lux: Uriellas Orden*, München, Evangelischer Presseverband für Bayern, 1992. That said, it does contain some important material.

37 The following observations are based on several transcripts of Uriella's revelations and copies of the journal *Der heiße Draht* (now called *Der reinste Urquell*), as well as a video production, *Uriellas Abenteuer mit Gott im Orden Fiat Lux!*, distributed by the group.

38 This period was, significantly, also an important time for Ashtar-related organisations.

39 See especially G. Wittek, *Das ist mein Wort A und Ω*, Würzburg, Universelles Leben, 1993. The latest survey of Universelles Leben (and its literature) is provided by Matthias Pöhlmann in R. Hempelmann *et al.* (eds), *Panorama der neuen Religiosität*, Gütersloh, Gütersloher Verlagshaus, 2001, pp. 567–72.

40 See the brochure *Auch die Brüder aus teilmateriellen Bereichen des Universums dienen im Erlösungswerk des Sohnes Gottes*, published by Heimholungswerk Jesu Christi (1981). Universelles Leben publishes a magazine entitled *Das Friedensreich*.

41 Walter Gaucher-Keller and Theres Gauch-Keller, *Aufruf an die Erdbewohner. Erklärungen zur Umwandlung des Planeten Erde und seiner Menschheit in der 'Endzeit'*, Ostermundingen, 1992. There is also an English translation entitled *Appeal to the Earth People*, Ostermundingen, 1996. Both editions are obtainable directly from the authors: W. and Th. Gauch-

Keller, Forelstrasse 54, CH–3072 Ostermundigen; the German text is also accessible on the Internet: http://www.ichbinliebe.de/aufruf.

42 See http://www.frankfurter-ring.org.

43 For an overview, see S. von Schnurbein, *Religion als Kulturkritik: Neugermanisches Heidentum im 20. Jahrhundert*, Heidelberg, Winter, 1992; F. Hundseder, *Wotans Jünger: Neuheidnische Gruppen zwischen New Age und Rechtsradikalismus*, München, Heyne Wilhelm Verlag GMBH, 1998; N. Goodrich-Clark, *Black Sun: Aryan Cults, Esoteric Nazism and the Politics of Identity*, New York, New York University Press, 2002.

44 F. Wegener, *Das atlantidische Weltbild. Nationalsozialismus und Neue Rechte auf der Suche nach der versunkenen Atlantis*, Gladbeck, Kulturförderverein Ruhrgebiet, 2001.

45 Ernst Zündel, Jan Udo Holey (Jan van Helsing) and 'old Nazi' Wilhelm Landig seem to be the major sources for legends about alleged Nazi saucers during the Third Reich, which are supposed to be hidden in the Antarctic.

46 See, e.g. www.luftarchiv.com/domain/ufo, or www.reichsflugscheiben.de Putting words like *Flugscheibe*, Nazi-UFO, *Haunebu* or *Vril* into Internet search engines will produce many other results.

47 http://www.freezone.de.

48 These ufological issues are developed under the heading *Schach der Erde*; see especially http://www.freezone.de/sde/sde_inh.htm.

49 See Ernst Benz's informed historical analysis of the UFO experience: *Außerirdische Welten*, especially, pp. 119–34; it was formerly entitled *Kosmische Bruderschaft. Die Pluralität der Welten: Zur Ideengeschichte des Ufo-Glaubens*, (1978).

50 Cf. A. Grünschloß, 'Cargo Cults', in Lewis (ed.), *UFOs and Popular Culture*, pp. 60–3. See also Garry Trompf's essay in Chapter 11 of this volume.

51 Euhemeros of Messana claimed, in antiquity, that nothing but ordinary 'men' became gradually deified because of their merits (*apotheosis*) and were, thus, faithfully revered as true 'gods'. Likewise, in the Paleo-SETI worldview, human religions are reconstructed as a cargo cult-like imitation of ancient humanoid astronauts, their deeds and technological devices.

52 For example, it is the declared goal of von Däniken to give ancient religious traditions and myths simply a 'technological and modern explanation': *Auf den Spuren der Allmächtigen*, München, Orbis, 1993, p. 189.

10

THE FINNISH UFO TRADITION, 1947–94

Jaakko Närvä

Several different views can be taken as to the beginning of the Finnish UFO tradition. Perhaps a good starting point is the year 1934, because during that year there was an impressive occurrence of UFO sightings in Scandinavia and Finland. However, a Finnish army investigation concluded that it was the result of mass psychosis.[1] In 1946 there was again a puzzling wave of UFOs experienced in Scandinavia, due to which the Swedish army was put on alert. Indeed, along with public interest, such was the official concern that several northern countries forbade the press to identify places where it was claimed that UFOs had been seen.[2] However, whilst these are interesting isolated events, I am going to begin with the year that is commonly considered to be the beginning of the modern UFO era, namely 1947.[3]

1947–60: background to the Finnish UFO movement

At the beginning of July 1947, Finnish newspapers reported strange sightings in the United States of America and some other countries.[4] The first Finnish reports of these events appeared on 6 July 1947, in the daily paper *Uusi Suomi*: 'In the middle parts of western America hundreds of people say that they have seen mystical "flying saucers", when at the same time many people around the country are speaking about "shining objects, which resemble a saucer" that have whistled across the sky at a high altitude.' The article also stated that the first report was provided by Mr Kenneth Arnold from Boise, Idaho, and that the flying saucers had been observed from the air, from the ground by several police patrols, by a group of people in Idaho, and by a person in the state of Washington.[5]

Following the ensuing media coverage, the Finnish press started to identify the locations of the 'flying saucer' sightings and to provide possible explanations for them. For example, there were speculations about secret weapons, about mass hysteria, and about weather balloons. A review of the newspaper reports at the time reveals a mixture of responses including puzzlement, neutrality, negativity and humour, but little that was particularly positive. Typical of many of the reports was that of one reporter who suggested that flying saucers might have originated from a well-built Soviet discus thrower.

Interestingly, it was not long after the Finnish newspapers had started to write about 'flying saucers' that Finnish people began to observe them. Indeed, the newspaper *Vapaa Sana* reported the first modern Finnish UFO sighting on 14 July 1947. Two men claimed that they had seen a 'flying saucer' above Helsinki.[6] In general, however, it was not until the 1950s that magazines began publishing articles about UFOs and discussions of UFO-related subjects became common in Finland.[7] (It should be noted that it was not until the late 1960s that the Finnish media began regularly using the term 'UFO'. And it is only from the early 1970s that we see the term widely used in Finnish society.[8])

Due to a wave of UFO sightings in several countries in 1952, new explanations were enthusiastically canvassed – e.g. UFOs were optical illusions or radar disturbances. In 1954, during the next international wave of sightings, there was again a rise in the publication of articles on UFOs. However, interestingly, this time the focus was on the alleged sightings of Martians in France, as a result of which Finnish newspapers became fascinated with the 'extraterrestrial intelligence hypothesis' (ETH). In 1957 there was yet again an international wave of interest in UFOs. This time the press spoke more about 'phenomena of light' and about unusual 'objects' than about 'flying saucers'. Indeed, a comparison of the 1957 reports with the earlier reports reveals a fairly blasé attitude to UFO sightings, if not one of mild boredom. Moreover, because the USSR had just that year launched the Sputnik satellite, Sputnik – as might have been expected – became the most popular explanation for UFO sightings. Certainly, from this point on, as far as the media were concerned, it became standard to explain UFOs in terms of the misinterpretation of physical phenomena. One of the reasons for this, it could be argued, is that, along with an acceleration of economic growth in Finland, there had been an increased emphasis on the importance of scientific and technical developments.[9] Hence, the general mood at this time regarding the supernatural and the paranormal was one of scepticism.

That said, there was quite a high level of Finnish curiosity in UFOs during the 1950s, whether sceptical or otherwise, although no actual UFO organisations were formed and no discussions were published.

Interestingly, there were perspectives which suggested an entirely different interpretation of UFOs than the one dominant at the time. In 1957, Ensio Lehtonen, the founder of the Christian publishing company Kuva ja Sana, provided an apocalyptic interpretation of UFOs in his book *Ajan Kello* (*The Clock of the Era*). Lehtonen argues that flying saucers are real, but they are not secret weapons, aircraft piloted by aliens or demons. Instead, Lehtonen points out that flying saucers are divine signs sent by God prior to the second coming of Christ.[10] Indeed, this wasn't Lehtonen's first religious assessment of UFOs. In 1954, in the magazine *Kipinä* (published by Kuva ja Sana), he published an article entitled 'Lentävät lautaset' ('Flying saucers'), which presented a similar view.[11] Toivo Pajala, in his 1958 book *Nykyajan tapahtumat Raamatun profetian valossa* (*Modern Events in the Light of the Prophecies of the Bible*), provides a very similar interpretation of flying saucers to that of Lehtonen. Basically, he states that, whatever flying saucers are, wherever they come from, or whether they are good or evil, they are divine signs that Jesus promised to send prior to his second coming.[12] In addition to this understanding of UFOs as divine signs, others believed UFOs held the key to certain biblical miracles. For example, Rev. Wiljam Aittala, in his book *Kaikkeuden sanoma avaruuskauden ihmiselle* (*The Message of Wholeness to Space Age Humanity*) suggests that the Bible includes descriptions about the inhabitants of other worlds. Aittala also claims that certain biblical figures travelled into space and had encounters with aliens, Enoch being the first human astronaut:[13] 'Enoch walked with God; and he was not, for God took him' (Genesis 5:24).

This is interesting since, from a contemporary perspective, positive interpretations of UFOs by Christians would be very unusual. It would seem that, as reflection on UFOs became more sophisticated and different theories were posited – including many occult theories, para-psychological theories, and theories which link UFOs with new religions and the New Age movement – such interpretations stopped.

1960–67: UFO hobbyists get organised

The first Finnish UFO club, a local group called Lentävät lautaset-kerho (the Flying Saucer Club), was founded in 1960 in Porvoo,[14] led by an economist, Joel Rehnström. In 1962 the group placed advertisements in newspapers requesting reports of Finnish UFO sightings. Although the result was poor, the efforts of Lentävät lautaset-kerho did constitute the initial steps of Finnish UFO research. Hence, the club can be considered the first organised attempt to investigate Finnish ufological phenomena. Also during 1962, on 21 November, the first national UFO association, Interplanetistit ry (Interplanetary Registered Association),[15] was founded with about forty members. Although the constitutive meeting decided to name the association Lentolautasliitto (The Union of Flying Saucers), probably due to demands of the Finnish registration authority, the name was changed the following year to Interplanetistit ry. A Christian priest, Arvi Merikallio, was selected as Chairman of Interplanetistit ry, with Joel Rehnström as Secretary.[16] Furthermore, 1962 also saw the founding of a publishing company by Joel Rehnström, Kustannus Oy Vimana, which published the first UFO books in Finland. These were translations of some influential UFO books, such as Desmond Leslie and George Adamski's *The Flying Saucers Have Landed* (*Lentävät lautaset – onko niitä?*).[17]

In the Spring of 1963, Interplanetistit ry (later called Helsingin Ufoyhdistys) presented its official position on UFOs.

1 The existence of flying saucers can be proven.
2 It is probable that members of space civilisations, who have already been in contact with some Earth people, are travelling to Earth by means of flying saucers.
3 It is possible that alien civilisations have a special message for humans.

1963 also saw the first edition of Interplanetistit ry/Helsingin Ufoyhdistys's magazine, *Lentolautaslehti* (*The Magazine of Flying Saucers*). In 1966 the organisation published one UFO book and, in 1967, changed the magazine's title to *Vimana*. At the end of the 1960s local branches were founded in Finland's thirteen regions. Helsingin Ufoyhdistys started to arrange seminars.[18]

There were some obvious reasons for the emergence of UFO hobbyists at the beginning of the 1960s, perhaps the foremost of which was that the scientific possibility of space travel had gripped the public imagination. On 12 April 1961, the Soviet cosmonaut Yuri Gagarin, in the spacecraft *Vostok 1*, became the first human to travel to space; in 1962, not only did the United States send *Mariner II* to observe Venus, but also the Soviet Union launched *Mars I*. The Finnish newspapers wrote enthusiastically about these missions and, particularly during the summer of 1962, speculated about the possibilities of extraterrestrial life. Second, science fiction became a popular genre in Finland at the beginning of the 1960s and consequently fuelled the Finnish imagination.[19] Finally, the material produced by the UFO tradition in North

America over the previous decade,[20] the growing stream of UFO literature in Finland, and a people naturally inquisitive about such
phenomena, all contributed to the significant rise of UFO hobbyists.

In 1965, Arvi Merikallio left Helsingin Ufoyhdistys because, in his
opinion, there were activities and beliefs in the association which were
not in accord with the spirit of the Bible. Merikallio also felt that the
rules of the association were not obeyed. A fundamental factor which
led to Merikallio's resignation was a dispute with a former ballet
dancer, Margit Lilius, who was theosophically oriented.[21] Following
Merikallio's resignation, an airline captain, Ilpo Koskinen, took over
the leadership of the organisation and Merikallio himself quickly
founded his own association, Suomen Planetistien Seura ry (Society
for the Planetists of Finland). Located in Vilppula,[22] it had, at its
height, several local branches and several hundred members.
Merikallio, convinced that the 'inhabitants of space' were both part of
the divinely ordained created order and part of God's plan for the
cosmos, preached that, at the final judgement, Christians will be
carried to heaven by flying saucers.[23] Again, whilst it may seem odd
that a Christian clergyman was able to incorporate UFOs into his
theology so easily, it should be remembered that he was by no means
alone in Finland at that time. For example, Eino Saares, a cathedral
dean, was both in broad agreement with Merikallio and an active
member of his organisation.[24] Indeed, such was the level of clerical
involvement in Suomen Planetistien Seura ry that it was dubbed 'the
UFO Club of Priests'.[25]

Margit Lilius was not only an adversary of Merikallio, but one of the
first Finnish contactees. In 1943, she claimed to have seen a UFO in
Oitti,[26] and, as a consequence of this experience, she says, she began to
search for 'the meaning of life'. At first, Lilius turned to theosophy, as a
result of which she travelled to the United States in order to study
under the guidance of Jiddu Krishnamurti. Lilius's first contact with an
alien occurred, she recalls, in 1955, in the middle of the rush hour in
Los Angeles. She established telepathic contact with an alien who
drove a cream-coloured Cadillac. Following this she was introduced to
an extraterrestrial teacher from the 'Brotherhood of Venus'. According
to Lilius, she was told that the mission of Venusians is to help humans
grow spiritually and to create a new psychology and philosophy by
uniting science and religion. Lilius travelled back to Finland in the
mid-1960s and brought with her *the Urantia Book*. (Interestingly, *The
Urantia Book* influenced Rehnström greatly, as well as several other
UFO activists in Helsingin Ufoyhdistys.[27]) Her own book, *Ihminen ja
avaruuden avautuminen* (*Man and the Opening of Space*) was published

in 1967 and was the first UFO book written by a Finn.[28] A few years later Lilius moved back to the United States.[29]

1968–78: the period of enthusiastic UFO investigators

In 1968, Tapani Kuningas, who had been active in Helsingin Ufoyhdistys, founded a sort of one-man research organisation and started to build a systematic network of UFO researchers.[30] Furthermore, a UFO research association, Turun Ufo (UFO of Turku), was founded in Turku[31] in 1968 – although it was not registered until 30 March 1971. In the memorandum of association it is stated that its purpose is to investigate 'UFOs', to collect data about them, and to disseminate accurate knowledge concerning them.[32] Reijo Sjögren, an active ufologist,[33] was elected as Chairman of the group. Turun Ufo was a very enthusiastic and proactive organisation. It established contact with the Swedish UFO association, UFO-Göteborg, and also with an American UFO organisation, the National Investigations Committee on Aerial Phenomena. Turun Ufo also arranged seminars and subscribed to foreign UFO magazines. Sjögren's own UFO book *Mies toisesta maailmasta ja muita ufoilmiöitä* (*A Man from Another World and other UFO Phenomena*)[34] was published in 1972.[35]

In the late 1960s the Finnish media had become interested in UFOs as a result of the international wave of sightings in 1967[36] and also, to a large extent, of the publication of Erich von Däniken's *Vieraita avaruudesta* (*The Chariots of the Gods?*). This UFO enthusiasim continued into the early years of the 1970s, fuelled partly by reports of an impressive wave of sightings over the Pudasjärvi area[37] during the years 1969–1971.[38] Investigations into this wave, which interested both Finnish scientists, the media and the international UFO community,[39] was led by Ahti J. Karivieri, a graduate engineer and one of the pioneers of Finnish UFO research, and Atte Särkelä, a local taxi driver who knew the geographical area well. Turun Ufo also assisted in the investigations, as did Oulun UFO-kerho (Oulu's UFO Club),[40] a newly-formed organisation which had been registered on 20 November 1969, and which Karivieri joined.[41] Basing his study on photographic evidence, Karivieri sought to locate some stationary cameras to observe the phenomenon, all of which were loaded with film sensitive to a certain kind of infrared light. His aim was to photograph, not only visible light phenomena, but also phenomena invisible to the human eye. The investigation was successful until, unfortunately, it met with difficulties when the importation of the film he needed was banned.

Subsequently, according to Karivieri, this particular type of film could only be used by American scientists researching infratechniques. His suspicion was that the imports were terminated at the request of the CIA. Indeed, he claimed that some of his films were deliberately destroyed in Kodak's laboratory in Stockholm where the films were processed. He was, he says, even seriously harassed, including having his phone tapped, because of his investigations into UFOs. Finally, Karivieri moved to Sweden to study.[42]

Although the magazine *Vimana* published its final issue in 1972,[43] that year a new monthly magazine was founded, *Ufoaika* (*The UFO Age*). Tapani Kuningas, who had already been significantly involved in UFO activities, became the editor-in-chief of *Ufoaika*.[44] Although initially the magazine concentrated solely on UFOs, because it was difficult to find enough material each month *Ufoaika* began to cover a range of paranormal phenomena and alternative sciences. To signify the broadening of focus, the magazine's name was changed to *Ultra* in 1974.[45] By this time Kuningas had also produced four informative books on UFOs.[46] In 1976, Kuningas was again busy, this time organising Rajatiedon yhteistyöryhmä (The Cooperative Group of Borderline Knowledge) in Tampere, as well as, on 8 February, the publishing company Kustannus Oy Rajatieto – which quickly became the publisher of *Ultra*. Kustannus Oy Rajatieto also founded a library and arranged a summer event for alternative spirituality called Ultrapäivät (Ultradays) in the resort of Kreivilä. Ultrapäivät quickly became an annual tradition and, in 1978, the publishing company also expanded into retail.[47]

Both Helsingin Ufoyhdistys and Turun Ufo grew well in the early years of the 1970s. For example, the membership of Helsingin Ufoyhdistys reached 758 in 1972 – a significant achievement for a Finnish UFO organisation – and Turun Ufo had over sixty members in 1973 – also not insignificant.[48] Although Merikallio's Suomen Planetistien Seura closed in 1972,[49] two new associations were founded in 1973 in Tampere: Tampereen Ufo ry (UFO of Tampere) was founded on 8 March and Tapani Kuningas' wife, Arja Kuningas, was elected as Chairman.[50] Suomen Ufotutkijat ry (UFO Researchers of Finland), which was perhaps the more important of the two organisations, was founded on 29 April, again by Tapani Kuningas,[51] who also became the first Chairman of the organisation. The aim of this new association was to realise Kuningas' desire for a network of UFO researchers.[52] Essentially, Suomen Ufotutkijat gathered together a number of Finnish UFO researches, groups and interested individuals in order to facilitate cooperation and the sharing of ideas and data.

Hence, very quickly, Suomen Ufotutkijat became an important and effective organisation for the development of Finnish UFO research.[53]

During the 1970s there was a clear effort made to establish Finnish UFO research as an academic discipline.[54] In 1973, Kalevi Pusa, a Licentiate in Philosophy and a UFO researcher, translated astronomer J. Allen Hynek's *The UFO Experience: A Scientific Inquiry* into Finnish.[55] Arguably the most important of Hynek's UFO books, this was understood to be a significant step forward in the establishment of ufology as a formal academic discipline.[56] A letter was written, mainly by Kalevi Pusa, to the President of the Republic Urho Kekkonen on 29 August 1975,[57] setting out the state of UFO research both in Finland and internationally. It described the attitudes different countries had taken to the phenomena, as well as the views of prominent scientists and politicians.[58] In a sense, the letter was a summary of the activities of Suomen Ufotutkija in the early 1970s. No reply was ever received.[59]

The year 1975 is also notable in Finnish UFO history for being the year when an alleged piece of a UFO was investigated.[60] At approximately 7.00 p.m., on Saturday 29 October 1964, Raimo Blomqvist, who was staying at his summer cottage on an island in Kallavesi, a large lake in southern Finland, witnessed a multicoloured, hazy object which was between 3 and 4 metres long with a solid, saucer-like centre. It seemed to hover over the edge of the lake, which was visibly rippling under it. A small piece of this 'light phenomenon' then fell into the water, hissing as it sank. Following this, the object glowed more intensely, vibrated violently and, in a second, disappeared over the horizon. After recovering from the shock of this experience, Blomqvist recovered the piece from the water and kept it. Over a decade later, in 1975, he related this incident to Finnish UFO researchers. Led by UFO researcher and graduate engineer Olavi Kiviniemi, the piece was analysed in Swedish and Finnish universities, as well as in some Finnish metallurgical laboratories. Investigations discovered that a small area in the middle of the piece was pure iron and that this was surrounded by different metallic compounds. It had five layers and included twenty-five primary elements, almost all of different metals. It was also evident that it had been subjected to very high temperatures for long periods of time and that it was slightly magnetic, but not radioactive. The possibilities of natural iron, iron meteorite, space junk or lava were excluded. Apparently the investigation concluded that the piece was probably an artificial object of some kind.

In 1973 and 1974, although there was a significant increase in the publication of UFO books in Finland,[61] it became apparent that public interest in the subject was waning.[62] However, it is interesting to note that this was also a transition period in that, gradually, Finnish UFO research began to take seriously parapsychological interpretations, a development which worried some UFO investigators.[63] However, even if the heyday of UFO research seemed to be coming to a close,[64] there remained a committed core of UFO enthusiasts to continue the tradition,[65] despite the fact that, unfortunately, Helsingin Ufoyhdistys had to close down its activities at the end of the 1970s – although it continued to exist as an organisation.[66]

Ancient astronaut theories, the emergence of contactees and Christian views in the 1970s

Erich von Däniken, a former hotel manager and perhaps the most famous ancient astronaut theorist, wrote a book in 1968, *Erinnerungen an die Zukunft* (*Chariots of the Gods?*), which became an international bestseller within a year. During the same year the book was also translated into Finnish (*Vieraita avaruudesta*) and both von Däniken and the book received a great deal of public attention in Finland. Indeed, such was the interest that, in 1969, *Vieraita avaruudesta* had to be reprinted several times.[67]

In the book, von Däniken claims that in the distant past, thousands of years ago, a civilisation from space visited Earth and created the human race. Our primitive ancestors, understandably, believed their creators to be gods. According to von Däniken, this can be demonstrated by an examination of archeological evidence and ancient religious texts.[68]

Von Däniken's second book, *Züruck zu den Sternen* (*Gods from Outer Space*), which was published in Finland as *Takaisin tähtiin* in 1970,[69] likewise attracted great public attention. As ever, the books gave rise to a stream of secondary literature which posited a variety of both interpretations and criticisms of his ideas. For example, the socialist daily paper *Kansan Uutiset* subjected *Takaisin tähtiin* to a marxist critique, claiming that it was propaganda aimed at misleading the working classes and distracting them from their struggle.[70] In 1973 von Däniken's *Tulimmeko tähtien takaa* (*Aussaat und Kosmos*) was published in Finland, and in 1974 *Kaikuja avaruudesta* (*Meine Welt in Bildern*).[71] However, although a further four Finnish translations of books by von Däniken were published between 1975 and 1979,[72] and although he visited Finland in 1977, making a few public appearances in Helsinki in November, by this time the general public interest in von Däniken had begun to subside. Whilst part of this decline was no doubt due to a general belief that his reputation as a competent researcher was questionable,[73] much of it simply reflected the general lack of interest in UFOs evident at the end of the 1970s. That said, whilst the 1970s saw the publication of other Finnish translations of books expounding the ancient astronaut hypothesis,[74] it was von Däniken's work which stimulated the most interest and laid the foundation for subsequent Finnish reflection in the area.

Along with the ancient astronaut hypothesis, another aspect of ufoism to become prominent in Finland during the 1970s, and an aspect that has a significant religious component, was the contactee phenomenon. One of the most important contactees during this period was Helge Lindroos, a masseur by profession. According to Lindroos, in 1945 three alien beings visited him and healed injuries to his eyes, upper back and right arm, all of which he had sustained during the Second World War. The aliens indicated that his sight had been healed in order to enable him to carry out his mission to humanity, the nature of which appears to be the communication of a broad range of alternative spiritualistic ideas. Two years later, in 1947, Lindroos, who was in Lapland at that time, again met some aliens. They showed him their spacecraft and talked with him for several days, revealing to him information about his past and future lives. They also imparted a range of teachings. For example, he was told that the human race was originally from God, that humans should learn to know themselves, that the most important way to learn truth is through personal experience. Lindroos, also a skilled healer, clairvoyant and inventor, stated that the soul is 'a piece of God within us all', and that humans have an aura which can be used by gifted healers (such as Lindroos himself) to diagnose ailments. Lindroos also claimed that he had built a number of machines, for which he had been offered large amounts of money by foreign organisations that had somehow found out about his work. For example, he had built a gauge which could read body temperature in a fraction of a second. However, because he didn't want to reveal the details of his inventions, he decided against taking the large amounts of money on offer.[75]

Interestingly, there were also some explicitly Christian ufological theories published in the early years of the 1970s that attracted quite a lot attention. For example, a pastor and longstanding representative of the Centre Party, Juho Tenhiälä, who also served as Minister for Social Affairs, wrote a book entitled *Usko ja ufot* (*Faith and UFOs*) in 1972. That the book provoked discussion was perhaps more to do with the identity of its author rather than with its content. Not only is *Usko ja ufot* clearly inspired by ancient astronaut theories, but also Tenhiälä reflects on the ufological significance of *Kalevala* (the Finnish national epic).[76] Indeed, he seems to argue that the creation myth of *Kalevala* is very similar to other creation myths, all of which can be explained in terms of ancient astronaut theories.[77] Similarly, Voitto Viro, an influential observer of supernatural phenomena, was outspoken in the early years of the 1970s on the subject of UFOs. This former vicar of Lauttasaari[78] argued that many biblical events could be explained ufologically and even suggested that Jesus might have been an alien.[79] Finally, Leo Meller, a follower of Ensio Lehtonen, the founder of the Christian publishing company Kuva ja Sana, is perhaps the most well-known Finnish Christian with ufological views. Meller had studied the UFO phenomena during the 1960s, he had been a member of Suomen Planetistien Seura and had written several enthusiastic UFO articles. Although he had remained religiously neutral throughout this period, in the early 1970s he began to construct a Christian worldview which, far from interpreting UFOs positively, understood them to be spiritually dangerous. In his 1973 book *Ufot ja maailmaloppu* (*UFOs and the End of the World*) he argues that UFOs and aliens are Satanic manifestations. They are part of a Satanic plan for world domination.[80] However, it should be noted that, whilst such Christian individuals attracted much attention as a result of their various interpretations, general speaking the Finnish clergy were cautious (or even dismissive) about the very existence of UFOs.[81] As in other countries, it is simply a subject in which the Church does not have a great deal of interest.

One can see many reasons why Finland witnessed great UFO enthusiasim in the late 1960s and early 1970s. The economy of Finland had not developed too well in the 1960s, partly because of the international economic depression which began in the middle of the decade. Also, there were demographic shifts, in that many people moved from the countryside to the cities. These factors resulted, not only in social restlessness in Finland, but also in a general rise in spirituality. Second, the beginning of the 1970s witnessed the emergence of new, Eastern-based religious movements in Finland,[82] thereby increasing the range of religious options and mystical thought for Finns. Third, during the 1960s there were enormous advances in astronomy and space science – including, of course, Neil Armstrong's famous first steps on the moon – which inspired public imagination concerning space.[83] Fourth, the UFO waves in the late 1960, particularly in Pudasjärvi, were significant for Finnish UFO activities. Finally, it is clear that the popularity of Erich von Däniken and his books greatly stimulated Finnish UFO enthusiasm.

Does Finnish ufology fade away during the 1980s?

Bearing in mind the decline of interest in UFOs at the end of the 1970s, one might expect ufology to fade away during the 1980s. In actual fact, the UFO hobbyists were active at the beginning of the 1980s.[84] This interest can, to some extent, be traced to a 1980 book published by Tähtitieteellinen yhdistys Ursa (Ursa Astronomical Association) entitled *Ufojen arvoitus* (*The Enigma of UFOs*). The book was written by two astronomers with a keen interest in ufology, Juhani Kyröläinen and Pekka Teerikorpi. *Ufojen arvoitus* is an overview of the history, the nature of, and the problems involved in, UFO research.[85] Its thesis is that, if serious UFO research is going to progress, it needs to be carried out at a multidisciplinary level. *Ufojen arvoitus* has since been lauded by both sceptics and the UFO community in Finland – not an easy feat to achieve.

The year *Ufojen arvoitus* was published, 1980, also saw the most famous abduction case in Finland. The abductee, Aino Ivanoff, worked as a teacher in an open college in Pudasjärvi. Her experiences were recovered during hypnosis sessions with the ufologist Ahti Karivieri. Her story, which is complex, convoluted and surreal, is perhaps worth summing up because, whilst being a part of Finnish ufology, it contains many religious features. The experience begins one evening at 11.00 p.m., after an evening class. Whilst driving home from the school she saw, three times, a red UFO in the sky. After seeing it for the third time, she records that she felt sleepy but, at the same time, inspired. She also remembers that the night appeared extremely black and that she felt more alone than ever. Suddenly she encountered a thick, strange fog, in the middle of which she saw two white and shining reindeer-like animals running in front of her car. After a while the car was lifted out of the fog and into the dark sky. Ivanoff felt doomed, terrified, puzzled and paralysed. Eventually, the car came to rest in a strange, dark red desert. She then recalls how she met some alien beings and a humanoid male, the most beautiful man Ivanoff had ever seen. He was like 'the Greek god Apollo in a boilersuit'. This alien stated that Ivanoff should not have been brought to this place. Subsequently, she was transported to another place, feeling peaceful during the journey, because the handsome alien was with her. Ivanoff eventually arrived at her destination, where she encountered a large group of strange little beings. Although initially unsettling, these friendly beings soon calmed her. However, Ivanoff later said something that the beings didn't appreciate, after which she was examined by a black-suited leader, who took five samples from her right upper arm and inserted a needle into her right temporal lobe. Having lost consciousness, she woke up in a quiet, dark tunnel. She then describes how she ran through the tunnel and arrived in the most beautiful garden she had ever seen. Then Ivanoff saw 'Him' – a Jesus-like, beautiful and gentle figure. He said that, although he knew Ivanoff wanted to stay in the garden, she must go because she had a mission to accomplish. Ivanoff returned to the tunnel, it suddenly disappeared, and she mysteriously found herself back in the dark red desert. She had no shoes and the sand burned her feet in a strange way. It didn't feel hot, but it still 'burned' somehow. Fortunately she quickly found her car. She also met Mauritze, the Apollo-like man, again. Although they felt deep and erotic love for each other, and although she wanted to stay, she says that she knew she had to go. She thus started driving and continued until she came to a castle. She stopped the car and entered the castle. Exhausted, Ivanoff rested in one of the rooms of the castle, and whilst in the room, 'Queen Viktoria' spoke to her about the dangers of nuclear weapons and the risky and irresponsible nature of those who manufacture them. Ivanoff then left the castle and began her journey home.

The next day, noticing that her wrist watch was two hours behind, she immediately realised that she had lost two hours during the night. She also noticed five prick marks in her right upper arm. Following this, from time to time she had fuzzy recollections and a red, glowing spot appeared on the back of her hand. She was also withdrawn after the experience and had loss of memory, fevers, strange rashes and shivers. Her ankles also started to bleed – and, apparently, have done so ever since. Nevertheless, whilst traumatic in some respects, these experiences also left her with psychic abilities and she subsequently became a prominent clairvoyant.[86]

Although there was a serious decline of interest in ufology after the early years of the 1980s, which led Turun Ufo to terminate its activities in 1983,[87] there were still some notable events. For example, in 1983, in the Helsinki area, Rajatiedon yhteistyöryhmä arranged a fair for alternative spirituality called Hengen ja Tiedon messut (The Fair of Spirit and Knowledge).[88] The fair has since become an important event for many UFO hobbyists and religionists. Also during the 1980s there were some investigations. For example, strange balls of light appeared in Hessdalen, Norway, a phenomenon which was studied in 1984 and 1985 by UFO researchers in several northern countries – assisted, to some extent, by university academics and the Norwegian army. That said, there weren't any notable results and the investigations don't seem to have had too much of an impact on the decline of Finnish UFO research.[89] Also significant for Finnish ufoism, was the publication of Tom Pellert's (a pseudonym) 1982 book entitled *Raamatun arvoitus ja Halleyn komeetta* (*The Enigma of the Bible and Halley's Comet*). This was the first Finnish book to provide a detailed ancient astronaut hypothesis.[90] As such, it led to quite a bit of religiously-inspired discussion within the Finnish UFO community. Moreover, the discussion was again fuelled when, in 1986, theologian Raija Sollamo systematically and thoroughly attacked Pellert in an article in the theological journal *Teologinen aikakauskirja*. She demonstrated how Pellert had wholly misunderstood and misinterpreted the biblical narrative.[91]

A new organisation which, although not a UFO association, was to have a significant impact on the Finnish UFO community was founded in March 1987. This organisation was the Finnish sceptics' association, Skepsis ry.[92] The sceptics had already tried to organise themselves in the 1970s, during a period of vigorous UFO enthusiasim. In particular, a group called Kriittinen tutkimusryhmä (Critical Research Group) was founded, which started to publish the magazine *Alfa*. The group attacked all alternative sciences and paranormal investigative activities, including ufology. Kriittinen tutkimusryhmä was disbanded at the end of the 1970s. However, after the publication of *Ufojen arvoitus* in 1980, Ursa's astronomy magazine *Tähdet ja avaruus* also began to focus on UFOs. By the middle of the 1980s *Tähdet ja avaruus* had started to adopt an explicitly negative perspective concerning such alternative sciences. The authors of sceptical articles in *Tähdet ja avaruus* contributed to the formation of Skepsis, which eventually started to work with Ursa.[93] Two years later, in 1989, Ursa published *Paholaisen asianajaja: Opaskirja skeptikolle* (*Devil's Advocate: A Guidebook for the Sceptic*). The book includes, for example, Dr Hannu Karttunen's influential and critical article 'Ufot, ifot ja pienet vihreät henkilöt' ('UFOs, IFOs and Little Green Men').[94]

Whilst scepticism was certainly popular during the latter half of the 1980s, there were also signs of the reappearance of positive ufology in Finland. At the vanguard of such ufology was the architect and UFO researcher Tapani Koivula who, having been influenced by Arvi Merikallio as a boy, had been interested in ufology for many years. He had, for example, helped with the investigations into the Pudasjärvi incident and was one of the investigators of the Norwegian Hessdalen phenomena.[95] In 1988, Koivula published his *Ufojen kosminen viesti* (*The Cosmic Message of UFOs*). This well-written book includes a history of UFO visitation, ufology and stories of contactees. The thesis of the book is that, not only are UFOs and aliens real, but also they come from other realities and are concerned for human welfare and the future of the planet. The aliens are trying to teach us via contactees. Certain official parties know about these aliens and their mission to humanity, but they keep it secret for their own purposes.[96] It seems clear that Koivula has now developed this thesis into a form of UFO-based New Age spirituality.[97] Indeed, from personal conversations I have had with him, I understand that he explicitly favours a New Age worldview.

The new rise of the Finnish UFO hobbyists

Around the time when Skepsis was founded and Koivula's *Ufojen kosminen viesti* was published, the medical doctor Rauni-Leena Luukanen-Kilde took her first steps on the path to an influential UFO career. Events can perhaps be traced back to 9 March 1985, when she was seriously injured in a car accident by the side of River Ounasjoki.[98] As a result of this road accident, she had to abandon her medical career. In autumn 1987, Luukanen-Kilde married a Norwegian diplomat, Sverre Kilde, and, in the same year, after an intriguing hypnosis experience, she became interested in UFOs. It wasn't long before Luukanen-Kilde was seen at UFO conferences, first as a visitor and then as a lecturer.

Whilst the car crash is clearly significant in Luukanen-Kilde's turn to ufology, in actual fact her interest in alternative belief systems stretches back into her childhood. She was born in Värtsilä, North Karelia, on 15 November 1939. Her father, Erkki Valve, was an economist and her mother, Eeva, a nurse. Soon after she was born, the family moved to Käpylä, Helsinki, from where Luukanen-Kilde has her first childhood memories. It was, she recalls, clear to her even at this early age that she was going to be a medical doctor. However, at the age of fifteen Luukanen-Kilde also became interested in alternative spirituality when one of her relatives explained reincarnation to her. Her subsequent interest in the religious and the paranormal continued into her medical career. After studying medicine at the universities of Oulu and Turku – where she met her first husband (hence the family name Luukanen) – she began her career as a provincial medical officer in Rovaniemi, Lapland, in March 1975.[99] Also at this time, she was working on a dissertation in the area of parapsychology – a task which has never been completed. Luukanen-Kilde was also active in Lapin Parapsykologinen Seura ry (Parapsychological Society of Lapland). Indeed, she was one of the founder members. In 1982, her first book *Kuolemaa ei ole*[100] (*There is No Death*) was published. This parapsychological book became quite popular in Scandinavia.[101]

As noted above, following her road accident and the demise of her medical career and the intriguing hypnosis experience, she focused on UFOs. Bearing in mind her previous interests in spirituality, it is perhaps not surprising that her first book to specifically address the subject of UFOs, *Tähtien lähettiläs* (*Envoy of Stars*), develops what might be called a New Age thesis.[102] In 1993, she published her third book, *Kuka hän on?* (*Who is S/He?*), in which she develops her ufological ideas. Essentially, her fundamentally spiritual understanding of ufological phenomena is based on the idea that the universe itself is a huge, super-intelligent living being. This being is *love* and is continuously creating new ways to express itself. Concerning humans, on the one hand, she argues that they are individual instantiations of this universal love, and indeed she develops what might be described as a love monism, and, on the other hand, she teaches that humankind is an experiment by this creative universal being. Incorporating the doctrine of reincarnation into this cosmology, she argues that humans are spiritually evolving over many lifetimes. They have been given both free will and the opportunity for numerous experiences. In accordance with much New Age thought, she argues that humans are currently moving into a far more developed spiritual 'dimension'. When we have fully entered this dimension there will be an understanding of both the potential and the meaning of free will. As a result we will learn to use it to create peace and harmony on Earth. However, currently we are not in a position to use our free will responsibly, and because our planet is in critical condition, it is placed under a certain amount of external control. This is where aliens are important for Luukanen-Kilde; they are crucial to the process, in that they are literally engineering human genes in order to accelerate the spiritual evolution of the race. Indeed, surveying the range of phenomena attributed to alien intervention, she even claims that cattle mutilations and crop circles must be part of the universal plan.

Luukanen-Kilde provides a rich illustrations of the so called 'Grays', which, she says, weigh about 20 kilograms and are between approximately 90 and 130 centimetres tall. They have thin bodies, large heads, big black eyes and no teeth or hair. Their skin is elastic and gray and, observed under a microscope, it is 'net-like'. They have weak muscles, their body fluids are colourless and they have no lymph follicles, lymphocytes, red cells or intestines. Aliens have always been here, she argues, and, in much the same way von Däniken argued, she claims that the Bible includes hundreds of references to these beings.

She has also developed conspiracy theories in which, for example, the government of the United States cooperates with the aliens. She claims that the US government has received a great deal of technical information and that there is an exchange programme between humans and aliens. Although leading politicians are well aware of this, it is kept secret because, if everything were revealed, not only would there be worldwide panic, but also the power structures of the world would change. In essence, there is a conspiracy of silence in order to maintain a status quo that favours powerful Western governments, particularly that of the USA. Luukanen-Kilde's mission is to expose this alien–government relationship because, she believes, not only are those conspiring to keep it secret corrupt, but also humankind is ready to meet the aliens.[103] More recently, in 1999, Luukanen-Kilde produced a more moderate statement which claimed, rather surprisingly, that, although the aliens exist, most UFO experiences are in fact of secret and unethical military experiments.[104]

In addition to Luukanen-Kilde's pronouncements and writings, the 1990s also saw a range of UFO activities in Finland, including programmes such as *Vieraita taivaalta* (*Visitors from Space*) directed by the flamboyant UFO enthusiast Juhan af Grann,[105] and events such as the three-year UFO exhibition in Oulu's Science Centre Tietomaa. Also, in 1991, Suomen Ufotutkijat received twenty-nine reports of UFO sightings, more than in any other year during the last decade. During the same year Suomen Ufotutkijat started to publish an annual report, a 1994 offshoot of which was the yearly book *Uforaportti*. Indeed, in 1992, Suomen Ufotutkijat recorded over a thousand reports of UFO sightings[106] – a particularly large number for a Finnish UFO organisation.

Also during the early years of the 1990s, Helsingin Ufoyhdistys, Tampereen Ufo and Turun Ufo became active,[107] as did a particular group of contactees, Kosmiset ystävät (Cosmic friends), founded in 1990 during Ultrapäivät.[108] This is, as far as I am aware, the first time contactees had organised themselves in this way.

In 1993, the second book produced by Finnish sceptics was published, *Katoavatko ufot? Ufoilmiön kriittistä tarkastelua* (*Do UFOs Disappear? Critiques of the UFO Phenomenon*). It addresses several notable UFO incidents in Finland, the SETI project and UFO religion.[109] Needless to say, it has provoked much discussion and was criticised by many in the UFO community for its dismissive approach.[110] In 1994, possibly as a result of the discussion caused by the book, for the first time there was a research course for UFO investigators held in Lautsia.[111]

The rising level of interest during the 1990s is apparent not only from the increased media coverage and the number of publications and activities, but it can also be gauged from the increasing membership of UFO organisations. For example, in 1992 Suomen Ufotutkijat had around 150 members. By 1994 this had increased to nearly 400 hundred.[112] As to the causes for this new rise in ufological interest, it might be explained in some measure by the following factors:

- The economic depression in Finland in the early years of the 1990s seems to have led to an increase of interest in spirituality and the paranormal.
- There has been a steady stream of UFO reports flowing in from Europe and Russia.
- Not only did the New Age movement become more prominent in Finland than it had been previously,[113] but it included UFO belief as well, leading to a connection between the UFO and New Age communities.
- As noted above, the flamboyant and impressive Juhan af Grann and Rauni-Leena Luukanen-Kilde significantly contributed to the popular interest in UFOs and aliens.
- The published critical views of sceptics clearly provoked both UFO activities and ufological enthusiasm.

The religious nature of the Finnish UFO tradition

The features John Saliba has identified in ufoism generally (psychiatric, psychological, science fictional, scientific and religious) are also applicable to the Finnish tradition.[114] One of the most prominent of the these features within Finnish ufoism has been its implicit and explicit religiosity. Although lacking any specific UFO groups, the general belief in UFOs and aliens in Finland tends to be religious (often drawing on traditional religions) with a technological and scientific gloss. Also mirroring much ufoism elsewhere, Finnish UFO belief tends to be informed by a variety of conspiracy theories.

Finnish ufoism has links with spiritualist and theosophical worldviews. (As discussed in several chapters within this volume, ufoism in general has links with spiritualist and theosophical worldviews.) For example, the theosophical Great White Brotherhood was believed to have been founded by Venusian masters millions of years ago and, through psychic contact, they teach and communicate through spiritually advanced individuals. We have seen that Margit Lilius even claims to have been introduced to a teacher from the Brotherhood of Venus.

Also, the theosophical understandings of karma, rebirth and spiritual growth[115] have all been absorbed into Finnish ufoism at some point. That this is so can be seen in the worldviews of Lilius, Lindroos and Luukanen-Kilde, as well as those of many contactees. We have also seen that Lindroos actually claimed to have both spiritual healing abilities and the information and intellectual ability to be able to construct machines more technologically advanced than any currently available on Earth. Furthermore, advanced knowledge has been revealed to Luukanen-Kilde – though, in her case, it concerns the paranormal and the spiritual nature of the universe. Indeed, as a result of her relationship with aliens, she claims to have – as did Lindroos – esoteric skills and knowledge. Interestingly, just as after a painful transformation process the shaman becomes wiser, more powerful and begins life as a healer and an adviser of his/her community,[116] we have seen that Aino Ivanoff's experience is somewhat shamanic in that, after a traumatic experience, she became a clairvoyant, an adviser of an esoteric community. We have also seen how Ivanoff's experience started with a vertical journey to a supernatural place, clearly reflecting change in her state of consciousness. Again, fruitful comparisons can be drawn with the shaman's different states of consciousness which are usually described as vertical journeys to supernatural places.[117] Naturally, Ivanoff is not the only UFO abductee whose experience seems shamanic in some respects. Indeed, arguably, similarities between shamanistic experiences and UFO abduction experiences are general.[118] Having said that, Ivanoff's abduction experience also has many theosophical elements within it, in that she speaks of meeting deities in space, such as Mauritze and the Jesus-like being, and she psychically receives message from 'Queen Viktoria'.

Whilst there are UFO researchers with little interest in the religious, many Finnish UFO enthusiasts, whilst possibly not UFO religionists in the strict sense of the term, do hold supernaturalistic and even explicitly spiritual UFO-based worldviews.[119] Certainly paranormal or spiritual theories are popularly used to explain UFO experiences.[120] As we have seen to be the case with Tapani Koivula, explicitily New Age ideas are often allied to ufology. On the other hand, we have seen that there are Finns, such as Arvi Merikallio and Leo Meller, who have sought to develop explicitly Christian ufological worldviews.[121]

NOTES

1   See T. Kuningas, *Ufojen jäljillä*, Helsinki, Kirjayhtymä, 1971, pp. 40–51. The UFOs of the year 1934 were called by the name *kummituslentokone* (phantom aeroplane).

2   See K. A. Kuure, J. Kyröläinen, G. Nyman and J. Piironen, *Katoavatko*

ufot? Ufoilmiön kriittistä tarkastelua, Helsinki, Ursa, 1993, pp. 16–18. The UFOs of the year 1946 were called by the name *aaveraketti* (foo-fighters) (p. 16).

3　See, for example, Kuure *et al.*, *Katoavatko ufot?* pp. 11–16; J. Närvä, 'Ufoilmiön uskonnollisia piirteitä', in J. Niemelä (ed.), *Vanhat jumalat – uudet tulkinnat. Näköaloja uusiin uskontoihin Suomessa*, Helsinki, University of Helsinki, 2001, p. 227; C. Peebles, *Watch the Skies! A Chronicle of the Flying Saucer Myth*, Washington and London, Smithsonian Institute Press, 1994, pp. 8–11.

4　See T. Kuningas, *Operaatio UFO*, Helsinki, Jaanes Oy, 1972, pp. 10–14; S. Virtanen, 'Lentävästä lautasesta outoon valoon. Ufoilmiö sanomalehtien palstoilla 1940-luvulta 1990-luvulle', unpublished dissertation, University of Tampere, 1998, p. 11.

5　J. Kyröläinen and P. Teerikorpi, *Ufojen arvoitus*, Helsinki, Ursa, 1980, p. 11. Arnold's sighting was central for the whole rise of the modern UFO tradition. One reason for this is Arnold's perceived reliability as a witness, in the postwar period when ex-servicemen commanded that sort of trust. (See Peebles, *Watch the Skies!*, pp. x, 8–11.)

6　Virtanen, 'Lentävästä lautasesta outoon valoon', pp. 10–16.

7　M. Kananen, 'Kun jumalat olivat humanoideja – Ancient astronaut – teorioiden tulo Suomeen', unpublished dissertation, University of Tampere, 1998, p. 12.

8　See Virtanen, 'Lentävästä lautasesta outoon valoon', p. 50; Kuningas, *Operaatio UFO*, pp.75–159. To find out the history of the term, see, for example, Närvä, 'Ufoilmiön uskonnollisia piirteitä', p. 228; Peebles, *Watch the Skies!*, pp. 34, 56.

9　Virtanen, 'Lentävästä lautasesta outoon valoon'; see also T. Kuningas, *Operaatio UFO*.

10　See E. Lehtonen, *Ajan Kello: Tihenevien ajan merkkien tarkastelua kuvin ja sanoin*, Helsinki, Kuva ja Sana, 1957, pp. 39–44.

11　Kananen, 'Kun jumalat olivat humanoideja', p. 68.

12　T. Pajala, *Nykyajan tapahtumat Raamatun profetian valossa*, Helsinki, Ristin Voitto, 1958, pp. 21–32.

13　See M. Kananen, 'Kun jumalat olivat humanoideja', p. 62.

14　Porvoo is a city about 40 kilometres to the east of Helsinki.

15　The current name of the association is Helsingin Ufoyhdistys – Interplanetistit ry (UFO Association of Helsinki – Interplanetary registered association); see R. Castren, 'Interplanetistien uudet haasteet', *Ultra* 5, 1996, p. 26; J. Kuningas, 'Suomalaisia rajatiedon yhdistyksiä', *Ultra*, 2002, vol. 5–6, p. 34. From now on I will use a short version of the current name of the association, which is Helsingin Ufoyhdistys. The abbreviation 'ry' means 'registered association'.

16　Kananen, 'Kun jumalat olivat humanoideja', pp. 14–15.

17　Others included George Adamski's *Olen ollut lentävällä lautasella* and Daniel Fry's *Lentävät lautaset kertovat*. See Kananen, 'Kun jumalat olivat humanoideja', pp. 15–16; see also D. Leslie, and G. Adamski, *Flying Saucers Have Landed*, New York, The British Book Centre, 1953; Virtanen, 'Lentävästä lautasesta outoon valoon', pp. 35–7.

18　Kananen, 'Kun jumalat olivat humanoideja', pp. 15–18.

19　See Virtanen, 'Lentävästä lautasesta outoon valoon', pp. 36, 39, 45.

JAAKKO NÄRVÄ

20 See Peebles, *Watch the Skies!*, pp. 1–146.
21 'Lilius' was her official family name when she died in 1991. She was the first classic ballet dancer in Finland. (See T. Kuningas, 'Moninkertainen pioneeri. Margit Lilius-Mustapa 1899–1991', *Ultra*, 1991, vol. 11, p. 4.)
22 Vilppula is located about 70 kilometres to the north of Tampere.
23 Kananen, 'Kun jumalat olivat humanoideja', pp. 62–3.
24 T. Äyräväinen, 'Suomessa 1994 toimivat ufotutkimusta harjoittavat yhdistykset', in L. Ahonen and T. Äyräväinen (eds), *Uforaportti*, Salo, Suomen Ufotutkijat ry, 1995, vol. 2, p. 175.
25 See Kananen, 'Kun jumalat olivat humanoideja', p. 62.
26 Oitti is located about 50 kilometres to the north of Helsinki.
27 See Kananen, 'Kun jumalat olivat humanoideja', p. 18; J. Rehnström, 'URANTIA ja *Ultra*', *Ultra*, 2002, vol. 1, p. 10.
28 Virtanen, 'Lentävästä lautasesta outoon valoon', pp. 46–7.
29 See T. Koivula, *Ufojen kosminen viesti*, Helsinki, WSOY, 1988, p. 358.
30 See Kananen, 'Kun jumalat olivat humanoideja', p. 22; T. Kuningas, 'Ufotutkimuksen vaiheita Suomessa, 30-luvulta 70-luvulle', in M. Kananen, T. Kuningas and H. Virtanen (eds), *Uforaportti 6*, Tampere, Suomen Ufotutkijat, 1999, pp. 98–109, 100–1.
31 Turku is the second largest city in Finland, located in the south west.
32 See Äyräväinen, 'Suomessa 1994 toimivat ufotutkimusta harjoittavat yhdistykset', p. 167.
33 See Kananen, 'Kun jumalat olivat humanoideja', pp. 31–2.
34 See R. Sjögren, *Mies toisesta maailmasta ja muita ufoilmiöitä*, Helsinki, Otava, 1972.
35 Äyräväinen, 'Suomessa 1994 toimivat ufotutkimusta harjoittavat yhdistykset', p. 167.
36 See Virtanen, 'Lentävästä lautasesta outoon valoon', pp. 50–56
37 Pudasjärvi is a commune located approximately in the middle of Finland.
38 See S. Lax, *Pudasjärven ufot*, Helsinki, Kirjayhtymä, 1972; Koivula, *Ufojen kosminen viesti*, pp. 102–9; Kuure *et al.*, *Katoavatko ufot? Ufoilmiön kriittistä tarkastelua*.
39 Äyräväinen, 'Suomessa 1994 toimivat ufotutkimusta harjoittavat yhdistykset', p. 115; see also Kuningas, *Operaatio UFO*, 1972, pp. 142–54. One incident in particular stimulated discussion. In Saapunki, Kuusamo (a city in northern Finland), there was a sighting of an impressive UFO, which left marks to the snow. Several parties studied the samples taken from the snow. The media became excited and UFO researchers became quite irritated because of Dr Birger Wiik's statement that the samples contained dish water. (See Koivula, *Ufojen kosminen viesti*, 105–8; Virtanen, 'Lentävästä lautasesta outoon valoon', pp. 65–6.) That said, the press seems to have been critical of Wiik's careless statement (p. 66).
40 See Koivula, *Ufojen kosminen viesti*, p.102. Oulu is a city in central Finland.
41 See M. Kananen, 'Oululaisen ufotutkimuksen kolme vuosikymmentä', *Ultra*, 1998, vol. 10, p. 36. The founder and first chairman of Oulun UFO-kerho was a decorator, Matias Päätalo.
42 Äyräväinen, 'Suomessa 1994 toimivat ufotutkimusta harjoittavat yhdistykset', pp. 115–19.
43 See Kananen, 'Kun jumalat olivat humanoideja', pp. 17, 32.
44 See Kuningas, 'Ufotutkimuksen vaiheita Suomessa, 30-luvulta 70-luvulle',

102–4. See also Kananen, 'Kun jumalat olivat humanoideja', pp. 25, 32.

45 See Kuningas, 'Ufotutkimuksen vaiheita Suomessa, 30-luvulta 70-luvulle', pp. 106–7; P. Mikkonen, 'New Age in Finland: A View Through Finnish New Age Magazines', in J. Kaplan (ed.), *Beyond the Mainstream. The Emergence of Religious Pluralism in Finland, Estonia, and Russia*, Helsinki, SKS, 2000, pp. 258–61. In 1973 the editorial office moved from Tampere to Kylämä, Kuhmoinen. Located in the south, Tampere is the third lagest city in Finland. Kuhmoinen is a commune located about 70 kilometres to the east of Tampere.

46 See T. Kuningas, *UFOja Suomen taivaalla*, Helsinki, Kirjayhtymä, 1970; *Ufojen jäljillä*; *Operaatio UFO, Muukalaisia ja humanoideja – suomalaisia havaintoja*, Helsinki, Kirjayhtymä, 1973.

47 T. Kuningas, '25 vuotta soihdunkantajana – Kustannus Oy Rajatieto syntyi vuonna 1976', *Ultra*, 2001, vol. 3, pp. 24–6.

48 See Äyräväinen, 'Suomessa 1994 toimivat ufotutkimusta harjoittavat yhdistykset', p. 175.

49 See Kananen, 'Kun jumalat olivat humanoideja', p. 63.

50 Äyräväinen, 'Suomessa 1994 toimivat ufotutkimusta harjoittavat yhdistykset', p. 171.

51 Tapani Kuningas, clearly a key figure in the development of Finnish UFO studies, was at the beginning of the 1970s studying social science in the University of Tampere. Unfortunately, the time spent on UFO research led to the abandonment of these studies. He did not have the time to write his thesis. He had signed a contract with the publisher Kirjayhtymä, became involved with the wave of UFO sightings during the winter of 1971 and, apparently as result of his work, moved to Kylämä. (Kuningas, 'Ufotutkimuksen vaiheita Suomessa, 30-luvulta 70-luvulle', pp. 103–4.) He also became the editor-in-chief of *Ultra* and was responsible for organising Suomen Ufotutkijat.

52 See M. Kananen, 'Suomalaisen ufotutkimuksen historiaa', *Ultra*, 1997, vol. 9, pp. 13–14; *Kun jumalat olivat humanoideja*, p. 33; Kuningas, 'Ufotutkimuksen vaiheita Suomessa, 30-luvulta 70-luvulle', pp. 104–6.

53 See Kananen, "*Kun jumalat olivat humanoideja*", p. 33; Kuningas, 'Ufotutkimuksen vaiheita Suomessa, 30-luvulta 70-luvulle', p. 105.

54 See Kananen, 'Kun jumalat olivat humanoideja', p. 104

55 See A. J. Hynek, *Ufot toden rajamailla*, Porvoo and Helsinki, WSOY, 1973.

56 See Kuningas, 'Ufotutkimuksen vaiheita Suomessa, 1977–1989', p. 136; Kuure et al., *Katoavatko ufot? Ufoilmiön kriittistä tarkastelua*, pp. 52–8; Kyröläinen and Teerikorpi, *Ufojen arvoitus*, pp. 18–31, 34–5.

57 See Kananen, 'Kun jumalat olivat humanoideja', p. 100.

58 See Koivula, *Ufojen kosminen viesti*, pp. 28–37.

59 Kananen, 'Kun jumalat olivat humanoideja', p. 35.

60 See Koivula, *Ufojen kosminen viesti*, pp. 92–3; T. Kuningas, T. E. Laitinen and M. Löfman, *100 ufoa Suomessa* Helsinki, Kirjayhtymä, 1994, pp. 87–91; Kuure et al., *Katoavatko ufot?*, pp. 114–15.

61 Eleven UFO books were published in 1973 and seven during 1974 (see Kananen, 'Kun jumalat olivat humanoideja,' pp. 50–3). According to Kananen eighty-nine UFO books were published in Finland during the years 1962–94. The books that Kananen has listed include both the ones which concern 'actual' UFO phenomena and those concerning ancient

JAAKKO NÄRVÄ

astronaut hypotheses. (See Kananen, 'Kun jumalat olivat humanoideja',
pp. 107–13.) Books are a signifigant source of information and inspira‑
tion for Finnish UFO hobbyists.
62 See Kananen, 'Kun jumalat olivat humanoideja', p. 34; Kuningas,
'Ufotutkimuksen vaiheita Suomessa, pp. 30‑luvulta 70‑luvulle', pp.
106–7.
63 See Kananen, 'Kun jumalat olivat humanoideja', p. 35.
64 See *ibid.*, pp. 34–6, 40, 44.
65 See T. Kuningas, 'Ufotutkimuksen vaiheita Suomessa, 1977–1989', in H.
Virtanen, M. Kananen and M. Repo (eds), *Uforaportti 1999*, Tampere,
Suomen Ufotutkijat ry, 2000, pp. 130–2.
66 Äyräväinen, 'Suomessa 1994 toimivat ufotutkimusta harjoittavat yhdis‑
tykset', p. 175.
67 See Kananen, 'Kun jumalat olivat humanoideja', pp. 18–21; see also E.
von, Däniken, *Vieraita avaruudesta*, Helsinki, Kirjayhtymä, 1993.
68 See Däniken, *Vieraita avaruudesta.*
69 See Kananen, 'Kun jumalat olivat humanoideja', p. 21; E. von Däniken,
Takaisin tähtiin, Helsinki, Kirjayhtymä, 1970.
70 See Kananen, 'Kun jumalat olivat humanoideja', pp. 21–2.
71 See *ibid.*, p. 26; E. von Däniken, *Tulimmeko tähtien takaa?*, Helsinki,
Kirjayhtymä, 1973; E. von Däniken, *Kaikuja avaruudesta*, Helsinki,
Kirjayhtymä, 1974.
72 The books were *Ilmestysten arvoitus*, *Todisteita tuntemattomasta*, *Olen oike‑
assa* and *Menneisyyden profeetta*. See Kananen, *Kun jumalat olivat
humanoideja*, pp. 36, 39–40. See also E. von Däniken, *Menneisyyden
profeetta*, Helsinki, Kirjayhtymä, 1979; *Olen oikeassa*, Helsinki,
Kirjayhtymä, 1978; *Todisteita tuntemattomasta*, Helsinki, Uusi kirjakerho,
1978; *Menneisyyden profeetta*, Helsinki, Kirjayhtymä, 1979.
73 Kananen, 'Kun jumalat olivat humanoideja', pp. 39–42.
74 The books were *Toisilta tähdiltä*, *Kun taivaat aukenivat* and *Tulivatko
jumalat tähdistä*. See *ibid.*, pp. 24, 28–9. See also J. F. Blumrich, 'Kun
taivaat aukenivat,' Helsinki, Kirjayhtymä, 1974; E. von Khuon, *Tulivatko
jumalat tähdistä*, Helsinki, Kirjayhtymä, 1979; P. Kolosimo, *Toisilta tähdiltä*,
Helsinki, Kirjayhtymä, 1971.
75 See Kuningas, *Ufojen jäljillä*, pp. 27–42.
76 See Kananen, 'Kun jumalat olivat humanoideja', pp. 24–5, 63.
77 J. Tenhiälä, *Usko ja ufot*, Hämeenlinna, Karisto, 1972, pp. 151–8.
78 T. Kuningas and V. Viro, 'Voitto Viro – totuudenetsijä ja elämän moniot‑
telija', *Ultra*, 1993, vol. 7–8, p. 4. Lauttasaari is a district of Helsinki.
79 Kananen, 'Kun jumalat olivat humanoideja', pp. 63–4.
80 See *ibid.*, pp. 70–3 and L. Meller, *Ufot ja maailmanloppu*, Loviisa,
Painoyhtymä Oy, 1973. As he had earlier claimed in the 1950s, in 1967
Ensio Lehtonen claimed in *100 merkkiä Jeesuksen tulemuksesta* that UFOs
were one of the signs of the Second Coming. See Kananen, 'Kun jumalat
olivat humanoideja', p. 68.
81 *Ibid.*, p. 64.
82 See M., Junnonaho, *Uudet uskonnot – vastakulttuuria ja vaihtoehtoja*,
Helsinki, SKS, 1996; Virtanen, 'Lentävästä lautasesta outoon valoon', p.
57.
83 See Virtanen, 'Lentävästä lautasesta outoon valoon', pp. 45–6.

84 See Kuningas, 'Ufotutkimuksen vaiheita Suomessa, 1977–1989', pp. 132–4.

85 See J. Kyröläinen and P. Teerikorpi, *Ufojen arvoitus*, Helsinki, Ursa, 1980.

86 See A. Ivanoff, *Punainen planeetta*, Suomussalmi, Myllylahti, 1999.

87 Äyräväinen, 'Suomessa 1994 toimivat ufotutkimusta harjoittavat yhdistykset', p. 170.

88 See T. Kuningas, '25 vuotta soihdunkantajana p. 24.

89 See Koivula, *Ufojen kosminen viesti*, pp. 124–31.

90 See Tom. Pellert, *Raamatun arvoitus ja Halleyn komeetta*, Helsinki, Tammi, 1982 During the same year Peter Kolosimo's book entitled *Ajaton maa* was also published in Finnish. See P. Kolosimo, *Ajaton maa*, Hämeenlinna, Karisto, 1982.

91 See Kananen, 'Kun jumalat olivat humanoideja', p. 46.

92 See K. Kuitunen, 'Skepsiksen ensimmäinen vuosi', *Ultra*, 1988, vol. 6, p. 16.

93 See Kananen, 'Kun jumalat olivat humanoideja', pp. 80–97.

94 See H. Häyry, H. Karttunen,and M. Virtanen (eds), *Paholaisen asianajaja. Opaskirja Skeptikolle*, Helsinki, Ursa, 1989; H. Karttunen, 'Ufot, ifot ja pienet vihreät henkilöt', in H. Häyry, H. Karttunen and M. Virtanen (eds), *Paholaisen asianajaja*, pp. 170–87.

95 See Koivula, *Ufojen kosminen viesti*, pp. 17, 102, 129–32.

96 See *ibid*.

97 See T. Koivula, *Viestejä*, Helsinki, Unio Mystica (karisto), 1996.

98 The river is located in northern Finland.

99 Rovaniemi is a city located in northern Finland.

100 See R.-L. Luukanen-Kilde, *Kuolemaa ei ole*, Helsinki, Weilin & Göös, 1982.

101 See T. Kuningas, 'Rauni-Leena Luukanen-Kilde, "Kuolemakaan ei vaienna minua"', *Ultra*, 1999, vol. 11, pp. 4–8.

102 See R.-L. Luukanen-Kilde, *Tähtien lähettiläs*, Porvoo and Helsinki and Juva, WSOY, 1992.

103 See R.-L. Luukanen-Kilde, *Kuka hän on?*, Porvoo and Helsinki and Juva, WSOY, 1993.

104 Kuningas, 'Rauni-Leena Luukanen-Kilde, "Kuolemakaan ei vaienna minua"', p. 8.

105 This programme was shown twice in 1992: 16 February and 10 August.

106 T. Kuningas, 'Ufotutkimuksen vaiheita Suomessa vuosina 1990–1994', in S. Laitala and M. Repo (eds), *Uforaportti 8: Milleniumin ufot*, Tampere, Suomen Ufotutkijat ry, 2001, pp. 124–7, 130–1.

107 See R. Castren, 'Interplanetistien uudet haasteet', pp. 26–7; M Kananen, 'Tampere aktiivinen rajatietokaupunki', *Ultra*, 1998, vol. 3, p. 10; T. Kuningas, 'Ufotutkimuksen vaiheita Suomessa vuosina 1990–1994', pp. 123–4, 125; Äyräväinen, 'Suomessa 1994 toimivat ufotutkimusta harjoittavat yhdistykset', p. 171.

108 See Kuningas, 'Ufotutkimuksen vaiheita Suomessa vuosina 1990–1994', p. 123. When I visited the group during the late years of the 1990s, the members of the group mainly discussed their UFO experiences.

109 See Kuure *et al.*, *Katoavatko ufot? Ufoilmiön kriittistä tarkastelua*

110 This is based on my discussions with UFO researchers. See also, for example, T. Kuningas, 'Ufotutkimusta ja -hutkimusta Suomessa', *Ultra*,

JAAKKO NÄRVÄ

1994, vol. 2, pp. 8–10.

111 See Kuningas, 'Ufotutkimuksen vaiheita Suomessa vuosina 1990–1994', p. 131. Lautsia is a village about a 100 kilometres north of Helsinki. When I participated in the event in Lautsia in the autumn 2001, it included a lot of presentations and discussion, but I would not say that it was still actually a research course. That said, there were several scientific views presented and I was also given a chance to talk about comparative religion and the study of UFO phenomena from an academic point of view.

112 Kuningas, 'Ufotutkimuksen vaiheita Suomessa vuosina 1990–1994', pp. 126, 131.

113 See Virtanen, 'Lentävästä lautasesta outoon valoon', pp. 86, 92, 97.

114 See Saliba, 'The Religious Dimensions of UFO Phenomena', in J. R. Lewis (ed.), The Gods Have Landed: New Religions from Other Worlds, Albany, State University of New York Press, 1995, pp. 16–22; 'UFO Contactee Phenomena from a Sociopsychological Perspective: A Review', in Lewis (ed.), The Gods Have Landed, pp. 207–14, 224–41.

115 M. Niinimäki, Teosofian juuret, Kylämä, Kustannus Oy Rajatieto, 1979, pp. 77–86.

116 See J. Whitmore, 'Religious Dimensions of UFO Abductee Experience', in Lewis (ed.), The Gods Have Landed, p. 71.

117 See K. Kärkkäinen, 'Ufokaappaukset ja ufokontaktiliike', Turku, Seminar Presentation, Department of Cultural Sciences, University of Turku, 1996, pp. 13–14.

118 Whitmore, 'Religious Dimensions of UFO Abductee Experience', p. 71.

119 See, for example, Koivula, Ufojen kosminen viesti; Kuure et al., Katoavatko ufot? Ufoilmiön kriittistä tarkastelua, pp. 52–8; Kuningas, Ufojen jäljillä, Kyröläinen and Teerikorpi, Ufojen arvoitus.

120 See, for example, Koivula, Ufojen kosminen viesti.

121 If a view includes both ufological and Christian concepts, it is sometimes difficult to tell whether it is essentially ufological, Christian, or both.

Part III

UNDERSTANDING NARRATIVES

11

UFO RELIGIONS AND CARGO CULTS

Garry W. Trompf

So-called 'cargo cults' are social movements focused on the preternatural arrival of European-style or internationally marketed commodities. The members of these movements are usually found in small-scale traditional societies that do not have access to such goods; hence the looking to a miraculous coming of 'new' riches. In fact, in the region where 'cargo cultism' is most common, the vast island world of Melanesia (from Irian Jaya to Fiji), contact with the outside world was generally so late that the items brought by European and Asian traders appeared the more extraordinary. Stone Age or lithic cultures encountered modern humanity at its highest levels of technological achievement. Already one may anticipate that 'unidentified Cargo' and its bearers could take on a comparable 'structure' to UFOs. In such a context, Cargo (capitalised; as also in the neo-Melanesian *Kago*) takes on numinous, other-worldly qualities, as if it has come out of another, quite different 'cosmic space'.

Comparabilities between cargo cultism and UFO religions, naturally, are at their sharpest when flying objects amount to astounding 'arrivals' in traditional societies. Thus, if we take the Melanesian case as pivotal, it is when aeroplane phenomena come into the story that an *eidos* of parallel structures strongly suggest itself. This first happens in 1917, in the Papuan Gulf District, during the First World War, a war that admittedly had little traumatic affect on the region (apart from Australia quickly seizing New Guinea from the Germans). The picture of an aeroplane was in the possession of Evara, leader of the so-called Vailala movement (sometimes called the 'Vailala Madness', and, after the American Indian Ghost Dance, perhaps the most highly publicised new religious movement among tribal cultures). The picture was from the cover of a paperback novel, and it depicted a white man descending down a rope ladder from a flying machine. The implication was that the whites and their objects mediated between the Vailala River villagers and the spirit world; the Europeans were either ancestors or close to them, knowing how new goods were made in the other order (above, or beyond the horizon). Evara allegedly communicated directly with the spirits through an imitation wireless pole; and at one point he was held to predict the coming of a great ancestor-guided ship from afar, which would disgorge promised Cargo on the beaches.[1]

Now, such connections between Melanesian religious hopes and air traffic as UFO-type phenomena have by now become fable in popular culture, especially through the film *The Sky Above, the Mud Below* (1962). This depicts virtually uncontacted New Guinea highlander response to planes overhead as apotropaic: rituals were performed to make sure the passing spirits did no harm, and later on, to ensure that they brought the precious valuables which were entering the area.[2] Variants of this scenario are known. Among the Papua highlander Fuyughe, as early as 1928, a local prophet by the name of Ona Asi predicted in an altered state that 'two great birds would fly across the Sauwo [Valley]!' an utterance fulfilled in the pioneering cross-Papua New Guinea flight by Ray Parer and a companion pilot a year later. In 1950 a mimic aircraft made from thatched materials was constructed in a remote district of the Madang highlands.[3] Not long before, in 1946, a group of Eastern Highlands Ke'efu first reached the crash site of a lost plane, and, having never seen Europeans, deduced that the thirteen dead whites inside were inert ghosts, and consequently sacrificed pigs to them.[4] Not far from the same area, some five years after, when the first cargo planes landed at Kainantu airport, local people were found encircling the shirts that the whites had laid out for their 'betterment' on the ground, reconciling themselves to the strange objects as if they were gifts from 'the world of the dead'.[5] The documentation could go on. As background to cargo cult activity, whites who travelled by land were still sometimes taken to have come from the sky;[6] while many group outbursts of cargoist expectation have involved the levelling of the forest into makeshift aerodromes to receive the ancestors' projected benison.[7] In the marginal Orokaiva area of Managalas, for another variation on the theme, various worship centres carry wooden aeroplanes on them instead of crosses.[8]

The author found the closest 'parallel incident' to a UFO-type encounter in an account by a geologist from Goroka Teachers' College (now University) of his helicopter expedition to the barely contacted Koroba area of the Southern Highlands in 1976. Landing on a ridge to inspect a geologically- intriguing outcrop, he noticed local people run away into hiding as he and the pilot came down. Out he stepped, dressed in a totally white explorer-scientist's outfit, and struck his pick-axe, in a moonraker mood, into the rock-face to secure a sample. Then, feeling like a visitor from outer space, he looked at the astounded half-hidden 'natives' surrounding him, got back with his findings into the cockpit, and flew speedly out of their sight![9] One can only imagine what feelings of wonder, mental confusion and exercises of imagination or explanation, followed this half-encounter among those on the ground. (That said, by now the amount of mining activity in the Southern Highlands will have changed many people's impressions. Rumours will have been heard, too, of how, during the gold rush at Porgera, highlanders would stake claims and pay for helicopters with nuggets just to get hot meals for themselves from the Mount Hagen stores!)

More important than such paradoxical incidents for structural comparison, however, are the known reasonings applied by indigenous Melanesians to justify their faith in the spectacular advent of Cargo. Whether airborne arrivals were involved or not, cargo cultists typically conceived of the new materials as deriving from their ancestors, or the collectivity of the departed. Although many traditional belief systems entailed deities, the ancestors were the ones taken to be crucially involved in securing the fecundity of the group: the living belonged in communities with the dead, and the latter were crucial mediators of group survival, let alone prosperity, from their privileged position in the spirit world. They possessed access to untold blessings; their powers were unlimited; they moved with untold quickness through space and time; they manifested in other life forms to bring signs to the living, often as birds, butterflies and other flying objects. It is small wonder that, with the emergence of cargo cultism, the ancestors have figured prominently. Certainly, the future promise of great bounty was often linked to the garbling or reinterpreting of mission talk about the End of the Known Order (or the Millennium). But if the Return of Christ 'on the clouds' was looked to, so also was the Return of the Ancestors with him (cf. Revelation 20:4 in any case), and in various cults in which tradition was more manifest than missionary influence the collective, dramatic return of the supportive ancestors was posited – albeit itself a new conceptual development facilitated by 'white man's talk' about a great future.[10]

Admittedly, the original bearers of technological innovation – the arts of horticulture, hunting, war, navigation and making canoes, for instance – were often taken as culture hero beings separate from the group's dead, yet none the less it was the deceased who passed down these inherited skills.[11] In a number of interesting cases, especially from western Papua New Guinea (some Trans-Fly people, the Kewa in the Erave area, the Mae Enga), there was recognition of spirits being in the sky or spirit villages in the sky realm; and, as with the first-mentioned groups, traditional items important for technology, such as stones (unknown in the inhabited swamplands), were held to be manu-factured by the dead in the sky and then sent through trade routes eastwards.[12] With characteristic presumptions that ancestors were the key to material wealth and technological know-how, there grew up in cargo cults (and the mentalities associated with them) the belief that the idea that the whites and other outsiders were intervening to take away all the Cargo which was originally intended to go from the ances-tors to the living indigenous Melanesians. Such views reflected local peoples' intense dissatisfaction at being unable to get access to the novel goods, and these antipathetic notions came into play *after* the actual 'contact period' when whites were themselves honoured as returning ghosts.[13] Movements thus grew up to get around an unac-ceptable deprivation, in a world in which relatively equitable exchange of valuables and foodstuffs was the long-inured norm. Cargo cults saw the development of rituals to get the direct attention of the dead – sometimes church-originated ritual practices were thought to hold the key – so that riches would bypass the intruders and go straight to the villagers – as they waited patiently at their would-be airstrips.

The allusion to mentalities suggests the need to make a working distinction between cargo cults and the mental ethos and set of atti-tudes that the author has called 'cargoism'. With cargo cults, a leadership – often a visionary or prophet-type figure – draws together group support on the basis of his or her heralding of transformation – and of a solution to both the enigma and inequity of the Melanesians' situation. The rituals required by such leaders seem to have justified the epithet 'cult', but cargo movements (or new indigenous religious movements expecting cargo), would do just as well. Cargoism is more widespread; it can manifest in the longings of many individuals who do not join any activist cult. The author has drawn a comparable distinc-tion between 'millenarism' as an apocalyptic habit of mind (or even ideology) and 'millenarianism movements', which comprise agitated groups expecting imminent, total, final and (usually) this-worldly salvation.[14] Various cargo movements have also been dubbed millenarian ones, because their dreams of Cargo are so great that they expect a complete end to the indigenes' known order. The members of the Pomio Kivung, for example, a continuing movement of East New Britain, believe that, when they return, the ancestors can by a mere wish create a city the size of New York around their very own

Jacquinot Bay.[15] In the main, however, cargo cultists have more limited dreams of dramatic change, and they could just as easily be called 'transformation movements'.[16] As for cargoist, millenarian and transformative *mentalités*, they are permeating styles of thought that bolster drives to obtain new commodities, to explain the puzzle of the whites and their goods (in the absence of any factory or exhibition of the items' manufacture), and to give confidence that local predicaments will be overcome at last.

Whereas cargo cults are sporadic and unevenly spread across the globe, cargoism and forms of millenarian hope are more widespread as mental configurations. Cargo cults have been very common in Melanesia, probably because of the very materialist nature of the autochthonous religions there. Ritual activity amounted to nothing if it did not yield material results – as expressed in great prestations of food and killed pigs (to which allied tribes were invited) or in military victory (in which enemies faced material vulnerability). But great expectations have arisen elsewhere on the globe, as when previously uncontacted peoples have seen outside marvels, even briefly, for the first time. The author has maintained, to illustrate, that the untraditional setting-up of scores of statues to face the sea on Rapanui (or Easter Island) was due to a fleeting sixteenth-century encounter with a lost Spanish caravel – or some passing 'spirit vessels'.[17] At other times cargo cults arise around the differences between types of goods, so that some highland Burmese villagers who were used to their own (not unimpressive) wares suddenly packed up for an agitated expedition into the mountains (during 1923) to await heaven-sent money and the preferred, seemingly miraculous, items and stock held by the Christian missionaries.[18] In the so-called 'Son of God' movement in Northern Rhodesia (1925–7), the rural followers of the prophet Tom Nyirenda looked for motor bikes and calico cloth (so much better than their own) to drop from the sky.[19] Among Polynesians, with their strong stress on a vertical cosmology, when prophets spoke of new commodities arriving in abundance, as on Rennell Island in 1936, they also looked 'to heaven'.[20]

Thus, while UFOs are overwhelmingly associated with the Western cultural contexts – with what Carl Jung recognised as the Europeans' notorious 'camera-mindedness' – such objects have structural counterparts across the globe. Out-of-space visitations, in any case, in dream and religio–visionary experiences, must be examined with care, because in traditional societies spirit(ual) messengers will seem to descend from the heavens *qua* the sky above, just as 'flying saucers' do.[21] 'UFO cults', however, that is to say new religious movements focused predominantly or in some significant way on extra-terrestrial visitations, have been almost exclusively found in Western contexts. We should note at the outset, of course, that they have been affected by a cultural ethos in which interest in objects travelling in outer space is very high – the world in which spacecraft are constructed and energetically publicised as being sent off the surface of the Earth, in which science fiction and cinematography about space travel and intergalactic contacts are most popular, and in which the possibilities of great changes brought from beyond the Earth's stratosphere are most widely imagined. Such a 'UFO culture', then, we may rightly comprehend as much more widespread, especially in Western contexts, as habitudes of thought and ideology, and it stands in relation to specific group outbursts of UFO cultic behaviour as cargoism does to cargo cults and millenarism to millenarian movements. The denoted ideational configurations, of course, always need to be recognised in and for working purposes abstracted from larger bodies and milieux of human thought. 'UFO-isms', for instance, if such shorthand may be allowed, can be viewed under the broader rubrics of 'New Age religion' and contemporary estoricisms.[22] They can also be examined within more specific 'areas of investigation', on the margins of aeronautical or cosmological studies – in connection with SETI programmes (the Search for Extra-Terrestrial Intelligence), let us say, or with branches of psychiatric, even theological, research.[23] And cargoism, millenarianism and UFO-ism, in any case, can overlap as thought complexes.

In the light of the above comments, UFO cultism as such presents a special difficulty of approach in terms of social groupings. This has to do with what we shall define as 'interest groups', made up of coteries or associations, sometimes loosely interlinked, that do not live at a high level of cultic intensity. Such a social variable if far less likely to occur with cargo cults; they can be pinpointed once a leader announces the approaching prospect, if not awesome imminence, of the Cargo. The variable however occurs with millenarisms because, whereas some millenarists wait with 'baited breath' for the millennium, others only look for 'the signs of the times' (as a Seven-Day Adventist magazine has it) and disdain agitated collective preparations for the transformative moment; although even in this latter case the epithet 'interest group' hardly applies to the less earnest types. When we consider UFO cult 'interest groups', these are made up of those who may agree about interpretations of the past in terms of extraterrestrial visitations, but do coagulate into any movement fixed on a future scenario of dramatic contact. Thus coteries affected by Erich von Däniken's manner of explaining ancient and mysterious archaeological sites, and the gap between primitive and civilised peoples, in terms of astronaut landings and sexual propagations, will not necessarily constitute any 'expectant assembly'.[24] This is also true, *inter alia*, of groups concerned to interpret biblical (or other worldly scriptural) passages as referring to spaceships.[25] On the other hand, interest groups focusing on historical (or more particularly ancient) encounters with UFOs may share hopes about the *return* of beings occupying space vehicles, notions that provoke or substantiate predictive activists, and at any rate generally contribute to the pool of ideas drawn on by 'adventists'.

Now, one can begin to grasp the structural (even unanticipated conceptual) connections between cargo cults and UFO religions when we realise that certain UFO groups in the West are looking eagerly for spectacular material blessings from the skies. Of course, we are not to forget that species of cargo cultism, let alone many forms of cargoistic thinking, also exist in the West. These do not always have a focus on outer-space blessings. The author remembers how individual Californian tertiary students set up in their college rooms shrines of the Japanese Namu-Myoho-Renge-Ko sect, before which they would meditate to ask for specific items – a television set, a new car, etc.[26] It is also possible to connect 'prosperity cults' in the West – movements deliberately proclaiming the acquisition of money as a surrogate salvation, or the Gospel as bringing concrete prosperity – as expressions of cargoism, at the least.[27] These provide relevant background to our interests here, but more important are images of some fantastic coming order in which final truth and breakthrough material benefits will arrive coupled together from beyond Earth.

Thus UFO 'cult groupings', when they congeal, characteristically focus on a transformative event, which is most commonly the ushering in of a this-worldly salvation. Of course, some of them do not seem to have that component – the Californian Heaven's Gate group, for instance, posited this world as only a 'virtual reality', so that a collective death of the 'elect' was necessary (in 1997) to gain access to the 'true' heavenworld (symbolised by the Hale-Bopp comet).[28] Others project the actual arrival of (a) spacecrafts(s) that will save the chosen from an utterly doomed world, so their future blessedness, whatever it is to be, will consequently lie quite beyond this world.[29] Such variability instructs us that UFO cults fall into a special category of their own and cannot be said to be coterminous with cargo cults and millenarian movements. But the intersections between ufological, cargoistic and transformative/millennial expectations are there to be considered. When there has been language of 'the new Golden Age', which is 'man's greatest opportunity' for 'perpetual peace', we want to know what is imagined to be borne, both psycho-intellectually and physically, by visitors from space (in this quoted case from the planet Clarion, taken by Truman Bethurum in 1959 to be *extra*terrestrial, even if other, more esoteric, interpreters held Clarion to be *inside* our Earth).[30] When there are assertions of landing that amount to 'a visible, physical event that would take place all over the planet over a period of nine days', we wish to know what beliefs have been held (in this case by the 'Light Affiliates' of British Columbia, in 1969) about both the truth content and technological implications of the momentous showdown, which supposedy heralded 'the Age of Aquarius'.[31]

Obviously, it is the new technology that connects directly the concept of Cargo we discussed at the beginning of this article. Taking our cue from the former Director of NICAP, Major Donald Keyhoe, however ambivalently various types of ufologists have taken his agenda, so-called 'flying saucers' are recognised as metallic (but of allegedly unknown metals); are intelligently controlled (but by an intelligence possibly outclassing human technical know-how); do not use 'fuel' according to our regular understanding of the process; manoeuvre and reach speeds 'beyond the comprehension of our best scientists here on Earth', and operate in an apparently limitless travel area.[32] By implication the arriving technology is unknown (or remarkably different to that previously known), and is therefore highly mysterious, perhaps even ready to bear the popular epithet 'miraculous'. The items are to be disclosed to earthlings as a dramatic 'revelation', as cosmically significant and therefore as carrying religious import. In this light, UFO technology – as presaged or promised by cultists, and laid bare for all to see in a grand *dénouement* – is structurally equivalent to the Cargo of cargo cults.

The suggestion of cross-cultural comparability between Cargo and UFO technology was first made by the author in 1990, when the author presented a long analysis of the impressive Californian commune called the Brotherhood of the Sun [Son], and then connected aspects of its eschatology with cargoist and millenarian dreams on the other side of the Pacific (in 'modern' Australia as well as a 'primal' Melanesia).[33] The recognition of comparable millenarian activities met no criticism – scholars were used to the same sociological point being made by such widesweeping investigators as Henri Desroche, Norman Cohn, Kenelm Burridge and the like.[34] But cargo cults were supposed to be more geographically confined, and so the parallelism on that count looked awkward.[35] Besides, a hidden embarrassment probably affected responses, because Westerners generally do not like to look at their own culture(s) as cargoistic or the seedbed of cargo cultism.[36] By 1998, however, the German scholar of religion and UFO movement investigator Andreas Grünschloß had picked up the author's earlier suggestion of structural equivalences as a theoretical reference point, and successfully applied it to a number of groups, starting with the Brotherhood of the Sun itself.[37]

The Brotherhood presents methodological problems from the start, however, because it is a millenarian, UFO and (on this new reading) cargo movement all in one, and is indeed possibly the most complex religion (or religious synthetism) on Earth.[38] A central point surrounding its leader, the 'messianic' Norman Paulsen (who self-aggrandised himself more and more as a surrogate Christ figure while the commune lived through the 1980s, its most ambitious yet crisis-ridden decade), was his role as 'a Builder'.[39] Paulsen presented himself as a cosmically crucial space traveller, who had been long involved in intergalactic conflict, and as a result had been 'space ship-wrecked many times and marooned on planets waiting to be picked up'. The 'Star Pilot', owned by the Sunburst or Brotherhood community he led, and acclaimedly the largest schooner off the Californian coast, was the terrestrial counterpart of his spaceship(s) and a sign that his divinely-called mission, begun 'over one million years ago', was going to be seen 'through to the end'.[40] The commune's 'Tajiguas' ranch (rather symbolically right next to President Ronald Reagan's) was conceived by Paulsen as 'a base station for Builders', in which 'young men and women could become space pilots or scientists, or [as a 'let-out'] to pursue whatever trade they felt drawn to'.[41]

What is going on here? Apart from the apparent megalomania, the leader and the group are located in a special mythic space-time, and what is projected for the future is 'the Return' of an Eden-like primordium, in which lost perfections are restored. The creators of this long-hidden mastery come out of an order which is both theosophically etheric and actually stellar, and so we find a coalescence of influences from H. P. Blavtasky's teachings of the earliest 'high planetary', spirito – etheric root races of humanity,[42] and more recent notions of alien life in outer space, all as a shadowy background to 'actual historical events', and claimed to be remembered by Paulsen as space warrior. He was, from the virtual beginning, it seems, involved in an intergalactic conflict that combines the idea of cosmic war between the forces of good and evil (with its roots in Genesis 6:3–5, the pseudepigraphical 1 Enoch and Theosophy) and the contemporary science-fiction culture of *Star Wars*. In this Paulsenian account, actual events begin 400,000 years ago, when the Builders arrive on Earth to create the first city on the now lost continent of Mu (at a location

around 800 miles west of Easter Island); and once on Earth, according
to what appears as a combination of Blavtasky's and von Däniken's
interpretations of the distant past, they stepped up the genetic evolution of the pre-existing 'primitives'.[43]

Here we can perceive what is very common in many new religious
movements across the globe, a mythological macrohistory explaining
how everything came to be, and, in New (space) Age thought, seeking
to better the Bible's account (or to expatiate what is only hinted at in
the conventional biblical narrative).[44] By postulating Mu (or
Lemuria), the Brotherhood ideology links ufological interests to
esoteric and New Age claims about lost civilisations, making it possible
that the inhabitants of both Mu and then Atlantis were in continued
possession of spacecraft and other superior forms of technology before
they were submerged when a giant asteroid hit the Earth (in 12,000
BC, the event that caused the Great Flood).[45] Much ink has been spilt
over lost civilisations, and, quite apart from connections made to UFO
phenomena, there has been much said about unrecovered technical
expertise that would explain such mysteries as the pyramid of Giza or
the great statues of Easter Island (so close to, and, in Brotherhood
ideology, a marginal remnant of Paulsen's imagined continent of
Mu).[46] James Churchward, of whom so little is known, made a veri-
table industry out of writing on the extraordinary technological and
psychical powers of Mu's inhabitants,[47] his claims being readily
absorbed into Paulsen's thought, but then readjusted to suit his space-
ship-oriented teaching, which was affected by Western American
books on desert UFO sightings and his own self-avowed entrance into
a saucer – so that his true identity could be (re)disclosed.[48]

Churchward's work also links to Rosicrucian and theosophic lines of
belief that, despite great catastrophes, spirit(ual) Masters – in Paulsen's
terms Builders – kept lost truths alive. Instead of India or Tibet (and
their Akashic records) still holding memorials of such treasures,
however, as in Churchward's views, for Paulsen it was flying saucer -
warriors who maintained the secrets of the universe (with the spatial
relations of the world religions, and certain archaeo-anthropological
details on the fringes of the Pacific – including Easter Island images,
and Meso-American pyramids and hieroglyphs – confirming that all
faiths and civilisations derived from Mu, dispersing both east and west
as fragments of a lost unity). In Brotherhood terminology, moreover,
UFO spacecraft were *mus*, survivals of continental Mu, and connected
to a Mothership.[49] The technology of Earth's most ancient civilisations
was thus still being kept up in practice, not just memorialised. Even
more significantly, *mus* and their inhabitants are taken to be God's

messengers or angels, and their more frequent appearances betoken a great transformation to come in the new Age of Aquarius and millennial time of Judgement.[50] The angelic world has here been humanised through UFO-ism; but the angels are super-humans in space (apart from Paulsen and his close disciples) linking the glorious past with a glorious future.

This mythic frame, though it is also a primary structure of paradise/unsatisfactoriness/paradise known across many cultures, recalls a significant feature of Melanesian cargo cults. In various cargo cult cosmologies, the old perfect time of creator beings and legendary ancestors was lost, to be followed by the brokenness of tribal conflict in a period that could even extend to include the injustices of colonialism. The lost perfection was to be restored – in Irian Jaya widespread terms such as *koreri* and *hai* denote peace, health, immortality, untold riches – with the stress being placed on the new possibilities presenting themselves externally: the newcomers and their goods from outside the indigenous cosmos.[51] Once the ambiguities of the present situation were resolved, what lay behind these external encounters would be truly revealed: the intended return of the ancestors, bearing untold gifts. The possibilities of the future, furthermore, amounted to the re-creation of primordial marvels – *in illo tempore*.

Of course the ancestral connection might not seem to work for Western contexts, in which veneration of the dead has been minimalised in ritual life. Yet it is a hidden assumption of scientific and technological thought, none the less, that all the skills, techniques and breakthroughs in knowledge are ancestral inheritances: unlike the animals, humans can 'increase their wisdom, their information, or their control over the environment from one generation to the next' because of what they receive from the past 'as *free gifts from the dead*'.[52] Viewing the Brotherhood of the Sun as a UFO cult, however, we see that the mainline terrestrial body of knowledge, especially 'science', has caused increasing problems, and will only produce widespread catastrophes, environmentally, economically and militarily, that require an apocalyptic solution.[53] Any future perfection will demand a *deus ex machina*, and if technology is to be part of the final solution, it will be as exponentially different from Western technology as Western technology is from Melanesian lithic cultures. This is why the present author wrote that 'the Cargo in this Millennium', as envisaged by Paulsen and his followers:

> cannot therefore simply be some superabundance of the technics and commodities already prevalent in the West, and

associated with 'greed for wealth and power', 'prestige [and] ...
the treadmill of competition' that are 'destroying any concept
of brotherhood.' It is rather a superior technology, an access to
materials currently unknown to humanity and an extraordinary harnessing of the universe's as yet unexploited powers.[54]

This superior technology can only arrive externally, extraterrestrially,
and in a miraculous(-looking) way parallel to the appearance of a
white-suited geologist, pickaxe in hand, out of a helicopter in the
Southern Highlands of Papua New Guinea. In much New Age jargon,
in any case, there has been a re-evaluation of the role of the dead, and
of 'the ladder of our ancestors' descending from other planets.[55] This is
why one is justified in linking UFO expectations to the phenomenon
of cargo cultism.

Grünschloß has proceeded beyond the Brotherhood case to test
more obvious instances of UFO cultism, some but not all of which
harbour the dream of some supranormal scientific disclosure. The
movement that split in 1997 into the Ground Crew Project (under
Valerie Donner) and the Planetary Activation Organization (under
Sheldan Nidle) is a crucial case in point. The split followed the failure
of Nidle's prediction, via telepathic channelling, that the 'Galactic
Federation' was sending 15 million spaceships to Earth, with the
extraordinary capacity to neutralise and beam up all earthly weaponry
into themselves. The Federation's astounding 'advanced technology'
could grant people 'full [and therefore peaceable] consciousness within
sixteen hours, replace our inferior communications systems, and transform Earth into a "galactic showcase" of ecological and sociological
equilibrium'.[56] Grünschloß's general findings are that:

> the hope for an imminent restoration of paradise within this
> world ('Heaven on Earth') [is] prevalent among UFO
> believers, [and that,] together with the expectation of a super-
> natural technology (here in the form of exotic, otherworldly
> Cargo from outer space) [it] can form a bridge between the
> scientific world view and an ecological esoteric religiosity.[57]

The special cargoistic component, in fact, draws the Western cultural
penchant for scientismic solutions, materialist comfort and the quests
for uncompromised physical wellbeing and happiness, back into the
sphere of *homo religiosus*, or more especially of New Age religion. The
attractions of UFO cultism, UFO-isms, or ufology in general, in fact,

are precisely their scientific *personae*, along with access to their belief worlds through the current sophisticated communications network.[58]

One has to be careful methodologically, however, in assessing the extent to which Cargo-type expectations are weak or strong in UFO movements. In the Raëlian grouping (founded 1973), for example, there is discourse comparable to that of the Brotherhood of the Sun about Master figures – in Raël's case the 'Elohim' making contact with us 'via PROPHETS, including Buddha, Moses, Jesus and Mohammed', and coming soon in spacecraft.[59] But talk of an extraordinary technology to accompany them is rather weak, compared to an emphasis on recovering lost spiritual truth and peace. It is more important for Raëlians that our own scientists have discovered DNA to tell us who our true creators are from the time of earlier UFO visitations.

Again, we must be appreciate that UFO-ist components in new religious movements do not have to be read as if anticipations of Cargo are automatically in view. In the iconography of the Brotherhood of the Sun, we note, spaceships, with angelic presences drawn pictorially as overshadowing and as integral to them, are taken as agencies of divine retribution (a well-known biblical motif). If the Brotherhood combine a sense of the Judgement with a new technological dawn, other movements more simply accentuate spaceships as destroyers of false civilisation. That has been the view of Elijah Muhammad, prophet leader of United States Black Islam, and it has been re-enunciated by the leader of the movement's most interesting sectlet, Louis Farrakhan.[60] Farrakhan has also struck up an accord with the Hopi Indians on this issue, from an indigenous American culture otherwise pacifist, but in this case wanting to let the divine will against invasive, exploitative white Americans be done.[61] Select coteries of the Hopi people, with whom members of the Brotherhood have sought relations (taking them to be survivors of Mu and reflective of the ancient 'Kingdom of the Sun'), are more interested in a return to uncomplicated ways and the peace of their mythic 'First World'.[62] For them, UFOs bespeak a millennial return, but not the Cargo.

In exploring the relationship between UFO-ist activity and cargo cultism, then, careful and methodologically sophisticated discernment will always be necessary. There should be no shame, however, in making both sociological differentiations *and* structural parallels in response to the complexities of data. Scholars ought to remain clear that the postmodernist reactions against philiosophic structuralism are not meant to preclude perceptive sociological and anthropological exercises in the comparison of social phenomena.[63] The opportunity

233

for fruitful comparative studies always remains, even if it demands cautious treatment and is highly challenging.

NOTES

1 F. E. Williams, *The Vailala Madness and the Destruction of Native Ceremonies in the Gulf Division*, Territory of Papua, Anthropology Report 4, Port Moresby, Government Printer, 1923, p. 29.
2 A documentary by P. D. Gasseau.
3 G. W. Trompf, 'Bilalaf', in G. W. Trompf (ed.), *Prophets of Melanesia*, Suva, Institute of Pacific Studies, 1981, pp. 40–1. Anonymous, 'They Still Believe in Cargo Cults', *Pacific Islands Monthly*, vol. 20, May, 1950, p. 85.
4 G. W. Trompf, *Payback: The Logic of Retribution in Melanesian Religions*, Cambridge, Cambridge University Press, 1994, p. 241.
5 R. M. Berndt, 'Reaction to Contact in the Eastern Highlands of New Guinea', *Oceania*, vol. 24, 1954, pp. 190ff.
6 See G. W. Trompf, 'Doesn't Colonialism make you Mad? The So-Called "Mur Madness" as an Index to the Study of New Religious Movements in Papua New Guinea during the Colonial Period', in S. Latukefu (ed.), *Papua New Guinea: A Century of Colonial Impact 1884–1984*, Port Moresby, University of Papua New Guinea Press, 1989, p. 257.
7 See, e.g., P. Worsley, *The Trumpet Shall Sound*, St Albans, Paladin, 1970, pp. 92, 121, 168–72, 198, 210–16, 255.
8 Anon., 'Getting to the People', *Family*, Anglican Church of Papua New Guinea, vol. 3, 1976, p. 9; cf. W. Houghton, 'Cargo Cults in the Managalas', unpublished typescript, Goroka Teachers College, Goroka, 1977, pp. 1–6.
9 G. W. Trompf, 'La teoria della meraviglia e i culti del cargo in Melanesia', trans. C. Camporesi, *Religioni e Società*, vol. 17, 43 2002, p. 34.
10 G. W. Trompf, *Melanesian Religion*, Cambridge, Cambridge University Press, 1990, pp. 46–8.
11 Following P. Lawrence, *Road Belong Cargo*, Manchester, Manchester University Press, 1964, pp. 21–6.
12 E.g. F. E. Williams, *Papuans of the Trans-Fly*, Oxford, Oxford University Press, 1936; cf. R. Lacey, 'A Glimpse of the Enga Worldview', *Catalyst*, vol. 3.2, 1973, pp. 37–47; Trompf, *Payback*, p. 276.
13 Cf., e.g., M. Leay, *The Land that Time Forgot*, London, Hunt & Blackett, 1937.
14 G. W. Trompf, 'Introduction', to G. W. Trompf (ed.), *Cargo Cults and Millenarian Movements*, Religion and Society, vol. 29, Berlin, Mouton de Gruyter, 1990, pp. 1–15. The description of millennial movements has been made famous by Y. Talmon in 'Millenarian Movements', *Archives Européennes de Sociologie*, vol. 7, 1966, p. 159.
15 G. W. Trompf, 'Keeping the *Lo* under a Melanesian Messiah: An Analysis of the Pomio *Kivung*, East New Britain', in J. Barker (ed.), *Christianity in Oceania*, ASOA Monographs, vol. 12, Lanham, University Press of America, 1990, p. 73.
16 A suggestion in M. Reay, *Transformation Movements and Associations in Papua New Guinea*, Political and Social Change Monograph, vol. 3, Canberra, Australian National University, forthcoming.

17 G. W. Trompf, 'Easter Island: The Site of the First Pacfic Cargo Cult?', in G. Casadio (ed.), *Ugo Bianchi: una vita per la storia delle religioni*, Rome, Calamo, 2002, pp. 441–65. The formally arranged Rapanui statues all face symbolically over ancestral *lands*.

18 For one account, see I. Kuhn, *Nests above the Abyss*, London, China Inland Mission, 1949, p. 123.

19 G. Shepperson, 'Nyasaland and the Millennium', in S. Thrupp (ed.), *Millennial Dreams in Action*, New York, Scribners, 1970, p. 157.

20 T. Swain and G. W. Trompf, *Religions of Oceania*, Library of Religious Beliefs and Practices, London, Routledge, 1995, p. 175; cf. pp. 122–32 for general orientation.

21 C. G. Jung, *Flying Saucers: A Modern Myth of Things Seen in the Skies*, trans. by R. F. C. Hull, New York, Signet Books/New American Library, 1969 [1959], chs 1–2.

22 See W. J. Hanegraaff, *New Age Religion and Western Culture*, Leiden, E. J. Brill, 1996, pp. 95–100.

23 E.g. A. Michel, *The Truth about Flying Saucers*, London, R. Hale, 1957; P. C. W. Davies, *We Are Not Alone*, London, Penguin, 1995; J. E. Mack, *Abductions*, New York, Scribners, 1994; F. J. Connell, 'Flying Saucers and Theology', in A. Michel, *The Truth about Flying Saucers*, New York, Criterion 1974, pp. 255–8.

24 E. von Däniken, *Chariots of the Gods?*, trans. M. Heron, London, Corgi, 1972. Different, if related, approaches are taken by A. Tomas in *We Are Not the First*, London, Sphere, 1972, and Z. Sitchin in *Genesis Revisited*, New York, Avon, 1990. Cf. also, for a relevant critical symposium, J. R. Lewis (ed.), *The Gods Have Landed*, Albany, State University of New York, 1995.

25 E.g. M. K. Jessup, *The Case for the UFO*, Garland, Varo Manufacturing Co., 1959; J. F. Blumrich, *The Spaceships of Ezekiel*, London, Corgi, 1974; cf. B. H. Downing, *The Bible and Flying Saucers*, London, Sphere, 1973; Sitchen, *Genesis Revisited* (the Bible); D. Leslie and G. Adamski, *The Flying Saucers have Landed*, London, Futura, 1977 (the 'Mahabharata'). Or even interpreting BVM sightings as UFOs, cf. D. Barclay, *Aliens: The Final Answer?*, London, Blandford, 1995, ch. 9.

26 Cf. Trompf, 'Introduction', p. 14.

27 E.g. G. W. Trompf, *Religion and Money: Some Aspects*, Adelaide, 1980, pp. 10–12 on Rev 'Ike', or Eikerokotter III; L. Lindstrom, 'Knowledge of Cargo, Knowledge of Cult', in Trompf (ed.), *Cargo Cults and Millenarian Movements*, pp. 255–6 (Oral Roberts).

28 The three 'Exit Statements' on Heaven's Gate's home page are discussed by A. Grünschloß in 'When We Enter into my Father's Spacecraft', *Marburg Journal of Religion*, vol. 3.2, 1998, p. 8 and n. 72. The German version of this article is found in D. Zeller (ed.), *Religion im Wandel der Kosmologien*, Frankfurt am Main, P. Lang, 1999.

29 Thus the Chicago-based coterie has been researched by L. Festinger, H. W. Riecken and S. Schachterm. See their *When Prophecy Fails*, New York, Harper & Row, 1964.

30 T. Bethurum, *Facing Reality*, Prescott, self-published, 1959, pp. 110, 126, 136–51. My rare copy is annotated by a reader adopting the esoteric quotation, quoting Charles Leadbeater; cf. G. J. Tillett, *The Elder Brother*,

London, Routledge & Kegan Paul, 1982, ch. 9.

31 S. Holroyd, *Briefing for Landing on Planet Earth*, London, Corgi, 1979; cf. Barclay, *Aliens*, p. 141 (quotation).

32 D. Keyhoe, *The Flying Saucer Conspiracy*, New York, Holt & Co., 1955; the succinct listing here taken from Betherum, *Facing Reality*, p. 103.

33 G. W. Trompf, 'The Cargo and the Millennium on Both Sides of the Pacific', in Trompf (ed.), *Cargo Cults and Millenarian Movements*, pp. 35–96.

34 H. Desroches, *Dieux d'hommes: Dictionnaires des messianismes et millénarismes*, Paris, Presse Universitaire de France, 1969; N. Cohn, 'Réflexions sur le millénarisme', *Archives de Sociologie Européennes* 5 (1958), pp. 103–7; K. Burridge, *New Heaven New Earth*, Oxford, Blackwell, 1969. The literature is extensively covered by G. W. Trompf in 'Millenarism: History, Sociology and Cross-Cultural Analysis', *Journal of Religious History*, 2000, vol. 24.1, pp. 103–24.

35 See especially O. Lake's review in *American Anthropologist*, vol. 94, 1992, pp. 510–11. He decides, despite his overall appreciation, that the material in *Cargo Cults and Millenarian Movements* as a whole 'does not settle Trompf's proposal regarding transoceanic parallels' of cargo cultism, and does not defend his 'premise regarding "similar predicaments".' Other reviewers in social scientific journals, however (e.g. *Archives de Sciences Sociales des Religions*, 1994) do not have the same quibbles about the parallelism – although one assessor, J. Barker, while he deems most articles do not 'Match the editor's [precise] billing' that cargo cultism and cargoism, not just millenarianism, are 'useful in cross-cultural enquiry', considers nevertheless that the editor's main case 'will inevitably remind us that the West has not only provided the hoped-for source of cargo for Melanesians, but was also the inventor of the concept of cargo cult' (review in *American Ethnologist*, vol. 21, 1994, p. 936).

36 *Pace* such radical thinkers as Marvin Harris, who took original Christianity to be a cargo cult (*Cows, Pigs, Wars and Witches*, London, Hutchinson, 1974, pp. 133–203), quite reductionalistically in my view – see my alternative view in 'When was the First Millenarian Movement? Qumran and the Implications of Historical Sociology', in A. Sharma (ed.), *The Sum of our Choices*, McGill Studies in Religion, vol. 4, Atlanta, Scholars Press, 1996, esp. pp. 243–4; Jonathan Z. Smith sees 'cargoistic structures' throughout religious life quite generally; see his *Imagining Religion*, Chicago, Chicago University Press, 1982, pp. 83–120.

37 Grünschloß, 'When we Enter into my Father's Spacecraft', pp. 1–18.

38 Trompf, 'Cargo and the Millennium', p. 37 *et passim*.

39 See Paulsen's autobiographical volume, *Christ Consciousness*, Salt Lake City, Builders Publishing Co., 1984, replacing his earlier *Sunburst: The Return of the Ancients*, Goleta, Sunburst, 1980 – p. 520 introduces the term 'Builders', which is essentially Masonic; see, e.g., J. F. Newton, *The Builders: A Story and Study of Masonry*, London, George Allen & Unwin, 1918.

40 Paulsen, *Sunburst*, pp. 522–3.

41 *Ibid.*, pp. 520, 522 – the square-bracketed section is the present author's.

42 For help here, see G. W. Trompf, 'Macrohistory in Blavatsky, Steiner and Guénon', in A. Faivre and W. Hanegraaff (eds), *Western Esotericism and the*

Science of Religion, Gnostica, vol. 2, Louvain, Peeters, 1998, pp. 274–86. For background in the primary literature, start with T. A. Barker (ed.), *The Mahatma Letters to A. P. Sinnett*, 3rd edn, C. Humphries & E. Benjamin (eds), Adyar, Theosophical Publishing House, 1962, p. 46.

43   See Trompf, 'Cargo and the Millennium', pp. 41–2.

44   On the concept of mythic macrohistory, see G. W. Trompf, 'Macrohistory and Acculturation', *Comparative Studies in Society and History*, vol. 31.4, 1989, pp. 615–48.

45   Paulsen, *Sunburst*, pp. 327, 354, 374–5, 381, 394, 387–402.

46   Start, for example, with S. Hutin, *Les Civilisations inconnues*, Paris, Arthème Fayard, 1961, esp. p. 2, ch. 4.

47   Out of Churchward's five-volume set, one is advised to start with his *The Lost Continent of Mu* (1931), but on technological stresses, note his *The Cosmic Forces of Mu* (1934) and *The Second Book of the Cosmic Forces of Mu* (1935), all now available: New York, Paper Library, 1968.

48   E.g., Paulsen, *Sunburst*, chs 11, 23.

49   N. Paulsen, *Brotherhood of the Sön*, Santa Barbara, Sunburst Industries, 1973, p. 21 (note: the pamphlet is unpaginated); *Sunburst*, p. 600, for his significant references to P. Tomkins, *Secrets of the Great Pyramid*, London, Allen Lane, 1973; *Mysteries of the Mexican Pyramids*, New York, Harper & Row, 1976.

50   For bearings, see Trompf, 'Cargo and the Millennium', pp. 47–51 and cf. Z. Sitchin, *The Twelfth Planet*, New York, Stein & Day, 1976, pp. 132–41, 156–7 on translating the ancient Sumerian word *mu* as spaceship.

51   For a preliminary orientation, see J. Pouwer, *Enkele aspecten van de Mimika-cultuur (Nederlands zuidwest Nieuw Guinea)*, The Hague, Staatsdrukkerij en Uitgeversbedrijf, 1955; G. W. Trompf, 'The Theology of Beig Wen, the Would-be Successor to Yali', *Catalyst*, vol. 6.3, 1976, pp. 166–74. Cf. F. C. Kamma, *Koreri: Messianic Movements in the Biak-Numfor Culture Area*, M. J. van de Vatherst-Smit (trans.), W. E. Haver Droeze-Hulswit (ed.), Verhandelingen van het Koninklijk Instituut voor Taal-, Land- en Volkenkunde, Translation Series, vol. 15, The Hague, Martinus Nijhoff, 1972 (*koreri*); B. Giay, 'Hai: Motif Pengharapan "Jaman Bagaia", *Deiyai* (Jayapura, Ind.), Sept.–Oct. 1994, vol. 4, pp. 5–8 (*hai*).

52   S. I. Hayakawa, *Language in Thought and Action*, London, George Allen & Unwin, 1974, p. 13 (emphasis in the original).

53   Consider the Brotherhood's use of Yogananda, *The Road Ahead*, Nevada City, Ananda Publications, 1973. Paulsen is taken as the true successor of Yogananda. See Trompf, 'The Cargo and the Millennium', pp. 35–6, 51.

54   'Particularly those of the Sun, so that men and women can truly "follow the simple laws of God and nature".' *Ibid.*, pp. 43–4, quoting *en route* Paulsen, *Sunburst*, pp. 206–7, 353–5; cf. S. Duquette, *Sunburst [Farm] Family Cookbook*, Santa Barbara, Sunburst Industries, 1978, p. 5.

55   Quoting B. Crowley and A. Pollock, *Return to Mars*, Melbourne, Matchbooks, 1989, p. 157 (note the faint allusion to Gen. 28:12).

56   Grünschloß, 'When we Enter into my Father's Spacecraft', p. 4.

57   *Ibid.*, p. 8.

58   Of background importance here is W. Braden, *The Age of Aquarius: Technology and the Cultural Revolution*, Chicago, Eyre & Spottiswoode, 1971.

59 Raël, *The Truth Finally Revealed* (pamphlet), Sydney, Australian Raëlian Movement, 2001, p. 2; A. Hansen, 'God in Space', *Union Recorder* (Sydney), vol. 75 (4 September 1995), pp. 8–9. On the theme of the Masters, especially as pervaded through Theosophy, see B. French, 'The Theosophical Masters', unpublished doctoral dissertation, University of Sydney, 2000 – to be published in the series *Gnostica* (Louvain, Peeters).

60 See D. Walker, 'The Black Muslims in American Society', in Trompf (ed.), *Cargo Cults and Millenarian Movements*, pp. 346, 350, 369, 381.

61 *Ibid.*, p. 381. See also D. Walker, 'Louis Farrakhan and America's "Nation of Islam"', in G. W. Trompf (ed.), *Islands and Enclaves*, Delhi, Sterling, 1993, pp. 71–100. Cf. Trompf, 'Cargo and the Millennium', pp. 46–7, 51–2.

62 See M. Behr, *From the Mesas*, Santa Cruz, University of California, Santa Cruz, 1975, pp. 1–2 – the volume was published for an exhibition in the Mary Porter Sesnon Gallery.

63 Using V. Descombes, *Modern French Philosophy*, trans. L. Scott-Fox and J. M. Harding, Cambridge, Cambridge University Press, 1980, ch. 3.

12

ALIEN DOUBTS

Reading abduction narratives post-apocalyptically

Jodi Dean

It's the end of the world as we know it

The link between aliens and apocalypse seems like an obvious one.
Examples include H. G. Wells's *War of the Worlds* and its contemporary reenactment in the 1996 movie *Independence Day* (also known
as *ID-4*).The coming of the aliens is the end of the world, the
judgement day when fire rains upon the earth. In *ID-4* this judgement is delivered with characteristic homophobia and puritanism:
the first character to 'get it' is gay and we see the most havoc being
visited upon the contemporary Sodom-and-Gomorrahs of New
York, Los Angeles and Capitol Hill.[1] And then there are UFO
cults. In the first influential academic study of one of these groups,
When Prophesy Fails, Leon Festinger, Henry Reichen and Stanley
Schachter examined a contactee cult waiting for a flood predicted
by 'the Space Brothers' who had reported the forthcoming deluge to
the group's leader, Mrs Keech.[2] A more recent example of an apocalyptic UFO cult is, of course, Heaven's Gate. This androgynous
group of peaceful California website developers and *Star Trek* fans
packed overnight bags and donned Nike sports shoes before leaving
their 'containers' (i.e. their bodies) to join the alien spacecraft
allegedly travelling in the tail of the Hale-Bopp comet. Finally, we
might consider the familiar strangeness of the alien icon so prevalent in contemporary popular culture. From the odd performance
art of SCHWA where aliens appear as icons for the inescapability of
corporate control, conspiracy and surveillance (the depth of the
conspiracy is reiterated in the acronym itself – it doesn't stand for
anything but appears as both the corporate publisher of the material
and as its unsettling content), to the skateboard accessory company
Alien Workshop, with its slogan '2001 Global Takeover', the ubiq-
uitous 'grays' and 'greens' (i.e. types of alien) suggest less an

alienation from than an acquiescent participation in marketing, media and event for their own sake. The alien icon, in other words, is a logo without a brand behind it, a logo that traverses the networks of contemporary culture fuelled by an inexplicable energy. It must be the end of the world when happy faces, Janet Jackson, anorexic Calvin Klein models and the cat in the hat have all morphed into aliens.[3]

These three examples of aliens and apocalypse appear in modes that Lee Quinby has analysed as technological apocalypse, divine apocalypse and ironic apocalypse.[4] In the first, the aliens use their superior technology to destroy (or attempt to destroy) the Earth. In the second, the aliens choose human prophets to whom they reveal their ultimate intentions or whom they select for salvation. In the third, as Quinby writes, 'Doomsday anxieties simply become banal.'[5]

But we might consider yet a fourth alien appearance also prevalent in contemporary American technoculture: alien abduction. If anything is apocalyptic, this surely must be. Abductees describe being brought into the light, being chosen as messengers to persuade humanity to transform itself or be damned as lab-rats or breeding stock for an unspeakable alien future. Like biblical prophets, abductees are often shown horrible images of destruction. Or they are seduced by promises of Earth's future membership in a galactic council, promises that hinge on our ability to unite in peace and harmonise our relations with the environment. Marked by cataclysm and revelation, the apocalyptic messages of abduction have circulated into popular media in the works of Whitley Strieber, David Jacobs, Budd Hopkins and Harvard professor John Mack.[6]

I want to complicate this apocalyptic rendering of alien abduction by emphasising the post-apocalyptic elements of the alien abduction discourse. I use the term 'discourse' in order to flag the practices, relations and technologies that have provided an environment into which abduction as an informational assemblage could be installed. Constituted around the suspicion that 'something is missing', that 'something needs to be explained', the abduction discourse compiles hope and fear, present and future, transformation and destruction in ways that sometimes unsettle the apocalypticism that tends to dominate cultural manifestations of the alien. *After the end*, something can happen and, indeed, much of the abduction discourse is an investigation into what happens *after* the 'world as we know it' has ended for the abductee and for the human species. The abduction phenomenon, says John Mack, reflects 'a growing realization that many of the catastrophic events of this century now ending have derived from radical secularism and spiritual emptiness'.[7] Through its attempts to understand what happens after the aliens have come, the abduction discourse pushes the compulsion to do something up against the suspicion that nothing can be trusted.

By highlighting the post-apocalyptic elements of abduction, then, I want to draw out an overriding doubt, a mistrust even, that is different from the irony and cynicism sometimes associated with post-apocalypse. In the discourse on alien abduction and, I would argue, contemporary technoculture more generally, the link between banality and doubt is often broken, such that lack of meaning connects neither with lack of vision nor inability to act. On the contrary, the very absence of a structure of meaning may paradoxically infuse efforts at agency. So I want, first, to bring out the post-apocalytic elements of abduction; second, to link these elements to the collapse of truth and certainty within the discourse; and third, to argue that this collapse of certainty and loss of closure be understood in terms of excesses that enable action.

Now what?

To begin reading abduction post-apocalyptically, I draw from the words of abductees. Here is David Caywood, an abductee from Michigan:

> First, it should be noted that I do not (or at least work to not) recognize the next moment or the one after that or the one after that, *ad infinitum* … as the 'future'. My new paradigm(s) in direct relationship to my abductions have shattered my former notions about space and linear time. So much so, that I have given up on the whole business and concluded that linear time models such as future, past and present are only useful when dealing with mortgage payments, time clocks, bus schedules, and while waiting for my next coffee break at work.[8]

This remark clearly expresses elements of the post-apocalyptic that James Berger explores in *After the End*. Caywood is attempting to navigate within the uncertainties of a shattered temporal and spatial reality. Abduction has destroyed his way of thinking, functioning as or representing 'ruptures, pivots, fulcrums, separating what came before from what came after'.[9]

The destruction of temporal reality is, not surprisingly, accompanied by a confusion of temporal sequence: before and after, cause and effect are unlinked, disarticulated.[10] In Caywood's words:

> At present (which is all there really ever was and is) our
> future or the 'future', is what I call 'trans-temporal'. Meaning
> it (the future) shifts from past to present and back again and
> does not exist except as a concept in higher-order mathe-
> matics, and the 'future' completely folds in on itself when
> viewed with the eyes of a quantum theorist. In other words,
> the future can be found as far back as we wish to look and as
> recent as a few moments ago.[11]

Not only do we see here the temporal inversion Berger describes, but
we find also the post-apocalyptic attempt to narrate what seems to
resist narration, the compulsion to speak the unsaid. Abductees often
emphasise that what they have experienced, or, in fact, what they are
reliving through hypnosis, can't be described, that it is an experience
they feel, but can't express, an experience beyond language.
Researchers acknowledge that abduction seems beyond human understanding. None the less, they all try to find, or develop, a way of
sharing their sense that reality has shattered.

In Caywood's remarks, as in those of most of the abductees I've
read, heard and spoken with, these compulsions to narrate an experience that seems to have happened and not happened, that takes place
(or doesn't) in dream, everyday reality, visions and some kind of other
dimension and that resists earthly temporality, manifest themselves in
two ways: through the reiteration of scientific authority, on the one
hand and through a grammar of the profound proclamation, on the
other. We might think of this reiteration of scientific authority and
prophetic proclamation as an example of the way post-apocalyptic
discourse links and re-links the remainders of meaning left over after
technological, divine and ironic apocalypse. Put somewhat differently,
all these apocalyptic modes continue in the discourse after the apocalypse, that is, after the abductee's world has collapsed, after the
invasion of the aliens and even after the end of Earth insofar as some
abductees claim that the aliens are visitors from the future come to bid
us to change our destructive ways. What the end of the world entails is
that these specific modes of apocalyptic thinking lose their hold on
meaning. The all-encompassing doubt that accompanies 'the end'
unchains the elements within each mode, enabling ever-varying and
unstable new links to be made between and among them.

In this vein, Caywood invokes the 'quantum theorist'. Mack writes,
'For many abductees the reproductive experiences ... are so vivid and
real that they use the language of genetic biology and speak of DNA
alteration and genetic harvesting ... '[12] Mack's subjects also use terms

like 'vibratory rates', 'transceivers', 'reprogramming' and 'cells' changing on a 'molecular level'. Throughout the abduction discourse, as in ufology more generally, an appeal to science for method, corroboration and authorisation marks the seriousness, the realness, of the events and experiences under consideration. Simultaneously, however, the very appeal to science re-inscribes uncertainty within the discourse's own terms: abductees doubt what has happened to them because they can't prove it; researchers continue to bash and berate one another for failing to come up with irrefutable evidence.

At the same time, abductees often use a language of proclamation in their attempts to communicate the depth, the significance, of their experience. Caywood told me, 'What will be found now will be found then.' Recounting 'information' that she 'remembered/received' from her alien encounters, Debbie Jordan intones, 'You have been blinded by your lives. You have let your negativity and your fear keep your inner eye closed. Do not fear. God is life, eternal. Our greater good is that which works together to bring to the Spirit that which belongs to it.'[13] Mack quotes an abductee, Karin: 'Food is sacred. Food is God. Food is love.'[14]

So far, in reading abduction for its post-apocalyptic elements, I've emphasised first the shattering of reality, understood in terms of ways of thinking about and experiencing the world, and second the attempts to describe and deal with this shattering, attempts often authorised through links to science and prophecy. I want to include one more idea here, that is, what Berger refers to as a turn to the primary, primal and immediate, the intrusion of the wild and untamed parts of self and world, world and universe. The wild side of abduction appears in the emphasis on sex, dreams, reptilians, the cosmos as trickster and, most importantly, native or ethnic others.

The sexual dimension of abduction is probably the most well known. Numerous abductees claim that aliens have extracted their eggs or sperm. Men and women alike tend to find the experience painful, frightening and humiliating, a violation even when accompanied by orgasm. Ejaculation seems to be a priority for the aliens. Abduction researcher David Jacobs, for example, has worked with a female subject who claimed that the aliens made her perform oral sex on a human male abductee in order to get a sperm sample from him.[15] Although the sexual dimension of abduction is nearly always focused on reproduction, there may be additional elements of erotic feeling, desire and orgasm. These are often the result of what is referred to as the alien's 'mindscan' procedure: the alien stares into the eyes of the abductee and makes these feelings arise. Why? Guesses include power, that is, alien efforts to control human subjects; curiosity, because the aliens have no sexuality of their own; and transformation or a kind of materialisation of the metaphors of hybridity and bridging that the aliens are trying to teach humans in order to enable humans to break out of Western metaphysics and save the planet. Mack quotes Eva: 'In one encounter I learned that the impregnation process I experienced … served as a process for the elevation of my conscious awareness into an individuated Being who is on a path of self-discovery back to God, learning and experiencing along the way wholeness, completion, nonattachment and most of all, humility.'[16]

Abductees often refer to their abduction experiences as 'dreams', although this does not mean that they understand their experiences to be less real. On the contrary, dreams provide direct access to what has happened to them, to how the world as they knew it ended and to what happens now. Sometimes abductees divide experience into multiple levels: 'waking reality', 'visions', 'the vibratory dimension' or 'astral plane' and 'dreams'. What is significant is the way that dreams and dream-like experiences provide insights which are more important, more primary, than everyday life. Like some psychoanalytic, psycho-therapeutic and New Age approaches to reality and consciousness, abduction works to uncover primary experiences that may have been forgotten or repressed.

Reptilians are one of the less well-known of the abducting aliens. They look like giant reptiles: I say, however, that the reptilians are instances of a kind of primal intrusion not simply because they look like reptiles, which is pretty good evidence on its own, but because abductees often interpret reptilian aliens in precisely this way. Mack describes what happened to Karin:

> Karin was convinced that an unpleasant and frightening encounter with ugly, scaly, lizard-like beings that she had not seen before occurred at a time when she was struggling with 'reptilian' energies and feelings toward a rough crowd of construction workers at the pub where she worked – people whose level of awareness she was also trying to raise through sharing her experiences … She drew this experience to her, Karin suggested, because she had been dealing with an angry, frustrated and judgemental part of herself and she saw a 'resonation' connecting the energy of the people at the bar,

'the reptilian things' in her encounter and negative or rageful elements of her own psyche that she was trying to integrate.[17]

Similarly, 'Greg' felt drawn to and repulsed by the reptilian because it seemed to represent 'the darkest, most ugly part of myself. I want to embrace it and ultimately heal it. I don't want to push it away because when I push it away, I push away a part of myself and I can't be whole.'[18]

If sex, dreams and reptilians suggest a post-apocalyptic intrusion of the primal, then the vision of a trickster cosmos highlights the elements of wildness and unpredictability appearing after the laws of nature have collapsed. Few abduction researchers can reconcile their findings with a mainstream physics with little tolerance for claims of multidimensional and galactic travel. Consequently, they are left arguing – and using the words of abductees to support these arguments – that the descriptions offered by scientists are inadequate, that they simply fail to do justice to the changing, living, inspirited character of the cosmos. Mack asks, 'Is it that the phenomenon itself is redolent of a kind of tricksterism that mocks our technology and the literalness of minds, which require material proof before they believe anything really exists?'[19]

Finally, the last example of the place of the primal and immediate in the abduction discourse involves the figure of the shaman, of the native other who authenticates the discourse. A couple of prefatory remarks: almost everything I have described up to this point can be found throughout the abduction discourse, in the work of various researchers and the testimonies of most abductees. Of course, there are differences in interpretation. Some researchers view abduction as a positive experience. They emphasise the election of abductees and the revelation offered by their encounters with aliens. Other researchers are more negative. They see abduction as a catastrophe; most of us are damned, abductees perhaps less damned than others. When read post-apocalyptically, this distinction between positive and negative abduction scenarios is not so important. What does become significant are the elements that enable the discourse overall to deal with the end, with the destruction of common sense, of everydayness. And, again, the elements that appear include the appeal to scientific authority, to prophetic grammar and to themes of primal immediacy. With regard to the last element, however, although nearly all researchers mention the trickster cosmos, reptilians, dreams and sex, Mack is virtually alone in talking about the shaman.

To be sure, ufology in general claims to be a global phenomenon – it has to because its concerns are the planet's concerns. All ufologists say that sighting reports come from all over the world. In fact, this is an important counter to the claim that flying saucers are simply the products of American sci-fi movies. MUFON (Mutual UFO Network) annual meetings always feature speakers from different countries with reports of extraterrestrial happenings – Mexico, Brazil and South Africa have been especially visible. None the less, only Mack has tied together the abduction experience with the altered states of the shaman and the oral and folkloric traditions of a particularly 'native' reading of 'indigenous' or non-Western cultures.

There are some good reasons for this: Mack received funding for what is a very expensive project (involving travel, translation, transcription). Few in the abduction community could mobilise this kind of capital. But more significant is the UFO community's own history: abduction as an alien contact phenomenon had a very difficult time gaining legitimacy in UFO circles. In the 1950s and 1960s some very visible contactees got a lot of popular media attention for their claims regarding the Space Brothers, trips to Venus and Saturn and interactions with alien visitors. Scientifically- minded UFO researchers felt that their work on flying saucers was stigmatised in that the general public lumped them together with the contactees – as occurred, for example, in the famous Condon Report, the evaluation of the Air Force Project Blue Book that reported that further work on UFOs was pointless. So, the research wing of the UFO community steered clear of contact reports, of channelling, of mysticism, of anything that hinted of what would come to be thought of as spiritualist or New-Agey. In this setting, abduction researchers acquired legitimacy through, on the one hand, an emphasis on their methods, on the scientific quality of their use of hypnosis and on the fact that their tests could be confirmed with lie detectors, and through, on the other hand, an emphasis on the trauma endured by abductees. Unlike contactees who had a great time zipping around in flying saucers, who thrived on their experiences, abductees were traumatised. They were victims. They neither invited nor enjoyed what was happening to them.

In this vein, abduction researcher Budd Hopkins resoundingly criticised John Mack at the 1997 MUFON annual meeting: 'Members of the Heaven's Gate cult maintained the extreme position that suicide was essential to leave this "depraved" planet so as to unite with alien beings on a "higher plane". But for anyone to accept the idea that we must bypass our fellow humans and look to the UFO occupants as the final source of ecological wisdom and spiritual growth is, unfortunately, to take a step along the same path.'[20] Hopkins argues that, when Mack looks at abduction as transformative rather than disastrous, he falls prey to the aliens' deceits. Mack takes them at their word, not realising that aliens can't be trusted.

In his alternative reading of abduction, Mack finds three major links between aliens and the shaman: the transformation experience, the dissolution of Western science's sharp division between the material and spiritual, and a sense of care for the ecological future of the planet. What strikes me, however, is the way Mack uses the native other to validate himself and his project. He looks for similarities between 'the reports of tribal people' and those of Americans. He also identifies 'a language of words and bodily expressions of intense feeling ... similar and relatively unmistakable across cultures'.[21] In his book, *Passport to the Cosmos*, Mack presents himself as the white man trusted by the native. He notes that Credo Mutwa, 'perhaps the best-known African *sangoma* or medicine man outside of his native South Africa', told him that 'most Africans are reluctant to talk to white people about extraterrestrial matters and that none of the established UFO groups in South Africa had bothered to talk to blacks'.[22] Moreover, Mack finds that 'medicine men and women' are 'usually pleased' with what he is doing for they see it as 'affirming tribal myths, legends and experiences. It is an example of a "white man" crediting matters that are sacred for them, that have been known in their cultures for centuries.'[23]

A conflation of emotional experiences, spiritual claims and native traditions, with little regard to history and much opposition to a unified Western scientific perspective, was apparent at the Star Wisdom Conference co-sponsored by PEER (The Program for Extraordinary Experience Research), Mack's organisation for inquiry into alternative experiences. Advertised as an exploration of contact with the cosmos bringing together 'Native Americans who describe contact with "star people" and Westerners who describe "alien abduction"' experiences, the featured conference speakers were astronaut Edgar Mitchell, Choctaw native elder Sequoyah Trueblood, Brazilian shaman from the Uru-wau-wau tribe Bernardo Peixota, Cherokee Chief and Tibetan Buddhist teacher Dyhani Ywahoo, John Mack, and various experiencers, individuals from Western culture who describe experiences with nonhuman intelligences. Rather than an exploration of contact, however, the conference was marked by a New Age eliding of a variety of different kinds of experience, different cultures and different histories under the sign of personal transformation via great emotional enthusiasm and an expression of concern for the planet. The weekend began with a ceremony of thanks to the spirit led by

Sequoyah Trueblood. It included discussions of quantum physics and tearful outbursts from abductees. One participant was selling fabulous crop circle photographs. The representatives of native peoples wore elaborate costumes. A woman in the bathroom told me about the time the aliens took her to a cave to talk to dolphins.

On the one hand, this pastiche of exoticised ethnicity suggests that, after the end, after the organising systems of Western science have collapsed, after the aliens or Spirit or Source have guided us beyond our current impasse, we will be one people. Here, the alien offers the perspective of the planet, the globe, the Earth. It should come as no surprise that Mack emphasises a link between abduction and environmentalism: the abduction experience allegedly inspires abductees to become more ecologically minded. The cosmic perspective provided by the alien is supposed to put us in touch with an essential, primal commonality. But the terms through which this unified planet is figured indicate the instability of its post-apocalyptic imagining. It's not so easy to think about the world after it has ended. Extreme emotions – sobbing, rage, erotic vibrations – link together the rather antagonistic discourses of science and spirituality. The claims to scientific authority suggest a generalisability, a universalisability, that can make the prophetic proclamations more than simply an isolated, subjective vision or religious experience. Their presence in the discourse, in other words, has globalising effects. Similarly, the claims to spiritual meaning, to profound transformative experience, correct the gaps and failures in science - its inability to deal with the excesses of emotion, experience and reality. Each compensates for the lacks and excesses in the other.

What sutures these two themes together is the shaman, the 'native', the indigenous other. Empowered by the secrets of age-old healing practices, by an inspirited relation to the world that enables him or her to conjure up the unseen forces that surround us, and by a willingness to accept the reality of extraterrestrial intervention in human experience, the shaman occupies the place where contradiction is embraced, encouraged, where it is a sign of sophistication, of a global perspective. Mack finds that 'Abductees and those, like myself, who work with them are often drawn to Native American spiritual leaders, for they appear to have a deep and enduring familiarity with the entities we call aliens and the role they have played in enabling them to maintain their own connection with the Creator.'[24] In the shamanic world or in the native traditions that Mack links together, morphings from animal to alien, from spiritual to material, from past to future, are familiar aspects of the multidimensional realities in which humanity is situated.

The shaman's apparent connection with primal, cosmic forces, with natures and cultures far removed from contemporary technoculture, thus attests to the meaningfulness of abduction. The abduction experience, especially in its ego-shattering dimension, is a non-ordinary state of consciousness, 'similar to the symbolic worlds of the shamans of indigenous cultures'.[25]

In *Passport to the Cosmos*, Mack gives details from the personal experiences of three shamans, one from the rain forests of Brazil, one a Native American activist and one, a South African healer. For the most part, these accounts are case histories, personal snapshots or screen images disconnected from any larger history. It reminds me of a television commercial for AT&T or a computer company, or of the Internet itself: there are one-to-one links between persons, links already disconnected from complicating networks of power, privilege and history.

Mack looks at all three shamans as 'bridge people'. All three have Western and 'native' backgrounds. All three have rejected their Western 'backgrounds' – Catholicism, university training, participation in the US military, indoctrination with Western values – to embrace a worldview that links multiple domains of reality and experience, aliens and mysticism, transformation and a sense of the global. What this entails in practice is Mack's insistence on the multiple, inextricable strands of myth, tradition, dream, ritual hallucination and possible exaggeration and confabulation. That is, his judgement as to what to believe in the words of the shaman rests on authenticity, precisely that authenticity provided by the authentic, primal, native. Western, commercial, scientific, and non-mystical, are automatically inauthentic. So even though the three shamans have Western training, what makes them 'real' is their rejection of the West. This rejection is a kind of purification that, even as it may cause the shaman personal pain, enables him to serve as the authentic link between scientific and spiritual. The shaman authenticates abduction, not because he has not been corrupted by Western media and provides an untarnished perspective, but because he rejects Western ways of knowing in favour of practices, rituals, legends and experiences that confirm the transformational potential that accompanies alien encounters.

Primal doubts

There is another dimension of the shaman or native important to a post-apocalyptic reading of abduction: the shaman is the figuration of doubt. Abductees express doubt all the time. They remain perpetually unsure if they really were taken into spacecraft by big-eyed alien beings or might just be imagining things. What Mack has done is situate shamans in the place of doubt or uncertainty, thereby transforming this doubt into a strength, a virtue, of the abduction experience itself.

For most abductees, acknowledging alien interference in their lives is painful and time-consuming. They are plagued by uncertainty. Their books are offered as testimonies to their experience. In painstaking detail, they document the fleeting, ambiguous evidence of abduction, the process of becoming abductees, of coming to think about their lives, experiences and memories in ways most of them would have dismissed or laughed at had it not happened to them. Abductee Anna Jamerson writes: 'I accept and reject their existence daily. I can believe in them when I know I have been abducted the night before, but that only lasts for a few weeks. When they become inactive for a month or so, I'm sure I made all this stuff up. I go back to denying that they are really abducting me … Beth calls it my denial phase. I go through it continuously it seems.'[26] Abductees' struggle over the real is interminable, ceaseless, an entangled process of tracing and retracing signs and events all the while knowing that certainty will hover just out of reach.

At the same time, certain pleasures accompany abductees' break with conventional reality. The trauma of their break with consensus reality is accompanied by the pleasures of knowing that things are not as they seem. Their enjoyment arises out of this alien knowledge's uncertainty and fragility; they know something the rest of us do not. They know that the reality which the rest of us take for granted is virtual, a screen for more complex processes and machinations comprehension of which remains just beyond our reach.

The persisting doubt that haunts the abduction discourse is manifest in the emphasis on 'becoming', the unceasing amassing of detail and the presumption of interconnection. First, I know of no case or case study where someone simply 'is' an abductee. All abduction narrative are marked by a profound ambivalence, by a person's inability to explain some odd memories, events or reactions to a movie, by their hypnosis and exploration of these memories, events or reactions and by their ongoing attempts to interpret and integrate the results of these explorations. Indeed, there is something profoundly misleading in thinking about abduction in terms of narrative at all. Not only is the narrative something put together after and during hours of research and exploration, but most abduction recollections are bits and pieces of disjointed image, sensation, feeling that the abductee has difficulty explaining. Few abductees are ever fully convinced that they know what has happened to them. For the most part, they are involved in a reiterative back-and-forth that mobilises doubt and reassurance into a never-ending, never-reconciled account of possibility.

This mobilisation of doubt is enacted through the accumulation of evidence, of bits and pieces of detail. Many abductees keep careful note of their menstrual cycles for signs of pregnancy with hybrid children. Many comb their bodies for evidence of scratches, punctures or 'scoop marks'. Researchers compile detailed cases of hundreds of experiences, recording their every thought and concern. At the same time, however, the vast compilations of data, of information, are confounded by an inability to determine not just what it all might mean or where it all might fit, but whether it is real or staged data. Many studying and experiencing abduction think that the telepathic and technological superiority of aliens enables them to produce experiences and memories. The aliens, in other words, can implant memories, visions and emotions. They can disguise themselves as owls, cats, even as Al Gore. All abductees report screen memories, memories that cover over what really happened. The drive for evidence is thus complicated by the troubling possibility that the evidence is not real. Put somewhat differently, doubt in abduction means that one cannot trust the very evidence one tries to accumulate. What is it evidence of? What does it prove? Any information could be misinformation or disinformation. Any information could be factual, reliable, well-supported and helpful.

What links doubt and detail is a presumption of interconnectivity. The abduction discourse relies on the notion that everything is or can be connected. Abductees link every odd or uncomfortable occurrence in their lives. They connect their computers' missing files with missing foetuses. They connect gazes from strangers sitting across a room with phones that ring once and then stop. They connect the emotions they feel when seeing a picture of a big-headed gray with enormous black eyes with their inability to remember details from their pasts. Beth Collings finds that none of the conventional explanations offered for abduction – 'coincidence', 'lucid dreams' or 'faulty human memory' – can 'justify the whole'.[27] 'Until something better comes along, something that can explain *all* the connecting events, we had no choice but to continue as we had been,' she writes, 'examining each unexplained event, comparing notes on shared memories, talking candidly with family and friends and keeping an open mind.' Collings takes the interconnections among discrete events as a given. She knows that they are linked, although she is uncertain as to how or why they are linked. The fact of linkage is the only thing about which she is certain.

Those UFO researchers trying to make sense of what they understand as the human–alien breeding project motivating abduction also presume a fundamental interconnectedness. They assume a chromosonal genetic compatibility between humans and aliens. How such interstellar hybridity is possible isn't baffling – we're all connected, linked to such an extent that reproduction can occur. UFO researchers also assume that abductions are interconnected with each other. Abductions affect families, occurring in successive generations. 'It's very much like an assembly line', says researcher David Jacobs.[28] Budd Hopkins adds that aliens bring people together deliberately, associating them through an intricate 'cosmic micro-management' that he calls 'controlled pairing'.[29] Each abduction has a link to another one; they are all part of something larger, something that links humans and aliens, earth and outer space.

Thoroughgoing uncertainty or, perhaps, humility, endlessly permutating images and experiences, the sense that everything is linked to every other – with these as key components of the abduction discourse, it is no surprise that Mack has been able to use the shaman as the native other of the extraterrestrial, as the exotic, mythic, authentic icon of the global and the cosmic. Viewed through a kind of eco-fantasy of being in touch with the primal, the shaman links the often discordant elements of scientific authority – he is a witch-*doctor*, after all – with spiritual transformation. Indeed, the hybridity inscribed in Mack's descriptions, in his emphasis on the ways that his shamans are bridging figures with a foot in two worlds, not the alien and the human, but the Western and the native, reconfirms the shaman as a figuration of doubt. He is never simply in one world, but always partially in another. Like the phenomenon itself, he cannot be fixed.

Acting uncertainly

Given the traumas of abduction, one might expect that abductees would become nearly paralysed with fear and uncertainty. If aliens are using them to breed hybrids, or if their worldviews really have collapsed, then how is it that they can continue within the ordinariness of everyday life? There are a couple of easy answers – people experience trauma every day and still go on, the abduction community provides a network of support – but these don't seem very satisfying. More convincing to me is the idea that the very instabilities in which they live, perhaps paradoxically, enable new kinds of action. The end of the world, in this reading of the abduction discourse, suggests the end of constraining systems of meaning, the end of confinement with a version of reality at odds with one's experience. I think of this kind of action as linking: after the end, abductees are freed to make previously unimaginable, or at least ridiculed, links. The images and terms they use are those left from technological and divine apocalypse. Now, however, they can be mixed and sampled with little regard for their narrative struggle.

And this takes me to that other strand of apocalyptic thinking that I seem to have neglected up to this point: ironic apocalypse. Rather than being convinced of the banality of everything and the pointless-ness of action, transformed abductees consider the potential for meaning in everything and stress the importance of action. They accumulate evidence – they gather information and make links – in the hope of finding meaning. Propelled by a sense of excess and lack, of an excess of meaning and potential and a lack of answers and certainty, they consider and reconsider, discover, search and go on. Their very scepticism makes them mobile.

To be sure, this action is configured within global corporate techno-culture, the same one that uses the idea that we are all connected as its slogan, that uses black faces and dancing feet to push the products and idea of an information age and that valorises personal transformation and self-remaking. Mack describes Isabel's attempt to meditate: 'I connected with all these different people all over the Earth.' She heard them talking all at once, voices from 'Australia, South America, Alaska and other countries'.[30] The action embraced by abductees may be deeply personal, part of their individual spiritual journey, occupation choice or decision to forego meat and to recycle. None the less, they tend to view their personal transformation as part of 'a collective shift in human consciousness and behaviour'.[31] If my consciousness changes, then so must everyone's, because I stand for, I represent, humanity. Armed by scientific and prophetic rhetorics, abductees' alternative experiences become, like the shaman's, exemplars of everyone's relation to the cosmos. The shaman links them to the earth, even as the alien draws them to the sky.

In the shamanic strand of the abduction discourse, action is either individual and personal or global and cosmic. Abductees don't have to organise or act collectively – although some may. They don't have to involve themselves with the political struggles of the 'indigenous peoples' in whose name they invoke myths, rituals and traditions. In their enthusiasm for an inspirited multiverse where we're all connected, they don't seem even to need to acknowledge the means through which earthly connections are established – money, corpora-tions, technologies, transportation and communication networks, histories of privilege. Indeed, these histories and technologies haunt the discourse overall and suggest why abduction has become such a prominent theme in popular networks of contemporary technoculture: even as change, hybridity and interconnection are globalisation's magic words, we aren't sure what they are conjuring up. After the end, action is possible, but we can't think of where it is going or know what it means. Under these conditions, we tend to oscillate between personal and cosmic. In the abduction discourse, this oscillation is enabled by the figure of the shaman.

NOTES

1 For compelling arguments regarding the apocalypticism of American puritanism and the homophobia of the religious right (as well as a reference to contemporary Sodoms and Gomorrahs), see L. Quinby, *Anti-apocalypse: Essays in Genealogical Feminism*, Minneapolis, University of Minnesota Press, 1994; and *Millennial Seduction: A Skeptic Confronts Apocalyptic Culture*, Ithaca, Cornell University Press, 1999.
2 L. Festinger, H. W. Riechen and S. Schachter, *When Prophecy Fails*, Minneapolis, University of Minnesota Press, 1956.
3 For a thorough account of aliens in contemporary technoculture, see my *Aliens in America: Conspiracy Cultures from Outerspace to Cyberspace*, Ithaca, Cornell University Press, 1998.
4 Quinby, *Anti-apocalypse*, pp. xv–xxii.
5 *Ibid.*, p. xx.
6 James Berger emphasises cataclysm and revelation within apocalypticism in *After the End: Representations of Post- Apocalypse*, Minneapolis, University of Minnesota Press, 1999, p. 38.
7 J. Mack, *Passport to the Cosmos: Human Transformation and Alien Encounters*, New York, Crown, 1999.
8 D. Caywood, 'What Futures May Come', personal email (11 October 1999). Mack (*Passport to the Cosmos*, p. 51) quotes abductees Andrea and Isabel regarding their abduction experiences. Andrea: it 'totally shook my belief system'. Isabel: 'it shatters everything that I was raised to believe.'
9 Berger, *After the End*, p. 5.
10 Berger writes that 'The narrative logic of apocalyptic writing insists that the post-apocalypse precede the apocalypse. This is also true of the logic of prophesy' (*ibid.*, p. 6).
11 Caywood, 'What Futures May Come'.
12 Mack, *Passport to the Cosmos*, p. 114.
13 D. Jordan and K. Mitchell, *Abducted! The Story of the Intruders Continues …*, New York, Carroll & Graff, 1994, p. 124.
14 Mack, *Passport to the Cosmos*, p. 142.
15 D. Jacobs, *The Threat*, New York, Simon & Schuster, 1998, p. 78.
16 Mack, *Passport to the Cosmos*, pp. 128–9.
17 *Ibid.*, p. 144.
18 *Ibid.*, p. 212.
19 *Ibid.*, p. 26; see also p. 10.

20 B. Hopkins, 'The UFO Phenomenon and the Suicide Cult – An Ideological Study', International UFO Symposium Proceedings, Seguin, MUFON, 1997, p. 248.
21 Mack, *Passport to the Cosmos*, p. 33.
22 *Ibid.*, pp. 185–7.
23 *Ibid.*, p. 32.
24 *Ibid.*, p. 280.
25 *Ibid.*, p. 277.
26 A. Jamerson and B. Collins, *Connections: Solving Our Alien Abduction Mystery*, Newberg, Wildflower Press, 1996, p. xx.
27 *Ibid.*, p. 228.
28 As quoted by Patrick Huyghe in 'The Secret Invasion: Does It Add Up?', *Omni*, Winter 1995, vol. 17.9, p. 60.
29 B. Hopkins, *Witnessed*, New York, Pocket Books, 1996, pp. 3–21.
30 Mack, *Passport to the Cosmos*, p. 238.
31 *Ibid.*, p. 237.

13

UFO BELIEFS AS SYNCRETISTIC COMPONENTS

Mikael Rothstein

A peripheral myth and its location

Proponents of what we may term 'the general UFO myth' (i.e. the claim that Earth is being visited by alien beings who travel in space-craft) will very often insist that the world's religions, not least their sacred texts, hold some kind of solution to the UFO enigma. And the reason is obvious, namely, the strange stories told today with regard to UFOs may well resemble stories of the past. This, however, does not mean that there is an unquestionable link between the myths of, say, Judaism or Buddhism and current UFO lore. Parallels between contemporary UFO beliefs and myths of ancient times depend entirely on interpretation. As it happens, such interpretations are usually presented by people outside the traditional religions, but within the dynamic, ever-changing UFO community. Thus any correspondence between religious myths and modern UFO stories only rarely reflects a Christian, Buddhist, Hindu or Jewish (or whatever religious) interest. Rather, the world's religions are taken into account in recently formed UFO-related belief systems. What is primarily addressed in the following is another story: the relatively rare incidents where the concept of UFOs is in fact taken into account by religions that other-wise have no direct focus on this issue. In other words, what is being discussed are religions with a touch of ufology.

A number of different religious groups, primarily focus their atten-tion on the notion of UFOs and may thus be termed 'UFO religions'. A number of other religious movements have quite different foci, but share with the actual UFO religions a certain interest in the subject, although in more subdued ways. In such cases the image of the UFO holds a position of limited importance in the theological or mytholog-ical systems, and may even be nearly imperceptible. Some of these religions are new or marginal groups which incorporate the concept of UFOs, or aspects of it, as a part of an emerging or newly developed belief system. In other instances ufological connotations are seen as mythological innovations within more conventional religions. In such cases ufological strands are incorporated into a traditional religious system and thus adapted to the structure and content of an already existing belief system. UFOs may be interpreted according to one of two obvious possibilities within, for instance, Christian mythology. They may become representations of either angelic beings, or of demons (as the examples in this chapter will show). This mechanism is actually well known in the history of religions. One particular set of beliefs is interpreted along another set – in much the same way as was done by the Romans, who interpreted foreign deities with specific reference to their own pantheon, a process known as *Interpretatio Romana*. In our case we can talk of UFOs as a guiding hermeneutical principle, or as a matrix for reinterpretation of traditional myth.

Such overlappings between different mythological spheres or systems are usually labelled 'syncretism'. In fact, strictly speaking, all religious systems are syncretistic. However, sometimes the process of the integration of one set of beliefs into another is especially apparent. The case of UFO beliefs as a new element in more conventional religious belief structures shows how a popular (and, at its outset, largely secular) myth becomes available for specific religious usage. On the other hand, however, we also see how religious interpretations of UFOs, to some people, seem to solve the riddle of the alleged phenomenon. The question is, then, whether UFO beliefs are used to rationalise traditional religious convictions or whether traditional religion helps people 'solve the enigma of the UFOs' – or, in scholarly terms, whether traditional religion provides a matrix for mythological elaboration regarding the alleged 'flying saucers'. At any rate, simultaneously at work, different belief systems meet and form new mythological patterns thus taking conventional religion, as well as UFO mythology, into new realms. While some people undoubtedly will identify UFO elements in, say, Christianity, as a theological deterioration, the syncretistic process is in fact an integral part of the social dynamics that make religion happen and indeed develop and thereby survive. It would be strange if something like this did not appear.

At the same time, though, it is important to notice that there is no single or universal pattern. Very often the syncretistic process is reversed, and a mythological system is reinforced by dissociating itself from a particular religious tradition and, indeed, becoming a competing belief system. This is also a consequence of the meeting of different belief systems and may thus be termed 'negative syncretism'.[1] In the current case this means that, even if many Christians are able to comprehend the notion of UFOs through Christian concepts (see p. 000), most Christians will probably reject this idea altogether and insist that UFOs (understood as alien spacecraft) belong to quite another realm, namely that of fiction. This is one of the reasons why UFO beliefs within religions with quite different theological or mythological focal points are not likely to become institutionalised or made formal doctrines of faith. Rather, notions of UFOs are destined to remain the private beliefs of individual members of a given religious group. Indeed, this is a typical feature of all religions. Formalised dogmatics never wholly correspond to what people *actually* believe. The question remains, therefore, where to 'locate' the religious belief of any religious group. Any belief system, in so far as it is defined or outlined, only represents a rather rough sketch of the actual worldviews of individual believers. The official texts and articles of faith of a religion rarely accurately reflect the beliefs of all its devotees. Nor is it enough to ask a random sample of members what they believe. Religious worldviews are viable social constructions that exist in ever-changing environments.

Concerning beliefs in UFOs and extraterrestrial visitation, it is quite obvious that the vast number of people who believe in such things are not members of actual 'UFO religions' such as the Aetherius Society, the Raëlian Religion, or Unarius. They are, on the contrary, 'ordinary' people with average religious affiliations or no religious affiliation at all. Among such people, some will keep apart their beliefs in UFOs and, say, Jesus as saviour, whilst others will merge the two mythic spheres into one, and claim that Jesus will in due time return to Earth in a spaceship. The eschatological doctrine of Jesus's return is, in such cases, embraced in the myth of the advent of a UFO.

The cognitive capacity of humans readily allows different belief systems to function simultaneously, even if they are in many ways contradictory. For instance, many people see no contradistinction between biblical religion and modern science, simply because the two are never contested. They are, on the contrary, entertained separately even if simultaneously. Much in the same way, most members of traditional religions, who consider UFOs to be alien spacecraft, will never or rarely relate this persuasion to their general religious worldview. People may well identify themselves as Christians, Jews or Muslims, and at the same time entertain notions of visiting aliens in strange spacecraft. Indeed, this author has conducted a number of interviews with Christians and Muslims in Denmark who believe in extraterrestrial visitation. Two informants (one Christian and one Muslim) had quite similar comments:

> God is the creator of the universe and of us, so why shouldn't He have created life elsewhere? I suppose that people are telling the truth when they say they have seen something strange in the sky or whatever. My response is: Yes, God probably also is the Father of those guys. And so what? I don't worship them. They are just another species or life form.
>
> (Male, 21 years old, Copenhagen 1999)

> I believe that there is life out there and that aliens have visited us on this planet. The universe is immense, remember that! This has no bearing on my life as a Muslim, but I don't know if God intended his laws to apply to them as well. I don't think so though.
>
> (Male, 23 years old, Copenhagen 1999)

Sometimes, however, individual members of religious groups do try to correlate elements from their religious traditions with elements of popular ufology. One such example I have come across is derived from the Bahā'ī religion.

The Bahā'ī religion

A semi-official homepage on the Internet which provides answers to questions posed by Bahā'ī believers and others illustrates an attempt to integrate faith and ufology. Following the public discussion of a particular UFO sighting where 'alien spacecraft' were reported manoeuvring over Mount Carmel, one member of the Bahā'ī community, Vafa Hashemi, wrote (quoted verbatim as found on the Internet; English is obviously not this person's mother tongue):

> SIGHTINGS [a television show] reported two weeks ago from Haifa, Israel. I witness video of Two UFOs were taken on the top of MT Carmel for 30 Minutes. Three Israel Jets try to intercept UFOs but their instruments were not function well. Sightings again will report on UFO Sighting on top of Mt Carmel. I do remember that when asked Bahá'u'lláh is there any life in other planets, He replied: For every star there is a planet and for every planet it has it's own Creatures. I will not

be wonders that UFOS already know about beautiful buildings
of Bahai on the Top of MT Carmel.[2]

Referring to the same statement by Bahá'u'lláh (the founder of the
Bahā'ī religion), another individual, Mike Talbert, writes the following:
'Could you explain what is meant here? Is he saying that every planet
has creatures? Or, is he saying that every planet which has life has its
own, particular set of creatures?' Whilst Bahá'u'lláh (who died in 1892)
could obviously not have been familiar with the modern concept of
UFOs, the point to note is that the question raises the general issue of
the existence of intelligent extraterrestrial life (regardless of whether
that life has actually travelled to Earth). The answer to the question
runs as follows:

> Yes, Mike, it is my understanding that when Bahá'u'lláh, in the
> book *Gleanings from the Writings of Bahá'u'lláh*, writes: 'Know
> thou that every fixed star has it's own planets, and every planet
> it's own creatures, whose number no man can compute'. That's
> exactly what He means. There is another comment by Abdu'l-
> Baha in the old 'Divine Philosophies' where, in speaking of
> other star systems he says, on pages 114–115 '...verily they are
> peopled, but let it be known that the dwellers accord with the
> elements of their respective spheres. These living beings do
> not have states of consciousness like unto those who live on
> the surface of this globe'.
>   Further it is emphasised that 'the power of adaption and
> environment moulds [these creatures'] bodies and state of
> consciousness, just as our bodies and minds are suited to this
> planet.'[3]

The first comment reveals an outspoken willingness to align traditional Bahā'ī positions with an element of ufology. However, referring to
the same event (i.e. the alleged sighting of UFOs over Mount Carmel),
the other commentator restricts his comments to a more general question of extraterrestrial life. It is interesting to observe, though, that the
question would probably not have been posed if the alleged UFO incident at that particular spot had not occurred. UFO sightings in general
may be of no significance to the man who asked for clarity regarding
Bahá'u'lláh's idea of extraterrestrial life, but when claims are made about
alien spaceship hovering over Mount Carmel, the interpretation of the
situation changes considerably, principally because this location is
invested with sacred significance in the Bahā'ī religion.

Of primary interest, though, is the fact that no information on UFOs whatsoever can be found in official Bahā'ī sources, whether in books or on the Internet. Hence, whilst UFOs are of no direct relevance to the Bahā'ī faith in its official form, it seems clear that some members of the Bahā'ī community have established a connection between their traditional religious authority (Bahá'u'lláh etc.) and popular notions of extraterrestrial life and UFOs. The important point to note, therefore, is that UFO lore has become distributed in such a way that many different religious traditions can be brought into the interpretation of apparently ufological phenomena, regardless of their official beliefs. Consequently, whilst it would be wrong to say that UFOs are part and parcel of the Bahā'ī religion in the narrow sense, it should be acknowledged that some believers do consider the concept of UFOs to be in accordance with statements of Bahā'ī theology. In such cases we might talk of 'relative syncretism' or perhaps 'private syncretism', as the moulding of different mythological systems is done by individuals with no formal support from a recognised or institutionalised religious body.

The Hopi Indians

Another brief example of this phenomenon has been described with relation to the Hopi people of Arizona, USA. In 1970 one of the lesser-known UFO prophets, Paul Solem, stepped into the arena and reminded people in the town of Prescott that, since 1948, he had been in close contact with space people and that an imminent disclosure of their intentions was at hand. For many years he had, among other things, claimed a close correspondence between the extraterrestrial beings and elements in Hopi prophecy, and, from time to time, had managed to gather small groups of interested Hopis around him. Thus, although not a Hopi himself, Solem presented himself as a superior authority in matters of Hopi religion. In 1969, after a series of UFO sightings in Prescott, the Hopi Chief Qötshongva had joined Solem. As the chief saw it, UFOs were not at all new to the Hopis. On the contrary, he believed them to play an important part in Hopi history. Why else should extraterrestrial images be inscribed into petrograph rocks near the Hopi mesas in Northern Arizona? Unfortunately Chief Qötshongva never benefited from his association with Paul Solem. The Venusians never arrived, and the chief was removed as leader by the Hopi Tribal Council for making them look foolish.[4]

The case is particularly interesting because the individual who takes the ufological turn is an official representative for his social group.

Usually UFO perspectives on traditional belief systems are suggested by people with no formal position. As it was, however, the political position of Qötshongva was not enough to keep his ideas alive.

Furthermore, it is necessary to take the general cultural setting into consideration when syncretistic mechanisms (official or private) are surveyed. It is, for example, of great importance to notice that elements of UFO beliefs only rarely occur in non-Western traditional religions, although a few examples can be found. This is a good indication that the UFO myth, whilst globalised,[5] is primarily a phenomenon of the Christian (and technologically most advanced) world, and that syncretistic mixes between traditional religious belief systems and UFO beliefs are more likely to appear in some cultural milieus than others.

Mormonism

A similar example of a religious belief system which may be related to current UFO tales is found in Mormonism/the Church of Jesus Christ Latter-day Saints. Mormonism was founded in 1830 over a century prior to the development of the modern myths of extraterrestrial life and alien visitation. From early on in the Mormon Church's history there were thoughts of life elsewhere in the universe. In one of the Church's sacred texts, *The Book of Moses*, there is a myth (an elaboration of material in the Hebrew Bible – Genesis 5:21–4) that tells of how Enoch's sacred city, Zion, with its entire population (including farms, houses, fields and cattle) was 'taken up' from the surface of the Earth by God (7:69). The town and its settlers were placed on another planet, Kolob (which is very close to 'the throne of God'), where death could not reach them and where their bodies were adapted to the local conditions in the 'higher world'. According to Mormon tradition, this was in the year 2948 BC when Enoch was 430 years old. After this event, Enoch and his friends became God's messengers to beings on other planets.

Mormons interviewed by this author (in 1999) had quite different opinions about how to understand this narrative. Some individuals understood it quite literally, while others saw it is as a parable. One informant argued that the story points to a possible link between 'acts of God and what people observe around the world'. Here, as in the Bahā'ī example above, the creative theological mind sees a possible combination between traditional beliefs and modern notions of interaction with extraterrestrials. However, to my knowledge, there is no support for the idea in the religious establishment of the Latter-day Saints. What is apparent is how flexible religious myths are. The narrative about the rapture of Zion, which is basic to Mormon theology, was conceived in a distinctly pre-ufological context, but once it is told in a modern, Western environment, it easily relates to UFO stories. In this case, UFO beliefs form a hermeneutical framework for religious inter-pretation, even if UFOs are absent in official Mormon doctrine.

The planet Kolob is important in Mormon theology. For example, in *The Book of Abraham* (the latter part of *The Pearl of Great Price*) the beginning of the third chapter focuses on Kolob and its meaning. It would seem that Kolob is the principal planet in a cosmic hierarchy of planets (3:9). Conditions on Kolob are in harmony with God's personal nature, as God is the cosmic ruler. It is worthwhile pointing out that this concept of a planetary hierarchy and superior intelligent life outside planet Earth allows for modern ufological notions along the lines of Mormon theology.

The Church of Scientology

Whilst ufology is rarely emphasised by the Church of Scientology, in fact it has been an element of Scientological thinking for a very long time. This, however, does not mean that the average member is specifi-cally occupied with UFOs or the idea of extraterrestrial life. It is certainly a part of the total fabric of scientological thinking and narra-tive, but not of prime importance. In some of L. Ron Hubbard's (1911–86) writings, the notion of alien races in distant universes is discussed in some depth, and it is described how the Thetans (a term used in Scientology to refer to their particular spiritual understanding of the human being) that eventually incarnated as human beings, come from other worlds to inhabit the Earth. In one of the narratives contained in Scientology's 'Operating Thetan' (OT) materials (i.e. texts designed for initiations into higher levels of Scientology's esoteric hierarchy), a space being is mentioned, a malevolent ruler named Xenu, who is said to have captured billions of Thetans in a giant ball of ice in the distant past.[6] Since they started to incarnate on this planet (which was then known as Teegeeack) some 75 million years ago, they have embarked upon a spiritual quest (which the Church of Scientology is now promoting).[7]

Other examples of ufological discourse are found in the so-called 'auditing reports' (i.e. logs taken during a special kind of ritual time-travel – a process of guided visualisation) that takes the individual back to earlier incarnations. In a published sample of such reports, anonymous participants allegedly recount lives beyond ordinary comprehension involving space rulers, star wars, spacecraft, robots and mysterious beings in other galaxies, often many trillions of years ago. This volume was published in 1950 as *Have You Lived Before This Life?* [8] and, to this day, the text has remained of great importance to scientologists as a common frame of reference. No doubt many scientologists have learned what to experience for themselves from working through this book. Ufological references in the spiritual recollections of active scientologists are therefore not simply a product of the mind developed in auditing therapy. Rather, the issue of extraterrestrial origin and contact is a vital mythological paradigm propagated through literature and interpersonal communication. Although it is never stated explicitly in the numerous materials made available to the general public, the issue of extraterrestrials and cosmic combats elsewhere in the Universe is not irrelevant to Scientology. The UFO dimension of Scientology's belief system is, to a certain extent, of an esoteric kind.

In this connection it is important to identify the foundations of the Church of Scientology's 'ufological connection', a task that is certainly not very difficult. The Church of Scientology was established at the peak of the contactee movement's popularity (1954), a simple fact that may explain why the concept of extraterrestrials etc. was of some importance to Scientology, even if many other new religions emerging at the same time did not address the issue. More importantly, however, the founder of the organisation, L. Ron Hubbard, earned his living as a relatively successful science fiction writer prior to his career as a religious leader. His fictional works, which include explicit descriptions of space rulers, spacecraft etc., whilst officially excluded from Scientology's canon of scripture, are highly praised and understood to be important texts, superseded only by his philosophical and religious writings.[9] Thus Scientology's UFOism has two sources of inspiration: the explicitly religious teaching closely connected with the auditing therapy; and, more indirectly, the cosmology described in Hubbard's science fiction novels. It is never claimed that the latter are anything but fiction, but there are remarkable similarities between aspects of Hubbard's explicitly religious thought and ideas developed in his novels. At any rate, the Church of Scientology displays an example of how one kind of cultural product can become translated into another kind, in that basic tenets of a religion's cosmology started out as exciting parts of an entertaining science fiction narrative. (Indeed Hubbard is not alone in this respect, since a similar process took George Adamski from the position of a non-successful science fiction writer, to a highly successful contactee.)

The ufological perspectives in Scientology has, in fact, no close relation to the concept of UFOs in the narrow sense of the term.

Rather, the broad ufological ideas that sweep through parts of the belief system serve to focus the attention on the core element in Hubbard's teaching, namely, the existence, eternity, plight and eventually freedom of the Thetans. By making a variety of mythological universes available, it becomes possible for scientologists to describe and explain the nature and life of the Thetans. In this sense, beliefs about space rulers in their spaceships become second-order beliefs (i.e. mythological elements that serve to support or explain something else which is considered to be at the core of the religious worldview). This is also why many Scientologists will, quite rightly, explain that the story about Xenu is in fact peripheral to their religious life. This is not to say that they deny the validity and significance of the myth. Rather, it is to say that it is not central to their primary belief system. All religious systems are socially negotiated in a way that will promote some mythological elements while leaving others on one aside, even if officially acknowledged as true and important. Having said that, it seems fair to say that ufological perspectives do play a part in the total fabric of the Scientology religion.[10]

ISKCON

Another example of a religion which relates to ufology is the International Society for Krishna Consciousness (ISKCON), popularly known as the Hare Krishna movement. The connection between ISKCON's Vaishnavite theology and ufology, however, is not so obvious and not directly official. When Bhaktivedanta Swami Prabhupada (1896–1977), the founder of ISKCON, brought Gaudiya-Vaishnavism to the West in 1965, he was presumably unaware of the ongoing UFO debate in the United States where he arrived. His biographer, Satsvarupa dasa Goswami, does not mention anything that could indicate any awareness of the concept of UFOs and nothing directly pertaining to the issue can be found in his writings. There is, however, a line of parallel themes in many of Prabhupada's writings, themes that were imported from fairly traditional Vaishnava theology. For one thing, Prabhupada frequently takes up the question of 'spiritual migration' to other realms or planets as it is discussed in classical Hindu philosophy. In this sense the very idea of interstellar or interplanetary travel is mentioned and any devoted ISKCON member may well feel inclined to expand on this theme in his or her own private reflections. Talks with devotees from different countries have revealed that this is often the case. It is beyond the scope of this brief article to provide statistics, but it seems as if Prabhupada's teachings in general are used by his followers to explain or rationalise many different beliefs (such as the existence of UFOs) that are not explicitly mentioned in ISKCON's sacred literature or other authoritative textbooks.

One of Prabhupada's disciples, Sadapuda dasa (whose original, pre-initiate name is Richard L. Thompson) has done more than the average devotee in this respect. Sadapuda has very straightforwardly related ufology to Prabhupada's teachings in a book based on the theory that UFOs are wholly explicable in terms of Gaudiya-Vaishnava theology. The book, *Alien Identities: Ancient Insights into Modern UFO Phenomena*, was published in 1993 by Govardhan Hill Publishing, an ISKCON publishing house, and was instantly received with enthusiasm by the general UFO community.

Sadapuda would certainly not have had his work published by Govardhan Hill Publishing if the ISKCON organisation had disapproved of the book's content. However, Sadapuda is no ordinary ISKCON member. He ranks among the intellectual heavyweights of the organisation and has, for quite a number of years, been very outspoken on questions of theology, science and education. Trained as a scientist himself, he has published extensively on the relation between Vaishnava theology and science, insisting that real science is encompassed in the theology of Prabhupada – and, in essence, nowhere else. He is well known and highly respected by ISKCON's devotees. Consequently, what he has to say about UFOs, therefore, will be generally understood as an authoritative position by an informed ISKCON authority.

According to Sadapuda, strange flying craft are described in detail in ancient Hindu texts such as the *Puranas*. UFOs, he argues, are in fact the vehicles of the gods, their *Vimanas*. He refers to a large number of religious texts in support of his thesis and suggests why these things are being seen, what they are doing, and where they originate.

Although new to the ISKCON community, this analogy between contemporary UFOs and the vehicles of the ancient gods is in fact not new. So-called astro-archaeological arguments have been presented for many years. Astro-archaeologists argue that there is a direct link between the gods of ancient myth and iconography and extraterrestrial visitation to Earth. The gods, it is claimed, are actually extraterrestrial beings which arrived on Earth and interacted with humans. The best-known exponent of this hypothesis is probably Erich von Däniken who launched his idea in 1968 in his book *Chariots of the Gods?*[11] More specifically, David Childress has argued for a link between UFOs and the *Vimanas* (and Atlantis!).[12] Both of these volumes appeared before Sadapuda's book was published. However, whereas authors such as von

Däniken and Childress believe that the 'gods' are in fact beings from other planets, Sadapuda holds that observations of UFOs are in fact encounters with the divine, or, rather, obvious indications of a divine presence or will confirming the tenets of Vaishava theology. He writes:

> According to ancient Vedic texts, there was a time when people of this earth were in regular contact with many different kinds of beings, from negative entities in the mode of darkness to great sages in advanced states of spiritual consciousness. The modern phenomena tend to confirm the Vedic picture, and this may also be part of the plan behind these phenomena. The teachings of the ancient sages are still available, but they have become eclipsed by the modern developments of materially oriented science and technology. Perhaps the time is coming when they will again be taken seriously.[13]

Indeed, the focus in Sadapuda's book is distinctive, in that it is not about what people see in the skies, but rather about spiritual experiences. The argument is based on the premise that the sacred texts of the Vaishnava tradition and Prabhupada's exegetical works are reliable objective accounts of the empirical cosmos. Hence, because UFO-like spacecraft are, as Sadapuda understands it, described in sacred texts, UFOs must, as a consequence, be objectively real.

One may wonder why Sadapuda has embarked on the potentially troublesome UFO journey at all? The answer probably has more to do with religious conviction and steadfast loyalty to the Vaishnava theology than anything else. In his work, Sadapuda has in many different ways tried to show how Prabhupada's teaching is superior to other understandings of the world, including the modern scientific worldview. By addressing the enigma of the UFOs, he seeks to contribute to the construction of an all-encompassing ISKCON explanation of the world. Once ISKCON's belief system is introduced, so it is believed, everything becomes intelligible. In this way Sadapuda's book is missiological in intention. The reader, who considers the arguments and is persuaded, is being introduced to the ISKCON worldview.

Christian perspectives

Christianity may also be interpreted from a ufological perspective. To some Christians, and to many ufologists who would not consider themselves practising Christians, encounters with UFOs can be found in the Bible. John Saliba summarises such beliefs in this way:

> Many incidences recorded during the exodus of the Israelites from Egypt provide excellent cases of multiple witness sightings. The parting of the Red Sea is said to have been caused by unidentified flying objects and the cloud that guided them across the wilderness (Exodus 13:21) is compared to contemporary cigar-shaped UFOs. In the same way, [Elijah's] ascension (2 Kings 2:11) in a 'chariot of fire' is one of the biblical narratives most often quoted to document the existence of flying saucers in biblical times. In the New Testament, the appearance of the angels to the shepherds at the birth of Jesus (Luke 2:9–13), the scene described at the baptism of Jesus (e.g., Matthew 3:13–17), and his ascension in a cloud (Acts 1:9) are all similarly explained as UFO experiences.[14]

The point is that it is claimed that the reality of UFOs is documented in the Bible.

Although few theologians have seriously considered the theological implications of UFOs, and although serious discussion about UFOs within the Christian community is not common, one should not assume that nothing at all is said about UFOs. Some Christian denominations, for example, primarily within the so-called fundamentalist wing of the Church, but also in the Charismatic movement, have provided interpretations of ufological phenomena. Essentially, such assessments of UFOs are negative and regard alien visitation as dangerous and demonic. In several cases UFOs are considered to be 'agents of Satan' or 'Satanic beings'. They are here, it is argued by such writers as John Weldon and Zola Lewitt, to distort peoples' minds in order that they may be confused when Christ returns.[15] Whilst, in a similar way to UFO religions, there is an identification of spiritual entities with UFOs, unlike the UFO religions, they are not saviour figures but rather they are here to enslave humans on behalf of Satan. Hence, unlike many Christians who reject the notion of UFOs as superstition or rational absurdity, such Christians interpret them in accordance with Christian demonology and argue that Satan is doing whatever he can to destroy God's plan of salvation. Consequently, the UFO is simply interpreted in terms of Christian demonology as a manifestation of the forces opposing good and God.

Another kind of theologically right-wing Christian approach to the issue of UFOs is found in a paper by Doug Potter entitled 'UFOs, ETs and the New Age: A Christian Perspective', initially read at the National Conference on Apologetics.[16] Potter's position is analytical rather than confrontational. He explicitly dissociates himself from religious preachers he considers to be heretical due to their explicit inclusion of ufological perspectives. He argues that nothing in his understanding of the Bible supports the thesis of extraterrestrial visitation. The following is Potter's statement regarding alien abduction:

> Reports of abductions usually include moral evils committed by aliens such as being taken against one's will, rape and other sexual abuses. If these alien beings were real, this would indicate that they have a need of forgiveness and redemption. But Scripture indicates that no one other than humans are in need of forgiveness and redemption.[17]

Whilst Potter rejects the reality of UFOs and alien beings, he takes UFO reports very seriously since they are manifestations of a negative psychological, possibly spiritual, phenomenon. Indeed, humans may lose their souls as a result of ufological involvement:

> … flying saucer watching is addictive and a waste of time. It leads to a suspension of disbelief. Many have become desensitized by the strangeness and lost their sanity. Thus, the dangers of pursuing UFOs are spiritual and physical. Alnor [a Christian author] wisely notes: 'The longer one makes a commitment to UFO research, the closer he or she is to dying and giving the God who made the planets an account of his life. It is a sin to waste time on unprofitable things'. Jn 9:4 says: 'As long as it is day, we must do the work of him who sent me. Night is coming, when no one can work'.[18]

The power of the UFO, even as a figment of the imagination, is strongly reflected here. Indeed, for Potter, it is the very idea that is disturbing. Hence, whereas some Christian apologists are concerned about UFOs because, as we have seen, they consider them to be ontologically Satanic, Potter interprets them in terms of a sinfully flawed understanding. In other words, UFOs are to be understood as manifestations of unacceptable, heretical ideas and thought processes.

In the final analysis, interpretations such as the above are informed Christian theologies of sin and the demonic. As such, and in a similar way to the positive ufological interpretations by writers such as von

Däniken, UFO sightings or reported encounters serve to confirm and strengthen particular worldviews. Indeed, as far as such Christians are concerned, the fact that UFOs attract interest in the occult subculture confirms their interpretation of UFOs as demonic and a consequence of sin.

The Family

A number of Christian sects have a more direct occupation with UFOs. One such group is the Family (formerly known as the Children of God and the Family of Love) whose theological emphasis is eschatological and apocalyptical. In essence, whilst the Family's history is one of sustained counter-cultural activity, the core teachings are, generally speaking, traditionally Christian, even if the emphases are often unique to this group.[19] The notion of UFOs, in this connection, remains a rather peripheral mythic element which is never highlighted by the group, nor by scholars (apart from an earlier study of my own[20]).

Whilst the founder of the Family, David Berg (1919–94), wrote about UFOs on several occasions, his particular interpretation of them is difficult to ascertain. For example, he designated UFOs 'circles of power', 'light', 'angelic beings', 'vehicles of angels', 'spirit beings', 'means for angelic transportation', 'carriers of the dead on their way to Heaven' and 'celestial machines'. Some of these designations seem to be mutually exclusive, and it is probably the case that Berg never arrived at a definite position. What he actually meant and to what extent the concept of UFOs is important to his religious thinking remains unclear. Furthermore, he claimed that 'the City of God' mentioned in Revelation 21 and 22 is 'God's space city', 'God's space vehicle' and 'the original flying saucer'. It is approaching, floating through the universe, Berg believes, and will arrive in the near future. Unlike the above Christian fundamentalist understandings of UFOs, Berg interprets them as manifestations of the angelic and even the divine. UFOs are essentially manifestations of God's presence and expressions of a higher spiritual reality.

As to why Berg considered it necessary to reflect theologically on UFOs, it is hard to avoid the conclusion that his thought was significantly shaped by his context. During Berg's days of glory in the 1970s, UFOs were a popular topic in the media. There was a great deal of public interest. Questions were asked and answers were sought after. During this period of heightened public interest, Berg claimed to receive a revelation regarding the UFOs directly from 'God, the creator of all things!' After all, no real prophet could be ignorant on the subject. Considering Berg's opposition to the conventional churches who either ignored the subject of UFOs or insisted that the phenomenon reflected demonic activity, it is arguable that Berg's position also served as a tool in his struggle against what was termed 'the system'. That is to say, arguably, he simply chose a contesting theological position. If this interpretation is correct, the social dynamics between the leader, his followers and the surrounding society led to Berg's ufological speculations. That is to say, his UFO beliefs were principally the product of political discourse more than anything else, an element in his ongoing effort to distinguish his movement from the established Church, to prove himself superior to the rest of the world in virtually every field of knowledge and understanding.

Today, members of the group seem not to pay too much attention to this aspect of Berg's teachings. It is considered to be a peripheral belief and, as such, of no great importance to their theology. Consequently, no theological elaboration has followed Berg's original remarks on the subject.

Final remarks

Initially being a secular myth, a response, according to many researchers, to Cold War fears in the aftermath of the Second World War, UFOs were soon given a largely theosophical interpretation by prominent contactees, most notably George Adamski.[21] From this point on it became an increasingly popular dimension in non-Christian mythology in the Western world, especially in what was to be known as the New Age movement. Apart from being a core doctrine of a number of specific UFO religions, today people from many different faiths have incorporated a belief in UFOs into otherwise non-UFO belief systems. UFOs must, therefore, be acknowledged as an important mythological innovation in contemporary religion. Indeed, whether in religious communities or not, the globalisation of the UFO myth as an independent area of belief is a most remarkable modern phenomenon.[22]

NOTES

1 M. Rothstein, *Belief Transformations: Some Aspects of the Relation between Science and Religion in TM and ISKCON*, RENNER Studies on New Religions, vol. 2, Aarhus, Aarhus University Press, 1996.
2 http://www.bcca.org/srb/archive/951021-951231/0690.html (1December 2001).
3 http://www.bcca.org/srb/archive/951021-951231/0982.html (1

December 2001).

4 See J. R. Lewis, 'Paul Solem', in J. R. Lewis (ed.), *UFOs and Popular Culture*, California, ABC-Clio, 2001, p. 276; A. G. Geertz, *The Invention of Prophecy: Continuity and Meaning in Hopi Indian Religion*, Aarhus, Brunebakke Publications, 1992, pp. 284f.

5 See M. Rothstein, 'The Myth of the UFO in Global Perspective: A Cognitive Approach', in M. Rothstein (ed.), *New Age Religion and Globalization*, RENNER Studies on New Religions, vol. 5, Aarhus, Aarhus University Press, 2001, pp. 133–49.

6 This narrative is contained in esoteric texts (designed for the OT-III course) and therefore not readily available from the Church of Scientology itself. Due to the massive anti-cult campaign against Scientology, however, the text is in fact available to outsiders. For easy access to this material see http://www.xenu.net/archive/OTIII-scholar/

7 For more on this, see A. Grünschloß, 'Scientology', in Lewis (ed.), *UFOs and Popular Culture*, pp. 266–8.

8 The book has subsequently been republished at least thirty times. This author refers to the Danish 1983 version: Copenhagen, New Era Publications, 1983.

9 One of the best indications for the appreciation of Hubbard as an author is seen in a sociological survey on the identity of members of the Church of Scientology in Denmark. They were asked whether L. Ron Hubbard meant most to them as 'an author' or as 'the founder' of a religion: 44 per cent answered 'author', while 56 per cent primarily venerated him as the 'founder' of their religion. The survey (started by the late Merethe Sundby-Sørensen, currently being continued by Peter B. Andersen and Rie Wellendorf) is available online at the home page of the Danish Data Archives as DDA-1605: http://www.dda.dk/).

10 See A. Grünschloß, 'Scientology', pp. 266–8.

11 E. von Däniken, *Chariots of the Gods? Unsolved Mysteries of the Past*, trans M. Heron, London, Souvenir Press, 1969. Original: *Erinnerungen an die Zukunft*, Ercon-Verlag, München,1968.

12 D. H. Düsseldorf, *Vimana Aircraft of Ancient India and Atlantis*, Illinois, Adventures Unlimited Press, 1991.

13 Sadapuda (Richard Thompson), *Alien Identities: Ancient Insights into Modern UFO Phenomena*, San Diego, Govardhan Hill Publishing, 1993, p. 414.

14 J. A. Saliba, 'The Religious Dimensions of UFO Phenomena', in J. R. Lewis (ed.), *The Gods Have Landed: New Religions From Other Worlds*, New York, State University of New York Press, 1995, pp. 32–3.

15 See J. Weldon and Z. Lewitt, *UFOs: What on Earth is Happening?* California, Harvest House, 1974.

16 D. Potter, 'UFOs, ETs and the New Age: A Christian Perspective', *Christian Apologetics Journal*, 1998, vol. 1:1, pp. 1–8.

17 *Ibid.*, p. 8.

18 *Ibid.*

19 See J. R. Lewis and J. G. Melton, *Sex, Slander and Salvation: Investigating the Family/Children of God*, Stanford, Center for Academic Publication, 1994.

20 M. Rothstein, 'The Family, UFOs and God: A Modern Extension of Christian Mythology', *Journal of Contemporary Religion*, 1997, vol. 12, pp. 353–62.
21 This perspective has been most thoroughly discussed by Robert Pearson Flaherty in his unpublished doctoral dissertation, 'Flying Saucers and the New Angelology. Mythic Projection of the Cold War and the Convergence of Opposites', Los Angeles, University of California, 1990.
22 See M. Rothstein, 'The Myth of the UFO in Global Perspective'.

14

APOCALYPTIC AND MILLENARIAN ASPECTS OF AMERICAN UFOISM

Daniel Wojcik

Beliefs about the apocalyptic and redemptive aspects of flying saucers and extraterrestrials have been an enduring part of American UFO culture for the past fifty years and these ideas continue to flourish in the new millennium. American UFO lore is vast and divergent, ranging from familiar narratives about mysterious men in black suits, cattle mutilations and crop circles, to abductions by invasive grey aliens and reptilian beings, beliefs about alien life beneath the Earth and ongoing conspiracy theories about massive government cover-ups, such as the alleged recovery of a crashed spaceship near Roswell, New Mexico, in July 1947. Despite the eclectic nature of American UFOism, a recurring theme is that UFOs and extraterrestrial entities will either invade planet Earth in the last days, rescue human beings from worldly cataclysm or help humanity transform the world and usher in a new age of peace and enlightenment.

American beliefs about the role of UFOs in the end-times share common concerns with other contemporary apocalyptic traditions, including a preoccupation with the threat of nuclear annihilation, environmental destruction and societal disasters; a sense of imminent crisis and the loss of confidence in the government to resolve current problems; cultural pessimism and an emphasis on conspiracies; and feelings of powerlessness and manipulation by external forces beyond one's control. Widely held beliefs by UFO enthusiasts exemplify the concept of millenarianism, defined as the expectation of imminent worldly destruction, transformation and collective salvation, to be brought about by other-worldly beings acting in accordance with a divine or superhuman plan.[1] Like previous millenarian worldviews, emergent UFO traditions often provide systems of meaning for understanding human existence and promise believers that the universe is ordered, that evil and suffering will be eliminated and that an age of harmony and justice will be established through the fulfilment of a cosmic plan.[2]

The flying saucer movement that arose in the 1950s and that continues today in varying forms is a syncretic phenomenon, composed of an assortment of earlier mythologies, religious traditions, occult teachings, scientific discourse and American popular culture, adapted and modified to express the concerns, fears and hopes of our era. As numerous researchers have asserted, American UFOism is essentially a religious phenomenon, with its own emergent mythology, legends and systems of belief, constructed from previous traditions about the supernatural, and affirmed and elaborated upon through personal encounters, visions, trance states, marvellous journeys and other numinous experiences.[3] As folklorist Robert Flaherty notes, unlike religious movements that have been promoted by ecclesiastical institutions, beliefs about UFOs have not been codified or co-opted by an institutional body, but have diffused at a grassroots level and then formulated into a variety of vernacular belief systems and traditions.[4]

Traditionally, the appearance of enigmatic objects in the heavens has been associated with divine portents and apocalyptic warnings and it was not long after Kenneth Arnold's sighting of nine large disc-shaped objects 'skipping' through the sky near Mt Rainer, Washington, on 24 June 1947, that people began speculating about the apocalyptic and millenarian meanings of these objects. According to some UFO enthusiasts, the wave of more than 800 hundred sightings that occurred in 1947 was directly related to the recent detonation of five atomic bombs (Alamogordo, Hiroshima, Nagasaki, Crossroads A and Crossroads B). The sightings were frequently reported to have occurred near nuclear power plants and it was commonly believed that nuclear bomb tests had drawn attention to planet Earth. Flying saucers, some said, had come to warn humanity of the dangers of atomic weapons, save us from destroying ourselves or from endangering life on other planets, similar to the plot of the film *The Day the Earth Stood Still* (1951), in which a saucer lands near the White House and the Christ-like alien Klaatu forewarns of the threat of atomic bombs. Some UFO enthusiasts speculated that the detonation of atomic bombs would cause a chain reaction that would disrupt the cosmos, while others maintained that extraterrestrials feared for their own lives because of the development of nuclear weapons.[5]

The UFO contactee narratives from the 1950s that describe encounters with benevolent space beings exhibit consistent eschatological themes that have informed subsequent beliefs about UFOs. Because the contactee experience is often positive and tends to involve repeated communications with familiar extraterrestrial entities, an extensive body of narratives and beliefs has emerged, giving

rise to assorted folk cosmologies and leading to the formation of religious groups. In the stories, the aliens often make contact in an
isolated location with an ordinary and unsuspecting person, bringing
the contactee aboard their craft and sometimes explaining its technology or taking the person for a ride. Unlike the pre-Second World
War conceptions of bug-eyed monsters from outer space depicted in
pulp fiction, the aliens encountered at the dawn of the atomic age are
human-like in appearance and are depicted as rational, benevolent and
beautiful beings with superhuman abilities. Coming from superior,
utopian civilisations, these beings often give messages through
telepathy that warn of imminent disasters because of the failures of
human beings and usually express concern with the condition of
humanity and planet Earth. The world is said to be in a state of crisis,
which is attributed variously to nuclear proliferation, ecological
destruction, societal breakdown, human ignorance, violence, cruelty
and selfishness. The contactee is then given a crucial mission: to warn
others of impending worldly catastrophe.[6]

The sense of imminent doom that usually pervades the early
contactee narratives is directly related to the threat of nuclear destruction. In the 1950s, four of the first flying saucer contactees who
received national attention – George Adamski, Truman Bethurum,
Daniel Fry and Orfeo Angelucci – all conveyed messages from space
people warning of the dangers of atomic bombs and radiation, and
these initial contactees have had a profound influence on subsequent
UFO lore. Nearly all of them were ordinary men who were self-
educated and came from working class,- manual labour backgrounds.
Their visions expressed the widespread apocalyptic fears of the time
about the inevitability of atomic war, and offered an escape from Cold
War apprehensions of imminent nuclear annihilation. In numerous
contactee accounts, the apocalyptic danger of nuclear weapons is
juxtaposed with utopian descriptions of the space people's utopian life
on their home planets where there was no war, poverty, suffering or
unhappiness. The space people frequently were said to live for thousands of years, while some were immortal and nearly all could be
reincarnated in another life.[7] Often earthlings were told that they also
had eternal souls which would survive physical death. This emphasis
on eternal life and reincarnation seems especially significant in the
context of the nuclear era, in which the bomb threatens perceptions of
symbolic immortality.

Apocalypse and planetary escape

Although many contactee narratives assert that the space beings are communicating with earthlings to prevent nuclear destruction and other disasters, in some instances worldly cataclysm is regarded as inevitable. A recurring idea in flying saucer lore is that a chosen few will be lifted off the planet before the Earth is destroyed, a belief that occasionally has given rise to small UFO groups that centre around a theology of imminent apocalypse and planetary escape. Perhaps the best-known case study of such a group is *When Prophecy Fails*, which focuses on a group in the 1950s led by Mrs Marian Keech, who said she was receiving channelled messages from space beings who warned of worldly flood disaster and promised to rescue believers and transport them to another planet prior to the cataclysm.[8]

The American UFO group that has received the most extensive media attention for its beliefs about inevitable apocalypse and planetary evacuation is Heaven's Gate, thirty-nine members of which killed themselves on 23–25 March 1997. Their collective suicide in the gated community of Rancho Santa Fe, near San Diego, California, was a media event – 'the worst mass suicide on American soil' – with the group portrayed as a New Age-UFO doomsday 'computer cult' of brainwashed devotees, sci-fi techno-millenarians, some of whom were castrated and all of whom were fans of the *X-Files* and *Star Trek*. Although so-called 'cults' are not typical within the UFO movement, and Heaven's Gate was much more dogmatic and authoritarian than most UFO groups, aspects of its belief system resemble ideas present in other apocalyptic UFO groups (and American apocalypticism in general), particularly the sense of fatalism for a world regarded as evil and doomed, an emphasis on demonic influences and conspiracies and the desire for salvation by otherworldly beings.

Like other UFO groups, the theology of Heaven's Gate consists of a synthesis of ideas borrowed from a range of traditions, including Christianity, Theosophy and New Age mysticism, melded together and reinterpreted. A central idea among this diversity of beliefs is that, by overcoming human attachments and living an ascetic lifestyle, one may escape from a corrupt and doomed world and ultimately be transported by a UFO to a higher realm. The group, which was started by Marshall Herff Applewhite and Bonnie Lu Nettles in the 1970s, came to be called the Human Individual Metamorphosis and later the Total Overcomers Anonymous (references to the goal of overcoming human attachments). The beliefs of the group changed over the years, especially after Nettles died in 1985, but a basic tenet was that aliens dwelling in the Kingdom of Heaven had planted human beings on Earth as a gardening experiment to grow souls.[9] Representatives from this Kingdom periodically make 'soul deposits' in the bodies of humans, preparing them to be transplanted to a higher evolutionary level. Applewhite considered himself a messianic representative from this higher level, like Jesus, who was incarnated into a human body and whose mission was to help earthly beings graduate from the human kingdom by overcoming human instincts, desires and attachments.

The secretive group disappeared from public view until 27 May 1993, when it placed an advertisement in USA Today entitled, 'UFO Cult Resurfaces with Final Offer', which declared that societal institutions and mainstream religions are controlled by an evil conspiracy and that the Earth would soon be destroyed and 'spaded under'. The passing of Comet Hale-Bopp in late March 1997 was embraced as a final prophetic sign, the 'marker' that believers had been waiting for, offering a sudden opportunity for planetary escape. Followers believed that the comet was being trailed by a gigantic spacecraft that would transport them to the 'Evolutionary Kingdom Level Above Human'; collective suicide was viewed as a means of evacuating an evil world, a way to shed one's physical 'container' and transport oneself onto this Next Level spacecraft and the Kingdom of Heaven.

Another recent UFO group in the United States that attracted extensive media attention for its predictions of worldly destruction is Chen Tao ('True Way'), also known as God's Salvation Church, which consisted of about 150 Taiwanese members who relocated to Garland, Texas, in 1997. The group initially settled in San Dimas, California, but then moved to Texas after the leader of the group, Hon-Ming Chen (known as 'Teacher Chen'), received a prophecy from God; Chen noted that 'Garland', when pronounced quickly, sounds like 'God's Land'.[10] The beliefs of the group involve a blend of Buddhism, Christian apocalypticism, Taiwanese folk beliefs and popular science, with an emphasis on the omnipresence of demonic forces and the redemptive role of flying saucers in human history.

In his treatise, 'God's Descending in Clouds (Flying Saucers) on Earth to Save People', Chen predicted that nuclear catastrophe and other disasters would begin in Asia in August 1999, but that believers would be safe in the United States, where they would eventually be evacuated in flying saucers by God. According to Chen, the world has suffered four great periods of tribulation, each of which has ended in nuclear war. In the past, human beings escaped the nuclear cataclysms in flying saucers and then later returned to live underground until the radiation dissipated.[11] Chen announced that God would soon warn humanity of impending nuclear apocalypse that would destroy most of the world, by appearing at Chen's home on 31 March 1998 at 10:00 a.m. and entering into Chen's body. Six days prior to that, on March 25, God would make a public announcement of his arrival, which would be seen on every television set in the world by tuning into Channel 18. Chen also declared that, as proof of God's presence at his home on 31 March, he would perform three miracles (turn invisible, make duplicates of his body to great people simultaneously and communicate with all visitors in their native language).

As the dates approached, the media speculated about the possibility of a mass suicide if God did not appear as predicted, similar to the Heaven's Gate tragedy, even though Chen condemned suicide as a demonic act. When 25 March arrived and God did not appear on Channel 18, Chen acknowledged his miscalculation, stating that his second prediction about God materialising in his home could be considered 'nonsense'; he then announced that the presence of hundreds of news reporters on the scene was God's way of spreading his message of salvation throughout the world. Although Chen acknowledged that his doomsday timetable was wrong, he continued to assert that worldly cataclysm was imminent and that God would rescue the faithful with flying saucers.[12]

Predictions of specific doomsday dates that characterise the beliefs of Chen Tao and Heaven's Gate are not typical within American UFOism, but ideas about imminent rescue of a chosen elect by space beings persist in the wider UFO movement today. For example, the publication *Psychic and UFO Revelations in the Last Days*,[13] is a collection of doomsday predictions conveyed to more than twenty UFO contactees, all of whom agree that worldly catastrophe is imminent, whether in the form of a global nuclear war, devastating ecological imbalances, natural disasters, land changes, plagues or a shift in the Earth's axis which will tip it out of its orbit and send the planet hurtling toward the sun. Although the world will soon go through a 'doomsday phase', the chosen ones will be physically removed from the planet.[14]

Similar to other catastrophic millenarian scenarios, the apocalypse anticipated within the UFO movement is often conceptualised as a cleansing of the world, to be followed by a terrestrial paradise of peace, fulfilment and harmony. The end-times predictions and evacuation scenarios in the flying saucer movement clearly resemble Christian 'rapture' beliefs about planetary escape prior to a period of worldly tribulation – although the criteria differ for who will be saved before the apocalypse. In some cases the chosen will be members of a specific

UFO group, or 'star children' and 'cosmic blends' – people whose ancestors mated with space beings eons ago; in other instances, those who believe in space beings as well as those who are spiritually attuned will be evacuated.[15]

UFOs, religious syncretism and the salvation of the chosen

The reworking and assimilation of previous beliefs into American UFOism is illustrated by the various UFO groups and publications which assert that Jesus will return in the rapture or in the second coming as the commander of a fleet of spaceships. One group of this persuasion is the Guardian Action International organisation, which is centred around the channelled messages of Ashtar, who is said to be a space being and commander of thousands of spaceships referred to as the Ashtar Command, which will descend prior to worldly catastrophe. When Jesus returns, according to one Ashtar Command leader named Romilar, 'He will lead the Armageddon, the armada of spaceships that will take those from this planet, who have been chosen.'[16] The Ashtar Command messages predict enormous cataclysms and warn of imminent doom, but hold out the slender hope that human beings will change their ways. Although catastrophe is imminent, believers are reassured that benevolent beings will rescue the chosen ones and later return them to repopulate the planet at some point in the future.[17]

Ideas about UFOs in the end-times have also been assimilated into the beliefs of the Nation of Islam, with the appearance of UFOs regarded by some as a doomsday sign, prophesied in the Bible, of an approaching apocalyptic battle involving the destruction of White America and the end of oppression.[18] According to Martha Lee, the original doctrine of the Nation of Islam was millenarian in its expectation of the downfall of the oppressive political institutions of the White world, and in its belief about the arrival of an African American millennium.[19] Like the ideologies of other Black Nationalist movements, these apocalyptic and racialist ideas were a response to continuing racism and discrimination and a separatist affirmation of black identity.

The early eschatology of the Nation of Islam focused on the 'Fall of America', predicted by the founder of the movement, the Honorable Elijah Muhammad, who maintained that there would be an imminent apocalyptic 'battle in the sky' as foretold in the biblical prophecy of Ezekiel.[20] Elijah Muhammad interpreted Ezekiel's vision of spinning wheels in the sky (Ezek. 1:4–28) as Allah's 'Mother Plane', an apocalyptic flying machine that is half a mile in circumference and that he describes as 'a small human planet made for the purpose of destroying the present world of the enemies of Allah ... The small circular-made planes called flying saucers, which are so much talked of being seen, could be from this Mother Plane'.[21] As Michael Lieb discusses, the idea of an apocalyptic UFO-like 'Mother Plane' or 'Mother Wheel' persists in the doctrines and beliefs of the Nation of Islam and has been emphasised by Louis Farrakhan, the current leader of the organisation, and frequently discussed in Farrakhan's newspaper *The Final Call*.[22] At a press conference on 24 October 1989, Farrakhan described his visionary encounter with a UFO, in which he was carried up into the Mother Wheel where he received messages from Elijah Muhammad, who warned of the war being waged 'against the rise of Black youth and Black people in America' and other oppressive aspects of American society.[23]

Another group that combines Afrocentric ideas with beliefs about the end-times role of UFOs, but also draws upon religious and cultural traditions cross-culturally, is the United Nuwaubian Nation of Moors (also known as the Ansaaru Allah Community and numerous other titles, most recently the Yamassee Native American Moors of the Creek Nation). The controversial founder of the group, Malachi Z. York (also known as Dwight York), claims that he is an extraterrestrial being from the Planet Rizq, located in the nineteenth galaxy called Illyuwn, and that his mission is to save his people from being killed before humanity destroys the Earth.[24] The group has its origins in the late 1960s and initially was a Black Nationalist movement, like the Nation of Islam, but with an emphasis on Sufism. Over time, the group has embraced beliefs from a range of world religions, and its identity has been influenced by an ever-changing assortment of cultural ideas, including Egyptian, Sudanese, African, American Indian, Jewish, Christian, Ethiopian and Islamic themes.[25] The group was originally located in Brooklyn, with a membership of more than 2,000 in the 1970s; in 1993, approximately 150 members of the group moved to Putnam County, Georgia, and built an Egyptian-themed religious community.[26]

Like many other UFO religious groups, including Heaven's Gate and the Raëlians, the Nuwaubians believe that extraterrestrial scientists created human life and civilisation. However, the Nuwaubian cosmology differs in that it teaches that people of African origin or with dark skin are the extraterrestrials' greatest creation, and that these chosen people have been tricked and oppressed by the other races on earth. York declares that he has been sent to educate oppressed people

DANIEL WOJCIK

of colour about their true origins and the nature of the cosmos, and that the chosen Nuwaubu people have the potential to communicate with the aliens and to become angelic, godlike beings called ELOHEEM, if they follow the teachings.[27] York says that the aliens will soon return to earth and evacuate 144,000 chosen ones (a number prophesied in the Book of Revelation) to the Planet Rizq, perhaps in 2003.[28] Similar to other American UFO groups, the Nuwaubians assert that human beings have de-evolved morally, psychically and spiritually and that the arrival of the extraterrestrials will restore various cosmic abilities and ensure the collective salvation of the righteous.

The belief that human beings are flawed and that the world is in a state of crisis and in need of extraterrestrial guidance characterises much of American UFOism. Numerous UFO movements warn that the human species has regressed and that worldly catastrophe is imminent, but assert that complete annihilation may be averted if people follow the directives of space entities. This conditional form of apocalypticism maintains that, if people change their behaviour as prescribed by superhuman beings – put an end to violence, become spiritually attuned or work for the transformation of planetary consciousness – the world may be saved. This view is exemplified by the Aetherius Society, one of the best-known and longest-lived UFO contactee groups, which has said for decades that imminent disasters may be averted through prayer and other spiritual practices. Based in Los Angeles, the Society was founded by George King, originally from England, who stated that he was selected as the primary channel for extraterrestrial messages transmitted from a being named Aetherius. According to King, he was contacted telepathically in 1954 by numerous Cosmic Intelligences orbiting earth in spacecraft and given messages concerning the salvation of the world: imminent worldly destruction may be avoided if the dangers of atomic weapons are acknowledged, and worldly redemption is possible through prayer and the promotion of the metaphysical teachings of the Cosmic Masters (including Jesus, Mars Sector 6 and Jupiter 92). King and his devotees use 'Spiritual Energy Batteries' that harness and amplify their prayers for world salvation; this 'Prayer Power', a form of psychic healing energy, is then discharged periodically to avert planetary catastrophes.[29]

In addition to the threat of earthly cataclysms, King declares that a constant threat of invasion by evil space beings exists and that the Aetherians and Cosmic Masters have fended off these nefarious invaders on various occasions.[30] In other messages, the Masters have promised that the Aetherians will be warned if the apocalypse should occur, so that they may gather at certain sacred, spiritually charged mountains to await rescue from above.[31] The goal of the society, however, is to prevent worldly annihilation, save every soul on the planet and transform planetary consciousness.[32]

Although the Aetherians, Guardian Action International, the Nuwaubians and other groups within the wider UFO movement may differ in terms of specific theologies and end-times scenarios, a fundamental belief shared by all of them is that a complete transformation of society and the human race is necessary to thwart humanity's destructive or oppressive tendencies. Human beings usually are depicted as an unenlightened or lower life form and extraterrestrials are said to be helping humanity attain a higher form of consciousness that will lead to the next evolutionary level of spiritual development and a new age of harmony and enlightenment.

The synthesis of ideas about spirituality and evolution, apocalyptic concerns and the attainment of immortality through futuristic technology finds full expression in the cosmology of the Raëlians. The group asserts that humanity will be transformed and saved by the arrival and guidance of superhuman beings and has become well-known for its support of human cloning research, known as 'Clonaid'. The Raëlian movement, which has more than 35,000 members worldwide, was founded in 1973 by Raël (born Claude Vorilhon) after an encounter with space beings.[33] In this and subsequent encounters Raël was informed that his mission is to warn humanity that it has entered into the 'Age of Apocalypse' since the bombing of Hiroshima and Nagasaki in 1945, and that human beings now must choose whether they will annihilate themselves in a global nuclear war or make a leap to a new planetary consciousness. Raëlians contend that human beings were scientifically created by extraterrestrials, called the 'Elohim', who fashioned humankind in their own image through the synthesis of DNA in their laboratories and then set human beings on Earth. The detonation of atomic bombs alerted the Elohim, our extraterrestrial parents, to the fact that humanity is now sophisticated enough to learn about its origins, if it does not destroy itself first. Raël, as the messenger of the Elohim and the last of forty Earth prophets, states that UFOs manned by the Elohim and the thirty-nine previous prophets (Jesus, Buddha, Mohammed, *et al.*) will arrive on Earth *if* an Elohim embassy is built for the space beings in Jerusalem by the year 2025. If not, the Elohim will not come and Earth will be destroyed.

Unlike many other UFO groups, the Raëlians do not emphasise planetary escape in the form of their physical bodies, but rather the perfection of life on Earth and a type of immortality achieved through a process of cosmic cloning. By attaining spiritual perfection, the Raëlians believe that they will alter and perfect their DNA; it is hoped that duplicates of themselves will be cloned by the Elohim for future space travel and settlement on virgin planets. In addition to saving themselves by being immortalised through cloning technologies, the Raëlians attempt to save the world by informing others of the teachings of Raël and the Elohim and by advocating the construction of an embassy in Jerusalem.[34] Their attempts to clone the first human being and their views on improving the human species through genetic engineering ultimately reflect the millenarian yearning for human perfection and a utopian, golden age on Earth.

Like the apocalyptic predictions of previous prophets, the techno-millenarian beliefs communicated by Raël, George King, Malachi Z. York and other UFO visionaries express the view that the future of humanity is determined by the arrival or guidance of superhuman beings, and that collective salvation is possible only if human beings act in ways prescribed by these messiah-like entities. Human beings, by themselves, are depicted as having contributed little to the development of human history and culture; the progression of civilisation, the spiritual development of planet Earth and the evolution of human beings have all been controlled or influenced by ETs. Such beliefs reflect a sense of powerlessness and the idea that, alone, humans are helpless and doomed; worldly salvation and transformation is possible only if human beings follow the mandates of superhuman entities who determine the fate of humanity and the planet.

Technological angels, apocalypse and American UFOism

The similarities between contactee beliefs and narratives about space beings and previous stories about intervention by supernatural entities such as angels have been noted by numerous researchers.[35] Like angels, the space beings are often depicted as superior other-worldly beings of light who are messengers, communicating God's principles or cosmic laws. Although encounters with angels tend to involve communications of a personal nature, the missives from space beings are often said to have global importance and concern planetary crisis and threats to the future of the human race. These messages frequently reflect the view that the planet can no longer sustain human life; that although planet Earth is hostile, the universe is friendly; and that superhuman beings with benevolent technology will rescue believers. Like the prophets of old, contactees warn of impending chastisements and worldly destruction unless humanity changes its behaviour, and they offer the hope of survival and salvation.

As Carl Jung suggests, space people are the equivalent of modern angels in technological guise who have emerged in popular belief traditions.[36] Jung believed that early UFO sightings were a direct result of Cold War anxieties; with the world divided into two hostile superpowers with nuclear weapons, people yearned for a divine resolution of the crisis. Although many people may have trouble believing that the human race will be saved by God's miraculous intervention, they are willing to believe in superhuman beings with advanced technology. Focusing in particular on visions of UFOs as luminous disks, Jung declared that flying saucers resembled mandalas, archetypal symbols of psychic totality and salvation found in mythologies through the world, that emerged from the collective unconscious and expressed people's yearning for harmony, reassurance and reconciliation in the atomic age.[37] As a vernacular religious response to the fears of the nuclear era, American flying saucer beliefs directly addresses apocalyptic fears, offering salvation by all-knowing beings with superior consciousness who oversee the fate of humanity. In contrast to the destructive technology of atomic weapons and the inescapable spectre of nuclear annihilation, UFOs represent a benevolent technology and the possibility of a golden age of peace and harmony. Just as the image of the mushroom cloud has become a master symbol of destruction in the modern era, the UFO has emerged as a folk symbol of hope and salvation, promising rescue by means of a technological rapture brought about by saviour beings descending from the skies.

American UFOism, like postwar beliefs in various other apocalyptic traditions, often expresses the idea that nuclear annihilation and other cataclysms are imminent and uncontrollable by human beings. Although earthlings are encouraged by the space people to stop using nuclear weapons and work to avert worldly cataclysms by promoting peace and harmony, a sense of fatefulness and impending doom is often pervasive. Helpless before the obliterating power of the bomb and other impending disasters, humanity sees its only hope of salvation in the planetary escape and protection offered by other-worldly beings. The apocalyptic aspects of UFO contactee beliefs exemplify the ways that traditions arise from eschatological and soteriological concerns in accordance with the cultural and mythic forms of the nuclear era.

DANIEL WOJCIK

Apocalyptic aspects of alien abduction narratives

The emergence, in the 1980s, of a variety of new UFO traditions that centre around the abduction of human beings by extraterrestrials further illustrates the ways that American apocalyptic beliefs have been transformed in response to the dominating concerns of the times. Alien abduction narratives are first-person accounts about encounters and capture by alien beings who are often described as small, grey-skinned creatures, with large triangular heads and bulging black eyes. Although such encounters have been discussed in UFO circles since the mid-1960s, the phenomenon was popularised after the publication of Whitley Strieber's book *Communion* in 1987,[38] which reached the top of the *New York Times* bestseller list in May that year. Strieber's account of his alleged abduction was followed by extensive coverage of the phenomenon on television and radio talk shows, and in a profusion of publications, including *Abduction: Human Encounters with Aliens* by Harvard psychiatrist John E. Mack,[39] *Close Encounters of the Fourth Kind* by journalist C. B. D. Bryan,[40] *Secret Lives: Firsthand Accounts of UFO Abductions* by historian David M. Jacobs,[41] and *Intruders* by ufologist Budd Hopkins.[42] Ufologists make bold claims about the pervasiveness of the abduction phenomenon, estimating that anywhere between 900,000 and 3.7 million individuals have been abducted.[43] Although abduction accounts have come from countries other than the United States, some researchers see alien abductions as primarily an American phenomenon, with no other nation expressing the same intensity of interest in the subject.[44]

Despite the wealth of literature on abduction encounters, the apocalyptic aspects of such experiences often have been overlooked by researchers, even though abductees themselves may assign an eschatological meaning to their experiences, which frequently deal with imminent worldly destruction, human destiny, transformation and a controlling power that oversees all existence. Some abductees (or 'experiencers') assert that the aliens are evil beings who have a sinister plan for world domination, or that they are amoral beings who are exploiting humanity for their own purposes in order to ensure the survival of their race. The other, more predominant, view asserts that aliens are benevolent beings or multidimensional entities that are warning us of imminent disaster or overseeing the evolution of humanity, either by interbreeding with human beings or by directing human consciousness to a more advanced level. This latter view has obvious redemptive themes. In some scenarios, the salvation of humanity will not be brought about through worldly cataclysm, but gradually through the genetic and spiritual perfection of human beings as directed by superhuman beings.

Although the abduction phenomenon has precipitated a variety of narratives, beliefs and interpretations, such accounts share features with previous legends of supernatural encounters, abductions and otherworldly journeys, particularly nightmare experiences, out-of-body experiences, shamanic journeys and traditional encounters with fairies, dwarves, demons and other diminutive mythological creatures.[45] In addition to their parallels with these earlier accounts, UFO abduction narratives have a consistent structure and are characterised by similar themes. First, aliens are interested in human reproduction and the genetic make-up of human beings, and abductees describe in vivid detail their often frightening encounters in which aliens conduct medical experiments. Abductees describe examinations, often of a sexual nature, in which they are penetrated or their body parts and organs removed and later reassembled.[46]

According to some, aliens submit abductees to this gruesome ordeal in order to procure genetic materials to create hybrid breeding pools in an attempt to save their own race or to develop a new breed of human beings that will survive after the current world is destroyed. Other abductees claim that the aliens come from a 'dying planet' that has been devastated by catastrophes and, because their planet and its inhabitants are no longer fertile, they seek human genetic materials to rejuvenate their race.[47] Some abductees assert that some sort of spiritual self-examination or transformation occurs after their encounter and say that the event was a turning point in their lives.[48] Abductees are then often given messages by the beings, which usually take the form of prophecies and warnings about worldly destruction, the end of the human race and the salvation of the planet, and which resemble those delivered to early flying saucer contactees.[49] In some cases, abductees have been shown images of the world blowing up and of an otherworldly metropolis being built by aliens for those evacuated prior to worldly destruction. Although warnings of the dangers of nuclear weapons persist, current abduction lore is preoccupied with apocalyptic scenarios involving environmental catastrophes, such as global warming, the destruction of the ozone layer, deforestation and pollution of the oceans, with many in the UFO movement believing that Earth.[50]Abductees are often informed that they have been chosen and that their experiences are part of a larger plan that is to be revealed at a later date. They are also told that humanity will survive the upcoming cataclysm in some way, if not through planetary escape then through the process of hybridisation in which a new alien–human being will be created.[51]

In addition to the themes of worldly destruction and salvation, feelings of complete powerlessness also pervade UFO abduction accounts. Unlike the benevolent Space People and Cosmic Masters encountered by early UFO contactees, the beings in abduction accounts are often depicted as intergalactic vivisectionists, all-controlling extraterrestrial genetic engineers who conduct torturous experiments on human beings in order to save the human race, which cannot be saved through human effort. Many abductees not only feel helpless but sense that, although aliens seem altruistic and courteous, in fact they are cold and indifferent, with little regard for human suffering or perhaps no understanding of it.[52] Abductees often feel that the aliens have a hidden agenda and that they have completely controlled the abduction and are controlling worldly events as well. As one abductee put it, 'They're doing things against our will. And the most frightening thing is, we have no control ... It doesn't matter what we do or think. They're going to do whatever they want anyway'.[53] In these accounts, the grey aliens forcibly abduct victims and dissect them as if they were laboratory rats; the abductees often emerge from these experiences feeling traumatised, exploited or abused. Some abductees even announce that beadlike objects have been implanted in their bodies for reasons of surveillance, control or further exploitation. In any case, future abduction may be imminent – it could happen at any time, to anyone. Despite the feelings of transformation that some abductees report, many accounts are characterised by an undeniable sense of helplessness and victimisation by overwhelming forces beyond one's control.

Whatever one makes of such narratives, they are consistently apocalyptic, reflecting fears of the imminence of the end of the world and the end of the human species. The narratives may resemble traditional experiences of initiatory death and transformation involving otherworldly beings, but the broader and more explicit message concerns the destruction of the world and the salvation of humanity. Although not yet formulated into a cohesive apocalyptic worldview, abduction lore shares features with other apocalyptic belief systems: it is characterised by a sense of powerlessness, perceptions of societal crisis and the belief in a superhuman plan or superhuman forces that are overseeing the salvation of humanity, in this case through extraterrestrial genetic engineering. Abduction narratives imply that the world is doomed unless the human race undergoes some sort of radical transformation that cannot be accomplished through human effort but only through the guidance of other-worldly or interdimensional entities.

Like the alien–human hybrid spawned in these narratives, abduction lore is itself a hybrid of religious and secular ideas, an amalgam of motifs about worldly destruction and salvation expressed in terms of futuristic technology, evolution and genetic manipulation. As super-human genetic engineers with omnipotent technology, the aliens are a secularised counterpart to God in some scenarios, while in others they are depicted as some sort of transcendent consciousness or power in the universe. Like the gods and goddesses of ancient times who mated with mortals to create hybrid heroes with extraordinary powers, aliens inter-breed with humans to create new beings who ensure the survival and transformation of humanity. In many abduction narratives, history is presented as the unfolding of a superhuman plan controlled by extraterrestrials, and abductees have a critical role in this plan: to warn humanity of imminent destruction and participate in crucial cosmic experiments involving the contribution of their blood, sperm and ova to help create a new hybrid race. In these accounts the sacred and the profane go hand in hand and salvation occurs through painful experi-ments and genetic recombination. Above all else, beliefs about aliens and UFOs assert that humans will survive worldly destruction as the result of superhuman guidance and ultimately transcend earthly exis-tence, gaining the technology and wisdom of the aliens and perhaps becoming superhuman beings themselves.

In addition to these abduction narratives that warn of imminent worldly catastrophes but offer the promise of survival and transforma-tion, there have emerged in recent years increasingly sinister UFO beliefs about malevolent aliens who are plotting to destroy the human race.[54] In some scenarios, the aliens are depicted as the demonic coun-terparts and enemies of the benevolent aliens, or as alien–human hybrids from dying planets who will invade and conquer the Earth in the future; in other scenarios, the aliens are already walking among us and preparing to colonise Earth. This recent UFO lore offers little chance of averting imminent worldly destruction or humanity's enslavement by aliens and is characterised by a sense of imminent crisis, overwhelming evil in the world, paranoia and manipulation by uncontrollable forces. These current UFO beliefs share many of the conspiratorial themes that pervade Christian apocalyptic traditions, such as a preoccupation with the rise of the new world order, the anti-Christ and conspiracy theories about the evil machinations of organisations such as the Trilateral Commission, the United Nations and the Bilderberg Group. One common theme is that the grey aliens and the MJ-12, a group of top-level scientists and military officers, are collaborating to establish a one-world dictatorship, and have already formed a 'Secret Government' that controls every aspect of politics, the military, industry, religion, commerce, banking and the media. Such beliefs assert that humanity ultimately will be enslaved or exterminated in concentration camps at the hands of the Greys, millions of whom now wait in underground bases to invade America from within.[55]

Unlike beliefs about aliens developing alien–human hybrids to ensure the survival of both races threatened with extinction, this recent lore has absolutely no redemptive themes. The evil aliens have superior technology and intelligence, as well as the help of the US government and the sinister Secret Government, a coalition that is all-powerful and which will enslave and exterminate humans, as the Grays conduct cruel experiments on the survivors. A sense of fatalism, nihilism and powerlessness are distilled and amplified in this UFO lore. Inexplicable and inescapable evil forces are everywhere; they are uncontrollable and the creeping tentacles of the conspiracy entwine with every aspect of human existence. By situating every event into a labyrinthine plan, UFO conspiracy theories provide reasons for perceived evils, directly address feelings of powerlessness and victimisation, and reflect the extreme level of alienation and hopelessness felt by some in American society today.

Progressive millennialism and UFO beliefs

Despite these increasingly sinister and unredemptive themes concerning malevolent aliens, beliefs about benevolent beings or forces that will help save humanity continue to be promoted within American UFOism. De-emphasising the idea of apocalypse and stressing notions of human evolution and progress, such beliefs assert that, if humans follow a cosmic plan prescribed by an extraterrestrial source, they will establish a terrestrial paradise. Relatively optimistic in emphasis, these ideas are an expression of 'progressive millennialism', characterised by the notion that collective salvation may be brought about gradually by human beings acting according to a divine plan or cooperating with the guidance of superhuman agents.[56] Progressive millennialism takes a variety of forms in American UFOism and is identified by the belief that, instead of the apocalypse, a sweeping change will occur involving a transformation of planetary consciousness, behavioural patterns, energy fields or the genetic code of all human beings.

This progressive millennialist view is exemplified by the '11:11 Doorway' movement led by Solara Antara Amaa-ra, who claims to channel messages from various extraterrestrial beings and declares that human beings are angels originally descended from various stars in the cosmos. According to Solara and her thousands of followers, a cosmic 'doorway of opportunity' for the salvation of humanity opened on 11 January 1992 and will close on 31 December 2011. During the twenty-year period, humanity will be given the chance to eliminate evil, spiritually cleanse and transform itself and then ascend to a new realm of consciousness. Like numerous other UFO and New Age millennialist movements, Solara claims that 144,000 believers must unite worldwide in 'conscious oneness' to attain some sort of spiritual critical mass, launching all of humanity into a higher level of consciousness that will usher in the Golden Age.[57] Although evil is acknowledged in progressive millennialist worldviews such as Solara's, the spiritual actions of human beings are believed to be essential for the elimination of evil and the salvation of humanity.

Solara's '11:11 Doorway' movement is similar in its beliefs to the Harmonic Convergence, perhaps the most famous example of New Age/UFO progressive millennialism. Coordinated by author José Argüelles, the Harmonic Convergence was celebrated by tens of thousands of people throughout the world on 16–17 August 1987. The event was centred around a variety of Mayan, Native American and Christian prophecies, the end of specific cycles of the Aztec and Mayan Calendars and purported cosmic occurrences and planetary configurations. According to Argüelles, the ancient Mayans were cosmic visionaries who left a 'galactic calling card' in the form of coded messages in the Mayan calendar that reveal how human beings may transform themselves and join the Galactic Federation after the Mayan calendar ends in 2012. In his book, *The Mayan Factor*,[58] Argüelles states that 16–17 August 1987 was a critical juncture in the history of the planet, a period of dangerous transition from one era to another during which the future of humanity would be determined. The world was to have plunged into a 'negative cycle' towards apocalypse unless 144,000 people or more participated in this rite of planetary passage, which was to restore Earth's solar and cosmic resonance. The event would create an atmosphere of increased spiritual understanding and trust with extraterrestrial and cosmic powers, triggering the Harmonic Convergence in which humanity would progress towards 'galactic synchronisation' and eventually join the federation of other enlightened planets after the aliens make contact in the year 2012.

Over the weekend of 16–17 August, individuals gathered at

renowned sacred sites such as Stonehenge, the Great Pyramid, Machu Picchu and Mount Shasta, where they chanted, meditated and engaged in various ceremonies in an attempt to transform the planet spiritually and connect humanity, the Earth and universal energies. In this scenario, human effort would not only prevent Armageddon but also activate the return of the spirit of the Aztec god Quetzalcoatl and all the gods and goddesses and heroes and heroines that have ever existed in the human imagination.[59] The archetypal divine energy of these beings was to be reborn in the hearts of all people on that date, instilling a new global consciousness resulting in a world in which humans beings live in harmony with each other and the environment. Organisers and participants of the Harmonic Convergence emphasised that their spiritual efforts during the two-day event saved the Earth from destruction and allowed the planet to pursue its cosmic destiny, preparing humanity for an evolutionary leap into the next dimension and the establishment of a new age in the year 2012.

The year 2012 is also a pivotal date in the psychedelically inspired UFO eschatology espoused by Terence McKenna (1946–2000), a philosopher and researcher of altered states of consciousness, who is known for his theories about the essential role of drugs in human evolution. McKenna advocated a type of neo-pagan, shamanistic, psychedelic spirituality, and his ideas have become popular among some in the neo-pagan community, members of the rave culture, those interested in entheogens and religious experiences and many others.[60] According to McKenna, the increase in reported UFO sightings and encounters marks the end of history and the transformation of human consciousness. UFOs represent the appearance of a 'transcendental object from beyond the end of history' that signals the complete disruption and transformation of the world as we know it in 2012; McKenna also asserts that certain drugs, especially psilocybin and dimethyltryptamine (DMT), allow contact with UFOs and extraterrestrial intelligences.[61]

McKenna has discussed extensively his encounters with a UFO and with alien creatures, and says that his own psychedelic experiences have led him to believe that psilocybin mushrooms are extraterrestrial organisms that arrived on planet Earth as spores, and that these mushrooms may contain an extraterrestrial intelligence that allows communication with alien intelligences.[62] McKenna contends that certain psychoactive plants provide shamanic and visionary experiences that are connected to UFO encounters, and that psilocybin in particular 'reveals an event at the end of history of such magnitude that it casts miniature reflections of itself back into time', which take the form of UFOs.[63] UFOs are not only manifestations of this approaching end-time transformation, they are also materialisations of what he calls the soul of humanity or 'the collective unconscious, the Overmind', that is revealing itself and that is controlling the development and destiny of the human species.[64] Disagreeing with widely-held beliefs about flying saucers coming from other planets, McKenna asserts instead that 'UFOs seem to come from eternity … The UFOs come from another dimension; one could say they come from beyond death. They come from a dimension somehow totally different from our own, but tied up with the human psyche in a way that is puzzling, alarming and reassuring – and shamanic.'[65]

McKenna based his prediction that history will end on 21 December 2012 (at 11:18 a.m.) on a 'time-wave' computer program that he developed based on shamanistic experiences, the I Ching and 'alien artifacts' that were revealed to him more than twenty years ago.[66] His program plots the precise moments in human history where great novelty as well as upheaval have occurred. According to McKenna's calculations, the Earth is in the final moments of a crisis and time as well as human advancement are now accelerating exponentially until the winter solstice in 2012 – the moment at which human accomplishment spikes to infinity. At that instant, history ceases and the Earth will be plunged into complete and incalculable novelty, an omega point of transcendence which could involve 'our departure from the planet, the triumph over death and release of the individual from the body'.[67] Although McKenna was unsure of the exact nature of this extraordinary event, he was convinced that it will involve an encounter with a transcendental or trans-dimensional object at the end of time and that UFOs foreshadow this transformative encounter.

The emphasis on an external cosmic event, associated with the year 2012 and extraterrestrial influences that will completely transform humanity, now pervades current American UFOism. This cosmic event is usually regarded as imminent and inevitable, and entirely beyond human control; a popular belief, for instance, is that planet Earth will pass through a galactic wave of light or a photon belt, resulting in the genetic and spiritual transmutation of humanity that will usher in a golden age. This scenario is promoted by the Planetary Activation Organization (known previously as the Ground Crew Project), founded by Sheldon Nidle in California in the 1980s. According to Nidle, who says that he channels messages from extraterrestrial entities from the planet Sirius, the Earth passed through an invisible high-energy, plasma-like photon belt sometime in the mid-

1990s, an event that is changing human beings genetically and allowing them to attain a new level of consciousness.[68] Nidle declares that this transformation is part of 'a great divine plan' by space beings who have been overseeing Earth's spiritual development and whose intent is to 'bring Earth humans into full alignment with their galactic brothers and sisters'.[69]

Nidle predicts a sudden mass landing of 15.5 million spaceships from the Galactic Federation, the extraterrestrial inhabitants of which will rapidly transform humanity and create a terrestrial paradise by the year 2012.[70] In Nidle's galactic version of the biblical narrative of the Fall, human beings are said to be the victims of various genetic mutations that have occurred through the millennia and that have caused the loss of certain cosmic capabilities. The Earth's passage through the photon belt is restoring these superhuman abilities, gradually transforming the genetic codes of all humanity from a double-helix DNA to a twelve-helix DNA pattern in the shape of the Star of David. As a result, the human body will regain its galactic ability to rejuvenate itself and overcome illness and ageing, and humans will be able to communicate telepathically with others as well as with plants, animals, the Earth (as Lady Gaia) and the deceased.[71] With the restoration of their lost genetic codes, human beings will become divine, a golden age will be established on Earth and earthlings will be reunited with their galactic forebears. Unlike catastrophic UFO scenarios in which only a select few are saved through planetary evacuation or alien–human interbreeding, the Planetary Activation Organization, like other progressive millennialist groups, promises that all of humanity may achieve collective salvation and the attainment of a terrestrial paradise.

One of the best-known UFO groups to have promoted this view since the 1950s is the Unarius Academy of Science in El Cajon, near San Diego, California. Led until recently by Uriel, 'Archangel and Cosmic Visionary' (otherwise known as Ruth Norman, 1900–93), the Unariuns[72] anticipate a spacefleet landing in the near future involving thirty-three spacecraft from the planets of the Interplanetary Confederation. Each spaceship will carry 1,000 intelligent beings, who will work with humanity to save our world, spiritually transforming Earth so that it will finally be advanced enough to join the other thirty-two enlightened planets. In anticipation of the arrival of these interplanetary beings, the Unarians work to spread the teachings of the Interplanetary Confederation in order gradually to transform the spiritual consciousness of humanity.[73]In contrast to apocalyptic beliefs that express a pessimistic view of the world as irredeemably evil, the

Unarians, like other progressive millennialist groups, regard current problems as conquerable by human beings working in harmony with superhuman agents or cosmic forces. Unlike apocalyptic worldviews that emphasise salvation for the righteous and the destruction for the evil 'others', progressive millennialism, at least within the UFO movement, tends to be less dualistic and to accept all humanity in its inclusive millennial embrace.

Although progressive millennialist traditions place more emphasis on human action in bringing about the millennium, and therefore appear less deterministic than other apocalyptic UFO worldviews, both forms of millenarianism reflect the view that history unfolds as part of a superhuman plan and that the fate of humanity is guided by external forces. Within this cosmic drama, human beings are said to have a preordained role to play and, through spiritual effort, genetic transformation and the guidance of the extraterrestrials, they will realise their destiny and perhaps become godlings themselves with the cosmic ability to create a golden age.

As the great diversity of these UFO beliefs indicates, American UFOism has become a Rorschach test of popular eschatological ideas. The range of UFO lore illustrates the protean qualities of apocalyptic traditions and the ways that new beliefs reflect the fears, hopes and preoccupations in American society. In an era plagued by the threat of nuclear weapons, environmental destruction, chemical and biological warfare, deadly viruses and other possible forms of extinction, the apocalyptic and millenarian aspects of UFO beliefs have an obvious appeal, directly addressing fears of collective death by offering the promise of salvation and the assurance that a superhuman plan underlies history. Steeped in images of catastrophe that reflect an awareness of our own endings and the widespread feeling that the world itself may be dying, such beliefs allay fears of human extinction, give expression to the desire for a meaningful narrative underlying history, and promise a perfect age of happiness and human fulfilment.

Although UFO traditions address issues of ultimate concern – the reasons for suffering and injustice, the awareness of death and the yearning for immortality, the nature of good and evil, human destiny and the fate of the world – the widespread belief that the world can be saved only by other-worldly beings may reinforce feelings of helplessness and serve as a substitute for confronting the actual problems that face humanity. Such ideas tend to deny the efficacy of human effort to improve the world and may encourage a passive acceptance of human-made crises and potential disasters. Within American UFOism, fatalistic beliefs about manipulation by evil aliens and inevitable worldly destruction have multiplied in recent years, yet optimistic beliefs about the transformative aspects of UFOs thrive as well, with people encouraged to bring about personal and societal changes and confront current crises. Whether or not more progressive or reformist UFO traditions arise in the third millennium, apocalyptic UFO beliefs predicting inevitable worldly cataclysm will proliferate as long as perceptions of overwhelming societal crises and uncontrollable evil exist.

Beliefs about worldly destruction and transformation have been an ongoing and significant part of American UFOism, existing at a grass-roots level for more than half a century. With the development of communication on the Internet through e-mail and newsgroups, UFO enthusiasts from around the globe now exchange ideas and debate topics ranging from the prophetic significance of ETs in the Bible, Hopi prophecies and *X-Files* episodes, to the relationship between UFOs, crop circles, cloning, the hollow Earth, weird Fortean phenomena and hyperspacial breakthrough in the year 2012. Given the dynamic nature of UFO traditions and the enduring appeal and explanatory power of such ideas, one need not be a cosmic visionary to predict that beliefs about the eschatological aspects of UFOs and extraterrestrials will continue to flourish and be transformed in the years ahead.

NOTES

1 C. Wessinger (ed.), *Millennialism, Persecution and Violence: Historical Cases*, New York, Syracuse University Press, 2000, pp. 6–9.
2 The word *apocalypse* (from the Greek *apokalypsis*) means revelation or unveiling, and this sense of a revealed, underlying design for history and humanity often characterises American eschatological beliefs about UFOs.
3 R. S. Ellwood and H. B. Partin, *Religious and Spiritual Groups in Modern America*, 2nd edn, Englewood Cliffs: Prentice Hall, 1988; R. S. Ellwood, 'UFO Religious Movements', in T. Miller (ed.), *America's Alternative Religions*, Albany, State University of New York Press, 1995, pp. 393–9; T. E. Bullard, 'UFO Abductions Reports: The Supernatural Kidnap Narrative Returns in Technological Guise', *Journal of American Folklore*, 1989, vol. 1, pp. 147–70; T. E. Bullard, 'UFOs: Lost in the Myths', in D. M. Jacobs (ed.), *UFOs and Abductions: Challenging the Borders of Knowledge*, Lawrence, University Press of Kansas, 2000; R. P. Flaherty, 'Flying Saucers and the New Angelology. Mythic Projection of the Cold War and the Convergence of Opposites', unpublished doctoral dissertation, Los Angeles, University of California, 1990; J. A. Saliba, 'The Religious Dimensions of UFO Phenomena', in J. R. Lewis (ed.), *The Gods Have Landed: New Religions from Other Worlds*, New York, State University of New York Press, 1995, pp. 15–64; J. Whitmore, 'Religious

Dimensions of UFO Abductee Experience', in Lewis (ed.), *The Gods Have Landed*, pp. 65–84; B. Denzler, *The Lure of the Edge: Scientific Passions, Religious Beliefs and the Pursuit of UFOs*, Berkeley, University of California Press, 2001, pp. 124–59. Brenda Denzler argues that the religious aspects of the UFO movement have often been overstated by scholars, and that the rhetoric in the UFO community is predominantly scientific. She concludes, however, that, despite the scientific and secularist themes, the beliefs and experiences of people in the UFO community frequently have religious and mythic overtones (see *The Lure of the Edge*, pp. 155–7).

4 Flaherty, 'Flying Saucers and the New Angelology', p. 5.
5 T. G. Beckley, *Psychic and UFO Revelations in the Last Days*, New Brunswick, Inner Light Publications, 1980, p. 8.
6 *Ibid.*, p. 5; Ellwood and Partin, *Religious and Spiritual Groups in Modern America*, p. 113.
7 D. Jacobs, *The UFO Controversy in America*, Bloomington, Indiana University Press, 1975.
8 L. Festinger, H. W. Riechen and S. Schachter, *When Prophecy Fails*, Minneapolis, University of Minnesota Press, 1956.
9 R. W. Balch, 'Waiting for the Ships: Disillusionment and the Revitalization of Faith in Bo and Peep's UFO Cult', in Lewis (ed.), *The Gods Have Landed*, pp. 137–66.
10 R. Perkins and F. Jackson, 'Spirit in the Sky', *Fortean Times*, April, 1998, vol. 109, p. 24.
11 *Ibid.*, p. 26.
12 *Register Guard* (Eugene, Oregon), 'God's a No-Show, So Group to Head Home', 26 March 1998, 4A.
13 Beckley, *Psychic and UFO Revelations in the Last Days*.
14 *Ibid.*
15 *Ibid.*, pp. 33–5.
16 T. G. Beckley, *The New World Order: Channelled Prophecies from Space*, New York, Global Communications, 1982, p. 55.
17 Beckley, *Psychic and UFO Revelations in the Last Days*, pp. 27–9; Tuella, *Project World Evacuation by the Ashtar Command*, New Brunswick, Inner Publications, 1993.
18 M. F. Lee, *The Nation of Islam: An American Millennial Movement*, Syracuse, Syracuse University Press, 1996, pp. 46, 87.
19 *Ibid*, p.2
20 *Ibid.*, p. 34.
21 *Ibid.*; D. Kossy, *Kooks*, Portland, Feral House, 1994, p. 27.
22 M. Lieb, *Children of Ezekiel: Aliens, UFOs, the Crisis of Race and the Advent of End Time*, Durham, NC, Duke University Press, 1998, pp. 6–7, 221–4.
23 Kossy, *Kooks*, p. 27; *ibid.*, pp. 209–13.
24 Nuwaubians, 'Brief History: Center for Anthroufology'. Available online: http://home.uchicago.edu/ryancook/un-nwtxt.htm (November 2002). It is not only the group's UFO ideology that has sparked controversy, but the alleged illegal activities of York and the Nuwaubians. In the 1960s, York served three years in prison for assault, resisting arrest and possession of a dangerous weapon, and the Nuwaubians have been accused of

various criminal activities including welfare fraud, extortion and building-code violations; most recently, York is in custody without bail for 208 counts of child molestation see S. Monroe, 'Space Invaders', *Time*, (12 July 1999), vol. 154.2, p. 32; Nuwaubians, 'Brief History'; Chapter 7 of this volume.

25 See Gabriel's discussion in Chapter 7 of this volume.

26 Nuwaubians, 'Brief History'.

27 *Ibid.*

28 Monroe, 'Space Invaders', p. 32.

29 R. Wallis, 'The Aetherius Society: A Case Study in the Formation of a Mystagogic Congregation', *Sociological Review*, 1974, vol. 22, pp. 27–44; D. Curran, *In Advance of the Landing: Folk Concepts of Outer Space*, New York, Abbeville Press, 1985.

30 Saliba, 'The Religious Dimensions of UFO Phenomena', p. 36.

31 Curran, *in advance of the landing*, p.64. In addition to UFO groups that venerate ETs in flying saucers who visit earth and make contact with human beings, numerous groups focus on Ascended Masters who exist on other planets and communicate through paranormal means, but do not visit earth in vehicles. One such group, which has been anticipating the end of the world for decades, is the Church Universal and Triumphant (the Summit Lighthouse), whose leader, Elizabeth Claire Prophet, channels apocalyptic and redemptive messages from the Masters. E. C. Prophet, *The Great White Brotherhood in the Culture, History and Religion of America*, Livingston, Summit University Press, 1987 [1976].

32 B. Sentes and S. J. Palmer, 'Presumed Immanent: The Raëlians, UFO Religions and the Postmodern Condition', *Nova Religio*, 2000, vol. 4.1, October, p. 86.

33 S. J. Palmer, 'Women in the Raëlian Movement: New Religious Experiments in Gender and Authority', in Lewis (ed.), *The Gods Have Landed*, pp. 106–7.

34 C. G. Jung, *Flying Saucers: A Modern Myth of Things Seen in the Skies*, trans. R. F. C. Hull, Princeton, Princeton University Press, 1978 [1959]; Ellwood and Partin, *Religious and Spiritual Groups in Modern America*; Flaherty, 'Flying Saucers and the New Angelology'; Saliba, 'The Religious Dimensions of UFO Phenomena'.

35 Jung, *Flying Saucers*.

36 *Ibid.*, pp.14–23.

37 W. Strieber, *Communion: A True Story*, New York, Avon, 1987.

38 J. E. Mack, *Abduction: Human Encounter with Aliens*, New York, Macmillan/Charles Scribner's Sons, 1994.

39 C. B. D. Bryan, *Close Encounters of the Fourth Kind*, New York, Penguin, 1995.

40 D. Jacobs, *Secret Lives: Firsthand Accounts of UFO Abductions*, New York, Simon & Schuster, 1992.

41 B. Hopkins, *Intruders: The Incredible Visitations at Copley Woods*, New York, Random House, 1987.

42 Bryan, *Close Encounters of the Fourth Kind*, p. 256; Whitmore, 'Religious Dimensions of UFO Abductee Experience', p. 67.

43 *Ibid.*, p. 80.

44 See Bullard, 'UFO Abductions Reports'; Flaherty, 'Flying Saucers and the New Angelology'; Whitmore, 'Religious Dimensions of UFO Abductee Experience'.
45 Bullard, 'UFO Abductions Reports', p.156; Whitmore, 'Religious Dimensions of UFO Abductee Experience', p. 70.
46 Bullard, 'UFO Abductions Reports', pp. 156–8.
47 Ibid., pp. 162–3; Whitmore, 'Religious Dimensions of UFO Abductee Experience', pp. 70–1.
48 Bullard, 'UFO Abductions Reports', pp. 156–7; Bryan, Close Encounters of the Fourth Kind, p. 421.
49 Ibid..
50 Bullard, 'UFO Abductions Reports', p. 157.
51 Ibid.
52 Bryan, Close Encounters of the Fourth Kind, pp. 277–8.
53 A sinister view of the UFO phenomenon is also embraced by numerous Christian prophecy interpreters, who regard aliens as demons or fallen angels who will be involved in an apocalyptic scenario in the last days. See H. Lindsey, Planet Earth – 2000 AD: Will Mankind Survive?, Palos Verdes, Western Front, 1994, pp. 68–71; I. D. E., Thomas The Omega Conspiracy, Herndon, Growth, 1986, p. 232; C. Missler and M. Eastman, Alien Encounters: The Secret Behind the UFO Phenomenon, Coeur d'Alene, Koinonia House, 1997.
54 C. Peebles, Watch the Skies! A Chronicle of the Flying Saucer Myth, Washington and London, Smithsonian Institute Press, 1994, pp. 257–8, 281–2.
55 C. Wessinger, How the Millennium Comes Violently, pp. 8–11. Progressive millennialism is not unique to American UFOism, but has been embraced by various groups, such as Christian postmillennialists, who preached the Social Gospel in the nineteenth century and declared that Christian principles would eventually prevail and defeat all evil, transforming the world into a place worthy of Christ's second coming. These postmillennialists had a reformist vision of the salvation of the world and worked to establish the millennial kingdom on Earth through good works – they contributed to the abolition of slavery and of child labour, the temperance movement and prison reform.
56 Solara Antara Amaa-ra, 11:11 – The Opening of the Doorway, Charlottesville, Starne-Borne Unlimited, 1990.
57 J. Argüelles, The Mayan Factor, Santa Fe, Bear & Co. 1987.
58 Ibid., p. 170.
59 See C. H. Partridge, 'Sacred Chemicals: Psychedelic Drugs and Mystical Experience', in C. Partridge and T. Gabriel (eds), Mysticisms East and West: Studies in Mystical Experience, Carlisle, Paternoster Press, 2003, ch. 7.
60 T. McKenna, The Archaic Revival: Speculations on Psychedelic Mushrooms, the Amazon, Virtual Reality UFOs, Evolution, Shamanism, the Rebirth of the Goddess and the End of History, San Francisco, HarperCollins, 1991; M. Lindemann, 'Highlights of Swiss UFO Conference', excerpt from CNI News, 5 July 1995, vol. 8.1. Available online:http://deoxy.org/t_swiss.html (November 2002).
61 McKenna, Archaic Revival, pp. 46–7, 206–7.
62 Ibid., p. 60.

63 *Ibid.*, pp. 64, 70.
64 *Ibid.*, p. 65.
65 Lindemann, 'Highlights of Swiss UFO Conference'.
66 McKenna, *Archaic Revival*, p. 92; *ibid.*
67 V. Essene and S. Nidle, *You Are Becoming a Galactic Human*, Santa Clara, S.E.E. Publishing Company, 1994.
68 *Ibid.*, pp. 234–5.
69 S. Nidle, 'Planetary Activation Organization (PAO) Message of Introduction'. Available online: http://www.paoweb.com/paomesg.htm (November 2002); B. El Masri, 'The Mass Landings. The Ground Crew Project'. Available online:http://www.portal.ca/groundcrew/crew/.
70 Essene and Nidle, *You Are Becoming a Galactic Human*, p. 58.
71 See R. E. Norman with C. Spaegel, *Preparation for the Landing*, El Cajon, Unarius Educational Foundation, 1987.

15

ATTITUDES TOWARD RELIGION AND SCIENCE IN THE UFO MOVEMENT IN THE UNITED STATES

Brenda Denzler

Early in 1992 I discovered what I'd been searching for since I had become a student of religion a decade earlier. It had occurred to me that it would be interesting to track one segment of United States culture through the change in the millennium, but for a long time I couldn't decide which segment I should watch. When I read a book entitled *Communion: A True Story*,[1] the account of Whitley Strieber's awakening to the realisation that he had had terrifying personal encounters with alien entities, I was, to say the least, intrigued. (To say the most, I was scared to death!) Following that with Budd Hopkins's *Intruders: The Incredible Visitations at Copley Woods*,[2] and then with Temple University historian David Jacobs's *Secret Life: Firsthand Accounts of UFO Abductions*,[3] it finally dawned on me that I had found the focus of my study.

Since May of 1992 I have been a participant-observer in the UFO community on as many different levels as possible. I have participated in relatively small UFO discussion and reading groups, have attended statewide Mutual UFO Network meetings and have gone to half a dozen major UFO conferences. Since the autumn of 1995 I have circulated a short questionnaire among members of the UFO community and since the autumn of 1996 a longer questionnaire among abductees only. I have met and corresponded with numerous people who report having had truly extraordinary experiences with UFOs and alien entities. And I have read extensively in the UFO literature. What I have learned about the UFO community in the United States is that its public image is based largely on an illusion and its internal condition is one of deep philosophical division over the roles of science and religion in the investigation and interpretation of UFO phenomena.

The part is not the whole

First, the illusion. The public (especially academic) image of the UFO community is an illusion because it is based on only a small fragment of the whole. Since the 1950s, most of the scholars who have paid any serious attention to the UFO movement, and certainly most of the press, have focused their attention on its most readily identifiable segment, the contactees – individuals who claimed to have had friendly, one-to-one chats with benevolent 'Space Brothers'. The messages for humanity given by these friendly visitors included, first, stern warnings about the grave dangers of our remarkable new techno-logical capabilities, given our moral bankruptcy as a species, and second, offers of fraternal assistance towards both our moral and our further technological improvement.[4] The religious dimensions of these encounters were not hard to see. In addition to the ethical concerns of the aliens, the very fact of contact assumed a cosmic significance for the experiencers as well as for those who took their messages seriously. At one point there were more than 150 contactee groups in the US devoted to studying and supporting the extraterrestrial teachings of their leaders.[5] Some of these followers made pilgrimages to historic contact sites or to the several educational and research centres set up by contactees at the behest of their alien benefactors.[6] One of the most successful of these centres was George Van Tassel's Integratron, located east of Los Angeles, for twenty-four years the site of a yearly flying saucer convention where many different contactees and their followers could gather to compare stories, sell books, give lectures and form networks. While the contactee scene added 'colour' to the UFO phenomenon and provided scholars with a wonderful workshop for studies of conversion, the persistence of belief and the genesis of new religious movements, it led many observers to overlook the rich diver-sity of opinion and experience that actually existed in the UFO community.

A typical example of this constriction of focus is the treatment by science historian James Gilbert in his otherwise excellent book, *Redeeming Culture*. Although he admits that not all UFO enthusiasts 'insisted on a religious interpretation of extraterrestrial visitors', he nevertheless characterises the UFO debates of the 1950s and 1960s as one in which ufology manifested religious interests, while UFO debunkers took the side of science. The only allusion he makes to the fact that during those years ufology had a number of well-qualified scientific supporters and offered scientific arguments in its own defence, is to note that there was a 'peril' to science when 'mainline

science appeared to stray into the UFO camp'.[7] The 'UFO camp',
Gilbert's characterisation notwithstanding, was actually composed of
scientists, non-scientists (many of whom tried to apply the scientific
method to their study of UFOs), sighters of UFOs, contactees (most of
whom had metaphysical interests before their reported contact experiences) and debunkers eager to declaim against the entire UFO
phenomenon as a kind of anti-scientific, irrational space-age substitute
for religion.[8] It was a community which, in its more successful organisational forms (such as the Aerial Phenomena Research Organization,
the National Investigations Committee on Aerial Phenomena and the
Mutual UFO Network), largely eschewed the contactees and their
messages because it saw itself as – and desired to *be* seen as – a community of inquirers who were deeply committed to the ideas that roughly
10 per cent of unexplainable UFO sightings represented a genuine
unknown (not misidentifications, hallucinations or hoaxes), and that
UFO phenomena should be studied with all the rigour of which
Western science was capable. The UFO phenomenon, by its very
nature, however, had within it the seeds of confusion, controversy and
conflict; the contactee movement and its unwelcomed equation with
the UFO community in general was just the first harvest.

Mysterium

The UFO community agrees in principle (being well-socialised in
Western ways) that science holds the keys to understanding the
mysteries of the universe. When asked whether they thought we could
hope to learn more about UFOs from science, from religion or from the
political arena, respondents to my short survey were six times more
likely to express high confidence in science than they were to express
high confidence in either politics or religion. Yet the actual *experience*
of a UFO encounter (and more than 60 per cent of the UFO community has had one) brings one face-to-face with a mystery whose
implications beggar the homocentric orientation of Western science.
Having such an experience has a discernible effect on confidence in
the ability of science to explain the phenomenon in general. In my
survey, 41.5 per cent of those who had never had an encounter and did
not know anyone who had, thought it was 'most likely' that we would
learn more about UFOs from science ('most likely' being the highest
value on a 5-point scale). Among those who had never had their own
experience but *did* know someone who had, only 29.5 per cent thought
it 'most likely' that we would learn more through science, and among

those respondents who had had UFO sightings themselves, only 25.5 per cent chose the 'most likely' category.

At the same time that the UFO experience weakens confidence in science as an adequate explanatory framework, it evokes a feeling of having encountered a greatly superior 'other'. Witnesses often describe their experiences as extraordinary, life-changing events – and the language of awe, the language of the dumbfounded, is a religious language. 'It changed my life ever since that day', one man wrote. A quarter of a century earlier he had spent five minutes watching a lighted disk hover thirty yards away from where he stood.[9] The net effect of a UFO encounter is to strengthen confidence in religion as an explanatory framework – but only somewhat. Within the UFO community in general, confidence levels in religion tend to be low. More than 75 per cent of survey respondents said that they doubted that we could expect to learn anything about the UFO phenomenon from religion. Of those who had never had a UFO experience and did not know anyone who had, only 1.7 per cent thought it 'most likely' that we would learn more through religion. Among those who had never had their own experience but *did* know someone who had, 3.1 per cent thought that religion might hold the key to greater understanding, while among those who had had their own sightings, 5.2 per cent gave religion the thumbs-up. These low levels of confidence in religion may reflect the fact that the UFO community in general has a low level of religious participation. More than 60 per cent of survey respondents participate very seldom in their religious communities, while in the US population, that figure is only 38 per cent. In short, while the UFO community has much more faith in science than in religion as an avenue for knowledge about UFOs, an actual firsthand encounter with the phenomenon tends to significantly undermine confidence in science at the same time that it somewhat increases confidence in religion. In other words, the *mysterium* in the *mysterium tremendum* of UFO encounters prevails.

The UFO community: abducted by the abductees

The greatest levels of confidence in religion combined with a diminished regard for science come from a segment of the UFO community that has achieved particular notoriety only in the last fifteen years – the abductees. Abductees report mostly nocturnal encounters with strange entities who paralyse the abductee, float her or him (58 per cent are women) out of parked cars or through bedroom walls and into a waiting UFO and perform medical-like manipulations on them.

Under the circumstances, abductees often liken these manipulations to rape. Men report having sperm samples taken; women report gynaecological and obstetric procedures after which they are shown extremely tiny babies who appear to be half human and half alien. Both sexes report having small implants painfully inserted, often through the nasal cavity and into the brain. They may then be allowed to dress and take a tour of the ship or have a conversation with their captors. Although the aliens at this point seem far less menacing, during the conversation abductees may receive mental images of planet-wide disasters, combined with warnings about our species' current course and exhortations for us to put a stop to the technological processes that are precipitating these catastrophes. Abductees report profound feelings of loss and despair, as well as the sense that they are being tasked by the aliens with some sort of role in the future survival of the human race.

Unlike its rejection of the claims of contactees, the UFO community has by and large accepted the claims of abductees as veridical events. In part this acceptance has been a natural outgrowth of evolution in the 'theory' of UFOs among ufologists. The acceptance of sightings as genuine events led, slowly and reluctantly, to an acceptance of entity sightings (but not entity contact). Once it came to seem reasonable that UFOs might have occupants and that those occupants might on occasion be seen, it gradually began to seem reasonable to believe that there might sometimes be interactions between those occupants and human witnesses. But the encounter claims of the contactees seemed too self-serving and too blatantly religious in nature to be believed. What made abduction stories more believable was the simple fact of terror. The encounters reported by abductees are traumatic – a violation of body and mind. Not only scientific curiosity, but also simple human sympathy for the suffering of experiencers, made abduction research a growing focus of interest in a UFO community that was already disposed to believe that Earth is being visited. Books on alien abduction became a growth industry in the publishing field as abduction researchers reported on some of their more interesting cases and offered new insights into the phenomenon, and as abductees began to tell their own stories. Small companies like Wild Flower Press and Greenleaf Publications were created to serve as publishers (and retailers) for UFO and abduction-related material.[10] In 1993 *Contact Forum*,[11] a newsletter for abductees, began production, followed in 1997 by *The Superstition Chronicles*.[12] Interestingly, although the major UFO research groups have independently published their own UFO reports and monographs for many years, they have published only sparingly on the abduction phenomenon. Besides the books by specialist publishers, most abduction information in print has come in the pages of UFO periodicals, most notably MUFON's monthly journal and the venerable British publication, the *Flying Saucer Review*.[13] On the Internet, discussion lists provide a cyber-venue where experiencers meet to discuss their abductions, offer coping strategies and, in general, find a kind of solace in numbers. Similarly, abduction-related websites disseminate the latest information to the abductee community, including links to literally hundreds of other UFO-related sites.

Given the levels of interest in and activity surrounding the abduction phenomenon, how many people claim to have had the experience? No one knows. Unlike contactees, many abductees prefer not to publicise their encounters. In my abductees' survey, 65 per cent said they had not talked to reporters, written about their experiences or appeared on radio or TV. (Talking to researchers like myself, however, is viewed as cooperation in the endeavour to learn more about what is happening, but abductees often hedge these communications about with restrictions safeguarding their anonymity.[14]) In addition to the reluctance of abductees to come forward publicly, numbering the abductees is complicated by the fact that many people who have signs and symptoms of abductions don't remember their encounters (although subsequent events may trigger recall). On this premise, a 1992 Roper Poll conducted for the Bigelow Foundation determined that as much as 2 per cent of the US population may have been abducted.[15] Within the UFO community itself, 21 per cent feel that they probably or certainly are abductees and another 14 per cent aren't sure. Thus, abductees form a sizeable minority in the UFO community – a minority whose influence on the shape and direction of discourse in UFO circles outweighs its numerical strength because of the unique nature of their experiences and what those experiences may portend for everyone else. It is in the search for answers to that question that the real battle is joined between scientific and religious approaches.

The level of confidence in science professed by abductees is about the same as that professed by people reporting a simple UFO sighting: approximately 26 per cent of both groups feel that science is 'most likely' to provide us with answers to the UFO mystery; and 42 per cent of abductees feel that science holds the key to understanding more about abductions in particular. Yet, ironically, 47 per cent disagree with the proposition that science gives us a good idea of 'the way things are'. In other words, abductees endorse science as a way of gaining more knowledge about their experiences, but mistrust the picture of reality that science paints. To some extent this mistrust has its roots in the UFO debates of the 1950s and 1960s when, in the name of science, UFO debunkers declared that all UFO sightings were hoaxes, hallucinations or misidentifications and impugned the reliability and integrity of UFO witnesses.[16] To some extent the mistrust is a result of a belief that science has ignored an important facet of reality: the non-physical world. Sixty-nine per cent of abductees agree with the statement that science must learn to deal with a non-physical world – which brings us to the realm of religion once again.

Unlike those who merely *see* UFOs, abductees have a higher rate of confidence in religion as a source of understanding the phenomenon. While 5.2 per cent of sighters gave religion a 'most likely' rating, 11.6 per cent of abductees on the short survey did the same. On the longer abductees' survey, 24.2 per cent agreed that religion holds the key to understanding more about abductions in particular. Why such high levels of confidence when compared to the UFO community as a whole? It is not that abductees are more religiously active than their UFO peers. Measures of their religious participation show that 70 per cent of them seldom do participate – a higher rate of non-involvement than for the general UFO community. Yet 54 per cent of abductees identify themselves as religious people. One possible explanation for the discrepancy between abductees' self-identification as religious people and their high rates of non-participation in religious activities lies in their experience of the *mysterium* of a UFO encounter: 50 per cent said that their practice of religion has changed since they became aware of their abduction experiences; while 57 per cent said that their ideas about religion have changed. It's not likely that these changes have occurred because, as good Westerners, abductees look more intently to science than to religion for explanations and the incompatibility of the two systems forces abductees to reconsider their faith: 65.9 per cent of them say that they have had no doubts about their faith because of a conflict between faith and science. In fact, 55.6 per cent do not think that there *is* any real conflict between faith and science. And therein lies the second harvest of the seeds of controversy inherent in the study of UFOs.

The marriage of science and religion in the crucible of UFO experience

The contactee movement of the 1950s and 1960s was at heart the assumption by students of spiritualism and Theosophy of a quasi-scientific, modern mantle – the UFO phenomenon. The apparently hard-edged reality of the UFOs and the superior levels of technological knowledge and, presumably, moral development of the UFO operators, dovetailed nicely with pre-existing worldviews that included infinitely wise spirit guides and Ascended Masters. It was a system of metaphysical beliefs to which the tangible 'miracle' of the technological and moral achievements represented by UFOs could be assimilated. The alien abduction movement of the 1980s and 1990s, however, was all miracle and no beliefs, according to abduction researcher Budd Hopkins. In other words, abduction experiences were incredible events lying well outside the frame of reference of most of those who reported them. Thus, many in the UFO community – particularly abductees – had to struggle to find a belief system that would accommodate the reality of UFO encounters. When they turned to mainstream science or to mainstream Western religion, the answers experiencers received proved to be disappointing. Mainstream religion, when it deals with the idea of alien life or with abductions at all, tends either to reject their reality (following the scientific opinion) or else to equate UFO encounters with demonic activity.[17] A well-known Christian evangelist, for instance, has said that according to the Bible abductees should be stoned for consorting with demons.[18] Mainstream science tends to reject the event-level reality of abductions in favour of psychological or sociological explanations. It does not want to stone abductees; it just wants to medicate or psychoanalyse and then dismiss them. Abductees often feel that neither approach bears true and satisfying witness to their experiences, but, equally, that neither approach in its general form and method can be rejected. So they search for a third alternative, which is a marriage of the two.

Presbyterian theologian Barry H. Downing has observed that the biblical understanding of faith is much like the relation of theory to science; that is, 'believing based on evidence without proof'.[19] If evidence is to be the criterion for believing, then the grounds for believing in UFO phenomena, he suggests, are stronger than the grounds for believing in many of the stories central to the Christian faith.[20] In other words, his solution to the religion–science tension in the UFO community is to rationalise religion along the lines of the scientific worldview in order to make the UFO phenomenon more nearly within the grasp of both disciplines. Other seekers after the third alternative emphasise, instead, the need for a change in the way we do science in the West. Harvard psychiatrist John Mack says that abductions are essentially all about a shift in a scientific paradigm which has engaged in '"the ultimate anthropocentric projection ..." a human self-aggrandizement' that places humanity at the centre of a cosmos that is otherwise lifeless and meaningless.[21] In order to plumb the depths of the abduction phenomenon, he advises, researchers will have to combine 'physics with comparative religion and spirituality'.[22] Note that Mack does not suggest combining physics with religion, but with comparative religion and with spirituality. There is a distinction made by many in the UFO community between religion and spirituality. To the chagrin of some, as abductees try to come to terms with their abductions, they sometimes begin to characterise the events as mystical experiences, 'a kind of ecstasy which ... can reach orgasmic proportions as they feel themselves open through their experiences ... to a divine source or creative center of being in the cosmos'.[23] This way of perceiving their experiences is supported by ideas that are prevalent in the New Age movement, to which many abductees turn for guidance.

While this is certainly not an interpretive move made by all abductees, it is the case with a sufficient number of them to cause concern in the UFO community. The mystical/spiritual approach to abductions, which can easily come to sound like just so much glib or pretentious New Age piety, is seen by some ufologists and abductees as a capitulation of abduction research (and by extension, perhaps the whole of ufology) to the sort of mentality in which the quest for a proper scientific understanding of UFOs is abandoned in favour of paranormal or other non-objective frameworks. As one abductee wrote, he was convinced that his family's abduction experiences were not events on the spiritual level, but real, physical events.[24] And real physical events require scientific investigation. A Mutual UFO Network state official cautioned that the turn to New Age ideas as a framework for understanding abductions threatened to turn that organisation into a cult. 'Personal, even if sincere, talks of otherworldly experiences ... add little or nothing to anyone's scientific understanding of whatever may be going on', he protested.[25]

But other ufologists are not so sure that a traditional scientific understanding should be the goal. Instead of seeing UFO phenomena as the subject of investigation *by* science, they view science as the subject of transformation by the phenomena. Often citing Thomas Kuhn's famous study of scientific change, these alternative science advocates see UFO phenomena as catalysts which will eventually shake science out of its bankrupt materialistic paradigm and into a more spiritually aware one. Abductee Betty Andreasson Luca states that the future of science and technological advancement lies in a spiritual direction – a fact, she says, the aliens are earnestly trying to convey to us.[26]

Of course, talk about challenges to the scientific paradigm is not the sole provenance of abductees. Philosopher Morris Berman also foresees the demise of science as we have known it, combined with a transformation of human consciousness. It is a vision with which many abductees can relate.

> Some collapse is inevitable, but this is not to say that destruction is necessarily the end point of it all … We may be on the verge of … a period of dynamic devolution, in which what is emerging is not merely a new society, but a new species, a new type of human being. In the last analysis, the present species [of egocentric individuals] may prove to be a race of dinosaurs.[27]

Ufologists think they may already know the circumstances under which that 'dynamic devolution' will come about. Budd Hopkins has observed that 'Our collective human ego is about to suffer the same profound dislocation it experienced centuries ago when Copernicus established that we were no longer the center of the universe … We will soon have to adjust to the idea that we may not even be the most advanced intelligence operating within our own atmosphere'.[28]

Sociologist Stjepan G. Mestroviæ echoing abductees' disenchantment with the traditional scientific worldview, asks, 'When will the Holy Inquisition of Science, as Unamuno called it, be over, when the irrational can be discussed openly?'[29] It is a question that ufologists and abductees have been asking of science and religion – and debating among themselves – for the last five decades. If they are no nearer a definitive answer than anyone else in our society, it is not for want of trying to find one.

NOTES

1 W. Strieber, *Communion: A True Story*, New York, Avon, 1987.
2 B. Hopkins, *Intruders: The Incredible Visitations at Copley Woods*, New York, Random House, 1987.
3 D. M. Jacobs, *Secret Life: Firsthand Accounts of UFO Abductions*, New York, Simon & Schuster, 1992.
4 See, for instance, D. Leslie and G. Adamski, *Flying Saucers Have Landed*, New York, The British Book Centre, 1953; G. Adamski, *Inside the Flying Saucers*, New York, Warner Paperbacks, 1955; G. Adamski, *Flying Saucers Farewell*, London, New York, Toronto, Abelard-Schuman, 1961, reprinted as *Behind the Flying Saucer Mystery*, New York, Paperback Library Inc., 1967; O. Angelucci, *The Secret of the Saucers*, Amherst, Wisconsin, Amherst Press, 1955; T. Bethurum, *Aboard a Flying Saucer*, Los Angeles, DeVorss & Co., 1954; T. Green-Beckley, *Messages from the People of the*

Planet Clarion: The True Experiences of Truman Bethurum, New Brunswick, New Jersey, Inner Light Publications, 1995; D. W. Fry, *The Curve of Development*, Lakemont, CSA, 1965; D. W. Fry, *To Men of Earth*, Merlin, Merlin Publishing Co., 1973; G. King, *The Days the Gods Came*, Los Angeles, The Aetherius Society, 1965; D. Kraspedon, *My Contact with Flying Saucers*, trans. J. B. Wood, London, Neville Spearman, 1959; reprinted as *My Contact With UFOs*, London, Sphere, 1977; H. Menger, *From Outer Space to You*, New York, Pyramid Books, 1967; R. E. Norman, *Preview for the Spacefleet Landing on Earth in 2001 A.D.*, El Cajon, California, Unarius Educational Foundation, 1987; Raël (Claude Vorilhon), *Let's Welcome Our Fathers from Space: They Created Humanity in Their Laboratories*, Tokyo, AOM Corporation, 1986; G. H. Williamson, *Other Tongues, Other Flesh*, Amherst, Wisconsin, Amherst Press, 1954; London, Neville Spearman, 1959, Albuquerque, New Mexico, B. E. Books, 1991; G. H. Williamson and A. C. Bailey, *The Saucers Speak! A Documentary Report of Interstellar Communication by Radiotelegraphy*, Los Angeles, New Age, 1954.

5 D. Jacobs, *The UFO Controversy in America*, Bloomington, Indiana, Indiana University Press, 1975, pp. 126–7.

6 See, for instance, B. and H. Reeve, *Flying Saucer Pilgrimage*, Amherst, Amherst Press, 1957.

7 J. Gilbert, *Redeeming Culture: American Religion in an Age of Science*, Chicago, University of Chicago Press, 1997, p. 233.

8 For an excellent perspective on the early decades of scientific interest in UFOs, see E. J. Ruppelt, *The Report on Unidentified Flying Objects*, Garden City, Doubleday, 1956. Ruppelt was the first director for the United States Air Force's Project Blue Book, a UFO data gathering and analysis effort instigated in 1951–2. For the work of serious, qualified scientists and engineers on the UFO problem, see E. U. Condon and D. S. Gillmor (eds), *Scientific Study of Unidentified Flying Objects*, New York, Bantam Books, 1969; P. R. Hill, *Unconventional Flying Objects: A Scientific Analysis*, Charlottesville, Virginia, Hampton Roads, 1995; J. A. Hynek, *The UFO Experience: A Scientific Inquiry*, New York, Ballantine, 1972; J. A. Hynek, *The Hynek UFO Report*, New York, Dell, 1977; J. A. Hynek and J. Vallee, *The Edge of Reality: A Progress Report on Unidentified Flying Objects*, Chicago, Henry Regnery, 1975; J. A. Hynek, P. J. Imbrogno and B. Pratt, *Night Siege: The Hudson Valley UFO Sightings*, New York, Ballantine, 1987; A. Michel, *The Truth about Flying Saucers*, trans. Paul Selver, New York, S. G. Phillips, 1956, New York, Pyramid Books, 1967; C. Sagan and T. Page (eds), *UFOs: A Scientific Debate*, Cornell University Press, Ithaca, New York, 1972, New York, Barnes & Noble, 1996; D. R. Saunders and R. R. Harkins, *UFOs Yes! Where the Condon Committee Went Wrong*, New York, New American Library, 1968; P. A. Sturrock, *The UFO Enigma: A New Review of the Physical Evidence*, New York, Warner, 1999; J. Vallee, *Anatomy of a Phenomenon: The Detailed and Unbiased Report of UFOs*, New York, Ace Books, 1965, reprinted as *UFOs in Space: Anatomy of a Phenomenon*, New York, Ballantine, 1974; J. Vallee *Forbidden Science: Journals 1957–1969*, Berkeley, North Atlantic Books, 1992; J. Vallee *The Invisible College: What a Group of Scientists Has Discovered About UFO Influences on the Human Race*, New York, E. P. Dutton, 1975. Another

excellent book emphasising the scientific aspect of UFO studies, though not written by a scientist, is K. D. Randle, *Scientific Ufology: How the Application of Scientific Methodology Can Analyze, Illuminate and Prove the Reality of UFOs*, New York, Avon Books, 1999.

9 Letter from G. L. Oliver, Jacksonville, Arkansas, reprinted in the *UFO Newsclipping Service*, September 1997, Issue No. 338, p. 12.

10 Greenleaf Publications, P.O. Box 8152, Murfreesboro, Tennessee 37133; Wild Flower Press, P.O. Box 190, Mill Spring, North Carolina 28756. It should be noted that the 'grandaddy' of UFO book distributors (founded in 1980) is Arcturus Books, Inc., 1443 S. E. Port St Lucie Blvd., Port St Lucie, Florida 34952. The fact that the market for UFO books can support three such enterprises indicates the magnitude of the popularity that UFOs and alien abductions has enjoyed since the late 1980s, although the advent of the book superstores has been handicapping the efforts of these small specialty booksellers to serve their unique marketing niche.

11 Contact Forum, c/o Wild Flower Press, P.O. Box 190, Mill Spring, North Carolina, 28756.

12 K. Kizziar, *The Superstition Chronicles: Adventures in the Paranormal*, AZ-Tex Publishing, P.O. Box 5903, Apache Jct., Arizona 85278.

13 *Flying Saucer Review*, FSR Publications Ltd, P.O. Box 162, High Wycombe, Bucks HP13 5DZ, UK.

14 42 per cent of abductees in my long survey said that they had cooperated with UFO and abduction researchers before.

15 This works out to approximately 3.7 million of the inhabitants of the United States. If the signs and symptoms of abduction apply worldwide, the number of potential abductees on this planet works out to a much, much higher figure. For a discussion of the survey and its results, see B. Hopkins, D. M. Jacobs and R. Westrum (eds), *Unusual Personal Experiences: An Analysis of the Data from Three National Surveys*, Las Vegas, Bigelow Holding Corporation, 1992; R. Hall, D. A. Johnson and M. Rodeghier, 'UFO Abduction Survey: A Critique', *Mutual UFO Network Journal*, July 1993, vol. 303, pp. 9–11, 14; B. Hopkins, 'The Roper Poll on Unusual Personal Experiences', in A. Pritchard *et al.* (eds), *Alien Discussions: Proceedings of the Abduction Study Conference Held at MIT, Cambridge*, Cambridge, Massachusetts, North Cambridge Press, 1994, pp. 215–18; and D. C. Donderi, 'Validating the Roper Poll: A Scientific Approach to Abduction Evidence', in Pritchard *et al.* (ed.), *Alien Discussions*, pp. 224–31.

16 For debunkers' comments on UFO witnesses as a population of emotionally disturbed people, see L. Grinspoon and A. D. Persky, 'Psychiatry and UFO Reports', in C. Sagan and T. Page (eds), *UFOs: A Scientific Debate*, pp. 233–46. For attacks on pro-UFO scientists as paranoid and egomaniacal individuals engaging in a 'neurotic rebellion', see M. Gardner, *Fads and Fallacies in the Name of Science*, New York, G. P. Putnam's Sons, 1952, pp. 12–15. For attacks on the credibility and character of modern-day abductees as 'little nobodies [without] much to attract people interpersonally', see M. Orne, 'Alien-Abduction Claims and Standards of Inquiry', *The Skeptical Inquirer*, Spring 1988, pp. 270–8; M. Orne *et al.*, '"Memories" of Anomalous and Traumatic Autobiographical Experiences: Validation and Consolidation of Fantasy through Hypnosis', *Psychological Inquiry*,

1996, vol. 7.2, pp. 168–72; R. Baker, 'Aliens Among Us: Hypnotic Regression Revisited', *The Skeptical Inquirer*, 1988, vol. 12.2, pp. 148–62; and S. Rae, 'John Mack's Abductees', *New York Times Magazine*, 20 March 1994, pp. 30–3.

17 J. L. Thompson, *Aliens & UFOs: Messengers or Deceivers?*, Bountiful, UT, Horizon Publishers, 1993. See also S. Casteel, 'Ron Felber of "Searchers"', *MUFON UFO Journal*, December 1995, vol. 332, pp. 19–20. The latter concerns the Mormon Church's reaction to the publicised abduction narrative of two of their members.

18 S. Porteous, 'Robertson Advocates Stoning for UFO Enthusiasts', *Freedom Writer Press Release*, Great Barrington, Massachusetts, 28 July 1997.

19 Downing's reference is to Hebrews 11:1: 'Now faith is the substance of things hoped for, the evidence of things not seen' (King James Version).

20 B. Downing, 'Faith, Theory and UFOs', in W. H. Andrus Jr. and D. W. Stacy (eds), *MUFON Symposium Proceedings: UFOs: The Hidden Evidence*, Seguin, Texas Mutual UFO Network, 1981, pp. 34–42.

21 J. Mack, *Abduction: Human Encounters with Aliens*, New York, Charles Scribner's Sons, 1994, pp. 420, 422.

22 *Ibid.*, p. 404.

23 *Ibid.*, p. 408.

24 Personal communication, Albert Franklin (pseudonym), 15 June 1999.

25 W. L. Garner J, 'MUFON Versus the New Age', *MUFON UFO Journal*, December, 1993, vol. 308, pp.13–14.

26 R. Fowler, *The Watchers: The Secret Design Behind UFO Abductions*, New York, Bantam Books, 1990, p. 340.

27 M. Berman, *The Re-Enchantment of the World*, Ithaca, New York, Cornell University Press, 1981, pp. 152, 298.

28 B. Hopkins, *Missing Time*, New York, Ballantine Books, 1981, p. 224.

29 S. Meštrović, *The Coming Fin de Siècle: An Application of Durkheim's Sociology to Modernity and Postmodernism*, London, Routledge, 1991, pp. 210–12.

16

JUNG ON UFOS

Robert A. Segal

If one can generalise, nineteenth-century psychologists were prepared to use their findings about the origin and function of religion to evaluate the truth of religion. By contrast, twentieth-century psychologists, like twentieth-century sociologists and anthropologists, tended to limit themselves to the origin and function of religion and to declare the truth of religion an issue beyond their ken, one to be considered instead by philosophers, theologians and natural scientists.

The origin and function of UFOs

C. G. Jung typifies the agnosticism of twentieth-century social science. He continually calls himself a mere psychologist. In the introduction to his famous little book on *Flying Saucers: A Modern Myth of Things Seen in the Skies*, he declares, 'As a psychologist, I am not qualified to contribute anything useful to the question of the physical reality of Ufos. I can concern myself only with their undoubted psychic aspect, and in what follows shall deal almost exclusively with their psychic concomitants.'[1] Jung offers two options and claims not to be qualified to say which is correct. The options are not: either UFOs are real, or they are psychological. Instead, the options are: either UFOs are real *as well as* psychological, or they are illusory and therefore *wholly* psychological. For, even if UFOs are real, those seeing them are still projecting onto them psychological – or, in Jung's preferred term, 'archetypal' – significance. If UFOs are not real, those purportedly seeing them are not merely magnifying but outright creating what they are seeing. As Jung puts these options:

> Thus there arose a situation in which, with the best will in the world, one often did not know and could not discover whether a primary perception was followed by a phantasm or whether, conversely, a primary fantasy originating in the

unconscious invaded the conscious mind with illusions and visions. ...In the first case an objectively real, physical process forms the basis for an accompanying myth; in the second case an archetype creates the corresponding vision.[2]

For Jung, it would be missing the point to say simply that, if UFOs are real, persons experience them because they are real – as if the persons were contributing nothing to the encounter. Similarly, if UFOs are not real, it would be missing the point to say simply that persons have made a mistake – as if the mistake were nothing more than a misimpression. Certainly the number of sightings worldwide argues strongly against the dismissal of the sightings as 'purely fortuitous and of no importance whatsoever':

When an assertion of this kind is corroborated practically everywhere, we are driven to assume that a corresponding motive must be present everywhere, too. Though visionary rumours may be caused or accompanied by all manner of outward circumstances, they are based essentially on an omnipresent emotional foundation, in this case a psychological situation common to all mankind.[3]

Jung the psychologist is fascinated not by whether UFOs are real but by what, real or imagined, they reveal about those who see them. Even if real, UFOs still have a substantially psychological origin and function, and it is these aspects of the experience that matter to Jung.[4]

For Jung, UFOs are either created or used by the unconscious to make contact with ordinary consciousness. Psychologically, UFOs represent an attempt by one domain to establish contact with another – not, however, an attempt by some civilisation in outer space to visit earth but an attempt by one part of the mind to visit another. UFOs come from *psychological* outer space and are on a mission to *psychological* planet earth. Persons who are cut off from their unconscious are the ones requiring the visitation:

The basis for this kind of rumour [of UFOs] is an *emotional tension* having its cause in a situation of collective distress or danger, or in a vital psychic need. This condition undoubtedly exists today, in so far as the whole world is suffering under the strain of Russian policies and their still unpredictable consequences. In the individual, too, such phenomena as abnormal convictions, visions, illusions, etc., only occur when he is suffering from a psychic dissociation, that is, when there is a split between the conscious attitude and the unconscious contents opposed to it. Precisely because the conscious mind does not know about them and is therefore confronted with a situation from which there seems to be no way out, these strange contents cannot be integrated directly but seek to express themselves indirectly, thus giving rise to unexpected and apparently inexplicable opinions, beliefs, illusions, visions, and so forth.[5]

The purpose of the visit by the unconscious is not to conquer ordinary consciousness but to reveal itself to ordinary consciousness. The ultimate purpose is to prod ordinary consciousness into trekking in turn to the unconscious and exploring it. An encounter on earth with a UFO can be shocking and terrifying, but for Jung r Jung is not, as in the saccharine movie *ET*, a merely alien-looking entity which at heart is just like us. A UFO is truly alien to ordinary consciousness, but not thereby antagonistic.

For Jung, it is moderns who are most severed from their unconscious and are therefore most in need of a visit. Moderns have lost religion, which previously had provided the fullest entrée to the unconscious, and have found no replacement for it. Priding themselves on being consummately rational, logical and scientific, they spurn religion as pre-scientific ignorance. Priding themselves on their ability to know and to control themselves, they spurn the notion of an unconscious as an affront. Jung thus observes that in reports of UFO sightings 'it is usually emphasized that the witness is above suspicion because he was never distinguished for his lively imagination or credulousness but, on the contrary, for his cool judgment and critical reason'.[6] The most level-headed fellow is invariably the one most detached from the unconscious, which therefore 'has to resort to particularly drastic measures in order to make its contents perceived'.[7]

Jung himself emphasises that sightings of UFOs have been especially prevalent in the 1950s, yet the modern severance from the unconscious goes back several centuries. What, then, is the cause of recent sightings? Jung offers at least three possibilities:

1   *The Cold War* The division of the world into West and East, and with it the fear of nuclear war, has spurred members of both camps to turn for help to the heavens, 'where the rulers of human fate, the gods, once had their abode'. 'Our earthly world is split into two halves, and nobody knows where a helpful solution is to come

from.'[8] Here UFOs arise to offer divine intercession in human affairs.

2 *Technological advance* The invention of planes means that 'today, as never before, men pay an extraordinary amount of attention to the skies'.[9] More grandly, it is 'at the very time when human fantasy is seriously considering the possibility of space travel and of visiting or even invading other planets'[10] that we can imagine the corollary: our being visited and even invaded by travellers from other planets.

3 *Overpopulation* Here space travel offers the possibility of resettlement for an ever-burgeoning population: 'It could easily be conjectured that the earth is growing too small for us, that humanity would like to escape from its prison ... Congestion creates fear, which looks for help from extra-terrestrial sources since it cannot be found on earth.'[11] Presumably, a visit to us by those from other planets facilitates our exploring other planets in turn.

Yet for all the weight that Jung accords these nonpsychological causes, he insists that the main cause remains psychological. The nonpsychological causes are too conscious and too rational to account for reports of UFOs, 'the apparent impossibility' of which 'suggests to common sense that the most likely explanation lies in a psychic disturbance'.[12] For all Jung's professed professional modesty – again, 'as a psychologist, I am not qualified to contribute anything useful to the question of the physical reality of Ufos' – he is prepared to declare that the belief in our being invaded by aliens 'is a purely mythological conjecture, i.e., a projection'.[13] Jung may not be precluding the reality of UFOs, but he is discounting the likelihood. The scientific implausibility of UFOs 'tempts' one 'to take them as a ninety-nine per cent psychic product and subject them accordingly to the usual psychological interpretation'.[14]

In short, Jung is claiming that UFOs are likely to be wholly the product of the unconscious. Because the unconscious projects itself onto the world, UFOs are experienced as if 'out there', but in fact they hail from the mind. And even if UFOs are real, the reality of them is for Jung almost incidental. They become convenient hooks onto which to foist projections, and it is in the projections, not in UFOs themselves, that the allure lies.

UFOs as myth

The belief in UFOs constitutes a 'living myth', the formation and spread of which we can therefore observe: 'We have here a golden opportunity to see how a legend is formed, and how in a difficult and dark time for humanity a miraculous tale grows up of an attempted intervention by extra-terrestrial "heavenly" powers'.[15] The belief qualifies as a myth because it is "widespread", because it involves an encounter with godlike personalities, because it arouses archetypal emotions of awe and fear, and because it explains physical events in the world. In addition, the belief often involves a story – about the creation of the saucers, about the creators of the saucers, and about the purpose of their visit. Above all, the belief both stems from the mind and serves the mind: 'A myth is essentially a product of the unconscious archetype and is therefore a symbol which requires psychological interpretation.'[16]

Should it turn out that 'an unknown physical phenomenon is the outward cause of the myth, this would detract nothing from the myth, for many myths have meteorological and other phenomena as accompanying causes which by no means explain them'.[17] The myth of Helios' driving his chariot daily across the sky may consciously arise to explain the rising and setting of the sun, but unconsciously it serves to express symbolically the course of the psyche, not of the sun. External events like the cycle of the sun and the cycle of vegetation are appropriated by the unconscious as vehicles for the manifestation of itself to consciousness. Similarly, a real UFO would offer an opportunity for the unconscious to manifest itself. As extraordinary an event as a visit by a real UFO in its own right would be, the unconscious would still be magnifying the experience, turning it into a myth.

Jung's demarcation between reality and myth is in fact blurry. Everybody witnesses the life cycle of vegetation, but only a few witness flying saucers. The death and rebirth of nature may be extraordinary, but the witnessing of a flying saucer is supernatural. Where the attribution of the death and rebirth of crops to the death and rebirth of a god is part of the myth and not part of the experience, those who claim to have seen flying saucers often claim to have encountered the superhuman occupants as well. In that case, what would be left as mythic and thereby left to psychology to explain? Jung himself is undeterred. As sceptical as he is about the reality of UFOs, he is also blasé. The reality would in no way encroach on the psychology.

Independent invention through heredity

One way that Jung argues for the wholly psychological nature of UFOs is by showing how commonly they appear in dreams and paintings, to which he devotes separate chapters of his book. Typically, he downplays the external world as a source of these appearances, repeatedly stressing that his subjects, some of them presumably his patients, have never seen a UFO, are not UFO aficionados, and in some older subjects had likely never even heard of UFOs. Throughout his writings Jung appeals to the frequency of similar strange phenomena worldwide to argue, first, that the phenomenon must be the product of independent invention rather than of diffusion from a single source and, second, that the phenomenon must arise from the mind rather than from the world.

Jung's most famous example of independent invention, that of the 'Solar Phallus Man', is of an institutionalised patient who believed that the sun had a phallus and that the movement of the sun's phallus was the cause of wind. Jung then came upon a comparable fantasy in a book describing the vision of a member of the ancient cult of Mithras. Assuming that the patient could not have known of the book – an assumption that has since been questioned – Jung forever after cited the similarity as a conclusive case of independent invention:

> The patient was a small business employee with no more than a secondary school education. He grew up in Zurich, and by no stretch of imagination can I conceive how he could have got hold of the idea of the solar phallus, of the vision moving to and fro, and of the origin of the wind. I myself, who would have been in a much better position, intellectually, to know about this singular concatenation of ideas, was entirely ignorant of it and only discovered the parallel in a book of Dieterich's which appeared in 1910, four years after my original observation (1906).[18]

Further, Jung uses this example as evidence of the distinctively Jungian version of independent invention: through heredity rather than through experience. Independent invention as experience means that every society creates myths for itself. Independent invention as heredity means that every society inherits myths. Of the Solar Phallus Man, Jung thus writes, 'This observation [of independent invention] was not an isolated case: it was manifestly not [to be sure] a question of inherited ideas, but of an inborn disposition to produce parallel thought-formations, or rather of identical psychic structures common to all men, which I later called the archetypes of the collective unconscious.'[19]

Contrast Jung's position to that of other theorists of myth – for example, Frazer and Freud. For Frazer and Freud, the similarities among myths stem from independent invention through experience. For Frazer, everyone is born with a need to eat, but the explanations of the source of food are not innate. Where moderns invent science to explain the source of food, 'primitives' invent myths. Because all primitives experience hunger, and because all primitives postulate gods to account for the source of food, myths are bound to be similar. But each primitive society invents gods and in turn myths on its own, in response to the similar experiences of its members. Frazer provides the quintessential statement of independent invention through experience: 'the resemblance which may be traced in this respect between the religions of the East and West is no more than what we commonly, though incorrectly, call a fortuitous coincidence, the effect of similar causes acting alike on the similar constitution of the human mind in different countries and under different skies'.[20]

For Freud, everyone is born with an incestuous drive that surfaces between the ages of three and five. Everyone experiences that drive individually. From one's forebears one inherits only the drive itself, not their experiences of it. Because everyone in society also experiences frustration in trying to satisfy that drive, myths are invented as one indirect, disguised, compensatory outlet for the blocked drive. Again, similar experiences are bound to give rise to similar myths. In *The Myth of the Birth of the Hero*, the classic application of Freud's theory, Otto Rank maintains that all hero myths even have a similar plot, yet one still invented by each society on its own.

Contrary to both Frazer and Freud, Jung contends that everyone is born not merely with a need of some kind that the invention of myth fulfils but with myths themselves. More precisely, we are all born with the raw material of myths, but material already elevated to the mythic level.

For Frazer, the myth-makers of each society start with the impersonal forces of the physical world and proceed to hypothesise gods to account for those forces and to invent myths to describe the actions of gods. For Freud, myth-makers start with a child and the child's parents and proceed to transform the child into a hero, the child's parents into royalty or nobility, and the conflicts between children and parents into hero myths.

For Jung, myth-makers start with the archetypes themselves – for example, the archetype of the hero. The archetype does not symbolise something else in turn but is itself the symbolised. In every society myth-makers invent specific stories that express those archetypes, but the myth-makers are inventing only venues for the manifestations of already mythic material. Symbols, not the symbolised, are invented. The figure Odysseus, for example, is either invented or used to serve as a Greek expression of heroism, which is not itself invented, the way it is for Frazer and Freud. The myth of Odysseus and the myth of flying saucers are passed on from generation to generation by acculturation, but the archetypes which they express are passed on by heredity.

For Frazer and Freud, experience, even if it is of innate needs, provides the impetus for the creation of myths. For Freud, for example, the experience of one's parents' reaction to one's incestuous drives spurs the creation of myth. For Jung, by contrast, experience provides only the occasion for the expression of already mythic material. Myths do not transform parents into gods or heroes but only articulate the experience of parents *as* gods or heroes – that is to say, as archetypal figures. Archetypes *shape* experience rather than *derive* from it. For example, the archetype of the Great Mother does not, as Freud would assume, result from the magnification of one's own mother but, on the contrary, expresses itself through her and thereby shapes one's experience of her. Similarly, flying saucers, even if real, express an archetype rather than create it.[21]

The unconscious manifests itself through projections onto the outer world only because consciousness would not recognise it otherwise. The external world is simply a circuitous but indispensable locus for the revelation of something internal. The unconscious manifests itself in the form of technological wizardry to grab the attention of moderns:

> The plurality of Ufos, then, is a projection of a number of psychic images of wholeness which appear in the sky because on the one hand they represent archetypes charged with energy and on the other hand are not recognized as psychic factors. The reason for this is that our present-day consciousness possesses no conceptual categories by means of which it could apprehend the nature of psychic totality. It is still in an archaic state, so to speak ... Moreover, it is so trained that it must think of such images not as forms inherent in the psyche but as existing somewhere in extra-psychic, metaphysical space, or else as historical facts. When, therefore, the archetype receives from the conditions of the time and from the general psychic situation an additional charge of energy, it

cannot, for the reasons I have described, be integrated directly into consciousness, but is forced to manifest itself indirectly in the form of spontaneous projections. The projected image then appears as an ostensibly physical fact independent of the individual psyche and its nature. In other words, the rounded wholeness of the Mandala becomes a space ship controlled by an intelligent being.[22]

because the UFO is unfamiliar, not because it is hostile. True, a UFO foThe hope is that moderns, having been dazzled by the experience, or seeming experience, of divine-like entities 'out there', will somehow come to recognise them as at least in part projections of divine-like entities within. Jung acknowledges the apparent incongruity in his assertion that the unconscious seeks to speak to consciousness yet speaks so symbolically that consciousness typically fails to grasp its message. He maintains nevertheless that 'a dream [or other vehicle] that is not understood can [still] have a compensatory effect, even though as a rule conscious understanding is indispensable'.[23] As critical of moderns as Jung is, he acknowledges that projection onto the external world is the way the unconscious has always reached humans. The difference between our forebears and us is that they had means of projection that we scorn – religion, including myth, most of all. At the same time, the fullest way to ensure that the message is imbibed is through analysis, which is a uniquely modern enterprise.

Synchronicity

There is yet a third option for Jung. Option 1 is that UFOs are real as well as psychological and that the unconscious seizes the occasion of their appearance to manifest itself. Option 2 is that UFOs are wholly psychological, the appearance itself being a concoction of the unconscious. Option 3 is the synchronistic one. As in option 1, UFOs are real, but the unconscious, rather than utilising the appearance of UFOs to manifest itself, creates in the mind something that parallels the appearance of UFOs 'out there':

The symbols of divinity coincide with those of the self: what, on the one side, appears as a psychological experience signifying psychic wholeness, expresses on the other side the idea of God.

This is not to assert a metaphysical identity of the two, but merely the empirical identity of the images.[24]

The psychological and the theological, the inner and the outer, parallel each other. The theological does not cause, or spur, the psychological (option 1), and the psychological does not cause the theological (option 2). The realms are wholly independent of each other. But their concurrence is more than sheer coincidence. It is a 'meaningful' coincidence. It is synchronicity. In Jung's favourite example of synchronicity, a resistant patient was describing a dream about gold jewellery in the shape of a scarab when a scarab beetle appeared at the window of the room. The appearance was so fortuitous as to be more than happenstance, for it helped break through the patient's resistance and thereby enableD the analysis to continue.

Taken synchronistically, an individual might dream about UFOs and the next day see one. The coincidence can also be collective: some individuals might dream about UFOs – or read about them or think about them – and shortly thereafter other individuals see UFOs. Where in option 1 the individual need not have first dreamed about UFOs, in option 3 the individual must have done so. Where in option 1 the individual projects archetypal significance onto the UFO, thereby contributing to the experience, in option 3 the individual projects nothing onto the UFO and instead sees a UFO that has appeared independently of the dreaming about UFOs. In synchronicity, what is going on in the mind occurs simultaneously, or almost simultaneously, with what is going on in the external world. By contrast, in option 1 what is going on in the mind affects what is experienced in the external world. In option 1 the experience of a UFO would be far less significant if there were no projection onto it of an archetype.

Jung is never clear about which option he is pushing. For all his apparent predisposition for the psychological option (option 2), he may be even more enamoured of either option 1 or option 3. In fact, in his chapter on 'Ufos Considered in a Non-Psychological Light', he argues that 'it remains an established fact, supported by numerous observations, that Ufos have not only been seen visually but have also been picked up on the radar screen and have left traces on the photographic plate'.[25] Here he seems to be concluding that UFOs are more likely real than not, so that he is rejecting option 2 in favour of option 1. But later in this same chapter he proposes the synchronistic option (option 3). Compounding the confusion, Jung's summary of option 3 conflates it with option 1:

It seems to me – speaking with all due reserve – that there is a
third possibility: that Ufos are real material phenomena of an
unknown nature, presumably coming from outer space, which
perhaps have long been visible to mankind, but otherwise
have no recognizable connection with the earth or its inhabitants. In recent times, however, and just at the moment when
the eyes of mankind are turned towards the heavens, partly on
account of their fantasies about possible spaceships, and partly
in a figurative sense because their earthly existence feels
threatened, unconscious contents have projected themselves
on these inexplicable heavenly phenomena and given them a
significance they in no way deserve. Since they seem to have
appeared more frequently after the second World War than
before, it may be that they are synchronistic phenomena or
'meaningful coincidences'. The psychic situation of mankind
and the Ufo phenomenon as a physical reality bear no recognizable causal relationship to one another, but they seem to
coincide in a meaningful manner. The meaningful connection
is the product on the one hand of the projection and on the
other of the round and cylindrical forms which embody the
projected meaning and have always symbolized the union of
opposites.[26]

In so far as synchronicity involves the projection of the unconscious
onto physical UFOs, it is indistinguishable from option 1.

The meaning of UFOs

For Jung, UFOs, real or not, are symbolic, and they symbolise parts of
the mind. Thus the dreaming of the appearance of not one UFO but
multiple UFOs symbolises multiple, unintegrated parts of the mind: 'we
could say that the unity of the self as a supraordinate, semi-divine
figure has broken up into a plurality'. 'The plurality of Ufos would
correspond to the projection of a plurality of human individuals,' but
with the symbol of a sphere 'indicating that the content of the projection is not the actual people themselves, but rather their ideal psychic
unity'.[27] What is symbolised is not, as for Freud, other persons, such as
family members, but sides of the personality. That multiple UFOs each
take the form of a sphere means that the goal is wholeness, or the
unification of the parts. The dream thus expresses not the present state
of the subject's psyche but the ideal state, to which the subject should
aspire.

True to form, Jung identifies the saucers as a symbol of an archetype

– here, that of the circle, or the mandala. Roundness means wholeness, and wholeness means the encompassing of opposites, especially the opposition between ordinary consciousness and the unconscious. Therefore the mandala stands for not just one of the many archetypes which compose the unconscious but for the overarching archetype, which encompasses not merely all of the unconscious but all of the psyche. The psychological state of wholeness is the ultimate state of the personality, the state which all humans should seek and which no human fully achieves. In Jung's terms, wholeness is the state of 'individuation', or 'selfhood':

> In so far as the mandala encompasses, protects, and defends the psychic totality against outside influences and seeks to unite the inner opposites, it is at the same time a distinct *individuation symbol* ... I have defined this spontaneous image as a symbolical representation of the *self*, by which I mean not the ego but the totality composed of the conscious *and* the unconscious.[28]

Epitomising perfection, roundness symbolises god: 'There is an old saying that "God is a circle whose centre is everywhere and the circumference nowhere". God in his omniscience, omnipotence, and omnipresence is a totality symbol *par excellence*, something round, complete, and perfect.' Moreover, appearances of god are 'often associated with fire and light'.[29]

As round objects, UFOs are symbols of god. But that way of putting it waxes theological rather than psychological. Psychologised, UFOs are symbols of the god *archetype*, which in turn symbolises the self archetype, which represents the ideal, fully realised psychological state, in which all opposites are, if not quite overcome, at least harmonised:

> On the antique level, therefore, the Ufos could easily be conceived as 'gods'. They are impressive manifestations of totality whose simple, round form portrays the archetype of the self, which as we know from experience plays the chief role in uniting apparently irreconcilable opposites and is therefore best suited to compensate the split-mindedness of our age.[30]

Jung adds 'on the antique level' because UFOs are a distinctly modern rather than ancient manifestation of the god archetype. True, there have been sightings since the Middle Ages and 'perhaps even in antiquity',[31] but most sightings have occurred since the Second World War. UFOs are *scientific* manifestations of the archetype. The unconscious selects symbols palatable to the modern ethos. Since, by definition, moderns reject religion for science – 'Consciously ... rationalistic enlightenment predominates, and this abhors all leanings towards the "occult"'[32] – the unconscious selects symbols of advanced technology to reveal itself to moderns:

> It is characteristic of our time that, in contrast to its previous expressions, the [self] archetype should now take the form of an object, a technological construction, in order to avoid the odiousness of a mythological personification. Anything that looks technological goes down without difficulty with modern man. The possibility of space travel makes the unpopular idea of a metaphysical [i.e., divine] intervention much more acceptable.[33]

Science and religion

Jung himself never sets science against religion. On the contrary, he sees science – better, science used psychologically – as a secular version of religion. UFOs may be the product of advanced technology, but they are manned by superhuman, godlike personalities, and they have come on a mission. Jung even calls the need for wholeness a 'religious instinct', which in modern times has lamentably been overshadowed by Freud's 'sex instinct' and Adler's 'power instinct':

> The only thing we cannot doubt is that the most important of the fundamental instincts, the religious instinct for wholeness, plays the least conspicuous part in contemporary consciousness because, as history shows, it can free itself only with the greatest effort, and with continual backslidings, from contamination with the other two instincts.[34]

Hence, when Jung proceeds to analyse dreams of UFOs, he turns to religion, especially to alchemy, for him key forerunner of his own analytical psychology. He uses his knowledge of pre-scientific, religious beliefs to elucidate UFOs, the meaning of which is as old as humanity: 'These symbolical ideas are archetypal images that are not derived from recent UFO sightings but always existed.'[35] A dream in which a 'plurality' of UFOs appears corresponds alchemically to a plurality of gods or souls – the fallen, split-up state of an initially and properly unified god, or godhead. Alchemists 'were consciously performing an *opus divinum* in that they sought to free the "soul in chains", i.e., to release the demiurge distributed and imprisoned in his own creation and restore him to his original condition of unity'.[36] But Jung then psychologises the alchemical parallel: 'the plurality of Ufos would correspond to the projection of a plurality of human individuals'. By individuals Jung again means 'not the actual people themselves, but rather their ideal psychic totality'.[37]

Conclusion

One would not turn to Jung to decide whether UFOs are real. One would turn to Jung to account for the belief that they are real *when one decides that they are not*. However open Jung himself is to the possibility of the reality of UFOs, and however compatible he deems the reality of them with the psychology of them, I daresay that most UFO buffs would consider enlisting Jung only upon concluding that the phenomenon is psychological *rather than* physical. Whether or not even then one accepts Jung's own psychologising of UFOs, he offers a way of fitting so extraordinary a phenomenon into the ordinary workings of the mind. For him, UFOs are not a novel or miraculous event. They are a modern expression of the eternal nature of the human mind.

NOTES

For his most helpful comments on this essay I want to thank Roderick Main of the University of Essex.

1 C. G. Jung, *Flying Saucers: A Modern Myth of Things Seen in the Skies*, tr. R. F. C. Hull, New York, Signet Books/New American Library, 1969, pp. 17–18. This book was originally published in German in 1958 and, with the addition of a brief 'supplement', was first published in English in 1959. My citations are to the 1969 paperback edition, which also has a foreword by Martin Ebon. The book appears in *Civilization in Transition, The Collected Works of C. G. Jung*, ed. Sir Herbert Read, Michael Fordham, and Gerhard Adler, tr. R. F. C. Hull, vol. 10, 2nd edn, Princeton, Princeton University Press, 1970, pp. 307–433. *The Collected Works* also contain a series of letters, dating from 1954 and 1958, that Jung wrote to several newspapers and to US Air Force Major Donald Kehoe, who headed a government investigation of UFO sightings: see Jung, 'On Flying Saucers', *The Symbolic Life, Collected Works*, vol. 18, Princeton, Princeton University Press, 1976, pp. 626–33. On Jung's agnosticism, see pp. 626–8.
2 *Jung Flying Saucers*, p. 17.
3 *Ibid.*, pp. 23–4.
4 Jung here is like continental atheists *vis-à-vis* English ones. Where English theists like Bertrand Russell seek only to expose religious belief as false,

continental atheists like Ludwig Feuerbach seek also to show what atheism reveals about human nature.

5 Jung, *Flying Saucers*, p. 24.
6 *Ibid.*
7 *Ibid.*, pp. 24–5.
8 *Ibid.*, p. 25. See also Jung, 'On Flying Saucers', pp. 626, 630–1.
9 *Ibid.*, p. 45.
10 *Ibid.*, p. 27.
11 *Ibid.*, p. 28.
12 *Ibid.*, p. 29.
13 *Ibid.*, p. 27.
14 *Ibid.*, p. 33.
15 *Ibid.*, p. 27.
16 *Ibid.*, p. 34.
17 *Ibid.*
18 Jung, *Symbols of Transformation, Collected Works*, vol. 9, pt. 1, 2nd edn, Princeton, Princeton University Press, 1967, pp. 157–8.
19 *Ibid.*, p. 158.
20 James George Frazer, *The Golden Bough*, abridged edn, London, Macmillan, 1922, p. 448.
21 On Jung's distinctive brand of independent invention, see my introduction to *Jung on Mythology*, (Princeton, NJ: Princeton University Press; London, Routledge, 1998), pp. 13–17.
22 Jung, *Flying Saucers*, p. 40.
23 *Ibid.*, p. 90.
24 *Ibid.*, p. 44. On synchronicity, see Jung, 'Synchronicity: An Acausal Connecting Principle' and 'On Synchronicity', in *The Structure and Dynamics of the Psyche, Collected Works, vol.* 8, 2nd edn Princeton, NJ: Princeton University Press, 1969, pp. 417–519 and 520–31. See also Robert Aziz, C. G. *Jung's Psychology of Religion and Synchronicity*, (Albany, State University of New York Press, 1990), and Roderick Main, introduction to *Jung on Synchronicity and the Paranormal* (Princeton, Princeton University Press; London, Routledge, 1997) pp. 17–36.
25 Jung, *Flying Saucers*, p. 114. See also Jung, 'On Flying Saucers' p. 627: 'The possibility of a purely psychological explanation is illusory, for a large number of observations point to a natural phenomenon, or even a physical one – for instance, those explicable by reflections from "temperature inversions" in the atmosphere.'
26 *Ibid.*, pp. 117–18.
27 *Ibid.*, p. 39.
28 *Ibid.*, p. 31.
29 *Ibid.*, p. 32.
30 *Ibid.*
31 *Ibid.*, p. 102.
32 *Ibid.*, pp. 32–3.
33 *Ibid.*, p. 33.
34 *Ibid.*, p. 48.
35 *Ibid.*, p. 88.
36 *Ibid.*, p. 39.
37 *Ibid.*

17

THE PSYCHOLOGY OF UFO PHENOMENA

John A. Saliba

The public interest in UFO phenomena can be documented not only by the many publications on the subject but also by explicit surveys, particularly those conducted by the Gallup Poll, conducted over the last 25 years. Such interest is not based on sheer speculation or science fiction, but rather on the growth of scientific knowledge about the universe.[1] Though the presence of life elsewhere in the cosmos has not been proven, it is certainly not far-fetched to assume that evidence of life in other solar systems will someday be discovered. And again, though the existence of intelligent life on other planets remains a matter of speculation, it cannot be dismissed out of hand. Similarly, although the possibility that intelligent life from elsewhere might be able to locate our planet Earth and travel to it might be somewhat remote, yet it cannot be completely ruled out. The three Gallup polls[2] that raised the question of the existence of UFOs are consistent in their results that up to 50 per cent of the population in the USA think that intelligent life exists elsewhere; though fewer, about 10–12 per cent, claim to have seen a flying saucer.[3] One of the questions asked by the three Gallup Polls was whether people thought that UFOs were real or not. Almost half of the respondents believed that flying saucers were real.

The question whether UFOs are 'something real, or just people's imagination' is quintessentially a psychological one. Given the fact that only about 12 per cent of the population claims to have had some kind of UFO experience and that the vast majority of UFO sightings have been proved to be natural phenomena, psychologists are bound to ask what psychological processes might be operative in the experience of UFOs. Why do some people have encounters[4] of one kind or another with UFOs and aliens, while the majority do not?

Psychological theories of UFO phenomena

One of the difficulties that psychologists face in studying belief in UFO phenomena is the fact that they cannot examine the objects of belief. Consequently, they tend to think that the reports of UFOs and extraterrestrial contacts tell us more about the contactees than about the flying saucers. Psychological studies thus focus on the mental and psychological states of contactees and on the positive and/or negative functions UFO beliefs and experiences have on the individuals who report encounters with extraterrestrial spacecraft and alien beings. Though most psychologists and psychiatrists tend to view those who experience UFO phenomena, particularly those who claim to have been abducted, as not quite normal individuals, there are two major approaches that dominate psychological literature. One interprets UFO experiences as free from any serious pathology and suggests that such experiences may have positive functions. The other sees such experiences as indicative of pathology, and thus encouraging beliefs in UFO contacts or supporting the claims of contactees is more likely than not to have a negative psychological impact on those individuals who need therapy. These functions are discussed in the context of several theories of the nature of UFO phenomena. Three of the most common theories[5] found in psychological literature are: UFOs are basically myths or folk tales; UFOs are the product of one's wishful thinking and can be attributed to fantasy proneness or hallucination; and UFO encounters are essentially errors in human perception that, for a number of reasons, can be explained as misinterpretations of natural phenomena.

UFOs as myth or folklore

One common approach to the study of UFOs interprets them as a kind of modern myth that portrays contemporary scientific knowledge about the universe or as folk tales that have many parallels with traditional folklore. In general, in psychology 'myths have been useful as source material that enriches our understanding of human behaviour, as well as increasing the validity of a psychological theory because it penetrates the mystery and increases our understanding of the myth'.[6] Under the influence of Sigmund Freud, many psychologists and particularly psychoanalysts have been inclined to study myths as a key to understanding the unconscious. The myths of Oedipus and Medusa have been typical, interpreted in the light of Freud's Oedipus complex or Zaslow's attachment theory. In such cases myths are seen as expressions of human neurosis.

The most elaborate effort to give a psychological explanation of myth is that of Carl Jung, who viewed mythological accounts as part of an inherited collective unconscious that manifests as universal symbolism and archetypes which, he held, help us understand human behaviour.[7] Jung begins his study by providing a brief history of UFOs before the modern era, and then treats the topic under three headings, namely: 'UFOs as Rumours', that is, as 'psychic products'; 'UFOs in Dreams'; and 'UFOs in Modern Painting'. According to Jung, stories of UFO sightings and contacts are important because they are indicative of some basic human psychic need or commonly felt danger. They are projections of the unconscious. They are symbolic archetypal images (like the masculine–feminine antithesis and the contrast between the higher world and the ordinary world of human beings) that express order, deliverance, salvation and wholeness in modern technological form. In dreams, UFOs are also related to the unconscious and portray widespread anxiety and insecurity. When depicted in modern painting, UFOs express the dominant trends of the age and stand for universal fear and anxiety and for the need to be healed and made whole. Jung, however, states that psychological explanations are not enough.[8] Psychological projections are not caused, but occasioned, by UFOs. Some writers, aware of the difficulties in giving a purely psychological interpretation of UFO encounters, have attempted to combine a social and psychological approach to explain the origin of the myth of flying saucers.[9]

UFO sightings and encounters, including abductions, have also been examined from a folklorist's perspective. Thomas Bullard, for example, looks at hundreds of accounts and reports of UFOs since 1947 and thinks that they have the ingredients of traditional folklore couched in scientific language.[10] He compares modern UFOs with similar phenomena in the ancient, medieval, Reformation and nineteenth century contexts, and concludes that current UFO sightings and contactees are part of a long folklore tradition. He develops a typology of the modern UFO phenomenon and relates it to parallel folklore accounts. Thus, for example, the experience of a vehicle being stopped in the presence of a UFO is similar to the account of a ghost that stops a horse. The main difference is that UFO stories are compatible with modern science and technology. Accounts of abductions by UFOs, therefore, 'update the content of supernatural kidnap traditions and assume their function'.[11] 'What matters here is not the ultimate nature of the reports but their status as narratives, their form, content, and relationship to comparable accounts of supernatural encounter'.[12] This approach assumes that UFOs, even if they are based on some empirically verifiable experience, are not objective phenomena and hence require some psychological and/or sociological interpretation. The same view, that abduction stories have a long history in folklore, is reiterated by Jacques Vallee, who points out that aliens were sometimes called 'fairies' or 'gods'.[13]

The study of UFO as myth or folklore means that the emphasis is shifted from learning about alien cultures and invaders to understanding what the stories tell us about ourselves and our culture. Thus, one recent anthropological study explored the Roswell UFO incident with the intention of finding out how the myth arose, why some people find it credible and assert that it is a factual account, and what one can learn from it about contemporary Western culture.[14] The psychologists would add that the study of the Roswell myth might also tell us something about the functioning of the human mind and the emotional make-up of those that contribute to the rise and maintenance of the story.

UFOs as wishful thinking or fantasy proneness

Another interpretation of UFO experiences is to see them as a type of wishful thinking. These experiences occur especially among those who suffer from fantasy proneness[15] and hallucinations.[16] Newman and Baumeister[17] maintain that UFO abduction accounts, like masochistic fantasies, 'both spring from a common source – the need to escape the self. Both masochistic and UFO abduction fantasies might derive from the excessive demands and stresses associated with the modern construction of the selfhood.'[18] According to them, stories of UFO abductions are spurious memories,[19] often made up under the influence of hypnosis.[20] Memories of abduction 'express the goal of escaping awareness of the self's most burdensome aspects, such as its needs for esteem and control'.[21] While pointing out that UFO experiences are not deliberate hoaxes and that the people who report them are not mentally ill, Newman and Baumeister state that 'a UFO abduction memory begins when someone with a prior interest in UFOs has an unusual experience, feeling or hallucinatory impression and then elaborates these impressions (often with the aid of a hypnotist) by drawing on his or her own latent masochistic fantasies'.[22] Fantasy proneness, which can be a sign of pathology,[23] seems to be a common explanation of UFO experiences, especially those of abductions. Spanos et al. found that the 'intensity of UFO experiences correlated significantly with the inventories that assessed proneness toward fantasy and unusual sensory experiences'.[24] The recall of UFO encounters is thus a kind of false memory that 'is reconstructive and organized in terms of current expectations and belief'.[25]

Many psychologists have taken issue with this view and seriously question both the inclination to fantasy proneness and the influence of hypnosis.[26] Banaji, for instance, finds Newman and Baumeister's comparison with masochistic behaviour unsupported by empirical evidence.[27] The hypothesis proposed instead focuses on the need of people to explain anomalous experiences and concludes that these experiences are not delusions. Others include belief in UFOs with other false beliefs and think that they may be, in part at least, the result of sleep disorders.[28] But these beliefs, which have positive functions, are not a sign of pathology nor are they caused by fantasy proneness. Still others prefer to explain the abduction experiences with reference to the 'misinformation effect'.[29] In other words, abductees construct their accounts from various sources, including sleep-related hallucinations, nightmares, media attention and hypnotic suggestion. Kenneth Ring modifies this view and argues that abductees are not more fantasy-prone than the average person, but they have 'encounter-prone personalities' and are similar to those people who have mystical or visionary experiences.[30] People who have UFO or deep religious experiences are able to enter into altered states of consciousness and become connected to 'another reality', which Ring labels 'the imaginal realm'. Abductees are people who have the capacity to see creatures from the imaginal realm, a realm that is not open to everyone and nor is it subject to empirical investigation.

Other psychologists have questioned the fantasy proneness theory. For example, both Basterfield and Powers surmise that the inclination to fantasise might explain some individual cases but does not account for the many stories of abduction.[31] Neither, according to other psychologists, can one explain tales of abductions by excessive hypnotic suggestibility.[32]

Jacobs completely rejects all psychological theories, including fantasy proneness and hypnotic suggestibility, since abductees relate detailed experiences of events that are frightening and that they would rather not have.[33] In Jacobs's view, no one would seek to create or fantasise about such an unpleasant experience as being abducted and experimented upon by aliens. Rather, he is inclined to think that the recollections of abductees are based on actual abductions by aliens. This same view has been articulated most forcibly by John Mack, who argues that the abduction experiences his patients related to him cannot be explained psychiatrically.[34] He assumed, in his counselling of individuals who had abduction experiences, that their experiences were real and that his patients needed therapy because they suffered traumatic results from a terrifying contact with aliens. In other words their trauma came, not from inside their psyche, but rather from an outside source. He writes:

> I have no reason for concluding as yet that anything other that what experiencers say happened to them actually did. The experiential data, which, in the absence of more robust physical evidence, is the most important information that we have, suggests that abduction experiencers have been visited by some sort of 'alien' intelligence which has impacted them physically and psychologically.[35]

Most psychologists do not agree with Mack's assumptions and would deny the claims of popular writers such as Bud Hopkins and Whitley Strieber, both of whom have argued that they are simply reporting empirical events.[36] In the final analysis, even though many psychologists and psychiatrists are willing to concede that the majority of UFO encounters are not evidence of pathology, they do believe that the cause of UFO experiences can be accounted for psychologically.

UFOs and human perception

A common theory often advanced to explain UFO phenomena is that they are a result of misperception. In other words, the experiences are totally or partly subjective, that is they are either pure hallucinations and/or the partial fabrications of eyewitnesses who are psychologically seriously impaired. Evans takes the Men-in-Black (MIB) phenomenon as an example of the hallucinatory nature of UFO experiences. Comparing encounters with aliens to visions of the Blessed Virgin and apparitions of ghosts or spirits, he concludes that they are all hallucinations 'projected as a result of the percipient's private fears, and given a specific shape or form based on prevalent notions of the CIA and other such agencies'.[37] This does not mean that the purported eyewitnesses are knowingly making up stories of UFO encounters. It does mean, however, that the fear of contactees can be diagnosed as some form of paranoia and thus indicates that they are suffering from some form of pathology. Bartholomew is much more negative in his views and includes certain UFO experiences as examples of 'mass psychogenic illness and social delusion'.[38]

Another view is that what contactees encounter has a definitive objective element. In other words, contactees actually see an unusual or rare physical phenomenon, but they unconsciously distort it, by allowing their cultural background, upbringing and previous knowledge of UFOs to influence and determine their perceptions.

One of the most elaborate and interesting theories along the above lines is the Tectonic Strain Theory, propounded by Michael Persinger and his associates. Persinger thinks that UFOs are but one type of 'anomalous luminous phenomena' (ALP) and has developed what he claims to be the only scientifically testable hypothesis called the Tectonic Strain Theory (TST), which states that '*most UFO phenomena* (not due to frank misobservation) *are natural events, generated by stresses and strains within the earth's crust*'.[39] In other words, the lights that are seen as UFOs are actually produced by stresses within the earth and hence most UFO reports should precede earthquakes. Research over the last 40 years has produced a wealth of observations which seem to support the theory, even though Persinger maintains that the TST has its limitations and has not been demonstrated conclusively.

Persinger and his associates do not dwell at great length on the mental and/or emotional state of those who claim to have seen UFOs and encountered aliens. Their theory, however, appears to corroborate the view that the interpretation of the luminous objects by UFO contactees is incorrect. The luminous objects are seen as flying saucers and are embellished by the perceptors' minds. Thus UFO sightings, though triggered by some physical phenomenon, are the result of some kind of misperception set into motion by social and/or psychological factors. The TST would explain UFO sightings not as wishful thinking nor as complete fabrication of the human imagination. UFOs are not illusory visions nor necessarily an indication of the sighters' personality problems. They are based on actual observable phenomena, namely, luminous lights. The belief system of the observers, however, transforms these lights into spaceships.

With regard to close encounters of the third and fourth kind (contactees and abductions), Persinger states that they are 'not critical to the verification of the TST'.[40] He compares such experiences with mystical and cosmic experiences and thinks they are normal, even though they may have anxiety, depression and dissociation as their cause. He even ascribes to them positive functions, such as an alteration of the perception of the self and the enhancement of the sense of purpose. Moreover, contactee and abduction reports are correlated with enhanced activities of the brain's temporal lobes. And, once again, Persinger sees this enhancement as normal, even though it heightens both creativity and suggestibility. It does not point to a higher incidence of psychiatric disorders.

Are UFO experiences, especially of abductions, a sign of psychopathology?

The conclusion that many psychologists draw from current studies is that those who have had UFO experiences, including abduction ones, are as a rule average, ordinary individuals who do not exhibit pathology and who therefore cannot be classified as paranoid or schizoid, even though some may suffer from identity disturbance or mild paranoia, or else have some unresolved personality issues.[41] Rodeghier states that abductees are not fantasy-prone; they exhibit no great level of heightened hypnotic suggestibility; they lie within the normal range and portray no signs of psychopathology.[42]

Most of the participants in the Abduction Study Conference held at the Massachusetts Institute of Technology appear to support this statement.[43] The common view advanced at this meeting, with few exceptions, was that abduction experiences are not delusional states and abductees are not more fantasy-prone than the average population. Hence, UFO experiences are not the product of psychopathology, even though some may suffer from post-traumatic stress disorder.[44] Boylan, for example, suggests that a new category, namely 'close extraterrestrial encounter syndrome' should be introduced and lists eighteen clinical features which may be present and require treatment.[45]

Newman and Baumeister propose the view that UFO abduction reports are not deliberate creations nor are they the outcome of mentally ill individuals. They suggest that 'the cognitive processes that lie behind UFO abduction memories conform to what is already known about the genesis of spurious memories ... and involve the need for an escape from self-awareness and loss of identity that have been shown in multiple spheres of motivated behavior and fantasy – particularly sexual masochism, which ... closely resembles in many aspects the UFO abduction experience'.[46]

Some researchers have tried to assess the personality traits of those who report UFO experiences. Parnell and Sprinkle applied the 'Minnesota multiple personality inventory' (MMPI) to over 200 individuals and concluded that there was no sign of psychopathology. However, the 'participants who claimed communication with extraterrestrials had a significantly greater tendency to endorse unusual feelings, thoughts and attitudes; to be suspicious or distrustful; and to be creative, imaginative, or possibly have schizoid tendencies.'[47]

Many psychologists and psychiatrists, however, look on UFO experiences as an outcome of pathology, such as psychotic or dissociation disorders, folies-à-deux, and Munchausen's syndrome. Some claim that such experiences are examples of mass hysteria. Consequently those who experience UFO sightings, contacts and especially abductions may need therapeutic treatment which, presumably, will lead abductees to realise that their encounter with aliens was not an objectively real one.[48]

Therapy for contactees

The question often raised in the study of UFO experiences is whether they are indicative of psychological illness that needs to be addressed in therapy. There seems to be agreement that, no matter what theory of UFO encounters one accepts, many UFO experiences, particularly those that include abduction, create serious personal problems for the abductees, problems, like post-traumatic stress disorder, that require therapeutic intervention. The therapy proposed, however, is usually based on one of the following theoretical assumptions.

The first starts with the view that UFOs do not exist and that consequently encounters with them are indicative of serious pathology. Some (e.g. Klass) have gone so far as to claim that those who claim to have been abducted by aliens are actually attention seekers.[49] Others have appealed to other abnormalities, such as cryptomnesia, hypnagogia, and hallucination. In other words, because encounters with UFOs are signs of pathology that existed prior to the UFO experience, such claims are nothing else but a modern expression of serious mental and/or psychological weakness or illness. Pathology, therefore, precedes the purported UFO encounters and abductees should be treated with some form of therapy.

The second assumes that those who relate UFO experiences, including abductions, are telling the truth. The trauma of real UFO encounters often results in pathological symptoms that require treatment. In this case, UFO encounters precede pathology. They are its cause, rather than its outcome. And since abductees are experiencing a unique type of mental and/or psychological problem, a specially developed 'alien abduction therapy' must be applied.

John Mack is probably the most well-known proponent of this view. In his controversial book which expounds his interpretation of UFO experiences and the treatment of purported alien abductees, *Abduction: Human Encounters with Aliens*, Mack identifies symptoms in abductees that are similar to those of childhood sexual abuse or satanic ritual abuse, and lists several symptoms that are specifically the result of alien abduction.[50] But he insists that problems caused by close UFO encounters are *sui generis* and, in spite of their similarities with other more commonly known psychological illness, must be treated differently. He rejects delusions or hallucinations as explanations. And he finds just as unsatisfactory those theories that explain memories of alien abductions as being a result of temporal lobe epilepsy or as some form of dissociation. He thinks that these memories do not result from either childhood sexual abuse or satanic ritual abuse. He lists the following five dimensions that are not accounted for by any of the above-mentioned theories:

1   The reports from abductees from all over the United States ... are highly consistent with one another among people who had no contact with each other ...
2   There are important physical signs that accompany the abduction experience ...
3   Abduction reports occur in children who are too young to have developed the psychiatric symptoms listed above ...
4   Although not every abductee sees a UFO into which he or she is taken, the phenomenon is consistently associated with sightings of unusual flying objects by abductees themselves and other witnesses ...
5   Psychiatric evaluation and psychological studies of abductees, including several of [Mack's] own cases, have failed to identify consistent psychopathology ...[51]

Mack has adopted his own type of therapy, similar to 'past-life therapy' or 'recovered memory therapy', during which hypnosis is often used. The assumption is that the abduction experience has been so traumatic that it has been suppressed and that the only way to cure the patient is to help him or her recall the original UFO experience. This approach has engendered a lot of discussion, particularly over the assumption that UFO experiences are as real and as easily documented as, for instance, physical abuse, and over the use of hypnosis as a technique for eliciting past memories.

A third approach finds flaws with both the above theories and promotes an 'agnostic' approach.[52] It avoids the issue of whether UFOs actually exist and whether UFO experiences are a result of pathology or its cause. Having the experience is not necessarily an indication of mental illness, but it may result in some pathological symptoms, such as increased anxiety, fear and helplessness. Psychologists and psychiatrists already have the necessary training to deal with these symptoms in counselling and therapy sessions without assuming or denying the empirical reality of UFO experiences.

Conclusion

The main task of psychology to not to determine whether encounters with UFOs and their alien inhabitants are based on the real presence of visitations from other galaxies. Rather, psychologists and psychiatrists are concerned with helping those whose experiences have had a negative effect on their mental, psychological and social functioning. The insistence by some psychologists (e.g. Mack and Jacobs) that UFO encounters, including abductions, are objective has, at times, shifted the debate away from psychological issues to the detriment of those who seek therapy.

Mack and the relatively few psychologists and psychiatrists who agree with him have found it necessary to argue in favour of the objective reality of UFO encounters. Yet their arguments have not persuaded most therapists and mental health-care professionals. The weaknesses of their arguments are self-evident. Thus, the fact that reports of abductees are similar is more easily explained with reference to the abundant cultural material with which people in Western culture have been bombarded for more than half a century. After all, the 'little green men' were part of science fiction long before they started abducting human beings. None of the physical signs that are said to accompany physical abduction can, from a medical standpoint, be definitely attributed to extraterrestrial sources. Moreover, the abduction reports by children are not detached from both parental and cultural influence. Indeed, the conclusion reached by many therapists that those who have had UFO encounters are not pathological, says nothing, in itself, about the objective reality of their experiences.

Recent debates have centred around UFO abductions because these experiences are obviously accompanied by stress, anxiety and other symptoms that require treatment. Yet psychological studies of those abductions are still in their infancy. Jacobson and Bruno state: 'We believe that more serious efforts to assess the frequency of major psychiatric disorders among abduction narrators are badly needed'.[53] Other encounters with UFOs are comparatively mild and, even if most of them can be explained away by hypnotic suggestibility, fantasy proneness and misperception, they are, in most cases, not indicative of any psychopathology.

As to whether UFO encounters are real or imaginary, this question

cannot easily be answered by psychological means, for these encounters are not subject to empirical verification. Consequently therapists
must compare them to other human experiences, which, like near-
death experiences[54] or satanic ritual abuse,[55] do not have an easily
identifiable objective reality. To the therapist they exist only as
psychological phenomena. UFO researchers can only study those
people who report these encounters and the sociocultural conditions in
which they flourish. Whether one needs to solve the problem of
whether UFOs are real may not, after all, be necessary. As Susan
Powers has remarked: 'For the purpose of therapeutic insight and interpretative work, the boundary between historical and narrative truth
may not be crucial'.[56] Since it is recognised by all that some UFO
experiences must be dealt with in therapy, psychologists and psychiatrists can apply various methods to deal with those symptoms that are
not unique to those who report being abducted by aliens. Powers has
suggested[57] that interventions proposed by, for example, Ochberg[58]
and Spiegel,[59] – namely, interventions that make use of the stories
patients tell – could be therapeutically beneficial.

It is also possible that psychological theories by themselves cannot
solve the mystery[60] of UFO encounters, since UFO beliefs might stem,
in part at least, from societal forces rather than from personal experiences.[61] Steven Lynn and his colleagues maintain that alien contact
and abduction accounts reflect the materials widely available in
Western culture. They state that such 'narratives may, in turn, be
prompted and shaped by leading questions and suggestions from therapists who are informed about UFO abduction narratives that serve as
explanations for puzzling or inexplicable symptoms and behaviors'.[62]
UFO encounters may be a product of, or partly influenced by, both
psychological and sociological factors, all of which must be taken into
consideration when dealing with those contactees who have recourse
to counselling or therapeutic intervention.

NOTES

1 See, for example, the following: T. L. Wilson, 'The Search for
Extraterrestrial Intelligence', *Nature*, 2001, vol. 409: no. 6823, pp.
1110–15; S. J. Dick, *Extraterrestrial Life and Our World View at the Turn of
the Millennium*, Washington, DC, Smithsonian Institution, 2000; *Life on
Other Worlds: The 20th Century Extraterrestrial Life Debate*, Cambridge,
Cambridge University Press, 2001; W. Alschuler and H. Zimmerman, *The
Science of UFOs: An Astronomer Examines the Technology of Alien
Spacecraft, How They Travel, and the Aliens Who Pilot Them*, New York, St
Martin's Press, 2001; S. Clark, *Life on Other Worlds and How to Find It*,
New York, Springer/Chichester, Praxis Publishing, 2000; M. D. Lemonick,

Other Worlds: The Search for Life in the Universe, New York, Simon & Schuster, 1999; P. Day, *The Search for Extraterrestrial Life: Essays on Science and Technology*, New York, Oxford University Press, 1998. Speculation about the possibility of life on other planets is paralleled by theories about the theological significance of the possible existence of other worlds inhabited by intelligent beings – see T. F. O'Meara, 'Christian Theology and Extraterrestrial Intelligent Life', *Theological Studies*, 1999, vol. 60, pp. 3–30.

2 Cf. G. Gallup, *The Gallup Poll: Public Opinion 1972–1977*, Wilmington, Scholarly Resources, Inc., 1978, pp. 213–16; *The Gallup Poll: Public Opinion 1987*, Wilmington, Scholarly Resources, Inc., 1988, pp. 52 ff.; *The Gallup Poll: Public Opinion 1996*, Wilmington, Scholarly Resources, Inc., 1997, p. 207.

3 A *Life Magazine* poll found that 54 per cent think that intelligent life exists elsewhere in the universe, while 30 per cent believe that aliens have visited the planet Earth. Further, 43 per cent think that UFOs are real and not imaginary, but only 1 per cent claim to have personally ever seen a UFO. This latter claim is significantly smaller than the one reported by Gallup, but the number of those who believe they have had a UFO encounter is still in the millions.

4 Four types of *close* encounters with UFOs are generally distinguished: (1) encounters of the first kind, when a flying saucer is seen at a distance of a few hundred feet; (2) encounters of the second kind, when the alien spacecraft has apparently left some tangible sign of its presence, such as a scorched area on the ground where it landed; (3) encounters of the third kind, when contact with aliens has been reported; and (4) encounters of the fourth kind, namely those that involve abductions. Other sightings of flying saucers are not usually included, since most of them can be explained as natural phenomena.

5 For other surveys on many different theories on UFOs see J. A. Saliba, 'UFO Contactee Phenomena from a Sociopsychological Perspective: A Review', in J. R. Lewis (ed.), *The Gods Have Landed: New Religions from Other Worlds*, Albany, State University of New York Press, 1995, pp. 207–50; P. D. Netzley, *Alien Abductions: Opposing Viewpoints*, San Diego, CA, Greenhaven Press, 1996; and L. Picknett, *The Mammoth Book of UFOs*, New York, Carroll & Graf, 2001, pp. 448 ff.

6 R. W. Zaslow, 'Myth', in Raymond J. Corsini (ed.), *Encyclopedia of Psychology*, Vol. 2, 2nd edn, New York, John Wiley & Sons, 1994, p. 448.

7 C. G. Jung, *Flying Saucers: A Modern Myth of Things Flying in the Skies*, Princeton, Princeton University Press, 1978.

8 *Ibid.*, pp. 146ff.

9 See, e.g., R. E. Bartholomew, *Ufolore: A Social Psychological Study of a Modern Myth in the Making*, Stone Mountain, GA, Arcturus Book Service, 1989.

10 T. E. Bullard, *UFO Abductions: The Measure of a Mystery*, Bloomington, IN, Fund for UFO Research, 1987.

11 T. E. Bullard, 'UFO Abductions Reports: The Supernatural Kidnap Narrative Returns in Technological Guise', *Journal of American Folklore*, 1989, vol. 1, p. 147.

12 *Ibid.*, p. 148.

13 J. Vallee, *Passport to Magonia: On UFOs, Folklore, and Parallel Worlds*, Chicago, Contemporary Books, 1993.

14 B. Saler, C. A. Ziegler and C. B. Moore, *UFO Crash at Roswell: The Genesis of a Modern Myth*, Washington and London, Smithsonian Institution Press, 1997.

15 R. E. Bartholomew, K. Baskerfield and G. S. Howard, 'UFO Abductees and Contactees: Psychopathology or Fantasy Proneness?', *Professional Psychology: Research and Practice*, 1991, vol. 22, pp. 215–22.

16 Cf., e.g., R. K. Siegel, *Fire in the Brain: Clinical Tests of Hallucination*, New York, Plume/Penguin Books, 1993; P. Klass, *UFO Abductions: A Dangerous Game*, Buffalo, Prometheus Books, 1989.

17 L. S. Newman and R. F. Baumeister, 'Not Just Another False Memory: Further Thoughts on the UFO Phenomenon Abduction', *Psychological Inquiry*, 1996, vol. 7, pp. 185–97.

18 L. S. Newman, 'Intergalactic Hostages: People Who Report Abduction by UFOs', *Journal of Social and Clinical Psychology*, 1997, vol. 16, pp. 151–77.

19 Cf. N. P. Spanos, *Multiple Identities and False Memories: A Sociocognitive Perspective*, Washington, American Psychological Association, 1996

20 The part played by hypnosis in accounts of UFO abductions is hotly debated. See, e.g., T. E. Bullard, 'Hypnosis and UFO Abductions: A Troubled Relationship', *Journal of UFO Studies*, 1989, vol. 1, pp. 3–40. See also the many comments on the topic made at the Abduction Study Conference: T. E. Bullard, 'Hypnosis and UFO Abductions: A Troubled Relationship', *Journal of UFO Studies*, 1989, vol. 1, pp. 3–40.

21 L. S. Newman and R. F. Baumeister, 'Toward an Explanation of the UFO Abduction Phenomena: Hypnotic Elaboration, Extraterrestrial Sado masochism, and Spurious Memories', *Psychological Inquiry*, 1996, vol. 7, p. 100.

22 L. S. Newman and R. F. Baumeister, 'Abducted by Aliens: Spurious Memories of Interplanetary Masochism', in S. J. Lynn et al. (eds), *Truth in Memory*, New York, Guilford Press, 1998, p. 285.

23 J. W. Rhue and S. J. Lynn, 'Fantasy Proneness and Psychopathology', *Journal of Personality and Social Psychology*, 1987, vol. 53, pp. 327–36; S. J. Lynn and J. W. Rhue, 'The Fantasy Prone Person: Hypnosis, Imagination, and Creativity', *Journal of Personality and Social Psychology*, 1986, vol. 51, 404–8; S. J. Lynn and J. W. Rhue, 'Fantasy Proneness: Hypnosis, Developmental Antecedents, and Psychopathology', *American Psychologists*, 1988, vol. 43, 35–44.

24 N. P. Spanos et al., 'Close Encounters: An Examination of UFO Experiences', *Journal of Abnormal Psychology*, 1993, vol. 102, p. 624. Some scholars consider UFO abductions as a type of anomalous experience, such as out-of-the body, Psi-related and mystical experiences. See, for example: S. Appelle, S. J. Lynn, and L. Newman, 'Alien Abduction Experiences', in E. Cardena et al. (eds), *Varieties of Anomalous Experience: Examining the Scientific Evidence*, Washington, American Psychological Association, 2000, pp. 253–82; and also K. Basterfield, 'Abductions: The Paranormal Connection', in Pritchard et al. (eds), *Alien Discussions*, pp. 149–50. For a thorough examination of the abduction phenomenon and theories proposed to explain it see S. Appelle, 'The Abduction Experience: A Critical Evaluation of Theory and Evidence', *Journal of UFO Studies*, 1996,

vol. 6, pp. 29–79.

25 N. P. Spanos, C. A. Burgess and M. F. Burgess, 'Past-Life Identities, UFO Abductions, and Satanic Ritual Abuse: The Social Construction of Memories', *International Journal of Clinical and Experimental Hypnosis*, 1994, vol. 42, p. 433. See also N. P. Spanos, *Multiple Identities and False Memories*.

26 See Newman and Baumeister, 'Toward an Explanation of the UFO Abduction Phenomena', pp. 99–126 and the responses to it in *Psychological Inquiry*, 7.2 (1996). See also the authors' reply: Newman and Baumeister, 'Not Just Another False Memory', pp. 185–97.

27 M. R. Banaji *et al.*, 'The Ordinary Nature of Alien Abduction Memories', *Psychological Inquiry*, 1996, vol. 7, pp. 132–5.

28 See R. M. Baker, 'Studying the Psychology of UFO Experiences', *Skeptical Inquirer*, 1994, vol. 18, p. 241.

29 E.g. S. E. Clark and E. F. Loftus, 'The Construction of Space Alien Abduction Memories', *Psychological Inquiry*, 1996, vol. 7, pp. 140–3.

30 K. Ring, 'Toward an Imaginal Interpretation of "UFO Abductions"', *Revision: Journal of Consciousness and Change*, 1989, vol. 11.4, pp. 17–24.

31 K. Basterfield, 'The Fantasy-Prone Personality Hypothesis', in Pritchard *et al.* (eds), *Alien Discussions*, Cambridge, North Cambridge Press, 1994 p. 371; S. M. Powers, 'Fantasy Proneness, Amnesia, and the UFO Abduction Phenomenon', *Dissociation: Progress in the Dissociative Disorders*, 1991, vol. 4, pp. 46ff.

32 E.g. M. Rodeghier, 'Psychological Characteristics of Abductees', in Pritchard *et al.* (eds), *Alien Discussions*, p. 298.

33 D. M. Jacobs, *Secret Lives: Firsthand Accounts of UFO Abductions*, New York, Simon & Schuster, 1992.

34 J. E. Mack, 'Why the Abduction Phenomenon Cannot Be Explained Psychiatrically', in Pritchard *et al.* (eds), *Alien Discussions*, pp. 372–4.

35 J. E. Mack, *Abduction: Human Encounter with Aliens*, New York, Macmillan, 1994, p. 434.

36 B. Hopkins, *Intruders: The Incredible Visitations at Copley Woods*, New York, Random House, 1987; W. Strieber, *Communion: A True Story*, New York, Avon, 1987.

37 H. Evans, *Visions, Apparitions, and Alien Visitors*, Wellingborough, Aquarian Press, 1984, p. 145.

38 R. E. Bartholomew, *Little Green Men, Meowing Nuns and Head-Hunting Panics: A Study of Mass Psychogenic Illness and Social Delusion*, Jefferson, McFarland & Co., 2001.

39 M. A. Persinger, 'The Tectonic Strain Theory as an Explanation of for UFO Experiences: A Non-technical Review of the Research, 1970–1990', *Journal of UFO Studies*, 1990, vol. 2, p. 105.

40 *Ibid.*, p. 128.

41 A. Clamar, 'Is It Time for Psychology to Take UFOs Seriously?', *Psychotherapy in Private Practice*, 1988, vol. 6, pp. 146–7; R. L. Sprinkle, 'Psychotherapeutic Services for Persons Who Claim UFO Experiences', *Psychotherapy in Private Practice*, 1988, vol. 6, pp. 151–7.

42 M. Rodeghier, 'Psychological Characteristics of Abductees', pp. 298–300.

43 Pritchard *et al.* (eds), *Alien Discussions*.

44 E.g. J. Stone-Carmen, 'A Descriptive Study of People Reporting Abduction by UFOs', in Pritchard *et al.* (eds), *Alien Discussions*, p. 313.

45 R. J. Boylan, 'Treatment of Close Extraterrestrial Encounter Experience', in Pritchard *et al.* (eds), *Alien Discussions*, pp. 330–1.
46 L. S. Newman and R. F. Baumeister, 'Abducted by Aliens: Spurious Memories of Interplanetary Masochism', in S. J. Lynn *et al.* (eds), *Truth in Memory*, New York, Guilford Press, 1998, p. 285.
47 J. Parnell and R. L. Sprinkle, 'Personality Characteristics of Persons Who Claim UFO Experiences', *Journal of UFO Studies*, 1990, vol. 2, p. 45; cf. J. Parnell, 'Measured Personality Characteristics of Persons Who Claim UFO Experiences', *Psychotherapy in Private Practice*, 1998, vol. 6, pp. 159–65.
48 E.g. R. E. Bartholomew, *Little Green Men, Meowing Nuns and Head-Hunting Panics*. Hall strongly disagrees with this view and states that attributing abduction experiences to mass hysteria is as anomalous as attributing them to actual encounters with aliens. R. L. Hall, 'Are Abductions Reports "Mass Hysteria"?', in Pritchard *et al.* (eds), *Alien Discussions*, pp. 377–81.
49 Klass, *UFO Abductions*.
50 Mack, *Abduction*, pp. 15–16.
51 Mack, 'Why the Abduction Phenomenon Cannot Be Explained Psychiatrically', pp. 372–3.
52 See D. Gotlib, 'Psychotherapy for the UFO Abduction Experience', *Journal of UFO Studies*, 1995–96, vol. 6, pp. 1–23.
53 E. Jacobson and J. Bruno, 'Narrative Variants and Major Psychiatric Illnesses in Close Encounters and Abduction Narrators', in Pritchard *et al.* (eds), *Alien Discussions*, p. 308.
54 See S. W. Twemlow, 'Misidentified Flying Objects? An Integrated Psychodynamic Perspective on Near-Death Experiences and UFO Abductions', *Journal of Near-Death Studies*, 1994, vol. 12, pp. 205–23. For responses to his paper see the *Journal of Near-Death Studies*, Summer 1994, vol. 12.
55 For example, consult the following: R. F. Baumeister and K. L Sommer, 'Patterns in the Bizarre: Common Themes in Satanic Ritual, Sexual Masochism, UFO Abductions, Factitious Illness, and Extreme Love', *Journal of Social and Clinical Psychology*, 1997, vol. 16, pp. 213–23; *et al*, Spanos, 'Past-Life Identities, UFO Abductions, and Satanic Ritual Abuse', pp. 433–46.
56 S. M. Powers, 'Specific Correlates of PTSD and Dissociation', in Pritchard *et al.* (eds), *Alien Discussions*, p. 320.
57 S. M. Powers, 'Alien Abduction Narratives', in S. Krippner and S. M. Powers (eds), *Broken Images, Broken Selves: Dissociative Narration in Clinical Practice*, Brunner/Mazel Publications, 1997, pp. 199–215.
58 F. Ochberg, 'Posttraumatic Therapy', *Psychotherapy* 28.1, 1991, pp. 5–15.
59 D. Spiegel, 'Dissociating Damage', *American Journal of Clinical Hypnosis*, 1986, vol. 29, pp. 123–31.
60 The 'mystery' dimension in UFO phenomena is recognised by several authors. See, for example, Bullard, *UFO Abductions*.
61 A. L. Patry and L. G. Pelletier, 'Extraterrestrial Beliefs and Experiences: An Application of the Theory of Reasoned Actions', *Journal of Social Psychology*, 2001, vol. 141, pp. 199–217; J. A. Saliba, 'UFO Contactee Phenomena from a Sociopsychological Perspective: A Review', in Lewis (ed.), *The Gods Have Landed*, pp. 212–25.

62 S. J. Lynn *et al.*, 'Rendering the Implausible Plausible: Narrative Construction, Suggestion, and Memory', in J. de Rivera *et al.* (eds), *Believed-in Imaginings: The Narrative Construction of Reality*, Washington, American Psychological Association, 1998, p. 130.

BIBLIOGRAPHY

G. Adamski, *Inside the Flying Saucers*, New York, Warner Paperbacks, 1955.

__ *Flying Saucers Farewell*, London, New York, Toronto, Abelard-Schuman, 1961; reprinted as *Behind the Flying Saucer Mystery*, New York, Paperback Library, 1967.

W. Alschuler and H. Zimmerman, *The Science of UFOs: An Astronomer Examines the Technology of Alien Spacecraft, How They Travel, and the Aliens Who Pilot Them*, New York, St Martin's Press, 2001.

Ancient Astronaut Society, *Kontakt mit dem Universum. Mysteries of the World*, CD ROM, Taufkirchen, Magellan Entertainment, n.d.

P. Andersson, 'Ancient Astronauts', in J. R. Lewis (ed.), *UFOs and Popular Culture*, 2000, pp. 20–5.

W. H. Andrus Jr and D. W. Stacy (eds), *MUFON Symposium Proceedings: UFOs: The Hidden Evidence*, Seguin, Mutual UFO Network, 1981.

O. Angelucci, *The Secret of the Saucers*, Amherst, Amherst Press, 1955.

Anon., 'They Still Believe in Cargo Cults', *Pacific Islands Monthly*, vol. 20, May, 1950, p. 85.

Anon., 'Getting to the People,' *Family* (Anglican Church of Papua New Guinea), 1976, vol. 3, pp. 8–9.

J. Appel, *The Homecoming (A Message From Antares)*, El Cajon, Unarius, 2000.

S. Appelle, 'The Abduction Experience: A Critical Evaluation of Theory and Evidence', *Journal of UFO Studies*, 1996, vol. 6, pp. 29–79.

S. Appelle, S. J. Lynn and L. Newman, 'Alien Abduction Experiences', in E. Cardena *et al.* (eds), *Varieties of Anomalous Experience: Examining the Scientific Evidence*, Washington, American Psychological Association, 2000, pp. 253–82.

J. Argüelles, *The Mayan Factor*, Santa Fe, Bear & Co. 1987.

Arieson, *The Visitations: A Saga of Gods and Men*, El Cajon, Unarius Educational Foundation, 1987.

T. Äyräväinen, 'Suomessa 1994 toimivat ufotutkimusta harjoittavat yhdistykset', in L. Ahonen and T. Äyräväinen (eds), *Uforaportti*, vol. 2, Salo, Suomen Ufotutkijat ry, 1995, pp. 167–76.

R. Aziz, *C. G. Jung's Psychology of Religion and Synchronicity*, Albany, State University of New York Press, 1990.

R. Baker, 'Aliens Among Us: Hypnotic Regression Revisited', *The Skeptical Inquirer*, 1988, vol. 12.2, pp. 148–62.

——, 'Studying the Psychology of UFO Experiences', *The Skeptical Inquirer*, 1994, vol. 18, pp. 239–42.

R. W. Balch, 'Waiting for the Ships: Disillusionment and the Revitalization of Faith in Bo and Peep's UFO Cult', in J. R. Lewis (ed.), *The Gods Have Landed: New Religions from Other Worlds*, Albany, State University of New York Press, 1995, pp. 137–66.

M. R. Banaji *et al.*, 'The Ordinary Nature of Alien Abduction Memories', *Psychological Inquiry*, 1996, vol. 7, pp. 132–5.

D. Barclay, *Aliens: The Final Answer?*, London, Blandford, 1995.

T. A. Barker (ed.), *The Mahatma Letters to A. P. Sinnett*, 3rd edn, C. Humphries and E. Benjamin (eds), Adyar, Theosophical Publishing House, 1962.

J. Barranger and P. Tice, *Mysteries Explored: The Search for Human Origins, UFOs and Religious Beginnings*, London, Book Tree, 2000.

R. E. Bartholomew, *Ufolore: A Social Psychological Study of a Modern Myth in the Making*, Stone Mountain, Arcturus Book Service, 1989.

——, *Little Green Men, Meowing Nuns and Head-Hunting Panics: A Study of Mass Psychogenic Illness and Social Delusion*, Jefferson, McFarland & Co, 2001.

R. E. Bartholomew, K. Basterfield and G. S. Howard, 'UFO Abductees and Contactees: Psychopathology or Fantasy Proneness?' *Professional Psychology: Research and Practice*, 1991, vol. 22, pp. 215–22.

R. E. Bartholomew and G. S. Howard, *UFOs and Alien Contact: Two Centuries of Mystery*, New York, Prometheus Books, 1998.

K. Basterfield, 'The Fantasy-Prone Personality Hypothesis', in A. Pritchard *et al.* (eds), *Alien Discussions: Proceedings of the Abduction Study Conference Held at MIT*, Cambridge, North Cambridge Press, 1994, pp. 370–2.

——, 'Abductions: The Paranormal Connection', in A. Pritchard *et al.* (eds), *Alien Discussions*, 1994, pp. 149–50.

R. F. Baumeister and K. L Sommer, 'Patterns in the Bizarre: Common Themes in Satanic Ritual, Sexual Masochism, UFO Abductions, Factitious Illness, and Extreme Love', *Journal of Social and Clinical Psychology*, 1997, vol. 16, pp. 213–23.

T. G. Beckley, *Psychic and UFO Revelations in the Last Days*, New Brunswick, Inner Light Publications, 1980.

——, *The New World Order: Channelled Prophecies from Space*, New York, Global Communications, 1982.

C. Bedell, *Concordex of the Urantia Book*, 3rd edn, California, Clyde Bedell Estate, 1991.

M. F. Bednaroski, *New Religions and the Theological Imagination in America*, Bloomington, Indiana University Press, 1989.

M. Behr, *From the Mesas*, Santa Cruz, University of California, Santa Cruz, 1975.

E. Benz, *Außerirdische Welten. Von Kopernikus zu den Ufos*, Freiburg, Aurum, 2000.

J. Berger, *After the End: Representations of Post-Apocalypse*, Minneapolis, University of Minnesota Press, 1999.

P. L. Berger and T. Luckmann, *The Social Construction of Reality*, Garden City, Anchor Books, 1966.

C. Berlitz and W. L. Moore, *The Roswell Incident*, New York, Grosset & Dunlap, 1980.

M. Berman, *The Re-Enchantment of the World*, Ithaca, Cornell University Press, 1981.

A. Besant, *H. P. Blavatsky and the Masters of Wisdom*, London, Theosophical Publishing House, 1907.

T. Bethurum, *Aboard a Flying Saucer*, Los Angeles, DeVorss & Co., Publishers, 1954.

——, *Facing Reality*, Prestcott, self-published, 1959.

H. P. Blavatsky, *The Key to Theosophy*, London, Theosophical Publishing House, 1889.

——, *The Secret Doctrine: The Synthesis of Science, Religion and Philosophy*, 2 vols, London, Theosophical Publishing House, 1888; Adyar, Theosophical Publishing House, 1978.

J. F. Blumrich, *Kun taivaat aukenivat*, Helsinki, Kirjayhtymä, 1974.

——, *The Spaceships of Ezekiel*, London, Corgi, 1974.

R. J. Boylan, 'Treatment of Close Extraterrestrial Encounter Experience', in A. Pritchard *et al.* (eds), *Alien Discussions*, 1994, pp. 327–34.

W. Braden, *The Age of Aquarius: Technology and the Cultural Revolution*, Chicago, Eyre & Spottiswoode, 1971.

D. Bradley, *An Introduction to the Urantia Revelation*, California, White Egret Publications, 1998.

P. Brierley, *UK Christian Handbook*, London, Christian Research, 1999.

C. B. D. Bryan, *Close Encounters of the Fourth Kind*, New York, Penguin, 1995.

T. E. Bullard, *UFO Abductions: The Measure of a Mystery*, Bloomington, Fund for UFO Research, 1987.

——, 'Hypnosis and UFO Abductions: A Troubled Relationship', *Journal of UFO Studies*, 1989, vol. 1, pp. 3–40.

——, 'UFO Abductions Reports: The Supernatural Kidnap Narrative Returns in Technological Guise', *Journal of American Folklore*, 1989, vol. 1, pp. 147–70.

——, 'UFOs: Lost in the Myths', in D. M. Jacobs (ed.), *UFOs and Abductions: Challenging the Borders of Knowledge*, Lawrence, University Press of Kansas, 2000.

——, 'UFOs – Folklore of the Space Age', in J. R. Lewis (ed.), *UFOs and Popular Culture*, 2000, ix–xxv.

K. Burridge, *New Heaven New Earth*, Oxford, Blackwell, 1969.

S. Casteel, 'Ron Felber of "Searchers"', *MUFON UFO Journal*, December 1995, vol. 332, pp. 19–20.

R. Castren, 'Interplanetistien uudet haasteet', *Ultra*, 5, 1996, pp. 26–7.

H. L. Cayce, *Earth Changes Update*, Virginia Beach, A.R.E. Press, 1980.

D. H. Childress, *Vimana Aircraft of Ancient India and Atlantis*, Illinois, Adventures Unlimited Press, 1991.

——, *Extraterrestrial Archaeology*, Illinois, Adventures Unlimited, 2000.

G. D. Chryssides, *Exploring New Religions*, London, Cassell, 1999.

——, 'Is God a Space Alien? The Cosmology of the Raëlian Church', *Culture and Cosmos*, 2000, vol. 4.1, pp. 36–53.

J. Churchward, *The Lost Continent of Mu*, New York, Paper Library, 1968.

——, *The Cosmic Forces of Mu*, New York, Paper Library, 1968.

——, *The Second Book of the Cosmic Forces of Mu*, New York, Paper Library, 1968.

A. Clamar, 'Is It Time for Psychology to Take UFOs Seriously?' *Psychotherapy in Private Practice*, 1988, vol. 6, pp. 141–9.

Clark (channeled by Katar), 'Back to School – Earth Revisited', *Open Channel: A Journal with Spirit*, November–December, 1988, vol. 2.

J. Clark, *The UFO Encyclopedia*, 3 vols, Detroit, Omnigraphics, 1996.

——, *The UFO: Book. Encyclopedia of the Extraterrestrial*, Detroit, Visible Ink, 1997.

——, *Extraordinary Encounters: An Encyclopedia of Extraterrestrials and Otherworldly Beings*, Santa Barbara, ABC-Clio, 2001.

S. Clark, *Life on Other Worlds and How to Find It*, New York, Springer/Chichester, Praxis Publishing, 2000.

S. E. Clark and Elizabeth F. Loftus, 'The Construction of Space Alien Abduction Memories', *Psychological Inquiry*, 1996, vol. 7, pp. 140–3.

N. Cohn, 'Réflexions sur le millénarisme,' *Archives de Sociologie Européennes*, 1958, vol. 5, pp. 103–7.

E. U. Condon and D. S. Gillmor (eds), *Scientific Study of Unidentified Flying Objects*, New York, Bantam Books, 1969.

F. J. Connell, 'Flying Saucers and Theology,' in A. Michel, *The Truth about Flying Saucers*, New York, Criterion, 1974, pp. 255–8.

R. J. Corsini (ed.), *Encyclopedia of Psychology*, 2nd edn, New York, John Wiley & Sons, 1994.

P. Cousineau, *UFOs: A Manual for the Millennium*, New York: HarperCollins, 1995.

B. Creme, *The Reappearance of the Christ and the Masters of Wisdom*, London, Tara Press, 1980.

B. Crowley and A. Pollock, *Return to Mars*, Melbourne, Matchbooks, 1989.

D. Curran, *In Advance of the Landing: Folk Concepts of Outer Space*, New York, Abbeville Press, 1985.

E. von Däniken, *Erinnerungen an die Zukunft. Ungelöste Rätsel der Vergangenheit*, Düsseldorf, Ercon-Verlag, 1968

__*Chariots of the Gods? Unsolved Mysteries of the Past*, trans. M. Heron, London, Souvenir Press, 1969.

349

——, *Return of the Gods: Gods from Outer Space*, trans. M. Heron, London, Souvenir Press, 1970.

——, *Takaisin tähtiin*, Helsinki, Kirjayhtymä, 1970.

——, *The Gold of the Gods?*, trans. M. Heron, London, Souvenir Press, 1973.

——, *Tulimmeko tähtien takaa?*, Helsinki, Kirjayhtymä, 1973.

——, *Erscheinungen: Phänomene, die die Welt erregen*, Düsseldorf und Wien, Econ-Verlag, 1974.

——, *Kaikuja avaruudesta*, Helsinki, Kirjayhtymä, 1974.

——, *Ilmestysten arvoitus*, Helsinki, Kirjayhtymä, 1975.

——, *Miracles of the Gods: A Hard Look at the Supernatural*, trans. M. Heron, London, Souvenir Press, 1975.

——, *Olen oikeassa*, Helsinki, Kirjayhtymä, 1978.

——, *Todisteita tuntemattomasta*, Helsinki, Uusi kirjakerho, 1978.

——, *Menneisyyden profeetta*, Helsinki, Kirjayhtymä, 1979.

——, *Auf den Spuren der Allmächtigen*, München, Econ-Verlag Gmbh, 1993.

——, *Vieraita avaruudesta*, Helsinki, Kirjayhtymä, 1993.

J. David (ed.), *The Flying Saucer Reader*, New York, The New American Library, 1967.

P. Day, *The Search for Extraterrestrial Life: Essays on Science and Technology*, New York, Oxford University Press, 1998.

J. Dean, *Aliens in America: Conspiracy Cultures from Outerspace to Cyberspace*, Ithaca, Cornell University Press, 1998.

B. Denzler, *The Lure of the Edge: Scientific Passions, Religious Beliefs, and the Pursuit of UFOs*, Berkeley, University of California Press, 2001.

V. Descombes, *Modern French Philosophy*, trans. by L. Scott-Fox and J. M. Harding, Cambridge, Cambridge University Press, 1980.

H. Desroches, *Dieux d'hommes: Dictionnaires des messianismes et millénarismes*, Paris, Press Universitaire de France, 1969.

S. J. Dick, *Extraterrestrial Life and Our World View at the Turn of the Millennium*, Washington, Smithsonian Institution, 2000.

——, *Life on Other Worlds: The 20th Century Extraterrestrial Life Debate*, Cambridge, Cambridge University Press, 2001.

D. C. Donderi, 'Validating the Roper Poll: A Scientific Approach to Abduction Evidence,' in A. Pritchard *et al.* (eds), 1994, *Alien Discussions*, pp. 224–31.

U. Dopatka, *Die große Erich von Däniken Enzyklopädie: Das einzigartige Nachschlagewerk zur Prä-Astronautik*, Düsseldorf, Econ, 1997.

B. Downing, *The Bible and Flying Saucers*, New York, Lippincott, 1968.

——, 'Faith, Theory and UFOs', in W. H. Andrus Jr and D. W. Stacy (eds), *MUFON Symposium Proceedings: UFOs: The Hidden Evidence*, Seguin, Mutual UFO Network, 1981, pp. 34–42.

L. Du Pertuis, 'How People Recognize Charisma: The Case of *Darshan* in Radhasoami and Divine Light Mission', *Sociological Analysis*, 1986, vol. 47, pp. 111–24.

S. Duquette, *Sunburst [Farm] Family Cookbook*, Santa Barbara, Sunburst Industries, 1978.

S. N. Eisenstadt, *Max Weber: On Charisma and Institution Building*, Chicago, University of Chicago Press, 1968.

R. S. Ellwood, *Islands of the Dawn: The Story of Alternative Spirituality in New Zealand*, Honolulu, University of Hawaii Press, 1993.

——, 'UFO Religious Movements', in T. Miller (ed.), *America's Alternative Religions*, Albany, State University of New York Press, 1995, pp. 393–9.

R. S. Ellwood and H. B. Partin, *Religious and Spiritual Groups in Modern America*, 2nd edn, Englewood Cliffs, Prentice Hall, 1988.

B. El Masri, 'The Mass Landings. The Ground Crew Project'. Available online: http://www.portal.ca/groundcrew/crew/messhum.htm (November 2002).

V. Essene and S. Nidle, *You Are Becoming a Galactic Human*, Santa Clara, S.E.E. Publishing Company, 1994.

H. W. Eu, *Divine Principle*, 2nd edn, New York, Holy Spirit Association for the Unification of World Christianity, 1973.

H. Evans, *Visions, Apparitions, and Alien Visitors*, Wellingborough, Aquarian Press, 1984.

L. Festinger, H. W. Riechen and S. Schachter, *When Prophecy Fails: A Social and Psychological Study of a Modern Group that Predicted the Destruction of the World*, Minneapolis, University of Minnesota Press, 1956.

Findhorn Foundation, *Catalogue*, Autumn/Winter, 1986–1987.

L. A. Fischinger, *Götter der Sterne: Bibel, Mythen und kosmische Besucher*, Weilersbach, Reichel, 1997.

L. A. Fischinger and R. M. Horn, *UFO-Sekten*, Rastatt, Verlagsunion Pabel Moewig KG, 1999.

R. P. Flaherty, 'Flying Saucers and the New Angelology: Mythic Projection of the Cold War and the Convergence of Opposites', unpublished doctoral dissertation, University of California, Los Angeles, 1990.

C. Fort, *The Book of the Damned*, London, John Brown, 1995.

R. Fowler, *The Watchers: The Secret Design Behind UFO Abductions*, New York, Bantam Books, 1990.

C. Fox, 'The Search for Extraterrestrial Life', *Life*, March, 2000, vol. 23.3, pp. 45–51, 54, 56.

J. G. Frazer, *The Golden Bough*, abridged edn, London, Macmillan, 1922.

B. French, 'The Theosophical Masters', unpublished doctoral dissertation, University of Sydney, 2000.

D. W. Fry, *The Curve of Development*, Lakemont, CSA Printers and Publishers, 1965.

——, *To Men of Earth*, Merlin, Merlin Publishing, 1973.

G. Gallup, *The Gallup Poll: Public Opinion 1972–1977*, Wilmington, Scholarly Resources, 1978.

——, *The Gallup Poll: Public Opinion 1987*, Wilmington, Scholarly Resources, 1988.

——, *The Gallup Poll: Public Opinion* 1996, Wilmington, Scholarly Resources, 1997.

M. Gardner, *Fads and Fallacies in the Name of Science*, New York, G. P. Putnam's Sons, 1952.

——, *On the Wild Side*, New York, Prometheus Books, 1992.

——, *Urantia*, New York, Prometheus Books, 1995.

W. L. Garner Jr, 'MUFON Versus the New Age', *MUFON UFO Journal*, December, 1993, vol. 308, pp. 13–14.

W. Gauch-Keller and T. Gauch-Keller, *Aufruf an die Erdbewohner: Erklärungen zur Umwandlung des Planeten Erde und seiner Menschheit in der 'Endzeit'*, Ostermundingen, self-published, 1992.

——, *Appeal to the Earth People*, Ostermundingen, self-published, 1996.

A. G. Geertz, *The Invention of Prophecy: Continuity and Meaning in Hopi Indian Religion*, Aarhus, Brunebakke Publications, 1992.

H. H. Gerth and C. Wright Mills (eds), *From Max Weber: Essays on Sociology*, trans. H. H. Gerth and C. Wright Mills, New York, Oxford University Press, 1946.

B. Giay, 'Hai: Motif Pengharapan "Jaman Bagaia"', *Deiyai* (Jayapura, Ind.), Sept.–Oct. 1994, vol. 4, pp. 5–8.

J. Gilbert, *Redeeming Culture: American Religion in an Age of Science*, Chicago, University of Chicago Press, 1997.

N. Goodrich-Clark, *Black Sun: Aryan Cults, Esoteric Nazism and the Politics of Identity*, New York, New York University Press, 2002.

D. Gotlib, 'Psychotherapy for the UFO Abduction Experience', *Journal of UFO Studies*, 1995–96, vol. 6, pp. 1–23.

G. Grandt, M. Grandt and K.-M. Bender, *Fiat Lux: Uriellas Orden*, München, Evangelischer Presseverband für Bayern, 1992.

T. Green-Beckley (ed.), *Space Gods Speak: An Ashtar Command Book*, New Brunswick, Inner Light Publications, 1992.

——, *Messages from the People of the Planet Clarion: The True Experiences of Truman Bethurum*, New Brunswick, Inner Light Publications, 1995.

L. Grinspoon and A. D. Persky, 'Psychiatry and UFO Reports,' in C. Sagan and T. Page (eds), *UFOs: A Scientific Debate*, New York, Random House, 1972, pp. 233–46.

A. Grünschloß, 'We Enter into my Father's Spacecraft,' *Marburg Journal of Religion*, 1998, vol. 3.2:www.uni-marburg.de/fbo3/religionswissenschaft/journal/mjr/ofogruen.html.

——, *Wenn die Götter landen … Religiöse Dimensionen des UFO-Glaubens*, EZW-Texte 153, Berlin, EZW, 2000.

——, 'Cargo Cults', in J. R. Lewis (ed.), *UFOs and Popular Culture*, Santa Barbara, ABC-Clio, 2000,

——, 'Scientology', in J. R. Lewis (ed.), *UFOs and Popular Culture*, 2000.

J. R. Hall, *Apocalypse Observed: Religious Movements and Violence in North America, Europe, and Japan*, London, Routledge, 2000.

R. L. Hall, 'Are Abductions Reports "Mass Hysteria"?', in A. Pritchard et al. (eds), *Alien Discussions*, 1994, pp. 377–81.

R. Hall,. D. A. Johnson and M. Rodeghier, 'UFO Abduction Survey: A Critique', *Mutual UFO Network Journal*, July 1993, vol. 303, pp. 9–11, 14.

W. J. Hanegraaff, *New Age Religion and Western Culture*, Leiden, E. J. Brill, 1996.

——, 'New Age Religion', in L. Woodhead et al. (eds), *Religions in the Modern World: Traditions and Transformations*, London, Routledge, 2002, pp. 249–63.

A. Hansen, 'God in Space,' *Union Recorder* (Sydney), 4 Sept. 1995, vol. 75, pp. 8–9.

F. Harris and B. Belitsos (eds), *The Center Within*, California, Origin Press, 1998.

M. Harris, *Cows, Pigs, Wars and Witches*, London, Hutchinson, 1974.

S. I. Hayakawa, *Language in Thought and Action*, London, George Allen & Unwin, 1974.

H. Häyry, H. Karttunen and M. Virtanen (eds), *Paholaisen asianajaja Opaskirja Skeptikolle*, Helsinki, Ursa, 1989.

Heaven's Gate, 'Time to Die for God? – The Imminent "Holy War" – Which Side are You On?' Available online: http://www.heavensgatetoo.com (24 September 1996).

P. Heelas, 'The Spiritual Revolution: From "Religion" to "Spirituality"', in L. Woodhead et al. (eds), *Religions in the Modern World: Traditions and Transformations*, London, Routledge, 2002, pp. 357–77.

Heimholungswerk Jesu Christi, *Auch die Brüder aus teilmateriellen Bereichen des Universums dienen im Erlösungswerk des Sohnes Gottes*, Heimholungswerk Jesu Christi, 1981.

C. Helland, 'Ashtar Command', in J. R. Lewis (ed.), *UFOs and Popular Culture*, 2000, pp. 37–40.

R. Hempelmann, V. Dehn and M. Nüchtern (eds), *Panorama der neuen Religiosität*, Gütersloher Verlagshaus, 2001.

J. Hick, *Death and Eternal Life*, Glasgow, Collins, 1979.

P. R. Hill, *Unconventional Flying Objects: A Scientific Analysis*, Charlottesville, Hampton Roads Publishing Co., 1995.

S. Holroyd, *Briefing for Landing on Planet Earth*, London, Corgi, 1979.

B. Hopkins, 'The Roper Poll on Unusual Personal Experiences', in A. Pritchard et al. (eds), *Alien Discussions*, 1994, pp. 215–18.

——, *Missing Time*, New York, Ballantine Books, 1981.

——, *Intruders: The Incredible Visitation at Copley Woods*, New York, Random House, 1987.

——, *Witnessed*, New York, Pocket Books, 1996.

——, 'The UFO Phenomenon and the Suicide Cult – An Ideological Study', *MUFON 1997 International UFO Symposium Proceedings*, Seguin, MUFON, 1997.

B. Hopkins, D. M. Jacobs and R. Westrum (eds), *Unusual Personal Experiences: An Analysis of the Data from Three National Surveys*, Las Vegas, Bigelow Holding Corporation, 1992.

W. Houghton, 'Cargo Cults in the Managalas', unpublished typescript, Goroka Teachers College, Goroka, 1977.

L. Ron Hubbard, *Have You Lived this Life Before?*, Copenhagen, New Era Publications, 1983.

P. Hughe, 'The Secret Invasion: Does It Add Up?', *Omni*, Winter 1995, vol. 17.9.

F. Hundseder, *Wotans Jünger: Neuheidnische Gruppen zwischen New Age und Rechtsradikalismus*, München, Heyne, 1998.

S. Hutin, *Les Civilisations inconnues*, Paris, Arthème Fayard, 1961.

J. A. Hynek, *The UFO Experience: A Scientific Inquiry*, New York, Ballantine Books, 1972.

——, *Ufot toden rajamailla*, Porvoo & Helsinki, WSOY, 1973.

——, *The Hynek UFO Report*, New York, Dell Publishing, 1977.

J. A. Hynek, P. J. Imbrogno and B. Pratt, *Night Siege: The Hudson Valley UFO Sightings*, New York, Ballantine Books, 1987.

J. A. Hynek and J. Vallee, *The Edge of Reality: A Progress Report on Unidentified Flying Objects*, Chicago, Henry Regnery Company, 1975.

D. Icke, *The Biggest Secret*, Ryde Isle of Wight, Bridge of Love, 1999.

A. Ivanoff, *Punainen planeetta*, Suomussalmi, Myllylahti, 1999.

D. Jacobs, *The UFO Controversy in America*, Bloomington, Indiana University Press, 1975.

——, *Secret Life: Firsthand Accounts of UFO Abductions*, New York, Simon & Schuster, 1992.

——, *The Threat*, New York, Simon & Schuster, 1998; London, Pocket Books, 1999.

—— (ed.), *UFOs and Abductions: Challenging the Borders of Knowledge*, Lawrence, University Press of Kansas, 2000.

E. Jacobson and J. Bruno, 'Narrative Variants and Major Psychiatric Illnesses in Close Encounters and Abduction Narrators', in A. Pritchard *et al.* (eds), *Alien Discussions*, 1994, pp. 304–9.

A. Jamerson and B. Collins, *Connections: Solving Our Alien Abduction Mystery*, Newberg, Wildflower Press, 1996.

A. James, 'The Aetherius Society Meeting', *UFO News UK*, 2001, vol. 1.8. Available online: http://www.ufoinfo.com/infonewsuk/v01/0108.shtml.

M. K. Jessup, *The Case for the UFO*, Garland, Varo Manufacturing Co., 1959.

John-Roger, *The Way Out Book*, Los Angeles, Baraka Press, 1980.

D. Jordan and K. Mitchell, *Abducted! The Story of the Intruders Continues ...*, New York, Carroll & Graff, 1994.

C. G. Jung, *Memories, Dreams and Reflections*, New York, Vintage, 1965.

——, *Flying Saucers: A Modern Myth of Things Seen in the Skies*, trans. by R. F. C. Hull, New York, Signet Books/New American Library, 1969 [1959]; Princeton, Princeton University Press, 1978.

——, *Symbols of Transformation*, in *Collected Works of C. G. Jung*, Sir Herbert Read *et al.* (eds), trans. by R. F. C. Hull, vol. 9, pt. 1, 2nd edn, Princeton, Princeton University Press, 1967 [1956].

——, *The Structure and Dynamics of the Psyche*, in *Collected Works of C. G. Jung*, vol. 8., 2nd edn, Princeton, Princeton University Press, 1969 [1960].

——, *Civilization in Transition*, in *Collected Works of C. G. Jung*, vol. 10, 2nd edn, Princeton, Princeton University Press, 1970 [1964].

——, *The Symbolic Life*, in *Collected Works of C. G. Jung*, vol. 18, Princeton, Princeton University Press, 1976.

M. Junnonaho, *Uudet uskonnot – vastakulttuuria ja vaihtoehtoja*, Helsinki, SKS, 1996.

F. C. Kamma, *Koreri: Messianic Movements in the Biak-Numfor Culture Area*, M. J. van de Vatherst-Smit (trans.), W. E. Haver Droeze-Hulswit (ed.), Verhandelingen van het Koninklijk Instituut voor Taal-, Land- en Volkenkunde, Translation Series, vol. 15, The Hague, Martinus Nijhoff, 1972.

M. Kananen, 'Suomalaisen ufotutkimuksen historiaa', *Ultra*, 1997, vol. 9, pp. 12–15.

——, 'Kun jumalat olivat humanoideja – Ancient astronaut – teorioiden tulo Suomeen', unpublished dissertation, University of Tampere, 1998.

——, 'Oululaisen ufotutkimuksen kolme vuosikymmentä', *Ultra*, 1998, vol. 10, pp. 36–7.

——, 'Tampere aktiivinen rajatietokaupunki', *Ultra*, 1998, vol. 3, pp. 4–12.

K. Kärkkäinen, 'Ufokaappaukset ja ufokontaktiliike', Turku, Seminar Presentation, Department of Cultural Sciences, University of Turku, 1996.

H. Karttunen, 'Ufot, ifot ja pienet vihreät henkilöt', in H. Häyry, H. Karttunen and M. Virtanen (eds), *Paholaisen asianajaja. Opaskirja Skeptikolle*, Helsinki, Ursa, 1989, pp. 170–87.

M. Katz, W. P. Marsh and G. G. Thompson (eds), *Earth's Answer: Explorations of Planetary Culture at the Lindisfarne Conferences*, New York, Harper & Row, 1977.

D. Keyhoe, *The Flying Saucer Conspiracy*, New York, Holt & Co., 1955.

E. von Khuon, *Tulivatko jumalat tähdistä*, Helsinki, Kirjayhtymä, 1979.

G. King, *The Practices of Aetherius*, London, Aetherius Society, 1957.

——, *Become a Builder of the New Age!*, London, Aetherius Society, 1963.

——, *The Days the Gods Came*, Los Angeles, Aetherius Society, 1965.

——, *The Five Temples of God*, Los Angeles, Aetherius Society, 1975.

G. R. King (G. Ballard), *Unveiled Mysteries*, Chicago, Saint-Germain Press, 1935.

R. G. Kirkpatrick and D. Tumminia, 'A Case Study of a Southern Californian Flying Saucer Cult', paper presented to the annual meeting of the American Sociological Association, San Francisco, California, August, 1989.

——, 'California Space Goddess: The Mystagogue in a Flying Saucer Group', in W. H. Swatos (ed.), *Twentieth-Century World Religious Movements in Neo-Weberian Perspective*, Lewiston, Edwin Mellen Press, 1992, pp. 299–311.

P. Klass, UFO Abductions: A Dangerous Game, Buffalo, Prometheus Books, 1989.

T. Koivula, Ufojen kosminen viesti, Helsinki, WSOY, 1988.

——, Viestejä, Helsinki, Unio Mystica (karisto), 1996.

P. Kolosimo, Toisilta tähdiltä, Helsinki, Kirjayhtymä, 1971.

——, Ajaton maa, Hämeenlinna, Karisto, 1982.

D. Kossy, Kooks, Portland, Feral House, 1994.

D. Kraspedon, My Contact With Flying Saucers, trans. J. B. Wood, London, Neville Spearman Ltd., 1959; reprinted as My Contact With UFOs, London, Sphere Books Limited, 1977.

I. Kuhn, Nests above the Abyss, London, China Inland Mission, 1949.

K. Kuitunen, 'Skepsiksen ensimmäinen vuosi', Ultra, 6, 1988, p. 16.

J. Kuningas, 'Suomalaisia rajatiedon yhdistyksiä', Ultra, 5–6, 2002, pp.33–7.

T. Kuningas, UFOja Suomen taivaalla, Helsinki, Kirjayhtymä, 1970.

——, Ufojen jäljillä, Helsinki, Kirjayhtymä, 1971.

——, Operaatio UFO, Helsinki, Jaanes Oy, 1972.

——, Muukalaisia ja humanoideja – suomalaisia havaintoja, Helsinki, Kirjayhtymä, 1973.

——, 'Moninkertainen pioneeri: Margit Lilius-Mustapa 1899–1991', Ultra, 1991, vol. 11, p. 4.

——, 'Ufotutkimusta ja -hutkimusta Suomessa', Ultra, 1994, vol. 2, pp. 8–11.

——, 'Ufotutkimuksen vaiheita Suomessa, 30-luvulta 70-luvulle', in M. Kananen, T. Kuningas and H. Virtanen (eds), Uforaportti, vol. 6, Tampere, Suomen Ufotutkijat, 1999, pp. 98–109.

——, 'Rauni-Leena Luukanen-Kilde, "Kuolemakaan ei vaienna minua"', Ultra, 1999, vol. 11, pp. 4–9.

——, 'Ufotutkimuksen vaiheita Suomessa, 1977–1989', in H. Virtanen, M. Kananen and M. Repo (eds), Uforaportti 1999, Tampere, Suomen Ufotutkijat ry, 2000, pp. 130–5.

——, '25 vuotta soihdunkantajana – Kustannus Oy Rajatieto syntyi vuonna 1976', Ultra, 2001, vol. 13, pp. 24–6.

——, 'Ufotutkimuksen vaiheita Suomessa vuosina 1990–1994', in S. Laitala and M. Repo (ed.), Uforaportti 8: Milleniumin ufot, Tampere, Suomen Ufotutkijat ry, 2001, pp. 123–31.

T. Kuningas, T. E. Laitinen and M. Löfman, 100 ufoa Suomessa, Helsinki, Kirjayhtymä, 1994.

T. Kuningas and V. Viro, 'Voitto Viro – totuudenetsijä ja elämän moniottelija' Ultra, 1993, vol. 7–8, pp. 4–9.

K. A. Kuure et al., Katoavatko ufot? Ufoilmiön kriittistä tarkastelua, Helsinki, Ursa, 1993.

J. Kyröläinen and P. Teerikorpi, Ufojen arvoitus, Helsinki, Ursa, 1980.

R. Lacey, 'A Glimpse of the Enga Worldview,' Catalyst, 1973, vol. 3.2, pp. 37–47.

P. Lagrange, 'Kenneth Arnold', in J. R. Lewis (ed.), UFOs and Popular Culture, 2000, p. 34.

W.-J. Langbein, *Astronautengötter: Versuch einer Chronik unserer phantastischen Vergangenheit*, Berlin, Ullstein Buchverlage GmbH, 1995.

——, *Götter aus dem Kosmos*, Rastatt, Verlagsunion Pabel Moewig KG, 1998.

——, *Am Anfang war die Apokalypse: Warum wir Kinder der Astronauten wurden*, Lübeck, Bohmeier Verlag, 2000.

D. Lavery, A. Hague and M. Cartwright (eds), *Deny All Knowledge: Reading the X-Files*, London, Faber & Faber, 1996.

M. LaVigne, *The Alien Abduction Survival Guide*, Newberg, Wild Flower Press, 1995.

P. Lawrence, *Road Belong Cargo*, Manchester, Manchester University Press, 1964.

S. Lax, *Pudasjärven ufot*, Helsinki, Kirjayhtymä, 1972.

C. Leadbeater, *A Textbook of Theosophy*, Adyar, Theosophical Publishing House, 1912.

M. Leay, *The Land that Time Forgot*, London, Hunt & Blackett, 1937.

M. F. Lee, *The Nation of Islam: An American Millennial Movement*, Syracuse, Syracuse University Press, 1996.

E. Lehtonen, *Ajan Kello: Tihenevien ajan merkkien tarkastelua kuvin ja sanoin*, Helsinki, Kuva ja Sana, 1957.

M. D. Lemonick, *Other Worlds: The Search for Life in the Universe*, New York, Simon & Schuster, 1999.

D. Leslie and G. Adamski, *Flying Saucers Have Landed*, New York, The British Book Centre, 1953; 2nd edn, London, Futura Publications, 1977.

——, 'Visitor from Venus', in J. David (ed.), *The Flying Saucer Reader*, New York: The New American Library, 1967, pp. 51–72.

D. A. Lewis and R. Schrekhise, *UFO, End-Time Delusion*, Green Forest: New Leaf Press, 1997.

J. R. Lewis, 'Approaches to the Study of the New Age', in J. R. Lewis and J. G. Melton (eds), *Perspectives on the New Age*, Albany, State University of New York Press, 1992, pp. 1–12.

——, *Encyclopedia of Afterlife Beliefs and Phenomena*, Detroit, Gale Research, 1994.

—— (ed.), *The Gods Have Landed: New Religions from Other Worlds*, New York, State University of New York Press, 1995.

——, *Seeking the Light: Uncovering the Truth About the Movement for Spiritual Inner Awareness*, Los Angeles, Mandeville Press, 1997.

—— (ed.), *UFOs A to Z*, Chicago, Contemporary Books, 1998.

—— (ed.), *UFOs and Popular Culture: An Encyclopaedia of Contemporary Myth*, Santa Barbara, ABC-Clio, 2000.

——, *The Encyclopedic Sourcebook of UFO Religions*, Amherst, Prometheus Books, 2002.

J. R. Lewis and J. G. Melton (eds), *Perspectives on the New Age*, Albany, State University of New York Press, 1992.

——, *Sex, Slander and Salvation: Investigating the Family/Children of God*, Stanford, Center for Academic Publication, 1994.

—— (eds), *Church Universal and Triumphant in Scholarly Perspective*, Stanford, Center for Academic Publication, 1994.

J. R. Lewis and E. D. Oliver, *Angels A to Z*, Detroit, Gale Research, 1995.

S. Lewis, 'The Lord of the Second Advent: the Deliverer is Here!', in F. Bowie (ed.), *The Coming Deliverer*, Cardiff, University of Wales Press, 1997.

M. Lieb, *Children of Ezekiel: Aliens, UFOs, the Crisis of Race, and the Advent of End Time*, Durham, NC, Duke University Press, 1998.

M. Lindemann, 'Highlights of Swiss UFO Conference', excerpt from *CNI News*, 5 July 1991, vol. 8.1. Available online: http://deoxy.org/t_swiss.html (November 2002).

H. Lindsey, *Planet Earth – 2000 AD: Will Mankind Survive?* Palos Verdes: Western Front, 1994.

R.-L. Luukanen-Kilde, *Kuolemaa ei ole*, Helsinki, Weilin & Göös, 1982.

R.-L. Luukanen-Kilde, *Tähtien lähettiläs*, Porvoo, Helsinki & Juva, WSOY, 1992.

——, *Kuka hän on?* Porvoo, Helsinki & Juva, WSOY, 1993.

S. J. Lynn *et al.*, 'Rendering the Implausible Plausible: Narrative Construction, Suggestion, and Memory', in J. de Rivera *et al.* (eds), *Believed-In Imaginings: The Narrative Construction of Reality*, Washington, American Psychological Association, 1998, pp. 123–43.

S. J. Lynn and J. W. Rhue, 'The Fantasy Prone Person: Hypnosis, Imagination, and Creativity', *Journal of Personality and Social Psychology*, 1986, vol. 51, 404–8.

——, 'Fantasy Proneness: Hypnosis, Developmental Antecedents, and Psychopathology', *American Psychologists*, 1988, vol. 43, pp. 35–44.

J. E. Mack, *Abduction: Human Encounter with Aliens*, New York, Macmillan/Charles Scribner's Sons, 1994.

——, 'Why the Abduction Phenomenon Cannot Be Explained Psychiatrically', in A. Pritchard *et al.* (eds), *Alien Discussions*, 1994, pp. 372–4.

——, *Passport to the Cosmos: Human Transformation and Alien Encounters*, New York, Crown, 1999.

R. Main (ed.), *Jung on Synchronicity and the Paranormal*, London, Routledge, 1997.

Mark-Age, *Reappearance of Christ Consciousness on Earth*. Available online: http://www.islandnet.com/arton/markage.html.

J. F. Mayer, 'Les Sauvers Venus de l'espace: croyance aux extraterrestres et religions soucoupistes', *Question de*, 2000, vol. 122, pp. 69–93.

D. McKenna & T. McKenna, *The Invisible Landscape*, New York, Seabury Press, 1975.

T. McKenna, *The Archaic Revival: Speculations on Psychedelic Mushrooms, the Amazon, Virtual Reality UFOs, Evolution, Shamanism, the Rebirth of the Goddess, and the End of History*, San Francisco, HarperCollins, 1991.

L. Meller, *Ufot ja maailmanloppu*, Loviisa, Painoyhtymä Oy, 1973.

J. G. Melton, 'The Contactees: A Survey', in J. R. Lewis (ed.), *The Gods Have Landed*, 1995, pp. 1–14.

——, 'Church Universal and Triumphant: Its Heritage and Thoughtworld', in J. R. Lewis and J. G. Melton (eds), *Church Universal and Triumphant in Scholarly Perspective*, Stanford, Center for Academic Publication, 1994.

J. G. Melton, J. Clark and A. A. Kelly, *New Age Encyclopedia*, Detroit, Gale Research, 1990.

H. Menger, *From Outer Space to You*, New York, Pyramid Books, 1967.

S. Meštrović, *The Coming Fin De Siècle: An Application of Durkheim's Sociology to Modernity and Postmodernism*, London, Routledge, 1991.

A. Michel, *The Truth About Flying Saucers*, trans. Paul Selve, New York, S. G. Phillips, 1956; London, R. Hale, 1957; New York: Pyramid Books, 1967; New York, Criterion, 1974.

P. Mikkonen, 'New Age in Finland: A View Through Finnish New Age Magazines', in J. Kaplan (ed.), *Beyond the Mainstream: The Emergence of Religious Pluralism in Finland, Estonia, and Russia*, Helsinki, SKS, 2000, pp. 225–71.

C. Missler and M. Eastman, *Alien Encounters: The Secret Behind the UFO Phenomenon*, Coeur d'Alene, Koinonia House, 1997.

S. Monroe, 'Space Invaders', *Time*, 12 July 1999, vol. 154.2, p. 32.

R. Montgomery, *Strangers Among Us: Enlightened Beings from a World to Come*, New York, Coward, McCann & Geoghegan, 1979.

——, *Threshold to Tomorrow*, New York, G. P. Putnam, 1983.

——, *Aliens Among Us*, New York, Fawcett Crest, 1985.

R. A. Moody, *Life After Life*, New York, Bantam, 1975.

——, *The Light Beyond*, New York, Bantam, 1989.

E. P. Moyer, *Our Celestial Visitors*, Pasadena, Moyer Publishing, 2000.

——, *Spirit Entry into Human Mind*, Pasadena, Moyer Publishing, 2000.

——, *The Birth of a Divine Revelation*, Pasadena, Moyer Publishing, 2000.

L. Mullins, *A History of the Urantia Papers*, Colorado, Penumbra Press, 2000.

J. Närvä, 'Ufoilmiön uskonnollisia piirteitä', in J. Niemelä (ed.), *Vanhat jumalat – uudet tulkinnat. Näköaloja uusiin uskontoihin Suomessa*, Helsinki, University of Helsinki, 2001, pp. 223–60.

E. Nesheim and L. Nesheim, *Saucer Attack!*, Los Angeles, Kitchen Sink Press/General Publishing Group, 1997.

P. D. Netzley, *Alien Abductions: Opposing Viewpoints*, San Diego, Greenhaven Press, 1996.

L. S. Newman, 'Intergalactic Hostages: People Who Report Abduction by UFOs', *Journal of Social and Clinical Psychology*, 1997, vol. 16, pp. 151–77.

L. S. Newman and R. F. Baumeister, 'Toward an Explanation of the UFO Abduction Phenomena: Hypnotic Elaboration, Extraterrestrial Sadomasochism, and Spurious Memories', *Psychological Inquiry*, 1996, vol. 7, pp. 99–126.

——, 'Not Just Another False Memory: Further Thoughts on the UFO Phenomenon Abduction', *Psychological Inquiry*, 1996, vol. 7, pp. 185–97.

——, 'Abducted by Aliens: Spurious Memories of Interplanetary Masochism', in Steven Jay Lynn *et al.* (eds), *Truth in Memory*, New York, Guilford Press, 1998, pp. 284–303.

J. F. Newton, *The Builders: A Story and Study of Masonry*, London, Allen & Unwin, 1918.

S. Nidle, 'A Message to Humanity from the Ground Crew Project. Planetary Activation Organization'. Available online:http://www.paowebcom/pao mesg.. htm (2001).

——, 'Planetary Activation Organization (PAO) Message of Introduction'. Available online: http://www.paoweb.com/paomesg.htm (November 2002).

M. Niinimäki, *Teosofian juuret*, Kylämä, Kustannus Oy Rajatieto, 1979.

E. Norman, *The Voice of Venus*, 6th edn, El Cajon, Unarius Educational Foundation, 1956.

R. E. Norman, *Thwarted: Effort to Destroy the Unarius Mission Thwarted*, El Cajon, Unarius Educational Foundation, 1984 .

——, *Testimonials by Unarius Students: To Help the New Seeker Conceive of the Various Benefits of Unarius*, El Cajon, Unarius Educational Foundation, 1985.

——, *Preview for the Spacefleet Landing on Earth in 2001 A.D.*, El Cajon, Unarius Educational Foundation, 1987.

——, *Biography of an Archangel*, El Cajon, Unarius Educational Foundation, 1989.

R. E. Norman with C. Spaegel, *Preparation for the Landing*, El Cajon, Unarius Educational Foundation, 1987.

R. E. Norman and Unarius Students, *Return to Jerusalem*, El Cajon, Unarius Educational Foundation, 1983 .

R. E. Norman and Vaughn Spaegel, *Who is the Mona Lisa?*, El Cajon, Unarius Science of Life, 1973 .

Nuwaubians, 'Brief History: Center for Anthroufology'. Available online: http://home.uchicago.edu/ryancook/un-nwtxt.htm (November, 2002).

F. Ochberg, 'Posttraumatic Therapy', *Psychotherapy*, 1991, vol. 28.1, pp. 5–15.

T. F. O'Meara, 'Christian Theology and Extraterrestrial Intelligent Life', *Theological Studies*, 1999, vol. 60, pp. 3–30.

M. Orne, 'Alien-Abduction Claims and Standards of Inquiry', *The Skeptical Inquirer*, Spring 1988, pp. 270–8.

M. Orne et al., '"Memories" of Anomalous and Traumatic Autobiographical Experiences: Validation and Consolidation of Fantasy Through Hypnosis', *Psychological Inquiry*, 1996, vol. 7.2, pp. 168–72.

T. Pajala, *Nykyajan tapahtumat Raamatun profetian valossa*, Helsinki, Ristin voitto, 1958.

S. J. Palmer, 'Women in the Raëlian Movement: New Religious Experiments in Gender and Authority', in J. R. Lewis (ed.), *The Gods Have Landed*, 1995, pp. 105–36.

——, 'The Raël Deal', *Religion in the News*, 2001, vol. 4.2, Summer, pp. 19–24. Available online: http://www.trincoll.edu/depts/csrpl/RIN.html.

S. J. Palmer and S. Luxton, 'The Ansaru Allah Community: Postmodernist Narration and the Black Jeremiad', in P. B. Clarke (ed), *New Trends and*

Developments in the World of Islam, London: Luzac Oriental, 1998, pp. 353–69.

A. Parfrey, *Cult Rapture*, Portland, Feral House, 1995 .

J. Parnell, 'Measured Personality Characteristics of Persons Who Claim UFO Experiences', *Psychotherapy in Private Practice*, 1998, vol. 6, pp. 159–65.

J. Parnell and R. L. Sprinkle, 'Personality Characteristics of Persons Who Claim UFO Experiences', *Journal of UFO Studies*, 1990, vol. 2, pp. 45–58.

C. Partridge, 'Sacred Chemicals: Psychedelic Drugs and Mystical Experience', in C. Partridge and T. Gabriel (eds), *Mysticisms East and West: Studies in Mystical Experience*, Carlisle, Paternoster Press, 2003, ch. 7.

A. L. Patry and L. G. Pelletier, 'Extraterrestrial Beliefs and Experiences: An Application of the Theory of Reasoned Actions', *Journal of Social Psychology*, 2001, vol. 141, pp. 199–217.

N. Paulsen, *Brotherhood of the Sön*, Santa Barbara, Sunburst Industries, 1973.

——, *Sunburst – Return of the Ancients*, Goleta, Sunburst Farms, 1980.

——, *Christ Consciousness*, Salt Lake City, Builders Publishing Co., 1984.

C. Peebles, *Watch the Skies! A Chronicle of the Flying Saucer Myth*, Washington & London, Smithsonian Institute Press, 1994.

T. Pellert, *Raamatun arvoitus ja Halleyn komeetta*, Helsinki, Tammi, 1982.

R. Perkins and F. Jackson, *Cosmic Suicide: The Tragedy and Transcendence of Heaven's Gate*, Dallas, Pentaradial Press, 1997.

——, 'Spirit in the Sky', *Fortean Times*, April, 1998, vol. 109, pp. 24–6.

M. A. Persinger, 'The Tectonic Strain Theory as an Explanation of for UFO Experiences: A Non-technical Review of the Research, 1970–1990', *Journal of UFO Studies*, 1990, vol. 2, pp. 105–37.

A. A. B. Philips, *The Ansaru Cult in America*, Riyadh, Tawheed Publications, 1988.

L. Picknett, *The Mammoth Book of UFOs*, New York, Carroll & Graf, 2001.

J. Porter, 'Spiritualists, Aliens and UFOs: Extraterrestrials as Spirit Guides', *Journal of Contemporary Religion*, 1996, vol. 11, pp. 337–53.

S. Porteous, 'Robertson Advocates Stoning for UFO Enthusiasts', *Freedom Writer Press Release*, Great Barrington, 28 July 1997.

M. Pössel, *Phantastische Wissenschaft Über Erich von Däniken und Johannes von Buttlar*, Reinbek, Roewohlt Tb., 2000.

D. Potter, 'UFOs, ETs and the New Age: A Christian Perspective', *Christian Apologetics Journal*, 1998, vol. 1.1, pp. 1–8.

J. Pouwer, *Enkele aspecten van de Mimika-cultuur (Nederlands zuidwest Nieuw Guinea)*, The Hague, Staatsdrukkerij en Uitgeversbedrijf, 1955.

S. M. Powers, 'Fantasy Proneness, Amnesia, and the UFO Abduction Phenomenon', *Dissociation: Progress in the Dissociative Disorders*, 1991, vol. 4, pp. 46–54.

——, 'Specific Correlates of PTSD and Dissociation', in A. Pritchard *et al.* (eds), *Alien Discussions*, 1994, pp. 320–3.

——, 'Alien Abduction Narratives', in S. Krippner and S. M. Powers (eds), *Broken Images, Broken Selves: Dissociative Narration in Clinical Practice*, Brunner/Mazel Publications, 1997, pp. 199–215.

A. Pritchard *et al.* (eds), *Proceedings of the Abduction Study Conference Held at MIT*, Cambridge, North Cambridge Press, 1994.

E. C. Prophet, *The Great White Brotherhood in the Culture, History and Religion of America*, Livingston, Summit University Press, 1987 [1976].

L. Quinby, *Anti-apocalypse: Essays in Genealogical Feminism*, Minneapolis, University of Minnesota Press, 1994.

——, *Millennial Seduction: A Skeptic Confronts Apocalyptic Culture*, Ithaca, Cornell University Press, 1999.

S. Rae, 'John Mack's Abductees', *New York Times Magazine*, 20 March 1994, pp. 30–3.

Raël (Claude Vorilhon), *Let's Welcome Our Fathers from Space: They Created Humanity in Their Laboratories*, Tokyo, AOM Corporation, 1986.

——, *The Message Given to Me by Extra-Terrestrials: They Took Me to Their Planet*, Tokyo, AOM Corporation, 1992.

——, *The Truth Finally Revealed* (pamphlet), Sydney, Australian Raëlian Movement, 2001.

Raëlian Church, 'Summary of the Messages: Scientists from Another Planet Created All Life on Earth Using D.N.A.'. Available online: http://www.rael.org (31 December 2001).

K. D. Randle, *Scientific Ufology: How the Application of Scientific Methodology Can Analyze, Illuminate, and Prove the Reality of UFOs*, New York, Avon Books, 1999.

A. Rawlinson, *The Book of Enlightened Masters: Western Teachers in Eastern Traditions*, Chicago, Open Court, 1997.

M. Reay, *Transformation Movements and Associations in Papua New Guinea*, Political and Social Change Monograph, vol. 3, Canberra, Australian National University, forthcoming.

T. H. Redfern, *The Work and Worth of Mme Blavatsky*, London, Theosophical Publishing House, n.d.

D. von Reeken, *Bibliographie der selbständigen deutschsprachigen Literatur über Außerirdisches Leben, UFOs und Prä-Astronautik*, Lüdenscheid, GEP, 1996.

B. Reeve and H. Reeve, *Flying Saucer Pilgrimage*, Amherst, Amherst Press, 1957.

J. Rehnström, 'URANTIA ja *Ultra*', *Ultra*, 2002, vol. 1, pp. 10–11.

J. W. Rhue and S. J. Lynn, 'Fantasy Proneness and Psychopathology' *Journal of Personality and Social Psychology*, 1987, vol. 53, pp. 327–36.

K. Ring, 'Toward an Imaginal Interpretation of "UFO Abductions"', *Revision: Journal of Consciousness and Change*, 1989, vol. 11.4, pp. 17–24.

S. Riordan, 'Channeling: A New Revelation?', in J. R. Lewis and J. G. Melton (eds), *Perspectives on the New Age*, Albany, State University of New York Press, 1992, pp. 105–26.

T. Robbins, *Cults, Converts and Charisma: The Sociology of New Religious Movements*, Beverly Hills, Sage Publications, 1988.

M. Rodeghier, 'Psychological Characteristics of Abductees', in A. Pritchard *et al.* (eds), *Alien Discussions*, 1994, pp. 296–303.

M. Rothstein, *Belief Transformations: Some Aspects of the Relation Between Science and Religion in TM and ISKCON*, RENNER Studies on New Religions, vol. 2, Aarhus, Aarhus University Press, 1996.

——, 'The Family, UFOs and God: A Modern Extension of Christian Mythology', *Journal of Contemporary Religion*, 1997, vol. 12, pp. 353–62.

——, 'The Myth of the UFO in Global Perspective: A Cognitive Approach', in M. Rothstein (ed.), *New Age Religion and Globalization*, RENNER Studies on New Religions vol. 5, Aarhus, Aarhus University Press, 2001, pp. 133–49.

E. J. Ruppelt, *The Report on Unidentified Flying Objects*, Garden City, Doubleday, 1956.

Sadapuda (Richard Thompson), *Alien Identities: Ancient Insights into Modern UFO Phenomena*, San Diego, Govardhan Hill Publishing, 1993.

W. S. Sadler, *A History of the Urantia Movement*:http://www.urantia. org/pub/ahotum.html

C. Sagan and T. Page (eds), *UFO's: A Scientific Debate*, Cornell University Press, 1972; New York, Barnes & Noble Books, 1996.

B. Saler, C. A. Ziegler and C. B. Moore, *UFO Crash at Roswell: The Genesis of a Modern Myth*, Washington & London, Smithsonian Institution Press, 1997.

J. A. Saliba, 'The Religious Dimensions of UFO Phenomena', in J. R. Lewis (ed.), *The Gods Have Landed*, 1995, pp. 15–64.

——, 'UFO Contactee Phenomena from a Sociopsychological Perspective: A Review', in J. R. Lewis (ed.), *The Gods Have Landed*, 1995, pp. 207–50.

——, 'The Aetherius Society', in J. R. Lewis (ed.), *UFOs A to Z*, Chicago, Contemporary Books, 1998.

——, 'The Earth is a Dangerous Place – The World View of the Aetherius Society', *Marburg Journal of Religion*, 4, 1999. Available online: http://www.uni-marburg.de/religionswissenschaft/journal/ mjr/saliba_main.html (6 November 2002).

D. R. Saunders and R. R. Harkins, *UFOs Yes! Where the Condon Committee Went Wrong*, New York, New American Library, 1968.

S. von Schnurbein, *Religion als Kulturkritik: Neugermanisches Heidentum im 20. Jahrhundert*, Heidelberg, Winter, 1992.

R. A. Segal (ed.), *Jung on Mythology*, London, Routledge, 1998.

B. Sentes and S. J. Palmer, 'Presumed Immanent: The Raëlians, UFO Religions, and the Postmodern Condition', *Nova Religio*, 2000, vol. 4.1, October, pp. 86–105.

G. Shepperson, 'Nyasaland and the Millennium,' in S. Thrupp (ed.), *Millennial Dreams in Action*, New York, Scribners, 1970, pp. 144–59.

H. Sherman, *How to Know What to Believe*, New York, Fawcett, 1976.

R. K. Siegel, *Fire in the Brain: Clinical Tests of Hallucination*, New York, Plume/Penguin Books, 1993.

J. L. Simmons, *The Emerging New Age*, Santa Fe, Bear & Co., 1990.

B. Singer and V. A. Benassi, 'Occult Beliefs', *American Scientist*, vol. 69, 1981, pp. 49–55.

Z. Sitchin, *The Twelfth Planet*, New York, Avon, 1976.

——, *Genesis Revisited*, New York, Avon, 1990.

——, *Divine Encounters: A Guide to Visions, Angels, and Other Emissaries*, New York, Avon, 1995.

R. Sjögren, *Mies toisesta maailmasta ja muita ufoilmiöitä*, Helsinki, Otava, 1972.

J. Z. Smith, *Imagining Religion*, Chicago, Chicago University Press, 1982.

A. Smyth, *The Occult Life of Jesus of Nazareth*, Chicago, The Progressive Thinker Publishing House, 1899; reprinted by Unarius in *The True Life of Jesus of Nazareth: The Confessions of St. Paul*.

Solara Antara Amaa-ra, *11:11 – The Opening of the Doorway*, Charlottesville, Starne-Borne Unlimited, 1990.

D. Spangler, 'The Role of the Esoteric in Planetary Culture', in M. Katz, W. P. Marsh and G. G. Thompson (eds), *Earth's Answer: Explorations of Planetary Culture at the Lindisfarne Conferences*, New York, Harper & Row, 1977.

N. P. Spanos, *Multiple Identities and False Memories: A Sociocognitive Perspective*, Washington, American Psychological Association, 1996.

N. P. Spanos, C. A. Burgess and M. F. Burgess, 'Past-Life Identities, UFO Abductions, and Satanic Ritual Abuse: The Social Construction of Memories', *International Journal of Clinical and Experimental Hypnosis*, 1994, vol. 42, pp. 433–46.

N. P. Spanos *et al.*, 'Close Encounters: An Examination of UFO Experiences', *Journal of Abnormal Psychology*, 1993, vol. 102, pp. 624–32.

D. Spiegel, 'Dissociating Damage', *American Journal of Clinical Hypnosis*, 1986, vol. 29, pp. 123–31.

L. Spiegel (Antares), *I, Bonaparte: An Autobiography*, El Cajon, Unarius Publishers, 1985.

R. L. Sprinkle, 'Psychotherapeutic Services for Persons Who Claim UFO Experiences', *Psychotherapy in Private Practice*, 1988, vol. 6, pp. 151–7.

M. J. Sprunger, 'The Future of the Fifth Epochal Revelation', in L. Mullins (ed.), *A History of the Urantia Papers*, Colorado, Penumbra Press, 2000.

B. Steiger, *Gods of Aquarius: UFOs and the Transformation of Man*, New York, Berkley, 1976.

J. Stone-Carmen, 'A Descriptive Study of People Reporting Abduction by UFOs', in A. Pritchard *et al.* (eds.), *Alien Discussions*, 1994, pp. 309–15.

R. Story, *The Space-Gods Revealed: A Close Look at the Theories of Erich von Däniken*, London, Book Club Associates, 1977.

W. Strieber, *Communion: A True Story*, New York, Avon, 1987.

D. Stupple, 'Mahatmas and Space Brothers: The Ideologies of Alleged Contact with Mahatmas and Space Brothers: the Ideologies of Alleged Contact with Extraterrestrials', *Journal of American Culture*, vol. 7, 1984, pp. 131–9.

P. A. Sturrock, *The UFO Enigma: A New Review of the Physical Evidence*, New York, Warner Books, 1999.

T. Swain and G. W. Trompf, *Religions of Oceania*, Library of Religious Beliefs and Practices, London, Routledge, 1995.

Y. Talmon, 'Millenarian Movements', *Archives Européennes de Sociologie*, 1966, vol. 7, pp. 159–200.

J. Tenhiälä, *Usko ja ufot*, Hämeenlinna, Karisto, 1972.

G. J. Tillett, *The Elder Brother*, London, Routledge & Kegan Paul, 1982.

A. Tomas, *We are Not the First*, London, Sphere, 1972.

E. Thomas, 'The Next Level', *Newsweek Magazine*, 7 April 1997.

I. D. E. Thomas, *The Omega Conspiracy*, Herndon, Growth, 1986.

J. L. Thompson, *Aliens & UFOs: Messengers or Deceivers?* Bountiful, UT, Horizon Publishers, 1993.

R. L. Thompson, *Alien Identities*, Alachua, Govardhan Hill Publishing, 1995.

P. Tomkins, *Secrets of the Great Pyramid*, London, Allen Lane, 1973.

——, *Mysteries of the Mexican Pyramids*, NewYork, Harper & Row, 1976.

G. W. Trompf, 'The Theology of Beig Wen, the Would-be Successor to Yali', *Catalyst*, 1976, vol. 6.3, pp. 166–74.

——, *Religion and Money: Some Aspects*, Adelaide, 1980.

——, 'Bilalaf', in G. W. Trompf (ed.), *Prophets of Melanesia*, Suva, Institute of Pacific Studies, 1981, pp. 12–64.

——, 'Doesn't Colonialism make you Mad? The So-Called "Mur Madness" as an Index to the Study of New Religious Movements in Papua New Guinea during the Colonial Period', in S. Latukefu (ed.), *Papua New Guinea: A Century of Colonial Impact 1884–1984*, Port Moresby, University of Papua New Guinea Press, 1989, pp. 247–78.

——, 'Macrohistory and Acculturation,' *Comparative Studies in Society and History*, 1989, vol. 31.4, pp. 615–48.

—— (ed.), *Cargo Cults and Millenarian Movements*, Berlin, Mouton de Gruyter, 1990.

——, 'Introduction' to G. W., Trompf, (ed.), *Cargo Cults and Millenarian Movements*, Religion and Society, vol. 29, Berlin, Mouton de Gruyter, 1990, pp. 1–15.

——, 'Keeping the *Lo* under a Melanesian Messiah: An Analysis of the Pomio *Kivung*, East New Britain', in J. Barker (ed.), *Christianity in Oceania*, ASOA Monographs, vol. 12, Lanham, MD University Press of America, 1990, pp. 59–80.

——, *Melanesian Religion*, Cambridge, Cambridge University Press, 1990.

——, 'The Cargo and the Millennium on Both Sides of the Pacific', in G. W., Trompf, (ed.), *Cargo Cults and Millenarian Movements*, Berlin, Mouton de Gruyter, 1990, pp. 35–94.

——, *Payback: The Logic of Retribution in Melanesian Religions*, Cambridge, Cambridge University Press, 1994.

——, 'Macrohistory in Blavatsky, Steiner and Guénon,' in A. Faivre and W. Hanegraaff (eds), *Western Esotericism and the Science of Religion*, Gnostica series, vol. 2, Louvain, Peeters, 1998, pp. 274–86.

——, 'Millenarism: History, Sociology and Cross-Cultural Analysis,' *Journal of Religious History*, 2000, vol. 24.1, pp. 103–24.

——, 'Easter Island: The Site of the First Pacfic Cargo Cult?', in G. Casadio (ed.), *Ugo Bianchi: una vita per la storia delle religioni*, Rome, Calamo, 2002, pp. 441–65.

——, 'La teoria della meraviglia e i culti del cargo in Melanesia', trans. by C. Camporesi, *Religioni e Società*, 2002, vol. 43, pp. 23–46.

Tuella, *Lord Kuthumi: World Messages for the Coming Decade*, Deming, Guardian Action Publications, 1983.

——, *Ashtar: A Tribute*, Deming, Guardian Action Publications, 1985.

——, *Project World Evacuation by the AShtar Command*, Utah, Guardian Action Publications, 1982; New Brunswick, Inner Publications, 1993.

——, *Ashtar: Revealing the Secret Identity of the Forces of Light and Their Spiritual Mission on Earth*, New Brunswick, Inner Light Publications, 1994.

——, *A New Book of Revelations*, New Brunswick, Inner Light Publications, 1995.

D. Tumminia, 'Brothers from the Sky: Myth and Reality in a Flying Saucer Group', UCLA, unpublished doctoral thesis, 1995.

——, 'How Prophecy Never Fails: Interpretive Reason in a Flying Saucer Group', *Sociology of Religion*, 1998, vol. 59, pp. 157–70.

D. Tumminia and R. G. Kirkpatrick, 'Unarius: Emergent Aspects of a Flying Saucer Group', in J. R. Lewis (ed.), *The Gods Have Landed*, 1995, pp. 85–100.

S. W. Twemlow, 'Misidentified Flying Objects? An Integrated Psychodynamic Perspective on Near-Death Experiences and UFO Abductions', *Journal of Near-Death Studies*, 1994, vol. 12, pp. 205–23.

Urantia Book, The, Illinois, Uversa Press, 1996.

Uriel and her students, *The Proof of the Truth of Past Life Therapy*, El Cajon, Unarius Publishers, 1988.

J. Vallee, *Anatomy of a Phenomenon: The Detailed and Unbiased Report of UFOs*, New York, Ace Books, Inc., 1965; reprinted as *UFOs in Space: Anatomy of a Phenomenon*, New York, Ballantine Books, 1974.

——, *The Invisible College: What a Group of Scientists Has Discovered About UFO Influences on the Human Race*, New York, E. P. Dutton, 1975.

——, *Forbidden Science: Journals 1957–1969*, Berkeley, North Atlantic Books, 1992.

——, *Passport to Magonia: On UFOs, Folklore, and Parallel Worlds*, Chicago, Contemporary Books, 1993.

G. Van Tassel, *I Rode a Flying Saucer! The Mystery of the Flying Saucers Revealed*, Los Angeles, New Age Publishing, 1952.

——, *When Stars Look Down*, 2nd edn, La Jolla, Trade Service Publications, 1999.

S. Virtanen, 'Lentävästä lautasesta outoon valoon: Ufoilmiö sanomalehtien palstoilla 1940-luvulta 1990-luvulle', unpublished dissertation, University of Tampere, 1998.

D. Walker, 'The Black Muslims in American Society', in G. W. Trompf (ed.), *Cargo Cults and Millenarian Movements*, 1990, pp. 343–90.

——, 'Louis Farrakhan and America's "Nation of Islam"', in G. W. Trompf (ed.), *Islands and Enclaves*, Delhi, Sterling, 1993, pp. 71–100.

R. Wallis, 'The Aetherius Society: A Case Study in the Formation of a Mystagogic Congregation', *Sociological Review*, 1974, vol. 22, pp. 27–44.

——, 'The Social Construction of Charisma', *Social Compass*, 1982, vol. 29, pp. 25–39.

——, 'The Sociology of the New Religions', *Social Studies Review*, September, 1985, vol. 1, pp. 3–7.

M. Weber, *Basic Concepts in Sociology*, H. P. Secher (trans.), New York, Philosophical Library, 1962.

——, *The Sociology of Religion*, Boston, Beacon Press, 1963 .

——, *Economy and Society: An Outline of Interpretive Sociology*, G. Roth and C. Wittich (eds), E. Fischoff (trans.), New York, Bedminster Press, 1968.

F. Wegener, *Das atlantidische Weltbild: Nationalsozialismus und Neue Rechte auf der Suche nach der versunkenen Atlantis*, Gladbeck, Kulturförderverein Ruhrgebiet e.v., 2001.

J. Weldon and Z. Lewitt, *UFOs: What on Earth is Happening?*, California, Harvest House, 1974.

C. Wessinger, *How the Millennium Comes Violently: From Jonestown to Heaven's Gate*, New York, Seven Bridges, 2000.

—— (ed.), *Millennialism, Persecution, and Violence: Historical Cases*, New York, Syracuse University Press, 2000.

J. Whitmore, 'Religious Dimensions of UFO Abductee Experience', in J. R. Lewis (ed.), *The Gods Have Landed*, 1995, pp. 65–84.

F. E. Williams, *The Vailala Madness and the Destruction of Native Ceremonies in the Gulf Division*, Territory of Papua, Anthropology Report 4, Port Moresby, Government Printer, 1923.

——, *Papuans of the Trans-Fly*, Oxford, Oxford University Press, 1936.

G. H. Williamson, *Other Tongues, Other Flesh*, Amherst, Amherst Press, 1954; London, Neville Spearman, Ltd., 1959; Albuquerque, B. E. Books, 1991.

G. H. Williamson and A. C. Bailey, *The Saucers Speak! A Documentary Report of Interstellar Communication by Radiotelegraphy*, Los Angeles, New Age Publishing Co., 1954.

T. L. Wilson, 'The Search for Extraterrestrial Intelligence', *Nature*, 2001, vol. 409, no. 6823, pp. 1110–15.

G. Wittek, *Das ist mein Wort A und Ω*, Würzburg, Das Wort, 1993.

L. Woodhead, P. Fletcher, H. Kawanami and D. Smith (eds), *Religions in the Modern World: Traditions and Transformations*, London, Routledge, 2002.

D. Wojcik, 'Mysterious Technology: UFOs and the Visionary Art of Ionel Talpazan', unpublished manuscript.

——, *The End of the World As We Know It: Faith, Fatalism, and Apocalypse in America*, New York and London, New York University Press, 1997.

P. Worsley, *The Trumpet Shall Sound*, St Albans, Paladin, 1970.

P. Yogananda, *The Road Ahead*, Nevada City, Ananda Publications, 1973.

R. W. Zaslow, 'Myth', in R. J. Corsini (ed.), *Encyclopedia of Psychology*, vol. 2, 2nd edn, New York, John Wiley & Sons, 1994, p. 448.

2012 Unlimited, 'Personal and Planetary Changes: Tools of the New Millennium'. Available online: http://www.2012.com.au/unlimited.html (November 2002).

INDEX